Alfred Lyall

# Asiatic Studies

Religious and social

Alfred Lyall

**Asiatic Studies**
*Religious and social*

ISBN/EAN: 9783744750646

Printed in Europe, USA, Canada, Australia, Japan

Cover: Foto ©Suzi / pixelio.de

More available books at **www.hansebooks.com**

# RELIGIOUS AND SOCIAL.

By Sir ALFRED C. LYALL, K.C.B., C.I.E.

SECOND EDITION.

LONDON:
JOHN MURRAY, ALBEMARLE STREET.
1884.

# PREFACE.

This book contains, in the form of chapters, eleven essays published by me during the past ten years; they were written in such intervals of leisure as could be spared by the constant and occasionally urgent preoccupations of official duties in India, and they have been thought to be worth the experiment of republication together. Ten of these essays relate to India, being mainly the outcome of personal observation in certain provinces and of intercourse with the people; one essay relates to China, with which country the writer has no direct acquaintance; and since they are all so far alike in their subject-matter that they deal with the actual character and complexion of religion and society in these countries at the present time, they may possibly be considered to have some useful bearing on the general study of Asiatic ideas and institutions. For throughout Asia, wherever the state of society has not been distinctly transformed by European influences, there is a fundamental resemblance in the social condition of the people, in their intellectual level, and in their habits of thought. And although India is in many respects a peculiar country, isolated and fenced off from the rest of the continent by broad belts of high and often impassable mountain country, so that it cannot be classed either with Eastern or Western Asia, yet it possesses, by reason of its extraordinary variety of peoples, creeds, and manners, a strong affinity with the widely different countries on either side of it; it partakes largely of the religious characteristics both of Western Asia, whence it has received Mahomedanism, and of Eastern Asia, to which it has given Buddhism, the pure outcome of Hindu theosophy; and it has preserved specimens of almost every stage in the history of Asiatic politics and the growth of Asiatic societies. No single first class country of Asia, therefore, so well repays examination; and it is just this part of Asia in which Europeans have had incomparably the best opportunities of accurate and continuous observation. The English know India as no other Europeans, since the Romans, have ever known an Asiatic country; in the long territorial struggle of modern times between Europe and Asia, their command of the sea enabled them to turn the flank of India's land defences, and by pushing up from the coast to establish themselves in the heart of Asia, at a time when the Cross and the Crescent were still contending fiercely on the Danube and the Caspian. Having thus occupied large provinces of Asia for more than a century, the English have been obliged, in building up their administration and consolidating their successive conquests, to look closely into the social and economical conditions of India, to consider the feelings of the people and to realize their political and religious idiosyncrasies; with the general result that by opening out India they have let a flood of clear daylight in upon Asia at large. The present small volume may possibly add something to the English store of information derived from Eastern experiences; it may aid toward the exact appreciation of Indian life and thought, and to a knowledge, through India, of Asia; and it may perhaps contribute materials of some special use to those who are engaged in the comparative study of religious and social phenomena generally. There may be nothing new in the ideas, to which reference is constantly made in this volume, that India, with its multiplicity of religions and tribes, and its variety of political groups, is the best surviving specimen, on a large scale, of the ancient world of history, the *Orbis veteribus notus;* and that the provincial administration as well as the foreign policy of the Roman empire are reproduced, in several notable respects, by our system of government in India. The conception is, of course, aided by the analogies to be found between the position of the Romans in some of their proconsulates and legations, and that of Englishmen in Bengal or in the Punjab; the administrative problems that arise are much the same, and they are often solved in a similar manner; insomuch that for the cases before our courts we can sometimes find very close precedents in those recorded as having been placed before Roman procurators or prefects. The consequence is that these ideas are continually recurring to the mind of any one who attempts to survey India at the present day, and to understand in what state the English found the country, and what they are now doing there. All such resemblances and comparisons help to bridge over the distance between the ancient and the modern world, and to give more distinct and familiar proportions to scenes and figures which appear strange and beyond our own experience when we read of them in history. We begin to feel the true religious atmosphere of past ages, and to realize their political aspects. We see that the polytheism of India still flows from sources and assumes shapes similar to those which produced the beliefs and worships of præ-Christian Europe; and we understand more clearly the situation that is created whenever a great empire is formed by the intervention of a nation pre-eminent in arms and civilization among backward and unstable communities.

Moreover, India not only presents a sort of picture in which we may recognize and examine for ourselves many of the features and incidents of early history; it also gives us a connected view of society in different stages, of various forms of tribal organization, of different systems of rule, and conceptions of sovereignty. The country affords a field of remarkable abundance for the collection and verification at first hand of living specimens of various types, especially for the study of early ideas on the subject of religion and rulership, and for observing the general movement of Asiatic society, which appears to be not unlike ancient European society in a state of arrested development. This field has been frequently and skilfully worked, by Sir Henry Maine and others, for the purpose of scientific research; and its exploration is of special value to those who, like the English in India, are going through a course of practical lessons in the great and prodigiously difficult art of dealing with races of backward and alien civilizations.

The first chapter in this volume, upon the religion of an Indian province, gives the conclusions formed by me upon the nature and condition of Hinduism in certain inland districts of India not very well known nor much visited, which, although they are administered by British officers, are not part of British India, and have preserved their local characteristics. Chapter VII., on the formation of castes and clans, was written after I had become acquainted with Rajputana, a country parcelled out among native States, and possessing a very rare and antique stratification of society, having still on its surface things that have been long overlaid or swept away in other parts of India.

Chapter VIII. gives a description of this country, and enters into some detail of its political history and social composition. Of the other chapters, that upon the origin of divine myths in India is, in effect, a somewhat venturesome attempt to resuscitate the discredited notions of Euemerus on the subject, and to suggest that some of the latest theories regarding the sources of ancient mythology have been extended too far. The writer, however, has no pretensions to scholarship, and can only claim to have analysed and registered the visible growth of myths in India as a phenomenon which cannot but throw much light upon the derivation of the heroic and divine legends of classic antiquity, in Europe as well as in Asia. In this chapter, and in others, some account is also given of the manner in which the myth-making faculty expands into the processes which evolve polytheism by the gradual elevation of heroes, saints, and remarkable personages to the higher honours of divinity. The rapidity with which their real history became transformed and their earthly origin is lost in the clouds, and the extent to which the evolution of deities is still going on after this fashion through a large portion of Asia, is perhaps not usually known or appreciated, even by students of primitive religions. It appears to be actively at work in China, under a curious and probably unique system of State encouragement and control, whereby the deifying processes are subordinated to administrative authority. Some illustrations of this system, and of the extent to which it prevails, are given in the sixth chapter; but the exact nature of the relations between the government and the religions of China can only be determined by those who know the country and have mixed with the people.

Chapter V. reproduces an Essay in which I ventured upon some dissent from certain views put forth by Professor Max

Müller, in a lecture delivered in Westminster Abbey, regarding the vitality of Brahminism, and its classification as a Non-Missionary religion. Professor Max Müller did me the honour of answering my remarks in an article which has since been republished in "Chips from a German Workshop," and I have now altered or toned down those parts of my original Essay which may have been written upon a misunderstanding of the Lecturer's position, or which at any rate I am not prepared to maintain against so distinguished an authority. All that I desire, with deference, to uphold is that Brahminism is a religion by no means dead or even moribund, but that, on the contrary, numbers are constantly brought within its pale, and are allowed to share more or less in its ritual. The last four chapters consist mainly of political discussions and speculations; they also contain references to controversies that were going on at the time when they appeared as articles, so that it is necessary to mention that they were all written not less than ten years ago. "Islam in India," for instance, is a review of a book published in 1871, and of course it does not nearly cover the extensive ground indicated by this heading to the chapter. Such questions as those relating to the present position and prospects of our Mahomedan fellow subjects in India, to their wants and feelings, and to the degree and manner in which they are likely to be affected, as a community, by the rapid advance of European civilization in India, require much more elaborate and comprehensive treatment, and are indeed closely allied to the momentous subject of the Future of Islam, upon which Mr. Wilfrid Blunt has recently published a dissertation of great interest. As to the chapter on our Religious Policy in India, it gives some retrospective account of what may be called, very roughly, the relations between Church and

State in British India, and its point is to argue that, taking the two leading theories on the proper relations between the civil government and religion to be, first, that which was advocated in Mr. Gladstone's book on Church and State, and, secondly, the contrary view propounded by Macaulay's review of the book, between these two opposed theories Asiatic custom and pablic opinion leans almost entirely to the side taken by Mr. Gladstone's book. In the final chapter, on the Religious situation in India, some broad speculations have been hazarded upon the probable course and outcome of religious development under the very singular combination of circumstances which have brought about the English empire in India. There can be no doubt that the religions of a country are necessarily acted upon by wide and deep political changes, by the substitution of peace and the rule of law for uncertainty and disorder, and by the sudden advance of a new civilization. Any speculations in this direction must inevitably be deeply coloured by the impression which pervades all political survey of India, and which is continually coming back on the spectator—as a scene in ordinary life suddenly brings to mind, and at times appears actually to reproduce, something that one has witnessed or read of before—the profound inpression of the analogy between the English dominion in Asia and the vanished empire of Rome.

The Essays, which originally appeared in the pages of the *Edinburgh Review*, No. 295, 1876 (Chap. VIII. of this volume) and of the *Fortnightly Review*, are now reprinted by the kind permission of the editors and proprietors of those journals.

A. C. LYALL.

# CONTENTS.

## CHAPTER I.

### RELIGION OF AN INDIAN PROVINCE.



## CHAPTER II.

### ON THE ORIGIN OF DIVINE MYTHS IN INDIA.

## CHAPTER III.

### INFLUENCE UPON RELIGION OF A RISE IN MORALITY.



## CHAPTER IV.

### WITCHCRAFT AND NON-CHRISTIAN RELIGIONS.

## CHAPTER V.

### MISSIONARY AND NON-MISSIONARY RELIGIONS.



## CHAPTER VI.

### RELATIONS BETWEEN THE STATE AND RELIGION IN CHINA.

## CHAPTER VII.

### ON THE FORMATION OF SOME CLANS AND CASTES IN INDIA.



## CHAPTER VIII.

### THE RAJPÚT STATES OF INDIA.

## CHAPTER IX.

### ISLAM IN INDIA.



## CHAPTER X.

### OUR RELIGIOUS POLICY IN INDIA.

## CHAPTER XI.

### THE RELIGIOUS SITUATION IN INDIA.

# ASIATIC STUDIES:

## RELIGIOUS AND SOCIAL.

## CHAPTER I.

### RELIGION OF AN INDIAN PROVINCE.

The actual religious condition of India, with its extraordinary variety of rites and worships, exemplifies the state of the civilized world in the ages of classic polytheism, before Christianity or Islam had arisen—A brief account of the religious beliefs in one province, Berar, may serve as a sample of Hinduism—Constant growth, movement, and change, of religious forms and conceptions—Classification, suggesting successive development, of the prevailing beliefs and liturgies, worship of things inanimate, of animals, of spirits, of ghosts, of divine incarnations, of the supreme Brahmanic gods—Some description of each class, with their connexion and the gradual evolution of deities from ancestral spirits, saints, heroes, and demi-gods—Successful wonder-working the selecting agency whereby this evolution is carried on; and the system of divine embodiment often the process of transmutation into and assimilation with the higher deities of Brahmanism—Probability that the existing state of Hinduism will not last long.

The general form and complexion of Hinduism is familiar enough to those who take interest in the subject of Asiatic religions. Many persons know that the Hindus are divided, as to their theology, into various sects, schools, and orders; that their orthodox Brahmanical doctrines express an esoteric Pantheism by an exoteric Polytheism; and that the mass of the people worship innumerable gods with endless diversity of ritual. A few students of India in England know a great deal more than this; but I doubt whether any one who has not lived among Hindus can adequately realise the astonishing variety of their ordinary religious beliefs, the constant changes of shape and colour which these beliefs undergo, the extraordinary fecundity of the superstitious sentiment—in short, the scope, range, depth, and height of religious ideas and practices prevailing simultaneously among the population of one country, or of one not very extensive province. It is not easy, indeed, for Europeans of this century to realise the condition even of a great continent in which there are no nationalities; or to perceive how in a mere loose conglomeration of tribes, races, and castes the notion of religious unity, or even of common consent by a people as to the fundamental bases of worship, can hardly be comprehended, much less entertained. For nationality is, as we know, a thing of modern growth; when Charlemagne restored the Western Empire, he swept within its pale not nations but tribes—Franks and Saxons, Lombards and Gauls—just as we have subdued and now rule, in India, Sikhs, Patháns, Rajpûts, and Marathas. It is therefore, perhaps, by surveying India that we at this day can best represent to ourselves and appreciate the vast external reform worked upon the heathen world by Christianity, as it was organised and executed throughout Europe by the combined authority of the Holy Roman Empire and the Church Catholic. From this Asiatic standpoint, looking down upon a tangled jungle of disorderly superstitions, upon ghosts and demons, demi-gods, and deified saints; upon household gods, tribal gods, local gods, universal gods; with their countless shrines and temples, and the din of their discordant rites; upon deities who abhor a fly's death, upon those who delight still in human victims, and upon those who would not either sacrifice or make offering —looking down upon such a religious chaos, throughout a vast region never subdued or levelled (like all Western Asia) by Mahomedan or Christian monotheism, we realise the huge enterprise undertaken by those who first set forth to establish one Faith for all mankind, and an universal Church on earth. We perceive more clearly what classic polytheism was by realizing what Hinduism actually is. We have been so much habituated in Europe to associate any great historic religion with the idea of a Church (if not in its mediæval sense, then in the sense of a congregation of the faithful), that most of us assign this kind of settled character and organic form to paganism, modern or ancient, so long as it is not barbarism. We are thus prone to assume that a people like the Hindus, with their history, literature, sacred books, and accumulated traditions, must by this time have built up some radical dogmas, or at least some definite conceptions of divinity, which the upper classes would have imposed on the crowd as limits to mere superstitious phantasy. For centuries Christianity has marched, along its entire settled frontier, with no other religion beside Mahomedanism, which has distinctive tenets and a firmly-set pale; therefore we do not readily appreciate the state of millions of Hindus to whom any such common bond or circumscription is altogether wanting. We can scarcely comprehend an ancient religion, still alive and powerful, which is a mere troubled sea, without shore or visible horizon, driven to and fro by the winds of boundless credulity and grotesque invention.

I have supposed, therefore, that it might be worth while to attempt a brief description of the actual condition, character, and tendencies of the religious beliefs now prevailing in one province of India. It will present, I believe, a fair average sample of Hinduism as a whole, like a pail of water taken out of a pond. But I do not purpose to draw the well-known figures of Brahmanic theology, nor to rehearse standard myths and heroic fables common to all India. The doctrine of Brahmanism, and the whole apparatus of its ceremonial, with its sects, orthodox or heterodox, flourish in this particular province much as they do in all others; I assume that the outline of them has been studied and understood. My present plan is to try whether the different superstitious notions and forms of worship which fall under everyday observation in an Indian district, can be arranged so as to throw any light upon recent theories as to the gradual upward growth and successive development of religion through connected stages. That the sphere of observation has, for the purposes of this essay, been mostly confined within provincial limits, is a condition not without certain advantages. By comparing different ages, diverse societies, and men under dissimilar physical environment, we may collect without difficulty every species and variety of superstition required to fit up our respective theories of religious evolution; and people have thus been accustomed to construct such theories upon materials drawn from an infinite diversity of habitations or races scattered over long periods of time. The convenience of ranging over such a wide field of selection may sometimes tempt us to ascribe to the customs and fancies of distant and greatly differing societies a closer relationship and inter-connexion than really exist. But if the living specimens can all be gathered from one country, then their affinity may seem more demonstrable, and the manner of their sequence or descent more intelligible. At any rate, the actual facts may be thus brought more easily under a connected view, and within compass of accurate research; while it may be interesting (setting aside all theories) to observe a whole vegetation of cognate beliefs sprouting up in every stage of growth beneath the shadow of the great orthodox traditions and allegories of Brahmanism.

The province (commonly called Berar) from which I have drawn my facts is situated nearly in the centre of India; it is almost identical in area with the present kingdom of Greece on the mainland; and it contains* 2,250,000 inhabitants, of whom 155,000 are Musalmáns, and the rest (of the natives) are loosely called Hindus. Now just as the word Hindu is no national or even geographical denomination, but signifies vaguely a fortuitous conglomeration of sects, tribes, races, hereditary professions, and pure castes; so the religion of this population of Hindus is at first sight a heterogeneous confusion. Without doubt much of this miscellany may be at once referred, for its source, to the composite character of its people. The Hindus proper, who can be ranged in known castes, have come in by migrations from North, South, and West; there is a strong non-Aryan leaven in the dregs of the agricultural class, derived from the primitive races which have gradually melted down into settled life, and thus become fused with the general community; while these same races are still distinct tribes in the wild tracts of hill and jungle. Nevertheless, the various superstitions have long ceased to correspond

* 1868.

with ethnic varieties; they have even little accordance with gradations of social position or of civil estate. Moreover, the characteristic which, after close examination, most strikes an European observer, is not so much the heterogeneity of the popular religion taken at a glance, as the fact that it is a thing which is constantly growing; that it is perceptibly following certain modes of generation, transmutation, and growth, which point toward and lead up from the lower toward the higher kinds of belief. Here, as everywhere in like conditions, the floating and molecular state of society has prevented religious consolidation; while again the multiformity of religion reacts continually upon the society, subjecting its constitution to a perpetual *morcellement*. And the wedges which have riven asunder and are keeping separate the general mass of the Indian people are furnished and applied by the system of Caste. The two great outward and visible signs of caste fellowship, intermarriage and the sharing of food, are the bonds which unite or isolate groups. Now Caste seems to be the stereotype mould which has in India preserved those antique prejudices of blood and religion that have been worn out or destroyed in almost all countries of equal or inferior civilization; and so far as caste is by origin Ethnological, Political, or Professional, its tendency in modern India is to subside and fade away out of active life. But to this threefold classification (by Professor Max Müller)* of the source of Indian caste must be added, I submit, a fourth term, Sectarian, meaning the castes which are produced by difference of religion, by new gods, new rites, new views, and new dogmas. While the three first-named sources are virtually closed, producing no fresh varieties, this fourth source is still open and flowing, and its effect upon the social fabric is still actively dissolvent. Where tribal and political distinctions are blending and amalgamating according to the ordinary operation of civilizing forces, this process is in India continually interrupted and foiled by the religious element of disseveration; the community, instead of coalescing, is again split up by divergences of doc-

* "Chips from a German Workshop."

trine, of ritual, or by some mere caprice of superstition, into separate bodies which eat and intermarry only among themselves, thus establishing and preserving isolation. New objects of adoration are continually being discovered and becoming popular; certain shrines get into fashion, or an image is set up, or a temple built; new prophets arise with fresh messages to deliver, or with fresh rules for a devout life. Holy men are canonized by the *vox populi* after death, or even attain apotheosis as incarnations of the elder gods; and these also have usually their recognised disciples. In fact, the chief among these moralists and miracle-workers are the founders of sects, and sects always tend to become sub-castes. Thus the objects of Hindu adoration are constantly changing, so that the Indian Pantheon, like the palace in the Persian parable, is but a caravanserai; the great dome of many-coloured glass endures with little change, but its occupants come and go. And these novelties of teaching or practice mark off the persons who adopt them; the devotees often become known by a separate denomination which denotes a peculiar discipline or tenet, or perhaps only the exclusive worship of one god or deified man. So that, if a metaphor may be borrowed from physical science, we may say that in India all Hindu religions belong to the *fissiparous* order; they have the property of disseverance into portions, each of which retains life and growth. And as the direction taken by the development of any considerable sect is toward the formation of a caste, the result is that continual piece-meal disintegration by religious anarchy of the mass of society, which I have endeavoured to describe.

We can perceive the vestiges of similar tendencies even in Great Britain, where very peculiar sectaries, like the Quakers, have lived and married for generations among themselves, and where any radical antagonism of creeds is still a serious bar to matrimony. But the state of things in India can only be realised by supposing that the Irvingites, for instance, should have become, as an inevitable and obvious consequence of their distinctive tenets, a class so far drawn apart from the rest of England that marriage beyond the communion would be of disputable validity, and dining with them would compromise the social and religious reputation of Anglican Churchmen.*

To give any intelligible account of beliefs and liturgies thus complicated, some system of classification appears necessary. I have therefore attempted to adopt one, though I do not pretend to much confidence in the hypothesis which it involves. Taking as the lowest stage of religious thought that conception which seems the most narrow and superficial, and proceeding upward as the ideas which I suppose to lie at the root of each conception become wider and more far-fetched, I should distribute the popular worship that can now be witnessed within Berar into the grades here following. It should be explained that these divisions in no way denote separate bodies of exclusive votaries, nor do they correspond even with any parallel steps of civilized intelligence or of social position. The average middle-class Hindu might be brought by one part or another of his every-day religious practice, within any or many of these classes, namely :—

1. The worship of mere stocks and stones and of local configurations, which are unusual or grotesque in size, shape, or position.

2. The worship of things inanimate, which are gifted with mysterious motion.

3. The worship of animals which are feared.

4. The worship of visible things animate or inanimate which are directly or indirectly useful and profitable, or which possess any incomprehensible function or property.

* Much might be suggested here (in support of what Sir Henry Maine has recently pointed out) upon the peculiar influence of the English law in arresting in India this process of constant change; in stereotyping institutions once found to exist, or perhaps only found by books to *have* existed, the facts having been long since transformed. A very notable example of this may be seen in the history and present state of the modern sect called *Brahmo Somâj.* They are philosophical deists, who disapprove of the common Hindu marriage ceremonies ; but for a long time it was not safe for the Brahmoists to disregard them, because any material omission of the customary rites might invalidate their marriage in an English court of law. Had no such court existed, they would probably have gone their own way, and become a sub-caste, with matrimonial rules of their own, which would have been recognised as perfectly valid, for Brahmists, by all Hindus.

5. The worship of a *Deo*, or spirit, a thing without form and void—the vague impersonation of the uncanny sensation that comes over one at certain places.

6. The worship of dead relatives and other deceased persons known in their lifetime to the worshipper.

7. The worship of persons who had a great reputation during life, or who died in some strange or notorious way—at shrines.

8. The worship, in temples, of the persons belonging to the foregoing class, as demigods or subordinate deities.

9. The worship of manifold local incarnations of the elder deities, and of their symbols.

10. The worship of departmental deities.

11. The worship of the supreme gods of Hinduism, and of their ancient incarnations and personifications, handed down by the Brahmanic scriptures.

This category comprises, I think, all the different kinds of Fetichism and Polytheism which make up the popular religion of Berar. With the inner and higher sides of Hindu teaching and belief known in the country I do not now pretend to deal, except so far as these doctrines (which are usually to be respected as profound and serious) have degenerated into mere idolatry of symbols, a relapse to which they are constantly liable. And with regard to the varieties of worship in the catalogue just finished, they are of course deeply tinged throughout by the strong skylight reflection of over-arching Brahmanism ; whence the topmost classes now pretend to derive their meaning immediately. Yet it may be said of all (except perhaps of the latest classes in the series) that these ideas are not so much the offspring of Brahmanism as its children by adoption ; they have not sprung out of any authoritative teaching or revelation which would control and guide their development, nor are they the decaying survivals either of a higher faith or of a lower superstition. They are living and fertile conceptions of species constantly germinating and throwing up new shoots, in the present age and in the country where they are found.

The worship of Stocks or Stones, for instance, is an active species which incessantly spreads and reproduces itself before our eyes, with different modifications that all eventually find their place and meaning in the general order of the people's religion. This worship has been placed in the lowest class, because it is taken to represent the earliest phase of Indian fetichism now existing. Let fetichism be defined as the straightforward objective adoration of visible substances fancied to possess some mysterious influence or faculty; then it may be supposed that the intelligence which argues that a stock or stone embodies divinity only because it has a queer, unusual form, expresses a low type of fetichism. And to this type I am disposed to refer, for their original idea and motive, all such practices as the worship of a stone oddly shaped, of a jutting bit of rock, a huge boulder lying alone in the plain, a circle of stones, a peculiar mark on the hill-side or a hummock atop, an ancient carved pillar, a milestone unexpectedly set up where none was before, with strange hieroglyphics, a telegraph post, fossils with their shell marks; in fact, any object of the kind that catches attention as being out of the common way. Now the Brahmanic explanation of this reverence for curious looking things, especially for things conical and concave, is always at hand and producible to the earnest inquirer after divine emblems or manifestations; but these interpretations appear to belong to a later symbolism, which is habitually invented by the more ingenious to account upon orthodox principles for what is really nothing but primitive fetichism rising into a higher atmosphere. I mean that this worship would prevail in India if the Brahmanic symbolism had never been thought of—does prevail, as a fact, in other far-distant countries. For the feeling which actuates the uninitiated Indian worshipper of stocks and stones, or of what are called freaks of nature, is in its essence that simple awe of the unusual which belongs to no particular religion. It survives in England to this day in the habit of ascribing grotesque and striking landmarks or puzzling antiquities to the Devil, who is, or has been, the residuary legatee of all obsolete Pagan superstitions in Christian countries. In any district of India such objects or local configurations as the Devil's Quoits (near Stanton), the Devil's Jumps (in Surrey), or the Devil's Punch-bowl (in Sussex), would be worshipped; similar things are actually worshipped all over Berar, and in every case some signification, either mythical or symbolical, has been contrived or sanctioned by some expert Brahman to justify and authorise the custom. Yet it seems certain that among the vulgar there is at first no *arrière pensée*, or second meaning, in their adoration. The worshipper requires no such motive, he asks for no sign, offers no prayer, expects no reward. He pays reverent attentions to the Unaccountable Thing, the startling expression of an unknown power, and goes his way. It is not difficult to perceive how this original downright adoration of queer-looking objects is modified by passing into the higher order of imaginative superstition. First, the stone is the abode of some spirit; its curious shape or situation betraying *possession*. Next, this strange form or aspect argues some *design*, or handiwork, of supernatural beings, or is the vestige of their presence on earth; and one step further lands us in the world-wide regions of mythology and heroic legend, when the natural remarkable features of a hill, a cleft rock, a cave, or a fossil, commemorate the miracles and feats of some saint, demi-god, or full-blown deity. Berar is abundantly furnished with such fables, and beyond them we get, as I think, to the regarding of stones as emblems of mysterious attributes, to the phallic rites, to the Saligram or fossil in which Vishnu is manifest, and to all that class of notions which entirely separate the outward image from the power really worshipped. So that at last we emerge into pure symbolism, as when anything appears to be selected arbitrarily to serve as a visible point for spiritual adoration. The present writer knew a Hindu officer of great shrewdness and very fair education, who devoted several hours daily to the elaborate worship of five round pebbles, which he had appointed to be his symbol of Omnipotence. Although his general belief was in one all-pervading Divinity, he must have something symbolic to handle and address.

It may be affirmed that the adoration of Things Inanimate having motion is, even in its rudest expression, more reasonable than the habit of staring with awe at a big stone, and may therefore be held to mark a slight advance towards higher levels. In Berar we have the worship of elements as fetich, of elements inhabited and directed by local spirits, and of elements with mythological origin or descent from the gods. Water runs up this whole gamut or scale of religious expression. The honours paid to a running brook, a hot spring, or to a river that alternately floods and falls—causing famine or abundance, bringing riches or ruin—are intended for the living water itself by a large class of votaries; and this notion of material identity seems preserved by the customs of bathing in sacred streams, of self-drowning, and of witch-dipping, which last custom resembles exactly that of England.* Suicide and witch-dipping in rivers present both sides of the same conception, acceptance or rejection by the divine element. Further on, the water-power is no longer deified nature, but controlled by a supernatural spirit, we have the kelpie who inhabits rivers under the form of a buffalo and personifies their effects. His name is *Mahisoba*, he has no image, but a buffalo's head is cut off and deposited on his altar. After this we ascend to mythologic fictions about the origin and descent of the greater rivers from the Hindu heaven, and to legends of streams turned, stopped, or otherwise engineered by interposition of the divine energy incarnate. The Southern Berar country is much tossed about by intersecting ridges and devious hill-ranges. The rivers pierce their way down from the watersheds by sharp angles and deep cuttings which suggest mighty forces. A torrent goes struggling and rushing through its channel choked by huge rocks and broken by rapids. The muffled roar of its waters, which cease not night or day, affect the mind with a sense of endless labour and pain; you might well fancy that the river-god was moaning over his eternal task of cleaving stony barriers and drawing down the tough basalt hills. Fire is a great Hindu Fetich, but it is nowhere in Berar generated spontaneously; and I believe that even the worship of *Agni*, the fire-god, has fallen to desuetude. The sun is the tribal god, as fetich, of the aboriginal *Korkus* who live apart among the northern hills of Berar; of course he is also worshipped by all Hindus under different conceptions and doctrines regard-

* It will be recollected that an old Frenchman was drowned in Essex, on suspicion of sorcery, so late as the year of grace 1863.

ing his personality. Tree-worship has a wide range. A tree is first reverenced as a thing to be feared, having sentient existence and mysterious potency, as proved by waving branches and weird sounds. Next, fruitful trees are honoured for yielding good fruits, which are bestowed yearly in more or less quantity according to some hidden caprice that may possibly be propitiated; then a particular species becomes sacred to a well-known god; or a great solitary trunk becomes the abode of a nameless impalpable spirit; or a dark grove or thicket may be his habitation. Soon this is perceived to be ground sacred to one of the acknowledged Hindu deities, with recognised titles and attributes; either by having got woven into some myth or local legend, or because some pious person sets up a temple therein, or because an anchorite fixes his hermitage there and devotes himself to a particular divinity. There are several thickets and clumps of trees in Berar, from which no stick is ever cut, nor even the dead wood picked up, though firewood is scarce and timber valuable. A temple or shrine will usually be found among the trees; but the sanctity of the spot does not necessarily derive from the building, the converse is more likely to be the case; and I conjecture that these dim and dusky retreats have usually been at first consecrated to the gods by some alarming accident or apparition which betokened the presence of a deity.

It does not seem hard to trace up thus in India, from the root of primitive tree-worship, the growth and ramification of the innumerable customs which, in the East, as once in England, ascribe essential virtues to certain trees in matters of ritual use and magic practice. In Berar different families are said to pay exclusive honour to certain kinds of trees; the rod of a special wood still divines water, and witches are scourged with switches of the castor-oil plant, which possesses sovereign virtue in the exorcising and dislodging of the evil power. It has been said that the English held hazelwood to be of specific efficacy in both cases, for detecting water and witches; while the Maypole and the mistletoe are supposed to be relics of early Keltic tree-worship. But in England the pedigree of these customs is dim, dubious, and disputable; the Church has for ages been denouncing and stamping out the ancient indigenous superstitions. Whereas in India the aboriginal autocthonic ideas of the country folk have been subjected to no persecution by dominant faiths, so that the entire concatenation of these ideas may be exhibited and tested within one province; the various practices and beliefs are alive before us; the sequence of them is close; we can collect the evidence of our eyes and verify it by cross-examination of devout believers, men far above the mental calibre of ignorant savages and rude peasants.

The worship of Animals, which by their appearance or habits alarm and startle human beings, is so obvious in its primitive reason, and so common throughout India, that it needs no detailed description for Berar. Of course, the tiger, wolf, monkey, serpent, and, above all serpents, the *cobra di capella*, are the most prominent objects of reverence. Some modifications and later aspects of the primordial instinct towards propitiation of a fearsome beast may be noticed. For instance, a malignant tiger's body may be possessed by the unquiet ghost of a dead man; or it may be the disguise adopted by a living sorcerer of evil temper. In another province an old witch, suspected of roving at night under a striped skin, had all her teeth knocked out to disable her. Here we have the transition from a simple Fetich to the idea of a disembodied spirit, and of possession. Then the idea gets completely superhuman; the tiger is an evil demon, without antecedent connection with humanity; and the terror spread abroad by such a pest become wholly preternatural has led to the institution of a departmental god, just as a violent epidemic necessitates a special administration to control it. Any application having reference to the ravages of a tiger, may be addressed to *Waghdeo*, though the particular beast who vexes you should also be cajoled with offerings. But the most complete and absolute elevation of an animal to the higher ranks of deified beings is to be seen in the case of *Hanumàn*, who from a sacred monkey has risen, through mists of heroic fable and wild forest legends, to be the universal tutelary god of all village settlements. The setting up of his image in the midst of an hamlet is the outward and visible sign and token of fixed habitation, so that he is found in every township. Ward, in his work on the Hindu religion, says that the monkey is venerated in memory of the demigod Hanumàn, which seems to be plainly putting the cart before the horse, for the monkey is evidently at the bottom of the whole story. Hanumàn is now generally supposed to have been adopted into the Hindu heaven, from the Non-Aryan or aboriginal idolatries; though to my mind any uncivilized Indian of this day, Aryan or Non-Aryan, would surely fall down and worship at first sight of such a beast as the ape. Then there is the modern idea that this god was really a great chief of some such aboriginal tribe as those which to this day dwell almost like wild creatures in the remote forests of India; and this may well be the nucleus of fact at the bottom of the famous legend regarding him. It seems as if hero-worship and animal-worship had got mixed up in the myth of Hanumàn. At any rate his traditions and attributes illustrate curiously the process by which a mere animal fetich, dreaded for his ugliness and half-human ways, soon rises to be an elfin king of the monkey tribe, next becomes a powerful genius, and latterly emerges into the full glory of divine *Avatár*, surrounded by the most extravagant fables to explain away the simian head and tail which have stuck to him through all his metamorphoses.

Some examples may be given of the simple and superficial indications which suffice to prove divine manifestations in animals. The goat has a peculiar trick of shivering at intervals, and this is taken to be the *afflatus*. In the North of India he is turned loose along a disputed border-line, and where he shivers there is the mark set up; the Thugs would only sacrifice a goat if the patroness *Devi* had signified acceptance by one of these tremors, but then they washed the animal to make him shake himself the quicker.* Obviously this habit (like the bray of an ass, which is one of the strongest omens) is ascribed to supernatural seizure, because it is uncertain, inexplicable, and apparently motiveless. I remark, in passing,

* Plutarch mentions that among the Greeks the test whether a goat was in a fit state for the sacrifice that preceded the interrogation of an oracle, was by cold water. If the animal did not shiver and shake himself when the water was thrown over him, the offering was not judged acceptable to the god.

that the scapegoat is an institution widely known and constantly used in India. The cat seems to be comparatively unnoticed by Indian credulity, though her squalling at night boded ill to Thugs; and it may be guessed that only in lands where the great carnivora have been exterminated does she keep up the last faint relics of primitive animal-worship. With wild beasts that are a real plague and horror she has no chance in competition for the honours of *diablerie;* but her nocturnal wanderings, her noiseless motions, and her capacity for sudden demoniac fierceness, distinguish her from other domesticated animals; so that her uncanny reputation still survives among the obscure pagan superstitions yet haunting us under the name of witchcraft.

The worship of Things and creatures beneficial might be classed apart from and after that of puzzling and menacing things, dead or alive, because the idea of gratitude and of boons attainable by propitiations seems a step in advance of the idea of averting ills. I have already alluded to the reverence paid to fruitful trees; and everyone knows that horned cattle, the wealth of a simple society, are adored throughout India. Comte remarks that this feeling has preserved certain species of plants and animals through the ages when no ownership existed to protect them; but after all they were really preserved by the universal appreciation of their value; and worship was only the savage man's expression of his sense of that value, combined with his ignorance of the laws which gave or withheld it.

Next after Plants and Animals, in the order of progress from the simple to the more complex notions might be placed the grotesque practice of worshipping Implements, Utensils, and generally the tools of the trade or craft by which one subsists. Not only does the husbandman pray to his plough, the fisher to his net,* the weaver to his loom; but the scribe adores his pen, and the banker his account books. Each sets up the thing

* Compare Habakkuk, i. 16, "Therefore they sacrifice unto their net," &c. Of this custom, the most sensational example was to be found among the Thugs, who used to worship the pickaxe which they carried for speedy burial of their victims on the spot of the murder.

itself as a fetich, does it homage, and makes offering before it. To ascribe to the implements the power which lies in the guiding hand or brain, is at least a thought farther fetched than to adore the generation of fruit on a tree, or the swelling udders of a cow; while the same fancy survives and is reflected over and over again in the legends of mediæval magic, of magic swords enchanted armour, seven-leagued boots, and the like. Moreover, it may be permissible to regard this tool-worship of the Hindus as the earliest phase or type of the tendency which later on leads those of one guild or of the same walk in life to support and cultivate one god who is elected, in lieu of individual tool-fetiches melted down, to preside over their craft or trade interests.

Up to this point I have been trying to classify the different kinds of worship of palpable objects, or, at farthest, of substances which by their shape or their qualities appear to evidence possession by a spirit, or the working of a superhuman occult power. The idea which suggests fear and (consequently) worship of Spiritual beings invisible, without form, name, or specific substantiality, is, I suppose, deeper and more abstract. It pervades the whole religious atmosphere of Central India. Every mysterious grewsome-looking dell, cavern, steep pass, and wild desolate hill-top or ridge has its *Deo;* never seen of man, but felt by those who visit the spot—by shepherds and herdsmen camping out far amid the melancholy wolds, or by travellers along the lonely tracks. The notion of fixed habitation in and identity with some object has now expanded into the notion of a *haunting.* But the whereabouts is sometimes marked by a heap of stones, sometimes by rags tied to a bush; occasionally by chains suspended mystically from a cliff or a tree; or the spirit wanders round a huge old banyan-tree or ruined temple.* As yet, however, he has

* Mr. Bowring, in his "Eastern Experiences" (1871), describes the Spirit-houses found in the Mysore forests—little sheds built over the white ant-hills, and dedicated (as I understand) to the wood-demons generally. Captain Forsyth, writing about the highlands of Berar, mentions that when the Gonds fell the wood on a hill-side, they leave a little clump, to serve as a refuge for the elf or spirit whom they have dislodged.

no name, no history or distinct origin, and his range is limited territorially. Yet within the uncertain limits of his haunt he can make himself very obnoxious if not duly propitiated; and fortunately there are always to be found pious men who have devoted themselves to decyphering (for a consideration) the signs of his displeasure.

This is, I conjecture, the dim *penumbra*, the vague floating *deisidaimonia*, which envelops embryonic conceptions of positive forms belonging to deities recognisable by name and character. We may surmise that this misty zone must have been passed through before a clearer air was first reached; before people gradually evolved out of these shadowy terrors the definite outline of their anthropomorphism. And this stage may perhaps mark the first imaginings of superhuman beings finally dissociated from their visible shells, that is, from their manifestations as individuals through natural substances, a stone, a tree, or a beast. The next step after this may be guessed to be the investing of this unseen intangible spirit with a man's individuality, though without a visible body; and thus the transition to anthropomorphism—from unseen spirits in general to unseen spirits in particular—is represented, as I venture to infer, by the worship of the ghosts of dead relatives. For it is easier to imagine that the active intelligence and familiar soul which have just left a corpse still exist round you in an invisible personality, than to abstract the notion of definite spiritual beings belonging by origin to an order quite distinct from humanity. Thus in Berar the aboriginal tribes, which are as yet little touched by Brahmanic doctrines, practise most elaborate and singular obsequies known by a name which may be accurately translated into the Irish term *wake*, meaning a vigil. The ceremony includes that very suggestive practice (known also to Brahmanic rites) of bringing back to his house the dead person's soul, supposed to have lost its home by the body's death. A stone, or some such object, is picked up at the grave, and carried reverentially back to the house, where it is worshipped for a few days, and then decently disposed of. There are also libations and a funeral banquet, sacrifices over the grave to an effigy, and the mourners sing an elegy, of which this is the curiously familiar burden—

> "Naked he came, and naked has gone.
> This dwelling-place belongs neither to you nor to me,
> To the life which has gone."

The ordinary funeral chant over a Hindu says, "He who spoke has gone;" and this idea, like the phrase so commonly used in all countries to express death—that the breath, the visible token of life, has departed—points to the flitting of something animated and even material. Though it issues forth from the corpse, it must be still somewhere, probably still hovering about its former home and friends. Now the direct motive and purpose of these earliest and most primitive mortuary rites are, I believe, the laying of the ghost; but from the wailing adoration of these Non-Aryan woodlanders, up to the ceremonious annual oblations and invocations of the high-caste Hindu, they are throughout more or less a kind of worship. And at this point we have to look for some explanation of the process by which other less narrow and less obvious ideas of supernaturalism may be conjectured to have developed out of this universal necrolatry. The reverent mind appears to me to rise, by a natural method of selection, from the indiscriminate adoring of dead persons known or akin to the worshipper's family during life, to the distinctive worship of persons who were of high local repute while they lived, or who died in some remarkable way. It would seem that the honours which are at first paid to all departed spirits come gradually to be concentrated, as divine honours, upon the Manes of notables; probably the reasoning is that they must continue influential in the spirit-world. For so far as I have been able to trace back the origin of the best-known minor provincial deities, they are usually men of past generations who have earned special promotion and brevet rank among disembodied ghosts by some peculiar acts or accident of their lives or deaths, especially among the rude and rough classes. With the communities of a higher mental level different motives for the selection prevail; but of this more hereafter. Popular deifications appear to have been founded, in their simplest form, on mere wonder and pity, as for mental and bodily afflictions; or an affecting incident, such as the death of a boy bridegroom (now the god *Dulha Deo*) in the midst of his own marriage procession; * or on horror at terrible and lamentable deaths, as by suicide, by wild beasts, by murder, or by some hideous calamity. Human sacrifice has always been common in India as a last resort for appeasing divine wrath, when manifested in a strange and inexplicable way; and it is suspected to be still the real motive of occasional mysterious murders. *Chând Khan* is a demon rather than a deity, but his tomb is worshipped on one bastion of every mud-fort in the Dekhan. The legend (without doubt founded on fact) is that a man thus named was buried alive under some bastion of which the building had been supernaturally thwarted until this sacrifice was made, when all hindrance and mysterious opposition ceased at once. Some years ago the piers of a railway bridge under construction in Central India were twice washed away, when nearly finished, by the floods; and a rumour spread abroad among the Bheels of the neighbouring jungles that one of them was to be seized and sacrificed by the engineers who had received such manifest proof of mysterious opposition to their work.

The Bunjâras, a tribe much addicted to highway robbery, worship a famous bandit, who probably lived and died in some notorious way. Any renowned soldier would certainly be worshipped after death, if his tomb were well known and accessible. M. Raymond, the French commander who died at Hyderabad, has been there canonised after a fashion; General Nicholson (who died in the storming of Delhi, 1857) was adored as a hero in his lifetime, in spite of his violent persecution of his own devotees, and there are other known instances of the commemoration of Europeans who have been feared or

* Compare the legends of Thammuz, Adonis, Ganymede, and Hylas. Mere grief at bereavement may be another motive. See "Wisdom of Solomon," xiv. 15: "For a father afflicted with untimely mourning, when he hath made an image of his child soon taken away, now honoured him as a god which was then dead. Thus, in course of time, an ungodly custom grown strong was kept as a law."

loved. Nor do I make out that the origin and conception of these local deities are at first connected with the Brahmanic doctrines by the unlettered and unsophisticated crowd who set up these shrines at their own pleasure. The immediate motive is nothing but a vague inference from great natural gifts or from strange fortunes to supernatural visitation, or from power during life to power prolonged beyond it, though when a shrine becomes popular the Brahmans take care to give its origin an orthodox interpretation. The saint or hero is admitted into the upper circles of divinity, much as a successful soldier or millionnaire is recognised by fashionable society, takes a new title, and is welcomed by a judiciously liberal aristocracy.

Between the class of dead men who are worshipped from feelings of admiration, surprise, pity, or terror, and the class of deified Saints, the line which might be drawn would, I consider, make a step upward. The common usage of adoring the spirit of a *Sati* (or widow who has burnt herself on the pyre of her husband) at the cenotaph put up on the spot, may perhaps be taken as an intermediate link; for she has been exalted both by the horror of her ending and the supreme merit of her devotion.*

Of the numerous local gods known to have been living men, by far the greater portion derive from the ordinary canonisation of holy personages. This system of canonising has grown out of the world-wide sentiment that rigid asceticism and piety combined with implicit faith gradually develop a miraculous faculty. The saint or hermit may have deeper motives—the triumph of the spirit over corrupt matter, of virtue over vanity and lusts, or the self-purification required of mediæval magicians and mystical alchemists before they could deal with the great secrets of nature; but the popular belief is that his relentless austerity extorts thaumaturgic power from reluctant

* Compare Euripides, "Alcestis," 995. "Nor let the tomb of thy wife be ccounted as a mound over dead that perish, but let it be honoured equally with the gods, for travellers to worship. And some one going up the winding path shall say, 'She once died for her husband, and is now a blest divinity (νῦν δ' ἐστὶ μάκαιρα δαίμων).'"

gods. And of him who works miracles do they say in India, as in Samaria they said of Simon Magus, "This man is the great power of God;" wherefore after death (if not in life) he is honoured as divine indeed. Now the word miracle must not be understood in our sense of an interposition to alter unvarying natural laws, for in India no such laws have been definitely ascertained; it means only something that passes an ordinary man's understanding, authenticated and enlarged by vague and vulgar report. And the exhibition of marvellous devotion or contempt for what is valued by the world stimulates inventive credulity. He who does such things is sure to be credited with miracles, probably during his life, assuredly after his death. When such an one dies his body is not burnt, but buried; a disciple or relative of the saint establishes himself over the tomb as steward of the mysteries and receiver of the temporalities; vows are paid, sacrifice is made, a saint's day is added to the local calendar, and the future success of the shrine depends upon some lucky hit in the way of prophecy or fulfilment of prayers. The number of shrines thus raised in Berar alone to these anchorites and persons deceased in the odour of sanctity is large, and it is constantly increasing. Some of them have already attained the rank of temples, they are richly endowed, and collect great crowds at the yearly pilgrim gatherings, like the tombs of celebrated Christian martyrs in the Middle Ages. But although the shrines of a Hindu ascetic and of St. Thomas of Canterbury may have acquired fame among the vulgar and ignorant by precisely the same attribute—their reputation for miraculous efficacy—yet the only point of resemblance between the two cases is this common inference from eminent sanctity in the world to wonder-working power in the grave. For whereas the great Catholic Church never allowed the lowest English peasant to regard St. Thomas or St. Edmund as anything higher than glorified intercessors, with a sort of delegated miraculous power, the Indian prophet or devotee does by the patronage of the Brahmans rise gradually in the hierarchy of supernatural beings, until his human origin fades and disappears completely in the haze of tradition, and he takes rank as a god. We see by this example of India what the Church did for the medley of pagan tribes and communities which came within her pale in the dark ages of anarchic credulity, before great Pan was quite dead. In those days, when, according to Milman,* saints were "multiplied and deified" by popular suffrage, when "hardly less than divine power and divine will was assigned to them," when the "wonder-fed and wonder-seeking worship" of shrines and relics actually threatened to "supersede the worship of God and his Son," it may be almost surmised that nothing but a supreme spiritual authority saved Christianity from falling back for a time into a sort of Polytheism.

But, in India, whatever be the original reason for venerating a deceased man, his upward course toward deification is the same. At first we have the grave of one whose name, birthplace, and parentage are well known in the district; if he died at home, his family often set up a shrine, instal themselves in possession, and realize a handsome income out of the offerings; they become hereditary keepers of the sanctuary, if the shrine prospers and its virtues stand test. Or if the man wandered abroad, settled near some village or sacred spot, became renowned for his austerity or his afflictions, and there died, the neighbours think it great luck to have the tomb of a holy man within their borders, † and the landholders administer the shrine by manorial right.‡ In the course of a very few years, as the recollection of the man's personality becomes misty, his origin grows mysterious, his career takes a legendary hue, his birth and death were both supernatural; in the next generation the names of the elder gods get introduced into the story, and so the marvellous tradition works itself into a myth, until

* "Latin Christianity," vol. vi. pp. 13, 417.

† A good instance will be found in the history of Mira Bâi, an authentic princess of the Jypore house, who is now worshipped by a sect as their patron saint. They say that she vanished from earth through the fissure of a rock. So did a woman in West Berar, not many years ago.

‡ In Affghanistan, certain villagers close to our frontier recently arranged to strangle a saint who abode among them, in order to secure his tomb within their lands. There is a similar story in Southey's ballads, of a design upon St. Romuald, which is styled by the Spanish chronicler a "determinacion bestial y indiscreta."

nothing but a personal incarnation can account for such a series of prodigies. The man was an *Avatár* of Vishnu or Siva; his supreme apotheosis is now complete, and the Brahmans feel warranted in providing for him a niche in the orthodox Pantheon.

It is scarcely worth while to enumerate for English readers the instances upon which this sketch of religious growth in Berar has been drawn out. This could be done only by giving a list of barbarous-sounding names of places and personages; but the details on which I rely could be produced, if want of space did not prevent it, and if they were of any value beyond the province. Of wonder-working saints, hermits, and martyrs (for Mahomedan and even Christian tombs are worshipped occasionally by Hindus) the name is legion. There are some potent devotees still in the flesh who are great medicine men, others very recently dead who exhale power, and others whose name and local fame have survived, but with a supernatural tinge rapidly coming out. Above these we have obscure local deities who have entirely shaken off their mortal taint; while beyond these again are the great provincial gods. Four of the most popular gods in Berar, whose images and temples are famous in the Dekhan, are *Kandoba, Vittoba, Beiroba,* and *Bâlâji.* These are now grand incarnations of the Supreme Triad; yet by examining the legends of their embodiment and appearance upon earth we obtain fair ground for surmising that all of them must have been notable living men not so very long ago.

Such is, so far as one can trust personal inquiry and observation, the regular process of Theogony, or the generation of local gods, which is constantly going on before our eyes in the districts of Central India. We have before us there the worship of dead kinsfolk and friends, then the particular adoration of notables recently departed; then of people divinely afflicted or divinely gifted, of saints and heroes known to have been men; next, the worship of demi-gods, and, finally, that of powerful deities retaining nothing human but their names and their images. It is suggested that all these are links along one chain of the development of the same idea; and that out of the crowd of departed spirits whom primitive folk adore, certain individuals are elevated to a larger worship by notoriety in life or death. At this point a different selecting agency comes into play, that of Successful Wonder Working; and it is by the luck of acquiring a first-class reputation for efficacious answers to vows that some few Manes emerge into a still higher and more refined order of divinity. This is the kind of success which has made the fortune of some of the most popular, the richest, and the most widely-known gods in Berar, who do all the leading business, and possess the confidence of the respectable and substantial professions. It should be remarked that the earliest start of even a first-rate god may have been exceedingly obscure; but if he or his shrine make a few good cures at the outset (especially among women and valuable cattle), his reputation goes rolling up like a snowball. One of the largest annual fairs in Berar now gathers round the grave of an utterly insignificant hermit. It thus becomes easy to perceive how the source of a far-flowing religion may be lost in obscurity; so that in later times, when the divinity or the sect has become famous, no one will accept the suggestion of a slight or humble, or accidental, origin for so great a development. The scholar explains the fact by some picturesque theory of mythical evolution; the devout believer builds up the traditions of some extraordinary life, full of miracles and mystic utterances.

Thus successful thaumaturgy, with lapse of time sufficient to evaporate the lingering flavour of mortal origin, are the two qualifications which lead to a high status among gods. But interest and a good connection open out short cuts to distinction for gods as well as for men. When the original saint or hero belonged in the flesh to a particular tribe, caste, or profession, in such case he may become the tutelary deity of that community, and is less dependent on continual proof of his efficacy, because the worship of him by his constituents is a point of honour, tradition, and *esprit de corps*. On the other hand, a god patronised exclusively by one trade or calling is liable to drop into a department, by contracting a speciality for the particular needs and grievances of his congregation.

But this is so far from being the natural ultimate mould into which polytheism falls, that gods now universally venerated have occasionally expanded, like Diana of the Ephesians, far beyond the circle of departmental practice. Comte's view of the development of polytheism is that man gradually generalised his observations of nature, grouping all the phenomena which resembled each other as the acts or characteristics of a Person; so that a cluster of similar Fetiches were amalgamated into one personification of the natural department to which they all belonged, which thus came forth as a god with special attributes. But this departmental system is only one side of polytheism, which in no time or country has been rigidly distributed into bureaux or portfolios with one supreme Jupiter, like the French Imperial Government. The Hindus, at any rate, have a multitude of gods very high in estimation and with a large *clientèle*, who preside over no special forces of nature, and have no exclusive province, but subsist solely upon their general reputation for good or bad influence over human affairs. The names of these deities are gradually noised abroad, the circle of their local notoriety widens, the crowd at their annual holy-day increases, the offerings attract Brahmans and the leading ascetic orders, who sing their praise, proclaim their miracles, and invent for them orthodox pedigrees. Soon a great prince visits, and perhaps endows, their temple; until at last the deity throws aside all separate functions, and is set up firmly as an all-powerful manifestation of the great Creators and Rulers of the Hindu universe.

On the whole, therefore, there is good evidence for concluding that the extravagant and unconscionable use made by Brahmans of their doctrine of divine embodiment is quite enough to account for the creation of the greater number of personal gods actually worshipped, without drawing upon any other source of polytheism. Nor are they always content with posthumous identification of a remarkable man as a god. They still occasionally refuse even to admit that the dissolution of the first mortal body was a sign that the god had departed from among them; and they employ that astonishing device, so notorious in India, of a perpetual succession of incarnations. At least two persons have been living within the last few years in Western and Central India who are asserted to be the tenements or vessels which the deity, who originally manifested himself in some wonderful personage, has now chosen for his abode on earth; and one native official well known in the Bombay Presidency, in whom the signs of divinity had been detected, was so harassed by an incessant following of devout folk that he became unable to do his business. This is, however, an inordinate use of the mystery. Its main employment is to keep up the prestige and privileges of the classical deities, by declaring all wonderful and famous personages to be embodiments of them; and thus have many great prophets and moral teachers been identified and absorbed, except those who actually attacked Brahmanism. One of the most numerous sects in Berar, and throughout the Dekhan, is that of the *Lingàyets;* they wear constantly the Linga, as Siva's emblem, and their founder was one *Chamba Basàpa*, evidently a great man in his day, who preached high morality, though probably tinged with mysticism. He is now commonly recognised to have been an incarnation of Siva, and his followers are merely a peculiar section of Siva-worshippers. The other leading sect among the trading classes of the Dekhan is that of the Jains, who adore certain deified saints that have traversed a series of metempsychoses. But the Jains deny the Vedas, and are distinctly, though not exclusively, heretical; so their saints have never been exalted or absorbed into the Hindu Pantheon.

Then we have in Berar an anomalous sect, called the *Mànbhaus*, part of whom are laymen, and the rest live by strict rule as wandering friars and nuns, clothed in black. Their teaching is quite anti-Brahmanical, and the consequence is that their founder, one Krishna, is declared by the orthodox to have been a Brahman who disgraced himself by a terrible *mésalliance*, not by any means an incarnation of the god Krishna, as his more enthusiastic and less exclusive votaries say. This real Krishna must have been a person of some mark; one of those true religious reformers who have arisen from time to time in India out of the humblest classes, and have caused great spiritualistic revivals.* Men of this temperament have constantly come forth in India, who, by their active intellectual originality, joined to a spiritual kind of life, have stirred up great movements and aspirations in Hinduism, and have founded sects that endure to this day; but it has almost invariably happened that the later followers of such a teacher have undone his work of moral reform. They have fallen back upon evidences of miraculous birth, upon signs and wonders, and a superhuman translation from the world; so that gradually the founder's history becomes prodigious and extra-natural, until his real doctrines shrink into mystical secrets known only to the initiated disciples, while the vulgar turn the iconoclast into a new idol.

But this line of disquisition would bring us out upon that other vast field of religious ideas in India which have for their base, not religion, but morality; and for their object, not propitiation of the unseen powers, but an ethical reformation. Upon that ground it is not possible here to enter, as in this essay I am only attempting to draw an outline of the external popular superstitions, and hazarding some conjectures as to the way in which this prodigious panorama of divine things and persons, the outward and visible manifestations of pantheism, has been constructed. Nowhere but in India can we now survey with our eyes an indigenous polytheism in full growth, flourishing like a secular green bay-tree among a people of ancient culture; and the spectacle may be thought to present many interesting features and analogies. It would seem as if the old order had been continually, though slowly, changing, giving place to new —as if the manifold deities from below had always been pressing upon the earlier divinities, until, like Saturn and Hyperion, they were more or less superseded. The classic personifications of the elements, and of their grand operations, are not now much in vogue as gods of the people. Even the Supreme Triad of Hindu allegory, which represent the almighty powers

* Compare the life and doctrines of Râm Dàss, the tanner; Dàdu, cotton-cleaner; Kabir, Mahomedan weaver; Tuka Ram, farmer; Nàm Deo, tailor.

of creation, preservation, and destruction, have long ceased to preside actively over any such corresponding distribution of functions. The direct or primary worship of these three divinities, especially of Brahma, the Creator (whose occupation has, obviously, more or less gone), is comparatively rare; and if it be true that in these outlying districts their original names have gone mostly out of ritual use, the reason may be that the original types have been melted down and divided piecemeal among a variety of emanations and embodiments, and that the highest offices of universal administration have thus been put into commission. Perhaps the gods who have suffered least from the wear and tear, during centuries of religious caprice, and who have longest held their ancient forms and places in the front rank of popular imagination, are the gods of heroic legend. The reason may be that the original kings and warriors out of whom these divinities have developed were especially powerful and famous in their time, and therefore cast a broader and stronger personal shadow upon tradition than the ordinary saint, prophet, or anchorite. They have also this peculiar advantage—that poetry has, of course, been a powerful agent in India (as in ancient Europe) for developing heroes into demi-gods, for spreading the fame of their deeds as gods, and for defining their attributes.

But although polytheism still prevails and multiplies throughout the land, and although the Brahmanic system, deep rooted and wide-spreading, shows no signs of vital decay, one may nevertheless venture to anticipate that the end of simple paganism is not far distant in India. The beliefs of the multitude are the reflections of their social and political history through many generations. Now that the Hindus have been rescued by the English out of a chronic state of anarchy, insecurity, lawlessness, and precarious exposure to the caprice of despots, they will surely introduce, at least, some ideas of rule, organised purpose, and moral law, into their popular conceptions of the ways of their gods towards men. It seems certain, at any rate, that wider experience, nearer and more frequent intercourse with the outer world, and the general education of modern life, must soon raise even the masses above the mental level that can credit contemporary miracles and incarnations, however they may still hold by the prodigies of elder tradition. And this will be enough to sever the tap-root of a religion which now, like the banyan-tree which it venerates, strikes fresh root from every branch, discovers a new god under every mystery and wonder. Moreover, the evidences of an incipient turning away from gross idolatry and a religion of the senses are already to be seen high and low, in the popularity among the wandering aboriginal tribes of certain spiritual teachers, in the spread among the middle classes of certain mystical opinions and of much floating scepticism, and in the perceptible proclivity toward the faith of Islam occasionally exhibited by some of the independent Hindu chiefs.

# CHAPTER II.

## ON THE ORIGIN OF DIVINE MYTHS IN INDIA.

Grote's conclusion, in the History of Greece, regarding myths—Remarks upon his argument—Comparative observation of heroic and religious myths of India may throw some light on the general subject of growth of myths—Leading authorities on mythology ascribe myths too largely to personifications of natural phenomena—Suggestion that the theory of Euemerus has been too entirely condemned, and that in India the deification of humanity is one main source of divine legends and of theogonies—The process of the generation and development of gods can be witnessed in India—Mythology develops into polytheism out of the mystery of death, out of wonder at the deeds, sufferings, and saintly character of remarkable men—The Heaven thus created is a reflection of the earth below, and religion rests upon the analogy of nature—Spiritual ascetics absorbed into materialistic divinities—General conclusion as to the various sources of the deities, their legends, and attributes.

Grote, in the first volume of his History of Greece, discusses in full the nature of myths, and he determines that the mythical narrative of Europe is a special product of the imagination and feeling, radically distinct both from history and philosophy. He refuses altogether to treat the myths as containing any evidence upon matters of fact. He does not deny, indeed he affirms, that myths may often embody real facts and the names of real persons; but his position is that we have no test whereby to distinguish fact from fiction in any particular myth of which corroborative evidence is not forthcoming, so that we must treat all as "matter appropriate only for subjective history."

Looking to the arguments used in support of this sentence on the myths, one may question whether the historian has not been too exacting in his demands for corroboration, and too peremptory in discarding all reliance upon internal evidence and analogies, when he thus condemns indiscriminately all stories which are not specifically propped up by external proofs. For Grote maintains that a narrative of credible incidents raises of itself no more presumption (in default of positive testimony) that the incidents occurred, than does a composition of Defoe: he says that it is plausible fiction and nothing more.* He considers even the highest measure of intrinsic probability to be of itself insufficient to justify one's believing that any of the facts related really occurred; it can only make one admit that they may perhaps have occurred. An assertion may be made, he observes, of a thing entirely probable, which yet no one need credit, as if a man should assert that rain fell in Massachusetts on the day of the battle of Platæa. Here Grote seems to be a little hard on the myths. For, first, it is very difficult to distinguish between plausible fiction (of the kind, for example, to which Defoe's History of the Plague belongs) and genuine history, in dealing with the records come down from ancient and uncritical ages; since extrinsic evidence thus preserved and transmitted is as likely to be plausible fiction as any other credible narrative, and we have very scanty means of actually sifting or testing any evidence whatever as to particular events or persons. If we may only receive as credible those ancient narratives which could not possibly turn out to be very plausible fiction, we shall be hard pushed for the trustworthy authentication of much early history, religious and secular. Secondly, the example of the supposed assertion as to simultaneous rainfall at Platæa and in Massachusetts is hardly fair. A man's assertion of an isolated fact of which he could not possibly have any positive knowledge, either directly or by hearsay, is a very different thing from affirming credible facts which might reasonably, and according to the known habits of the people who relate the facts, have been handed down by tradition from the persons who witnessed them to those who related them. And, lastly, I venture to think that Grote's purely sceptical attitude ignores a great deal of collateral evidence in favour of myths being ordinarily formed round a nucleus of facts, any other formation being exceptional. At any rate, if one may rely upon comparative observation of the growth of myths in various parts of a country

* History of Greece, Chapter XVI., page 413, small edition.

in which they spring up like mushrooms, a very great number of the myths of Indian polytheism and hero worship have grown straight up from a fact at their roots.

However, Grote did not deny that myths, taken in a mass, contain real matter of fact; he only said that in any particular myth you cannot distinguish fact from fiction, so he rejects them all as useless for the purpose of history. He would probably have admitted Defoe's History of the Plague to be some kind of evidence that a plague did break out somewhere at some time; he would not have attempted to explain the whole story as some travesty of early imaginations. Whereas some of the comparative mythologists would remove all foundation in fact whatsoever from the figures and incidents of early Aryan myths, especially of divine myths. The whole province of myths has been occupied and annexed under the standard of philology. And of all myths the divine myth is universally taken to be most demonstratively a baseless fabric, to be founded on a class of facts utterly different from those which it purports to relate. The highest authorities in comparative mythology appear to trace almost the whole of this class of figures and narratives into personifications of the worship of inanimate Nature. Professor Max Müller, in his essay on Comparative Mythology, wrote *—

"If we want to know whither the human mind, though endowed with the natural consciousness of a divine power, is driven necessarily and inevitably by the irresistible force of language as applied to supernatural and abstract ideas, we must read the Veda; *and if we want to tell the Hindus what they are worshipping —mere names of natural phenomena, gradually obscured, personified and deified*— we must make them read the Veda. It was a mistake of the early Fathers to treat the heathen gods as demons or evil spirits, and we must take care not to commit the same error with regard to the Hindu gods. *Their gods have no more right to any substantive existence than Eos or Hemera, than Nyx, or Apatê.* They are masks without an actor—the creation of man, not his creators; they are *nomina* not *numina*—names without being, not beings without names."

And in another essay on the Manual of Mythology, Mr. Cox receives the very lenient warning that we ought to be prepared even in the legends of Hercules or Theseus "to find some grains of local history on which the sharpest tools of com-

* "Chips from a German Workshop," article Comparative Mythology. (*Italics mine.*)

parative mythology must bend or break." "It does not always follow," Professor Max Müller observes, "that heroes of old who performed what may be called solar myths are therefore nothing but myths." Nevertheless "the general agreement which has of late years been arrived at by most students of mythology, that all mythological explanations must rest on a sound etymological basis,"* has been so entirely accepted and made so comprehensive by writers of the books on this subject which are most widely read, that it seems likely to obliterate all other explanations from the popular mind. This is especially the case as to divine myths, which contain so much that is obviously incredible that people are the easier convinced that all these stories are imaginary from first to last, and the figures in them mere phantoms of sun and mist. Even Grote, who did not commit himself to the theory of solar myths, uses the fact of the existence of divine myths as undeniable proof that myths need have no basis in fact, but may be pure creations of the mythopœic faculty. For, at any rate, he argues (in opposition to those who affirmed the mythopœic faculty to be never creative) the divine legend is often purely imaginative, not merely in Greece, but in other countries also. These legends, he considers, derive their origin "not from special facts misreported and exaggerated, but from pious feelings pervading the society and translated into narrative by forward and imaginative minds . . . . legends in which the generating sentiment is conspicuously discernible, *providing its own matter as well as its own form.*" † "To suppose," Grote adds in a note to another passage, "that these religious legends are mere exaggerations of some basis of actual fact—that the gods of polytheism were merely divinized men with qualities distorted or feigned—would be to embrace in substance the theory of Euemerus." ‡ Now to embrace Euemerism is also an unpardonable heresy against comparative mythology.

But while it would be undoubtedly a grievous error to em-

* "Chips from a German Workshop."

† History of Greece, Chapter XVI.

‡ History of Greece, Chapter XVI., note to page 394.

brace the theory of Euemerus as a "Key to all Mythologies," on the other hand I venture to suggest that it cannot be left out altogether as an exploded notion "astonishing in writers who have made themselves in any degree acquainted with the results of comparative grammar."* If one may be permitted to offer an opinion formed upon some extensive observation of the working of the mythopœic faculty in India—perhaps the only ancient country which still keeps alive a true polytheism of the first order—I should say that in constructing the science of religion we might do worse than make room for the theory of Euemerus. In the details of his treatment of the myths his method of rejecting all that was to his mind impossible or incredible, and piecing together out of the residuum a plausible version of the story, seems indefensible. But Euemerus is said to have been an Asiatic traveller; and if we may judge from what goes on before our eyes in Asia now, there is a great deal to say for his main theory which "represented both gods and heroes as having been mere earth-born men, though superior to the ordinary level in respect of force and capacity, and deified or heroified after death as a recompense for services or striking exploits." Indeed, this quotation from Grote describes very nearly the conclusions that would be drawn from looking narrowly at the process of the generation of gods in India at the present day; and if there be ground for supposing that this process has been going on more or less in India for thousands of years, the effect is worth considering. It is probable that the loose presumptuous way in which Euemerus applied his method has brought his theory into unmerited disrepute, and has thus thrown it too much into the background now-a-days. His mistake lay in treating his theory as a master-key which would disclose the inside of all mythologies, though this is a mistake rarely avoided by anyone with a theory on the same subject, for the latest writers appear very intolerant of any rival theory in any corner of the same field, and are not satisfied until they have hunted it clear off the ground; so that even the best and soundest of modern

* Mythology of the Aryan Nations, page 171.

theories suffer in this way by overstraining. For example, this theory of Euemerus is, I believe, rejected altogether by the more thorough-going comparative mythologists. The view maintained in the Mythology of Aryan Nations as to the origin and course of divine myths, stated briefly, appears to be that primitive Aryans began with personifying the great processes of Nature, went on to deify in the image of man the impersonated phenomena, and to distribute their attributes; then made the gods actors in legends which accepted in real earnest and converted into earthly incidents such metaphors as of light striving with darkness, and the like; and, finally, settled their full-blown gods and demi-gods down upon earth with local habitations, names, and human biographies. Now the Euemeristic theory would, speaking roughly, invert this order of development and begin at the other end, tracing the local hero of real life through different stages up to the great deity who wields the forces of Nature. And the main objection to either system seems to be that its author insists upon an exclusive monopoly of the whole province of myths; that it leaves no room for the other; that because it does explain a part of mythology it has been applied to the whole; that it endeavours to explain not only mythology in one phase or at one period, but the whole general course of its evolution into actual polytheism. Upon this subject the comparative method and philology have thrown a flood of light; nevertheless the high authorities who appear to assign to the whole family of divine Aryan myths their birth-place in the personifications of inanimate Nature may be unaware of the quantity and weight of evidence that an Euemerist could even in these days produce on his side. They seem to exclude too absolutely from their survey of the main springs of mythology and religion that copious and deep flowing foundation of belief, the direct deification of humanity; the fact that men are incessantly converting other men into gods, or embodiments of gods, or emanations from the Divine Spirit, all over Asia, and that out of the deified man is visibly spun the whole myth which envelops him as a silk-worm in its cocoon. This very remarkable operation of human credulity is little mentioned by mythologists, and yet to omit careful account of it, or to treat it as merely the last stage of a personified Nature worship, appears to involve risk of a wide misunderstanding of the whole birth and growth of primitive belief. Moreover, this miscalculation at the starting point would be likely to lead us astray further on, so that we might miss the structural connection between early incoherent forms of religion and those which are later and more concentrated. It should be remembered that all the great Asiatic religions which have lifted the world up out of polytheism derive straight from remarkable personages; that the authentic history of all such personages has invariably become surrounded by every kind of subsequent legend, and discoloured by the refracting lights of popular imagination, whereby the sifting out of the real facts has become very difficult. It is also to be borne in mind that there prevails a constant tendency to question and explain away the historic humanity and substantial individuality of persons recognised as being of divine character or origin. Sakya Muni, the founder of Buddhism, has been disguised by the Brahmans as a great Avatàr or embodiment of Vishnu—the younger Burnouf actually interprets Christianity, on etymologic grounds, to be a Fire worship; [just as Kápila, the reputed founder of the Sankhya philosophy among the Hindus, is affirmed by learned Hindu commentators to have been an incarnation of *Agni*, because one of the meanings of his name is Fire], and the speculations of Strauss are well known.

Before, therefore, we undertake to tell the Hindu what he is worshipping, and to assure him that his gods are mere names of natural phenomena, I think we are bound to consider them in the actual field of observation, how they grow. We shall at least find a good deal of evidence to be collected in favour of Euemerism in India itself. For there it is certain that the popular polytheism of the present day is constantly growing up and developing out of the worship of holy or famous men who have actually existed. The universal and incessant practice throughout India (and one may say throughout Eastern Asia) of deifying remarkable personages, will account for the origin of almost all divine anthropomorphic narratives and for many of the gods now in vogue, and it certainly seems to warrant us in allowing for a much larger proportion of authentic fact than is usually admitted in compounding a theory as to their beginning and evolution. In a former chapter some attempt was made to describe the process of turning men into divinities, by which saints and heroes are gradually promoted until they reach the highest and mistiest summits of godship; and subsequent enlargement of observation in different provinces of India has created a deep impression that in Europe there is now no adequate conception of the extent to which and the force with which this intense and habitual working of the primitive mind toward deification must have affected the beginning of religions. In this stage of belief the people construct for themselves Jacob's ladders between earth and heaven; the men are seen ascending until they become gods; they then descend again as embodiments of the divinities; insomuch that it may be almost doubted whether any god, except the Vedic divinities and other obvious Nature gods, comes down the ladder who had not originally gone up as a man, and an authentic man. The ascent of the elder Hindu deities is shrouded in the haze of past times; but several of the most eminent (Siva and Krishna for instance) are still vulgarly reported to have been men; and there are instances in plenty of men who have actually started up the ladder by consent and testimony of the whole neighbourhood, and have re-appeared as acknowledged divinities. To quote examples would be only to give a list of provincial deities, more or less obscure; but one might safely say that a great number of verifiable men are now worshipped as gods in various parts of India, and the number is constantly added to. The Indians worship everything created, but above all things men and women; and anyone can notice that nothing impresses the primitive or the uncultivated mind like human personality or character. Nature worship itself, in its most striking form, is only maintained among the crowd by anthropomorphism, while the actuality and sympathetic attraction of a real known person gives him the immense advantage of local popularity. And this intense impression left by human personality is seen to be stronger as scrutiny descends into the lower stages of superstition. The aboriginal tribes are completely under its dominion; they cannot shake it off at all, and are haunted by their incapacity to get rid of powerful masters in life or death. If they attribute storms or sunsets to a sort of personified agency they are sure to attribute it to the agency of some real man whom they or their fathers have known. The process of Brahmanizing which these tribes are undergoing in India of course greatly increases the supply of gods from the Euemeristic source; for as these poor non-Aryans, innocent of the abstracting faculty, do actually worship men, so the homely jungle hero comes eventually to get brevet rank among regular divinities, whenever his tribe is promoted into Hinduism.

The upper class of Brahmans are prone to deny the existence of this process, and to prefer that the proselytizing which goes on should be understood as involuntary on their part and merely superficial; they would be willing to keep their Olympus classic, and above the heads of these low-born intruders. But the local Brahman has to live, and is not troubled by any such fine scruples, so he initiates the rude Gond and Mina (non-Aryans of the jungle) as fast as they come to him for spiritual advice, sets them up with a few decent caste prejudices and gives to their rough unfinished superstitions some Brahmanic shape and varnish. This is vexatious to the refined Vedantist of the towns, but the same thing goes on everywhere; for a lofty and refined orthodoxy will not attract ignorant outsiders, nor will it keep the mass of a people within a common outline of belief. And so the high and mighty deities of Brahmanism would never draw the non-Aryan, if he were not invited to bring with him his fetish, his local hero or Obi man, his were-wolf and his vampires, all to be dressed up and interpreted into orthodox emanations. In one part of Rajputána the Minas (an aboriginal tribe) used to worship the pig. When they took a turn toward Islam, they changed their pig into a Saint called Father Adam, and worshipped him as such; when the Brahmans got a turn at them, the pig became identified as the famous Boar Avatàr of Vishnu.

While these things are going on before one's eyes, insomuch that any striking personage appears tolerably sure of divine honours and a miraculous biography after death, it is difficult not to allot the first place among the different methods of manufacturing gods to this process. Without doubt the Vedic deities and a good many others which prevail in India have been produced by finer and more intelligent handicraft; but for a rough propitiatory worship, adapted to everyday popular needs and uses, the quantity and quality of the deified men appear to satisfy a large demand and to give them an immense circulation. It should be remarked, however, that the description of Hinduism given in this chapter applies throughout to the worship of the mass of the population of India, which is mainly rural; and that the difference between the worship of the country and of the towns is very considerable whenever polytheism extends over a wide area, and is not under the influence of cities as orthodox centres. Probably some such distinction as is implied by the word pagan has always existed to some degree in India.

In short, though no one would deny the strong influence of Nature worship upon primitive religions, yet the part played by inanimate phenomena must not be overrated. Early superstitions derive much from the heavens above, from the sky, the storms, the seasons, and from light and darkness. The great Nature gods still reign in India, if they do not govern; and their influence is felt over a wide range of legend and liturgy. But all the vitality and the concrete impressive figures which stand forth in the front rank of a popular Asiatic religion appear to come direct out of humanity below, out of the earth, as the scene of the exploits, sufferings, and passions of mankind, which are above all things of absorbing interest to man. That the two sources of mythology meet and are blended, there can be no doubt; the Nature god sometimes condenses into a man and is precipitated upon earth; the hero or saint often refines and evaporates into a deity up in the skies. And thus it may, perhaps, be said that a polytheistic religion forms itself after the manner of a waterspout, which to the looker on appears to be by the dipping down of the clouds from the sky, and the uprising of the waters which cover the earth, whereby is created a continuous column which may seem to lead up from earth to heaven, or down from heaven to earth, according to the fancy of the wondering spectator. The bowing down of the clouds toward the earth may illustrate the human personification of the great mysteries of the elements of the inanimate forces as seen in the changes of the sky; the uplifting of the sea water toward heaven above is the elevation to divinity of the incidents of human life, far sounding actions, wonderful adventures, pathetic striving, and the like. Where the waters of the earth end and those of the sky begin, one can tell precisely neither in the water-spout nor in the religion, after it has formed; the precise point of contact disappears, and one can only guess by watching the process of formation upon other occasions. But whereas many persons appear to hold that this column which holds up the heaven of a primitive polytheism is almost entirely let down from the sky, the lesson of Indian observation is that it rises much more directly from the earth, that man is mainly the base as well as the capital.

That the theory of Euemerus applies more extensively to modern Asiatic polytheism than it did to the polytheism of ancient Europe, may well be true. It may be that Nature worship, conscious or unconscious, prevails more largely in one stage than in another of popular religion; and that the Indians have passed out of that stage; that the old personifications have been superseded and have retired into the background. Indeed there is such a crush and jumble of new gods constantly pushing themselves forward up the Jacob's ladder in India that without fresh blood no old established deity could long maintain predominance. New and improved miraculous machinery is constantly introduced, and the complex and changing nature of human wants and grievances requires a popular god to keep abreast with the times. Such a thing for instance as vaccination needs in these days to be accounted for; and the question is whether such new wonders are to be accepted and absorbed or denounced. Fresh blood may be obtained by the simple expedient of a new embodiment of the old fashioned divinity if the competitor is a new and remarkable personage, or by a new attribute if it is a physical discovery. In this manner the elder gods may well have been driven back into the sky by the swarm of earth-born deifications. But the leading gods of ancient Greece and Rome seem to have always been more obvious personifications of inanimate Nature than has for many centuries been the case in the popular liturgy of India. Coote's theory of the evolution of polytheism by the grouping of physical phenomena into a personage (which is in effect identical with the theory of the evolution of all divine myths from Nature worship) appears mainly drawn from classic polytheism, wherein the great heads of natural departments were universally known and adored, more or less consciously. These are the deities with which Euemerism has nothing to do, and which Euemerus should not have tried to explain away into men, for he did not understand their constitution and made altogether a wrong diagnosis. As to these, so far as one can understand their position in India, it would appear that the departmental god, immediate or derived, occupies no very forward place in modern Brahmanic polytheism. Without doubt the Vedic personifications are still held in high reverence, and the system agrees with classic polytheism in deifying a few of the more important vital functions, which are, however, still represented by unmistakable concrete symbolism, very different from such delicate personifications as Aphrodite or Lucina. And natural phenomena are still largely worshipped in concrete, as the Sun or Fire. But it may be affirmed that the vast majority of the deities really in vogue are magnified non-natural men, without any defined speciality, who subsist and flourish by absorbing and taking credit for, not the powers of nature, but the devout or heroic exploits of men.* And this difference, if it exists, between the constitution of Asiatic and of classic polytheism may, perhaps be explained by saying that the more

* They also draw largely upon the dangerous characteristics of animals; but this is a branch of the subject which is not here touched, though here also comparative mythology seems to have made an arbitrary and somewhat unjustifiable annexation of the whole province. To those who live in a country where the people are convinced that wicked people and witches constantly take the form of wild beasts, the explanation of Lykanthropy by a confusion between Leukos and Lukos seems superfluous and very far fetched.

imaginative and incomparably more æsthetic Greek had reached a later stage of polytheism, in which people are satisfied with personifying movements of Nature, that his symmetrical and poetic taste led him to group the attributes of the sea, for instance, artistically under one name, and actually to adore his beautiful creation. Whereas the Hindu, grotesque and irregular in his conceptions, more gross in his sensuous ideas, but at the same time more profoundly spiritual, more oppressed by the mystery of life and death, requires something closer to human sympathies for his worship. Between a bad climate and worse governments he has usually had a hard and precarious lot upon earth; he would demur from his own experience to the sentiment that kings and priests can make or cure but a small portion of the ills which man endures; on the contrary, he would assert the exact contrary, taking the priests to be agents of the gods, and taking, as he does, many of the gods as representing merely another phase of the powerful men who do what they choose with him on earth. These personages, whether in the visible or invisible world, are a great burden to his weariful existence, and are the chief causes of his anxiety to escape from it; he by no means looks forward to meeting them in some future world and singing their praise; what the Hindu desires is to escape from them altogether and to attain either absorption or extinction. He canonizes or deifies his distinguished men, not always by way of distributing orders of merit or titles for past services, but often because he really thinks they were and are the embodiments of power and could still do him a mischief. And the extraordinary difficulty which the Hindu finds in conceiving a way of escape out of his own personal existence is only one proof of the very strong impression made upon him by individual personality and character. He will not realize the dismissal to shades below of a hero, nor will he leave him drinking nectar with a purple mouth up above, only to re-appear when called in to solve knots worthy of a god. His favourite doctrines of transmigration and incarnation bring the individual constantly back upon earth in the flesh. Thus he constantly turns his men into gods, and his gods back into men; he discovers a living man in whom the god actually resides, or he builds a temple to a god with an authentic human biography, in either case with equal confidence. All this may rest upon pantheism, or the belief that the primal energy is the same everywhere in a storm, a cow, a man, or a god. But it none the less follows that this divine energy is most directly concerned with humanity when it is run into the mould of a human creature. Borgias and Catilines are, in India, more important and impressive representatives of heaven's design than even storms and earthquakes; and, therefore, for one personification of storms and earthquakes, the Hindu deifies a hundred Borgias or successful Catilines. These considerations may be allowed to support an argument that the working divinities of Hinduism are much more largely supplied by the deification of authentic men than may ever have been the case in classic Europe, and consequently that the theory of Euemerus affords a good explanation of the origin of a great part of Asiatic polytheism.

It is worth remarking that Buckle, in comparing the Hindu and Greek religions, lays stress upon a view of their respective characteristics which is almost exactly contrary to that which has here been suggested. He is illustrating the influence of physical laws on religion; and in this place his errors on matters of fact are so great as to inspire grave mistrust of the process of searching a library for facts to suit a comprehensive theory, "According to the principles already laid down," says Buckle, the deification of mortals "could not be expected in a tropical civilization, where the aspects of Nature filled man with a constant sense of his own incapacity. It is, therefore, natural that it should form no part of the ancient Indian religion;" and he then quotes Colebrooke, who said that the worship of deified men is no part of the Vedic system, as if the remark applied to Indian religion generally; while he goes on to point out that in Greece the deification of mortals was a recognized part of the national religion at a very early period. But what Colebrooke really said was that the worship of deified heroes is a later phase, not to be found in the Vedas; though the heroes themselves, not yet deified, are therein mentioned occasionally. Buckle had evidently never heard of that very remarkable and still flourishing offshoot of Buddhism, the Jaina faith, which is nothing else but the worship of deified men; and when we consider that the deification of men is universally characteristic of the cults of all the wild non-Aryan tribes in India, we see how completely Buckle's theory, that this deification implies a superior respect for human powers, breaks down under accurate observation. The bloodiest and most degrading superstition in all India, that of the Khonds, is saturated with the idea that men become gods, and the worship of the dead, which is embryonic polytheism, is an almost universal characteristic of the earliest superstitions in all countries.

And thus, to resume the course of our subject, mythology develops into polytheism very largely out of the primitive habit of astonishment at the deeds and sufferings of real men, out of the tragedy of life, the mystery of death, and the universal attraction exercised over man by superior men. The elemental personifications exist, but they retain no monopoly of attributes, for a large proportion of every wonderful event or appearance is claimed for the local hero; whether it be storm, earthquake, or cholera, it is just as likely to be attributed to some notorious person living or just dead, as to an established god, or to one of the primal deities who are constantly re-appearing in the Avatàrs or embodiments of famous gods or heroes. Later on in the apotheosis come the stories of monstrous and fantastic miracles, which are mainly nothing more than fictions invented for advertising a deity and attracting attention, like a huge pictorial programme of a circus stuck up in a country village. These amazing excrescences create no proper prejudice at all against the actuality of their hero, for no hero ever appeared in Asia who was not at once daubed over with a thick coating of the marvellous, which may be in some cases, however, mere conventional exaggeration, mainly intended to amuse and attract. No one is seriously taken in by the magnificent coloured painting of the circus performer driving twenty horses abreast; it only means that anyone who goes within the booth will find that something rather novel and curious is really performed. And the end of this deification is that a magnified non-natural man is deposited in Olympus with a large credit to his account for whatever has been latterly going on in his neighbourhood upon earth, and an accumulated capital stock of miracles which are sometimes pure delusions but often facts grievously distorted. Then in latter days when the atmosphere of belief has changed, and when public opinion is become clarified on such matters, people are astounded at finding a deity with such a history quietly seated up aloft, and they try to evaporate him or to explain him away with all possible ingenuity. Hence a variety of metaphors and mystifications employed particularly by the more cultivated and intellectual polytheists; but it is very rare to find anyone of the superior classes who will acknowledge that the god is simply the natural outgrowth of the deifying process going on around them. They will say of a man that he is the embodiment of a god: they encourage the people to turn men into gods, and they are reluctant to allow that their gods are men. The moralists are puzzled by the apparent want of moral purpose or ethical decency about the god, forgetting that they who fashioned him went upon the analogy of their own experience and of the hourly processes of nature, and that the god was never intended to be a model, or a reforming ruler and teacher of mankind, only a distorted image of some passages in human existence. And, lastly, in order to get rid of the intense anthropomorphism of polytheism, philosophers expound that it is necessary to the laws and processes of the human mind, that it is absolutely indispensable in order to make certain transcendental ideas conceivable to the faculties. But, in fact, man usually obtains the human figures for his heaven by a very much more material operation, by taking rough casts, as one might say, of famous personages in the flesh, and subsequently modelling and re-modelling the plastic shape to suit his fancy or his moral sense. Of course it does not logically follow that because every real hero and saint is divinized, therefore every divine personage was once a real hero or saint, and the point contended for in this chapter is only that comparative observation establishes a strong presumption in favour of some such inference, where no other explanation is manifest.

From this point of view, therefore, the professors of the science of religion who maintain that divine mythology was originally formed in the sky out of Nature worship, where it gradually condensed and was precipitated in the shapes of polytheism, may be perhaps said to have omitted due attention to the antecedent process of evaporation upward. The cloud land is first filled by emanations from the earth. And, from a different stand point of observation, the metaphor suggested by this constant transmutation of human forms into divine images, and by their refraction again upon the sight of men wondering, is that of a mirage. In countries and climates where, as in India, the phantastic phantasmagoria of divine shapes or scenes in the heavens above answers very closely to what is actually going on, or supposed to be going on, among men upon earth below, the phenomenon of deification is easily explained and understood. One watches the reflected forms take shape and colour, and fade as the sun grows strong enough to dispel the intellectual mist out of which they are produced. In such circumstances it is impossible not to suspect the fallacy of drawing an argument in favour of the credibility of a divine narrative from its natural analogy with the known order of things in the world, and of demonstrating that because strange and unaccountable things are known to occur upon earth, therefore any incident not more strange and unaccountable, reported as from heaven, is credible. This is to affirm that the reflection is as substantial as the thing reflected. The peculiarity of the religious mirage is that it remains long after the scenes upon earth which it caught up have past away; for a primitive belief retained among cultivated people is like the survival in the sky of a mirage long after the landscape which it reflected, with the early light and the hazy atmosphere which transmitted it, have changed. If this survival were physically possible, then, since the appearance still remaining in the sky would have no longer even a fanciful or refracted resemblance to things among the people on earth, they would wonder how it came there, the phenomenon would appear mysterious and inexplicable, mystic and symbolical, as a divine myth appears to later generations. Whereas those who have seen a religious mirage in its earlier stages perceive that the human forms visible in the heavens are mostly the great shadows cast by real personages who stood out from among the primitive generations of men upon earth. They are fantastic *silhouettes*, and they fade away as the mists clear; but they almost certainly reflect and preserve in outline an original figure somewhere once existent upon earth, though they may be now no nearer the scale of humanity than the spectres of the Brocken.

For the purposes of the science of religion, and as a study of further developments, it is worth while observing how the spiritualists of India, the preachers of pure morals and of subjective creeds, are hampered and entangled by this gross materialism of the people. No spiritual teacher of mark can evade being reckoned a god (or a visible embodiment of divine power) by the outer-ring of his disciples, and an atheist or blasphemer by his enemies; he may disown and denounce, but the surrounding atmosphere is too strong for him. When the lower class of priests discover that in his secret teaching he is against them, they are apt to invent vindictive and scandalous accounts of his birth and social conduct. They may excommunicate him, and prudently, for in all countries the spiritualist is impelled to attack, as empty formalities, injurious to religious brotherhood and equality, those caste rules and prejudices about physical purity or impurity which are so inveterate in all early theologies. And if the new sect openly defies caste, it will be persecuted. The common people, on the other hand, amid much vague awe of the professional Brahman, never allow him a monopoly of their religious custom; nor does the Brahman himself set up as agent for the only genuine repertory of divinities, or declare all others to be spurious. Uniformity and consistency in creeds are inventions of the logical and thorough-going European mind; and though religion is the only general question which really interests the Asiatic people, yet they have never organised either their ideas or their institutions up to that point of precision which naturally breeds active intolerance. To the mass of Hindus it is quite simple that they shall indulge their fancy in following after any new deity or saint who is likely to do them a good turn, without troubling themselves whether this latest dispensation is in accordance or collision with their regular everyday ritual. So they insist on recognizing the spiritualist as a fresh manifestation of Power, and they worship him accordingly. This does not much offend orthodoxy, which has no great objection to adding to the number of deities; but the esoteric doctrines, which probably drown all priesthoods and gods together in the depths of some mystic revelation, are much more likely to get their authors into trouble. Hence arise the secret fraternities, the symbols and masonic signs, by which nearly every spiritual sect intercommunicates. These things are used to save the teacher from his friends as well as from his enemies; the melancholy ascetic may be seen sitting and enduring the adoration of the crowd; he does not encourage them, but he does not much attempt to undeceive them. His secret, his way of life, his glimpse behind the curtain before which all this illusive stage play of the visible world goes on, his short cut out of the circle of miserable existences, these things he imparts to those disciples whom he selects out of the herd, and whom he sends abroad to distribute the news. When he dies he is canonized, and he may fall into the grip of the Brahmans after all, and be turned into an embodiment of a god, but his society may also survive and spread on its spiritual basis. Unluckily secret societies founded on the purest principles are unsafe institutions in all ages. They are of course regarded suspiciously by every government, and with very good reason; for their movements in Asia are sure to grow into political agitation whenever they acquire any impetus. And in India there is such a perceptible tendency of spiritual liberalism to degenerate into licence—there is so much evidence of the liability of the purest mysticism to be interpreted by way of orgies among weaker brethren—that one may guess scandalous stories about private gatherings of the initiated to have been not altogether without foundation in any age or country.

Whether a spiritual ascetic shall succeed in founding a sect with inner lights, or only a fresh group of votaries which adore him as a peculiar manifestation of divinity, seems to depend much upon all kinds of chance. Sometimes both conceptions of him survive, and thus we get that duplex formation so common in Eastern religions—the esoteric doctrine and the exoteric cult. There is one widely spread sect in India (though not many English know it) which outwardly worships Krishna, an incarnation of Vishnu, and sets up his image in the house; but their real point of adoration is an obscure enthusiast who founded the sect not very long ago, and who is now in the semi-miraculous stage. By the outer-disciples he is certainly held to be himself an embodiment of Vishnu; but, so far as can be made out, the initiated still know him to have been a spiritualist who scorned gods and Brahmans. But, as times go on, these two branches out of one stock, the worship of a divinity and the inner revelation, become twisted up together, so that the reputed miracles are used to authenticate the spiritual message, and the spiritual message is put forward as an adequate motive to explain the miracles. Then of course the message itself is subjected to incessant changes and enlargements; for, being always at its first delivery a very simple message contained in a few deep abstruse sayings, it is very soon required to explain everything in this world and the next. Here comes in the living tradition which fills in details, and provides fresh formulas to supply fresh needs. This duty falls upon the successors who are elected as chiefs of the sect, upon whom the mantle of the founder is supposed to have fallen; sometimes, indeed, they are proclaimed to be successive incarnations of the god who first appeared in the founder. But this is only where the spiritual side of the peculiar doctrine has been very much darkened, either intentionally or by ignorance.

All these transitions in the working out of religious creeds and dogmas are visible in India at the present day. We can perceive how the religious ideas of a great population do not develop regularly and simultaneously through regular stages in one direction or from one starting-point; but that ideas, simple and complex, physical and metaphysical, moral and immoral, grow up together in a jumble, the strongest growth absorbing the weaker ones. In India of course the whole atmosphere is gradually changing, but we have yet to see how this will modify the old belief. Speaking broadly and excluding Europeanized societies, it may be said that nowhere as yet in India has morality become essential to the credibility of a divine narrative. Perhaps, indeed, the course of ideas in modern India may never lead up to this necessity, and the Hindus may retain their primitive notions of malignant deities as being reasonably in accordance with the perceived analogies of nature, and as furnishing quite as good an explanation of the prevalence of evil in this world as any hitherto discovered by philosophers. For Mill's conclusion, that of accepting a Divinity, but doubting His omnipotence, is, whatever he may say to the contrary, a kind of philosophic return toward the idea of popular polytheism, a distribution of divine powers. And the main practical objection to its becoming popular is that it in no way satisfies the religious feeling of desire for perfect trust and dependence which is peculiar to Christianity and Islam. In Hinduism also this feeling is universal, but vague and indefinite, not belonging necessarily to the conception of the gods. That belief in a moral purpose and a just Providence should be rooted in the Hindu mind, side by side with all these absurd mythologies, is only one of the numerous anomalies natural to polytheism, which should neither derange nor confirm any theory about the origin of the mythology. Yet the co-existence in the same community of irrational and monstrous myths with sublime conceptions of the ways of God toward men has not only been marked as a puzzling contradiction, but has been used as evidence that the source of divine myths was never really religious belief, that it is to be found in metaphoric expressions. It seems to have been argued that because Eumæus in the Odyssey speaks reasonably and reverentially of God, therefore his generation could not actually have invented or believed the undignified and scandalous stories about the gods. And consistency is saved by the theory that the scandalous stories were only distorted Nature myths. Nevertheless it is quite certain and open to proof that a pagan will invent and worship the most indefensible gods, and will simultaneously believe vaguely in a moral purpose and a supreme dispensation of justice and judgment to come. Any Hindu will call on God to attest the justice of his cause, precisely as a Christian might; though at the same time he worships any number of specific divinities who have no pretensions to moral ideas. And the real explanation of the contradiction is that the specific god is seldom anything more than a glorified supernatural image of a man, not necessarily virtuous at all, only undoubtedly powerful. The innumerable gods of Hinduism are deified ghosts, or famous personages invested with all sorts of attributes in order to account for the caprices of nature. This is the state of the vulgar pagan mind; by the more reflective intelligence the gods are recognized as existent and as beings capable of making themselves very troublesome, whom it is therefore good to propitiate, like men in office. At the same time a devout pagan trusts that there is something better beyond and above these gods, and that the moral purpose works itself somehow straight in spite of their capricious influences; at any rate there is death, absorption, or annihilation by which one may escape that dread of the gods which troubles the life of man down to its inmost depths. But whether the Hindus tend toward improving their popular divinities into rational gods or into moral gods, or into gods inconceivable yet credible, or toward sinking them all in the ocean of pantheism or of materialism, we may be sure that both the fantastic demi-gods and the mystical spiritualists will have their acts and sayings melted down and recast to suit the exigencies of the times. All sorts of fictions will be employed to manage the further transition by gentle gradients and breaks, to serve for a curtain behind which the costumes are changed and the scenes shifted. And it is probable that later on scientific inquirers from a distance (either of space or time) will become so puzzled by the anomalies and contradictions thus produced, not only by the original confusion of belief, but also by the processes which these beliefs and the narratives of their origin have undergone in being adapted to different levels of credulity or conscience, that they will distrust altogether the actuality of the human leaven which is at the bottom of these fermentations. People will show how the divine narratives grew up and were pieced together out of unconscious allegory, poetic symbolism, personification of nature, or disguise of language, and will decide, because these are necessary conditions to the existence and transitions of a divine myth, that its hero has no more authentic human origin. Yet the Hindu at any rate, with his strong sense of personality after death and of the necessity for providing a fresh tenement for the soul disembodied, has certainly built up the greater part of his inhabited pantheon out of the actions and words of real men; and he mostly follows, not will-o'-the-wisps and distorted metaphors, but the deep footsteps left by extraordinary men in their passage through the world. He cannot believe that these souls have gone for ever; he is continually recalling them and worshipping them; he will not let the heroic shade depart to the shades below ὃν πότμον γοόωσα, but translates him at once into a present spirit.

To conclude. It has been thought worth while to lay so much stress in this paper upon the fact that the actual gods of Asiatic polytheism have been mostly men, because the broad impersonal theories now in vogue about the origin and development of religious belief usually ignore this fact, more or less. Because an immense quantity of superstitious gossip about the gods, of fairy tales, folk lore, and the like, are evidently fables, built up out of mere words, therefore the extreme comparative mythologist appears to infer that the central divine figures round which all this floating fable gathers are also nebulous and unreal. To dissipate the stories which cluster round a god, and to dissipate the god himself, are two distinct operations; and it is not always clear whether the mythologists observe this distinction in dealing with strange outlandish deities, though it is well known nearer home. This may be a mistaken view of the extent to which comparative mythology desires to go, for it is difficult to ascertain positively how far the writers would actually carry their dissolving process; but certainly the general drift of some standard works upon mythology appears to imply that polytheism gradually grew and took shapes out of mere abstractions and the habit of metaphoric talk. If this were accepted as a comprehensive explanation of the worship and multiform gods of the Hindus, for instance, it would, I think, entail a wrong apprehension of the beginning and development of primitive beliefs. For there appears to be sufficient ground for contending that such beliefs do not form themselves upon the personification of natural phenomena or by accidental linguistic coincidences so much as by deifying authentic men. And the popularity of the impersonal explanations seems to be very much connected with the exigencies of the transitional state of religion in Europe, which requires all stiff dogmas and clear cut individualities to be softened down into a haze. However this may be, within the domain of religion, as sometimes within that of history, there may be danger of carrying too far the method which obliterates the influence of persons, and ascribes all movement to general causes, physical or metaphysical. Those who are masters of the subject may preserve their own understanding of the true proportion in the general landscape of each religious period that should be allotted to the great figures in the foreground; but upon the unlearned the effect is apt to be hazy, and a broad view is mistaken for a dead flat. Certainly it would be to depopulate and take a great part of the life out of Indian polytheism if we could suppose that it consisted only of an aggregate of fortuitous impersonations of inanimate Nature.

# CHAPTER III.

## INFLUENCE UPON RELIGION OF A RISE IN MORALITY.

Religion regarded by primitive and civilized men respectively from two different stand-points—In Europe religion could not now stand apart from morality; in India there is still no necessary connection—In India morality unable to advance without the concurrence of religion, which adopts and authorizes useful and progressive ideas as soon as they become popular, thus accommodating itself to the gradual improvement and enlarged ideas of mankind—As moral sentiments and notions of utility thus develop, the religion which accepts them becomes more refined and more rational; and the sacred books lay down consistent rules adjusted to new ideas and uses—Influence of morality tends to modify the capricious and malevolent character of early divinities, while the recognition of order and regular sequence lessens their direct responsibility for the world's affairs—Difficulty of introducing moral systems without leaning for support on divine sanction, which is the basis of all authoritative teaching, and of all claims, temporal or religious, to legislate or command—Titles of Indian dynasties run back by presumption to divine origin—British Government alone in India rests on purely secular rights and its own power—Question whether physical conditions of India permit any great national or moral changes.

THE British Empire has so much concern with great Non-Christian populations, whose religious ideas and institutions are being rapidly transformed by English notions of law and morality, that the influence upon religious beliefs of a rise in morality may be almost as interesting a question as the recent discussion* of the influence upon morality of a decline in religious belief. It is possible, moreover, that some far-away connection may be recognized between the two subjects and that the examination of one may throw some light upon the other.

At first sight the two stand-points from which religious belief is regarded by primitive and by civilised men respectively, appear as wide apart as possible. In Europe a large

* In the "Nineteenth Century." Nos. 2 & 3, April and May, 1877.

majority still holds that morality could not endure without the authority of religion; but most people also admit that a creed which should be found not useful to morality would fall into disuse, would, in fact, cease to be believed, and would thus dissolve of itself. In India, on the other hand, few people would admit that their religious beliefs were necessarily connected with morality, and a good many might even say that morality would be none the better for such a connection. If primitive men were asked the use of their beliefs, they might in substance reply that theology is like navigation or astrology, or any other empiric art which helps one through the risks and chances of the voyage through sensitive existence, that it is the profession of interpreting signs and tokens of the divine caprice, and of propitiating powerful deities, who take a sort of blackmail upon human prosperity. Nevertheless the real difference between the two stand-points may perhaps be expressed by saying that, whereas a civilised religious belief cannot do without the sanction of accepted morality, in primitive times morality (or at least expediency and utility) must seek the patronage of some accepted religious belief. In Europe morality can, on the whole, dictate terms to theology, and though both sides still equally dread an open quarrel, yet theology has most to fear from a dissolution of partnership. In Asia theology is still the senior partner with all the capital and credit, and can dictate terms to morality, being for the most part independent of any necessary connection with it; for Asiatic theology transacts with the gods all matters touching the material interests of humanity, and in this very speculative business, as in many others, morality is by no means essential. It is well known that the primitive mind finds relief from the perplexity caused by things passing its understanding, in the theory that the gods swarm all round men, and are incessantly interfering, either to help or to hinder. From the promulgation of a code which is to direct society in the minutest particulars, down to the swallowing of a drug or the moment of starting on a journey, every act of life, great and small, requires the assent of the divinities, and is assumed to be done after ascertaining their good pleasure, through stewards of the mysteries. It follows naturally that with a paramount authority so close at hand, and so constantly meddling irresistibly, no man can act with independence or on his own judgment; he must obtain the proper sanction of theology for all that he wants to do. Theology is thus the most essential and comprehensive of all sciences, since it teaches men how to obtain the sanction without which no step in advance, however useful or expedient, can be ventured upon by mankind. An ethical reform, a sanitary improvement, a new medicine, any useful discovery or moral axiom, must first be presented at the court of the gods before it can be received into society; and the priest acts as Lord Chamberlain. Moreover, it constantly happens, as in mundane courts, that disagreeable and immoral candidates for court favour get presented by help of powerful patronage; certain practices and rights are introduced and sanctioned by theology which run directly counter to elementary morality and even to a sense of natural expediency. The excuse is that it has been the gods' good pleasure to ordain and sanction these practices; but it will almost always be found that they are really founded upon some selfish material interests, and are not, as they are usually supposed to be, merely whimsical superstitions as to what will please the gods, or as to what is right and proper.

In short, all novelties and changes, whether the move be forward or backward, must be undertaken by theological word of command, and the gods get the credit or discredit. Perhaps the best example of a selfish device obtaining vogue under the cloak of a necessary rite is afforded by the famous practice of a widow becoming *sati*, or burning herself alive with her dead husband, which is undoubtedly, as Sir H. Maine has pointed out, connected with the desire of the husband's family to get rid of her right, if she is childless, to a tenancy for life upon her husband's land. Among the great families it is also connected, as may be easily observed still in certain parts of India, with the wish of an heir to employ this simple plan of freeing himself from many inconveniences and incumbrances entailed upon him by the bequest of a number of step-mothers who cannot marry again. Other instances might be given;

but though this habit of lending the names of the gods to dubious transactions and conspiracies to defraud has always prevailed more or less, yet it may be affirmed that on the whole we find the primitive deities almost as often patronizing good as evil. Theology is usually well pleased to grant its patents to improvements and to adopt simple discoveries, in expediency or even in ethics, so long as the inventor or moralist is professedly submissive, dedicates the work and ascribes all the glory to the proper quarter. And this is readily done in a state of society when no sort of venture or enterprise has the slightest chance of being well received or becoming popular unless the gods appear in the prospectus. A good example of the address with which elementary science avails itself of theological protection may be taken from the practice of medicine, which has to be carried on very largely, in the old fashioned provinces of India, under the name and colours of theology, which is here so confidently supreme that it does not even condescend to stipulate for any concealment of the material processes. One may observe the native practitioner, learned in charms and simples, openly mixing a drop of croton oil with the ink with which he indites his charm for a purge, and the patient swallows the paper pill in cheerful reliance upon the combined effect. Many other practices, ascertained empirically to be fit and expedient, have become in course of time so overgrown and concealed by the religious observance in which they were originally wrapped up, that it is now very difficult to extract the original kernel of utility, and one only hits upon it by accident, when in trying to abolish what looks like a ridiculous and useless superstition, the real object and reason are disinterred and sometimes prove worth knowing. Thus the rule of burying Hindus who die by smallpox or cholera is ordinarily expounded by priests to be imperative because the outward signs and symptoms of those diseases mark the actual presence of divinity; the smallpox is not the god's handiwork, but the god itself manifest; but there is also some ground for concluding that the process of burying has been found more wholesome against contagion than that of the hurried and ill-managed cremation which prevails during a fatal epidemic. If vaccination could only be ordained theologically, it would have an immense success in India; but the English insist on explaining it otherwise, and thereby set theology against it, raising grave suspicion of witchcraft, or at any rate of contraband and unauthorized practices. All elementary methods of natural science which are practised independenly of the religious authority are thus stigmatized; and as the gods gradually acquire some tincture of morality, any very discreditable and mysterious misfortunes to pious and innocent people are traced to the same source. Men attribute their failures and mishaps to the gods; the gods pass on to the sorcerer the blame of those accidents which it is not quite convenient to explain; the system is not favourable to a development of self-reliance, but the people are not by any means so blindly superstitious as they pretend to be, and both gods and sorcerers yield like prudent ministers to an advance of public opinion.

In fact the more one watches the actual working and disposition of primitive religion, the more one is impressed by its elasticity and accommodating changeableness. So long as the single principle of the supreme authority of the gods is left undisputed, it may be invoked for the sanction or support of any practice or belief upon which men are tolerably agreed; and it may be used like steam as a prime mover of any machinery constructed by ingenious mortals. The extraordinary variety and multiformity of polytheism largely represents the endeavours of the vagrant imagination of the people, much aided by priests and other astute leaders of society, to bring their religious ideas into working correspondence with their earthly needs. Discoveries of social utility are brought out as revelations from on high; and necessary changes in the way of life, for good or for bad, are shown to be distinctly ordained; while as all the credit is given to theology, it is easy to see what enormous influence that science continues, so long as its position is unchallenged, to accumulate. Comte has noticed with his usual insight into the minds of primitive people the manner in which a religious belief adapts itself to genuine social and political needs; and personal observation proves that this goes on rapidly and incessantly in the loose incoherent formations of the earliest types. As the state of society improves, the religious beliefs seem to develop themselves by a sort of natural selection. We may here put aside mere ritual and the innumerable forms of worship which are only devices for propitiating the unseen, and which continue to be used, like the post-office, just as long as people have reason to believe that their messages arrive and are answered, but no longer. The early religious beliefs are not only propitiatory, but contain rules of conduct by which a man is to be guided in all circumstances of his existence; the main difference between earlier and later religion being that the first looks almost as entirely to man's material as the second does to his spiritual well-being. And as it has been truly remarked in regard to the latest forms of religion that any religious movement is doomed to sterility if it cannot assimilate some philosophical element, if it is not what the age calls moral and reasonable, so also, in early religions, an ordinance or rule of conduct will only endure and develop if it is founded on some true notion or conjecture of material utility or expediency. If it is useless or harmful, a simple caprice or inspiration, it will not last. In the midst of countless random and whimsical guesses at what is fit and suitable, among various tricks and pretexts meant to give a religious colour to some selfish interest, those religious commands alone survive long and develop which are or have been somehow connected with the real needs of the people to whom they were delivered. The moral and material progress of a country goes on pushing before it the religious beliefs and shaping them to suit it on exigencies; while theology slowly and reluctantly repeals and disowns the rules which become obsolete, or which are found to have been issued under some very inconvenient and undeniable error of fact. Morality is not yet essential to religion, but if an inspired command turns out to be a blunder as well as a crime it is shortlived, and will soon be amended by a fresh ruling. Nevertheless the gods in no way admit themselves to be bound by human views of morality, while the functions of popular religion very much resemble, in their highest range, the functions of a modern government; its business is confined to procuring material blessings, warding off evil, contending against such physical calamities as famine or pestilence, and codifying rules of social utility which have been verified by experience. As the scene of its operation is principally the visible world, the scheme of future rewards or punishments is not an essential part of the system; for such a scheme must not be confounded with vague beliefs in places of refuge for disembodied spirits, which may be either different kinds of limbo from which the ghost issues forth and meddles again with the world, or Elysian shades for heroes, or an Olympus to which dead magnates ascend on special promotion to apotheosis. There are heavens and hells in Indian theologies; but it is remarkable that a doctrine which in highly civilised religions is usually regarded as the most important, and is certainly the most impressive upon the masses, is in primitive religions of comparatively insignificant effect, and appears to make no such mark upon popular imagination as to influence conduct in every-day life. The reason may be that the Indians, as a mass, still consider religion as the supreme authority which administers their worldly affairs, and not as an instrument for the promotion of moral behaviour; and although, like Job's comforters, they are fond of connecting misfortunes with sins previously committed in the same or in an antecedent existence, yet this law is still supposed to operate within the sphere of the visible world.

As the confirmed perceptions of utility develop moral sentiments, these colour slightly the notions regarding the gods, who are soon credited with some indignation at wrong doing, at any rate when the sufferer is one of their clients or devotees. But the idea is still that the gods punish or avenge in this life by material curses, or aid by lending a material hand at critical moments; and thus as they begin to be affected by the sight of a good man struggling with adversity, the feeling develops that virtue ought to be divinely helped against vice. Nevertheless the primeval thinkers very soon observed that as a matter of fact the gods appear to be often on the side of the wicked, or at least against the innocent; and here comes in the complication between sin and evil which runs through all phases of religious speculation, from Buddha to J. S. Mill, the problem of justifying the ways of the unseen powers which are assumed to be governing human affairs. The earliest and most simple attempts to account for evil are by assuming that the gods must have in some mysterious way been offended; whence comes the institution of the scapegoat so well known in India in plagues of cholera, which embodies that idea of expiation which has had such immense development in the history of religions; and the various receipts for discovering Jonah, the man with a contagious curse, not necessarily a moral offender, but only one who has incurred the divine wrath, who is also common throughout all Asia. Next follows the advanced notion that this offence against the gods is not only some insult or sacrilege, as when Ulysses killed the sacred oxen, but is a moral sin, an offence against society of which the gods take magisterial cognizance. Job's comforters try hard to prove to him that he must be reaping the fruit of his own guilt, and in all times the early theologian has made desperate endeavours to connect misfortune with misconduct, though often driven to explain the connection by references to ancestral stain, or to the hypothesis of something done in a previous existence. But the more vigorous and daring minds rejected these subterfuges; and finding themselves landed in the dilemma between the omnipotence and the perfect justice of divinity, they solved it in different ways. Buddha held firmly to morality, threw over the gods altogether as immoral and troublesome powers from which a philosopher has to escape as fast as he can, and objected even to heaven as a final resting-place, on the ground that you are never safe so long as you own a sentient existence. Nothing but *Nirváṇa*, or being blown out like a lamp, will set men finally beyond the reach of the demon who afflicts them with sensation. This teaching was, however, a moral and metaphysical doctrine vastly above the heads of the people; and practical common-sense Hinduism has never allowed questions as to the moral character of the gods to be sufficient reason for turning one's back on them or refusing to deal with them. Philosophers may have concluded privately that the gods are either incompetent or ill-disposed, a class of beings who must be endured and ignored; but the people have always made the best of their divinities so long as they did not oppose themselves to reasonable improvements in the moral standard, adapted themselves to circumstances, and recognized governments *de facto*. Mere peccadillos attributed to one or two out of many gods are of little account. Arthur Young ridicules a Frenchman who denounced to him the profligacy of Louis XV.; and he says that Frederick the Great was a much more objectionable despot, because it is infinitely less important to the commonwealth that a king should take a fancy to his neighbour's wife than that he should fancy his neighbour's provinces. This view, though questionable, is precisely that taken by polytheists of their divinities; so long as the gods do not bring some tremendous misfortune upon the country they need not be particularly moral; their speciality not being the direction of morals, as in later faiths, but the distribution of temporal blessings and curses.

This process by which the divinities absorb and sanctify useful ideas and convenient reforms evidently tends to improve and elevate the whole religion in its legislative department; but as the creeds thus refine and cleanse themselves the authoritative revelation comes to be recorded in writing and gets into professional hands; which of course makes an important change of type. The scripture is much less easily questionable, the rules become more precise and consistent, and consequently much less elastic; the change is analogous to that whereby a scientific code supplants judge-made law and free construction of precedents. Interpretation of holy writ necessarily supersedes, or greatly restricts, oracular delivery of messages and traditions; and a favourable reading of texts, even under the cloud of a sacred language, is not so easy to negotiate as a fresh oral inspiration, though the latter is largely retained to help out the former. Nevertheless as the world changes gradually for the better, these concessions and compromises have to be managed; since there are always impatient reformers who will arise to denounce the *parole morte* if it falls too much behind the times, and will come forward with a new prophet, a new symbol, or a new revelation more in accordance with actual needs and convictions. And the sects and diverse creeds thus generated represent the constant oscillations of ideas and opinions beyond and below the orthodox standard—not only the high but also the low water-marks of the restless tides of superstition, because occasionally there is a relapse into some grotesque or immoral belief decidedly below orthodox level. When a liturgy becomes established and recognized on a wide scale, as is the high-class Brahmanic ritual, it is sure to be more decent and respectable than less public worships of a looser structure; and though it may become flat, stale, and emotionally unprofitable, it retains the support of all quiet respectable conservatives.

Now it is to be observed that even Brahmanism has never yet been forced into admitting openly any necessary connection with morality. It has sanctified a good many rules of life and conduct which are decorous and expedient, but these are issued theologically; and the ethical Hindu reformer who insisted on the paramount necessity of a moral object and reason for his beliefs has had to leave the pale. That righteousness is better than sacrifice has not yet been openly acknowledged by the high church of Hinduism; its ultimate teaching points directly, not to a moral Providence of any kind, but to Pantheism, which has no ethical basis. Pantheism and final absorption are not merely esoteric doctrines; they underlie and give form to the common popular beliefs, and are thoroughly accepted by men of ordinary intellect and culture. In the West the Jews had distinctly founded religion upon righteousness before Christianity came to confirm and perpetuate the connection; and the new religion further satisfied and strengthened morality by the doctrine of a final state of rewards and punishments, beyond which consummation no one desired to go, because this was a sufficient explanation. Whereas in the East morality has never been strong enough to demand of theology a satisfactory explanation; and no such terminus as a single future state satiates the deeper Indian sense of immensity. The Hindu fancy does not repose eternally in a heaven or a hell; he must go on through an endless rotation of existences until absorption or extinction stave off his pertinacious logical craving for knowledge of the "whence and whither." In his country the moral purpose running through countless ages has never been demonstrable enough to serve as a final cause; while the incessant flux and change of religious ideas and shapes support that analogy between the nature of things human and of things divine which is the origin of all primitive religions, and makes the gods appear as ephemeral as mortals. Mr. Swinburne's Hymn to Proserpine represents the attitude of the pagan worshipper who refuses to abandon the old gods, consoles himself for their overthrow by declaring the modern creed just as transitory as the ancient one, will not adore the new divinity, "but standing, looks to the end." This is the true spirit of philosophic paganism; but the popular religious beliefs must obey the pressure of slowly rising moral influence, and if the social condition of a people continues to advance, this process goes on until at last the authority of morals becomes as necessary to theology as at first the authority of theology was to morals. We may some day find in India, as elsewhere, theology completely subordinated to morality; indeed there are already indications of a tendency towards this inversion of original parts, though the mental and material impediments to be surmounted are still considerable.

Here it is obvious that the acknowledgment of the duty of moral government must expose the old divinities to great danger; they are very much in the same predicament with hereditary despotic rulers who are forced to admit the rights of man; there is no knowing how the admission will be used against authority and prescription. The analogy from nature, which is the root of all natural religions, becomes gradually subjected to a severe strain, because it is difficult to reconcile this analogy with a moral purpose, and yet this analogy is really what makes all early religions credible, since they are built up out of actual observation and experience of the stern and incomprehensible working of natural laws. This is a solid, and for the time being an incontestable basis for inferences about supernatural beings who administer the visible world; whose acts and behaviour prove them to be careless and cruel; but on the other hand these observations disagree widely with a presumption of moral government, and so whenever the ethical reformer attempts to take his stand on morality as a divine institution, he is instantly challenged to show his authority for any such belief. A theological authority of course he must have, or he must give up all hope of popularizing his teaching; while in times of material distress and disorder, and in countries where "the amazing waste in nature, the destruction and misery" * are quite unaccountable and prevail on a large scale, the difficulty of making credible the moral government and benevolence of divinity is perhaps rarely realized by people in more comfortable and enlightened parts of the world. So the analogy from nature constantly trammels the advance of morality, and drags back the higher moral teaching into the slough of despond; because the people still insist upon inferring the nature of the gods from their experience of the misery and disorder of human life, which the gods are supposed to regulate. In a country subject to wars, famines, pestilences, and scandalous tyrannies, and in a state of thought which attributes directly to the divinities all the remarkable accidents or events of life, the resistance offered to an advancing morality by natural religion is constant and powerful; it is the incessant gravitation of the earthborn deities whom morality endeavours to lift up.

It is only when, as time goes on, the gradual perception of the order and sequence of things withdraws from the divinities by tacit consent a great deal of direct responsibility for the course of affairs, that the road ahead is cleared for morality to advance without parting company with theology. The old gods may either fall below the raised level of public opinion, and become discreditable, or they may be provided with an improved set of attributes. Some powerful religious reformer steps in, and strikes a religious note above the ordinary level. His strength lies in this—that he collects, and as one might say, edits, puts into popular shape and effective form, all the ideas and feelings about purer morals and worship which have been floating about, usually in the form of sayings and maxims, on the highest surface of the popular mind; these he delivers as his message from heaven, and sanctions it by

* Butler; Analogy.

a more refined ritual. Nevertheless the difficulty of a religious reform lies always in this, that to improve religion it is also necessary to rehabilitate the divinities, seeing that no reformer will be listened to at all by the masses unless he can prove his warrant from the powers that be, and can produce his signs and tokens. When Elijah challenged the priests of Baal, he put the authenticity of his authority upon a palpable and immediate issue to be judged by all men. And as in certain states of society the ordinary visible facts are usually against any one who attempts to prove that the gods are good, while the extraordinary signs and tokens are not always on the better side, the reformer runs great danger if he pushes ahead too fast. He exposes his communications with natural religion, and endangers his theologic base; orthodoxy closes in round him with all the strength of prescription and of the sacred writings that have recorded in ancient days the words of gods speaking with men, so that the new notions have to fight hard to keep their ground. Yet they do keep it if the conditions of existence are favourable, for the influence upon general morality, and thus upon theology, of changes in the material conditions of a people's existence, is very observable. J. S. Mill writes in his autobiography that he is "convinced that no great improvements in the lot of mankind are possible until a great change takes place in the fundamental constitution of their modes of thought;" but to those who watch the effect upon Indian modes of thought of continuous peace and good government the converse view seems equally true and even more important. A great improvement in the lot of a people begins immediately to affect the sources of their ideas, since it must obviously touch the springs of the natural religions which simply reflect and record mankind's lot upon earth, represented as the ways of gods with men, and which change with the world's aspect, as shadows vary with changes of the substance.

The problem, then, for all these indigenous beliefs which have grown up and been moulded by their environment, is to admit the influence of morality brought about by change of circumstance and mental atmosphere, and to rise gradually without losing their footing upon their native earth, or their authority derived from religious prescription. And the problem, conversely, for morality is to raise and shape these beliefs without disowning them abruptly or breaking off from them; for the stay and sanction of theology are still absolutely essential, and the morality which lets go its hold of them must fall. It is not necessary, however, to conform to a powerful orthodoxy and to allow the moral or material improvements to be stamped with the one trade-mark without which no principles are genuine; the Brahmans are ready enough to say of any new discovery or doctrine that it is the same concern, and the law of patents in theology is very loose. But a moralist must not go so far as to deny altogether the prescriptive authority, or he will surely be attacked in a way which will make it very hard for him to hold his ground *coram populo*. A very good example of the danger of too rapid an advance over the ramparts of superstition may be drawn from the fortunes of a well-known sect called the *Brahmo Somáj*. This sect professes an exalted deism, which was imported from Europe by its founder about fifty years ago, and has taken some root in Bengal, where it suits the taste of the educated classes to whom orderly government and the comforts of civilization have suggested a refined and mild ideal of the divine governor of their world. At first the Brahmists attempted to hold by the Vedas, but this involved them in sundry inconsistencies, and the more advanced section appears to have staked its creed upon pure *à priori* assumptions of a just and benevolent deity. They abjure the "gross materialism" of ancient religions, they reject dogmas and traditions, and desire their disciples to look at the objects round them in the world for evidences of divine power, intelligence, and mercy. Their principal leader declares that "the physical sciences give us better and higher conceptions of God and His government of the world than we could otherwise possess." "Few will deny," he says, "that the material universe is a great religious teacher, that the sublime and beautiful in nature exercise a vast influence on the mind." That the world around us is a great religious teacher, and that religious men feel awed and subdued by the aspect of nature, are obvious truths; but most persons who judge by history, observation, and experience, would flatly deny that these feelings necessarily make for righteousness, or that the physical forces and processes of the universe prove the divine benevolence. If anyone considers closely the nature and complexion of religions which have encompassed the hearts of great nations, and reviews their origin and progress, it is easy to perceive that a faith which contains mere pious fervent sentiments and high moral lessons has never, as such, taken hold of an entire people. Such a faith has usually been preserved, in all ages of culture, by the refined intellectual minority, with a distilled aroma of the popular creed, just sufficient to indicate its origin. But Dr. Newman is right in saying that religion, properly so called, has hitherto been synonymous with revelation, that it has ever been a message, a history, a vision.* And in point of fact the Brahmists have made no substantial progress, probably because the sect can appeal to no authoritative warrant or prescriptive sanction; while throughout the greater part of India experience and observation of the natural world tell directly against the assumption that the deity is either just or benevolent. The argument from the analogy of nature which Butler applied so unanswerably to the deism of his time, is as effective when used by Hinduism against the optimistic speculations of India; indeed in India the deist is very much more puzzled than in England to explain upon his theory the condition and prospects of mankind; for if the visible world is directed by the divinities, as both sides agree, there can be no doubt that in Asia the system is at least very incomprehensible. And between the two explanations offered, of terrible and capricious, or of just and benevolent deities, the probabilities and *primâ facie* look of the case appear to the simple folk very much on the side of the former; so that we begin to see that Butler's famous argument from the analogy of nature is connected with the ideas that lie at the roots of all religions which have grown up out of this very analogy, that is, at the roots of all natural

* Grammar of Assent.

religions. He revived in logical form the unconscious train of thought out of which all beliefs are more or less evolved; he proved that the irresistible and pitiless working of natural laws warranted the inference of any degree of stern severity in the character of the administrator; and it is precisely in this demonstration that lies the strength of natural religions. Butler set this out for the first time forcibly and scientifically, and the position is doubly impregnable when held by those who are not concerned, as Butler was, to prove that a moral and beneficent government of the world is nevertheless credible. Whenever morality and the refinements of an improved state of life begin to press in upon the older and rougher conceptions of divinity, we shall always find theology entrenched behind the undeniable concordance of what is recorded about the gods with what is seen of their doings in the visible world; so long, that is, as they are allowed to be responsible for what is done. Morality can carry this entrenchment either by relieving them of their direct responsibility or by dissolving connection with them; both very perilous manœuvres for morality to attempt in almost every part of the world as it now is, and certain to be ruinous in Asia. In the present state and prospect of ideas in Asia, morality would be cut off from its base, and would lose all its leverage, if men were persuaded to abandon their certain belief in the constant intervention and the supreme influence of present divinities, if they were convinced that for ages they had built themselves fanes of fruitless prayer. Any sudden rupture of continuity in the established order of beliefs would be hazardous; while, on the other hand, theology, if not openly bombarded, is accessible to terms, compromises, and propositions for an alliance, and will even consent to march several stages on the same road with morality, provided that theology has nominal command of the whole force.

After this manner, therefore, does the gradual and constantly interrupted advance of moral and material improvement influence the religious beliefs, which adapt themselves good humouredly to newfangled ideas upon decency and the like, so long as their infallibility is not openly defied. Yet to this general rule that for every social reform must be given theologic authority, the legislation of the British Government forms one great exception; because instead of seeking diligently to find sacred warrants for its acts, this government eliminates with minute care from its laws any kind of reference to or recognition of religious belief as an authority. This is one of those curious contrasts which modern India exhibits at every turn. On one side of a river we may have a British legislature proclaiming incessantly and laboriously its total freedom from any taint whatever of theological considerations; on the other we may have a native ruler obliged to explain as sedulously that what he does is entirely supported by sacred authority, or by prescription resting ultimately upon such authority. British law-giving only defers to prescription in so far as it respects customs and prejudices that are tolerably harmless; but native administrators can do nothing important without attaching it to prescription; and the most powerful and unanswerable prescription is obtained by tracing back a rule to a divine mandate. This is, as has been already observed, the reason why morality is still so entirely dependent upon religious beliefs, and the same necessary connexion holds good between religion and all social and political movements; except only when the prime mover is the British Government, which alone in Asia is strong enough to put out a measure upon its intrinsic merits. Indeed the British legislature goes much further, for it has fixed bounds within which theologic authority shall have no jurisdiction at all, and morality, or at least expediency, shall reign triumphant. Nor is this objected to by the people, which in fact desires mainly to find out where lies a supreme incontestable power in temporal matters, and if the British Government is strong enough to assume that position, and to undertake responsibilities and duties usually laid upon the gods, there can be no reason why the *de facto* providence shall not have their allegiance. On the other hand the responsibilities thus assumed are enormous, for one of the conveniences of the old theocratic system was that disasters or afflictions might be shifted by the government on to the shoulders of the priests, who usually passed them on downward, if uncommonly damaging, to the sorcerers or to any class unpopular at the moment. Now the British Government, having thrown aside these lightning-conductors, is much more exposed than a native ruler would be to shocks from famines or other widespread misfortunes; and in fact the native newspapers already indicate that the tendency to cry out upon government when the world goes in any way wrong, is actually becoming immeasurable. Cholera, famine, and great sea inundations, when they are not made the text of invectives against the British Government, do at least in some confused way bring upon it great discredit, not apparently from the idea that the gods are angry with the government which has ignored them so persistently as to have pretty well established its independence of them, but upon the dim feeling that the government has undertaken the gods' business and is breaking down. And the multifarious functions assumed by a modern administration (so far beyond the simple *régime* of an ordinary Asiatic ruler, who merely collects revenue and keeps an army) lay it wide open to every kind of imputation against its wisdom and its benevolence; it is like a great divinity in whom are absorbed and concentrated a great number of attributes.

This feeling, moreover, when we consider it, must be admitted to be the natural outcome of the movement and direction given to ideas by the British Empire in such a country as India. We have in many ways openly undertaken the business and liabilities usually left by Asiatics, at least in form, to divine authority; the science of administration is supplanting the science of theology, the cool scorn of the English legislature, and its force, are fatal to the predominance of divinity, whose sphere of action contracts perceptibly under that influence. Rules of conduct which hitherto have rested upon theologic sanction, gradually drop the connection with theology when they come to be adopted and enforced by a penal code; while theology is forced, to save its credit and avoid awkward collisions, to drop rules of misconduct which the code prohibits. Under these favourable auspices the reformation of religious beliefs, pushed forward by a morality so powerfully backed up, is likely to be abnormally rapid, and one is almost inclined, out of pure cautious conservatism, to question whether the assertion of independence by morality and its annexation of the old theologic dominions may not go on too fast. In Europe we already find a party declaring that morality and theology are about to dissolve their long partnership, and debating only as to the probable consequences, whether there will be the confusion of an interregnum or a revolutionary period, and whether the great enterprise of the civilization of mankind can be carried on when the security of religion, and the confidence which it inspires, shall have been withdrawn. Those who regard theology as an essential basis of morals may be right in maintaining that the affairs of the world can never prosper without the support and guidance of some such belief; but in Europe the transition is at least gradual, and the carefully recorded results of observation and experience are steadily limiting the sphere of any but human responsibility and action. It is at least possible in Europe that morality may take up the position and the responsibilities for temporal affairs and the material interests of mankind, which theology has very nearly relinquished, and may manage to go forward upon her own score and venture; but even with the aid of British penal codes this would be a very perilous venture in India. In Asia prescriptive authority, which necessarily means divine authority, is the only explanation upon which the Hindu mind, so primitive yet so restlessly inquiring, can find rest and release from uncertainty; and morality must still be content with playing a secondary rôle in subordination to the religious beliefs.

As with moral and ethical explanations, so it is with political and social institutions, they must have their basis on religious prescription, except where the British Government undertakes to demonstrate practically that the thing must be so. The pedigree of a rule or a right must be traced far away up into the mists of the past, up to a myth or a divine message; its origin must transcend man's understanding and his memory, or the title becomes incomplete and disputable. One would suppose that the title by which the Chiefs of Rajpût clans of Central India hold their dominion would be ancient enough, for their possession has lasted many ages, and their lineage is accurately preserved; and yet to this day the Chiefs of the oldest States obtain a sort of religious investiture, upon each accession, from some representative of the aboriginal races whose land the Rajpúts took centuries ago. The most important States in India are of very modern origin, dating back no earlier than the first establishment of the English dominion: but the elder Hindu dynasties, which lay claim to great antiquity, seem to lie under the necessity of either attaching the beginning of their line to that other line which they cut short, or of carrying the chain of inheritance back to a conquering demi-god, or else of quoting a special revelation in their favour, as when Islam conquers under a divine mandate. The right is thus asserted in a form acceptable to the customary apprehension of the people; nor has any despotism in Asia ever attempted to do without some such religious warranty, excepting only the British Government which is itself a sort of incarnation of inexplicable power. In short, the whole notion of rights is still so closely tied up with the religious beliefs that any premature endeavour to sever the connection would be a very delicate operation.

In all this there is, of course, nothing very new. Religion has in all countries at one time been the basis of society; and the divine right of kings is not a very old story in England. Morality and religion everywhere act and react upon each other; everywhere the slow improvement of the world has produced dynastic revolutions among gods and kings, and the traditional beliefs must accommodate themselves to the change of circumstance. But in India the peculiarity of the situation is that very primitive religious beliefs are being unexpectedly overtaken by an unusually high tide of public morals and spreading knowledge, which have come upon them without due warning; and the nature gods are confronted by penal codes and modern education in a sudden way that is hardly fair. They have no time to reform, hardly time to change their costume; it is even questionable whether they will easily manœuvre their retreat out of the material into the spiritual world, give up the distribution of material blessings, and fall back upon future states of existence over which their power cannot be tested. It has already been noticed as a characteristic of the phase of religious beliefs hitherto prevailing, that the doctrine of heaven and hell, though well known and accepted in Hinduism, has not exercised any great influence over the people. The ordinary worshipper looks for material blessing or ban; the philosopher accepts heaven and hell not as departments of reward or punishment, but as places of purification whereby a soul may be cleansed of its sensations and become absorbed again into the Infinite, or escape into nothing. Both these conceptions arose out of a thorough distrust of the gods, the people dealing with them just as far as they could see (or thought they could see) that worship was answered by works, the philosopher renouncing them and all their works as completely as he dared. Nevertheless if these beliefs are prematurely submerged, we may have an awkward break in the continuity of theologic development, and it is not quite clear how this may affect morals. We may after all find morality in India, as elsewhere, looking dubiously at the ladder she has kicked down, and seriously alarmed at the decline of religious beliefs which has been the necessary consequence of her own rise. Or it may be that those are right who insist that Asia has always been too deep a quicksand for Europe to build upon it any lasting edifice of morals, politics, or religion; that the material conditions forbid any lasting improvement; that the English legions, like the Roman, will tramp across the Asiatic stage and disappear, and that the clouds of confusion and superstition will roll up again. Then after all the only abiding and immovable figure in the midst of the phantasmagoria will be that of the Hindu ascetic and sceptic, looking on at the incessant transformation of men into gods and gods into men, with thoughts that have been caught by an English poet, and expressed in lines that have a strange Asiatic note—

"All ye as a wind shall go by, so a fire shall ye pass and be past;
Ye are gods, and behold, ye shall die—and the waves be upon you at last.
In the darkness of time, in the deeps of the years, in the changes of things
Ye shall sleep as a slain man sleeps, and the world shall forget you as kings."

* * * * * * * * * *

# CHAPTER IV.

## WITCHCRAFT AND NON-CHRISTIAN RELIGIONS.

"Witchcraft is as the sin of rebellion."

Inquiry into distinction between witchcraft and the lowest types of religion—Suggestion as to difference of origin and principle—Religion works invariably through some agency supposed to be divine; witchcraft works independently of priests and deities, and probably begins with some accidental discoveries of natural laws—Witches persecuted in polytheist countries because their underworking is contraband, unaided by recognized supernatural powers or methods—Resemblance of practices and devices of witch finders in India to those formerly used in Europe—Cruelties inflicted on witches because they are supposed to be personally the cause of calamities; also, because the priests shift on to witches the blame of all inexplicable evils which the gods cannot or will not cure—As religion becomes purified and elevated, this shifting process increases, and witchcraft becomes more degraded and detested—Men go to witches for disreputable purposes, or when the gods fail to help—Witchcraft protected by the British Government in India; is possibly the lowest phase of empiric observation and inquiry, and thus superior to mere vague supernaturalism.

To those who live in a country where the belief in witchcraft still pervades all classes, from highest to lowest (though of course the pressure of the superstition is far lighter upon the uppermost layers of society), the study of this delusion by autopsy of the living subject is most interesting. For we have all learnt the history of European witchcraft: how the fear of it once overspread the whole land, and faith in it was a cardinal doctrine with church and state, with kings and judges; how it gradually faded, until the notion of such a thing has at last become ridiculous to all but the most ignorant; and how this virulent mental disease was expelled, not by refutation or any special remedy, but by a gradual change in the conditions of existence which had engendered and fostered it. We know, in fact, the precise position of witchcraft under the Christian dispensation; and we understand the view taken of it by our different churches in different ages; but this essay is meant to carry the inquiry further back, and to seek for more light upon the origin and development of the craft or practice of sorcery, by looking into its relations with the non-Christian religions, and by attempting to ascertain the place which it holds among those very superstitions with which Christians have constantly identified it.

Witchcraft has been usually supposed to be a very low and degraded phase of religion. Now this is largely true of the art in Europe, where the great Christian churches for ages combined to stamp out the relics of ancient paganism, which they denounced and furiously branded with the opprobrium of hideous sorcery, until the wretched, half-heathen serfs did actually turn devil worshippers; but the question is whether in a country that is altogether pagan, witchcraft is only one form of what we call Religion, or a different species altogether. Was there any plain distinction known among the ancient Greeks, for example, between the slaying of Iphigenia upon the altar at Aulis to obtain a fair wind, and a magical ceremony for the same object? Most people would agree that some distinction has always been recognised, though they might not find it so easy to explain. If we try whether any aid toward a satisfactory explanation is obtained by carefully looking at what goes on before our eyes in India, it seems possible to distinguish a radical separation, from the very outset, between witchcraft and the humblest form of what in India is called Religion.

Witchcraft appears to have been, from the beginning, the aboriginal and inveterate antagonist of religion or theology, and hardly less so in the most primeval ages of barbarous superstition than it was in the days of our King James I. It may be supposed to have arisen from an exceedingly dim and utterly confused glimpse of the secrets of Nature; to have begun with the first notion that such secrets exist and can be known, and that things which we do not comprehend may be brought to pass without the results being inseparably connected with the divine agency. In the rudest stage of religion, the line between the most abject fetichism, perhaps only the worship of certain queer objects, and withcraft is very difficult to be traced by us to whom from our great intervening intellectual distance both kinds of superstition seem indistinguishable in type and character; yet even in this lowest grade of primitive society their separation is decipherable. One may venture to affirm that the difference between devotees and magicians, between those who propitiate gods visible or invisible, and those who use mysterious mummery not necessarily addressed to any object or subject at all, exists and can be verified from the earliest times. As a matter of fact, witchcraft is more feared and more practised by the lowest Indian tribes than by any other classes; and though one does not at first sight perceive how they can discern or point it out to themselves, amid all the monstrous rites and grotesque terrors of their lawful beliefs, yet they always lay their finger upon it without hesitation. There seem always to have been some faint sparks of doubt as to the efficacy of prayer and offerings, and thus as to the limits within which deities can or will interpose in human affairs, combined with embryonic conceptions of the possible capacity of man to control or guide Nature by knowledge and use of her ways, or with some primeval touch of that feeling which now rejects supernatural interference in the order and sequence of physical processes. Side by side with that universal conviction which ascribed to Divine volition all effects that could not be accounted for by the simplest experience, and which called them miracles, omens, or signs of the gods, there has always been a remote manifestation of that less submissive spirit which locates within man himself the power of influencing things, and which works vaguely toward the dependence of man on his own faculties for regulating his material surroundings. Those two antagonistic ideas, of dependence on supernatural will and of independence, can, I think, be found to demarcate Witchcraft and Religion, from the Alpha down to the Omega of their long history, which is a chronicle of incessant war, growing fiercer and fiercer as the two forces developed and became organised, and as the two principles diverged and discovered their mutual antipathy. Science had also a stage when it consisted of unreasoning observation, and in the earliest beginning of that stage it must have been very like witchcraft. The man who first hit upon the conditions under which fire can be invariably got by rubbing sticks, probably ceased to pray for fire as he must have prayed when the result was very uncertain; or perhaps the more reverent minds continued to rub and pray; while the bolder and busier men gradually discarded their vows as they became convinced that rubbing was alone effective. But this association of cause and effect, of rubbing sticks with fire, and the like, instead of suggesting the scientific method, only caused the undisciplined savage experimentalist to speculate rashly, to jump at most unwarrantable conclusions, and to connect together things which have no affinity whatever. The imagination of primitive man was limited or steadied by no true reasoning; one consequence was to him just as likely as another. If rubbing a stick produced fire, an utterly amazing result, without the aid of any sacrifice or other invocation of gods, why should not two knives laid crossways on a threshold, or a bit of red string over the lintel of a door, bring down or avert disease? or why should not certain charms carved on the door-post make the whole house collapse? All these things are only questions of experiment, and one successful operation goes a long way to establish confidence in the method. If disease has once been stopped by incantation, why not always, or at least usually? Especially if a wise woman has cured an ulcer by applying a few simples, and muttering unknown words, or has averted a hailstorm by hanging up mystic rags and observing the wind, there are no limits to reasonable faith in her. In this manner the first person who picked up a little physical knowledge beyond his fellows was tempted to trade upon it enormously beyond his real capital, because the boundless credulity of his neighbours inspires equal belief in himself, and if he can do one inexplicable thing he may be able to do anything else; the peculiarity of his practice being that he does everything without the aid of the gods. And this it is that makes him a Witch as distinguished from the successful propitiator of fetich.

Witchcraft is thus supposed to begin when a savage stumbles

upon a few natural effects out of the common run of things, which he finds himself able to work by unvarying rule of thumb. He thence infers that he has in some wonderful way imbibed extra-natural power, while he has only picked up accidentally one or two of the roughest keys which open the outer lid of the physical world. He has hit upon a rudimentary materialism; and, while he fancies himself to be entering upon a mysterious department, in which he can do without the popular fetich, he in fact becomes a Fetich unto himself; for he thinks that the virtue lies in his own self (which is partly true), not in the essential conditions of the things which he sees and handles. His characteristic must have been always this, that he *has* some real knowledge, or faint tincture of it; and that while the vulgar crowd round him ascribe all strange coincidences to the spite or favour of idols and demons, the witch makes bold to dispense with divine intervention, and to rely on his own arbitrary tricks for producing not only a few simple effects, which he has verified, but all sorts of absurd exploits which he aims at by mere guess work; one thing being to him just as probable or improbable as the other. The practice and the pretensions of the sorcerer are very nearly as preposterous as those of the most unsophisticated keeper of idols. Yet the cardinal distinction between the fetich witch and the fetich worshipper is the same as that between the witch and all priesthoods in all times; the former stands aloof from the ordinary adoration of supernatural powers, asking nothing from capricious gods, exercising an art for the most part as blind and irrational as rites performed to a river or a rock, but yet founded upon and clinging to the idea that his power lies somewhere within his own control, and is not vouchsafed by the good pleasure of the popular divinity. Fetichism is the adoration of a visible object supposed to possess active power; it ascribes, as Comte says, to all phenomena ideas of vital energy and power drawn from the human type; in short, the fetich (a river, for instance) is a mysterious being whom you try to make friends with, as you would with a man who is plainly too strong to be frightened. But Fetichism also, as Comte further remarks, admits slavishly that man can only hope to influence nature by worship, not by work; and it sets up an order of specialists in the business of enlisting this irresistible supernatural agency. Whereas witchcraft does after its dim, blundering fashion, from the very first stumble away in the contrary direction; in order to avert floods or attract water it does not propitiate the river god or the running stream; it employs for these purposes some utterly random and senseless ceremony of its own devising, which nevertheless might probably be traced back with infinite trouble to some scrap of real knowledge, or traditional observation, or hap-hazard coincidence. The witch is like a savage, who might pick up a lucifer match-box, and should imagine that the power of lighting the matches was peculiar to himself, thence inferring that he was gifted with miraculous powers, and could command the lightning. He is only just superior to his fellows, who would fall down and worship the box.

A witch, therefore, may be thus defined. He is one who professes to work marvels, not through the aid and counsel of the supernatural beings in whom he believes as much as the rest, but by certain occult faculties and devices which he conceives himself to possess. In so far as he does really possess a trifling store of superior skill and useful tricks, he is the *savant* of his time; in so far as he merely pretends and guesses, he is a crazy charlatan. By applying constantly this definition we may reduce into order our ideas of the relative position of witchcraft towards all phases of religion. First, we grasp the real distinction, even in fetichism, between the witch and his brother practitioner upon a fetich, or between the witch and the *Shâman* who rolls about the ground and screams out his oracle; and this line between adoration, inspiration, vows, or oracles, on one side, and thaumaturgy by occult incomprehensible arts on the other side, divides the two professions from bottom to top. Secondly, we see why the said witch is so violently persecuted even in the earliest times, when there is no church to proscribe him, nor morality to denounce his ways. So long as people ascribe to their gods all inexplicable and unforeseen calamities as well as blessings, and so long as everyone is allowed to worship his fetich, spirit, or idol, after his own fashion, the cruelties of superstition are confined mainly to barbarous propitiatory sacrifices, in which the victim is sometimes human. If these offerings will not appease the gods there is nothing else to be done in that direction. But the pretensions of a successful witch suggest the idea that a human being, who is within reach of your hand to seize, wields mysterious power to afflict his fellow-creatures; and this conviction it is which has always caused, indeed in India it still causes, horrid cruelty. While the priest, or fetich keeper, or oracle monger, is held in reverence, as the ambassador of a power on whom it is hopeless to make war, the witch is always feared, and usually detested; because the priest disclaims all responsibility for the ills inflicted by his angry or malevolent deities, whereas the witch can be made to pay with his person. Moreover, he has also often to pay for all the shortcomings of the popular fetich; since a priest who has the credit of his establishment at stake will usually attribute any failure in the efficacy of prayer, or of vows, to the malignant influence of his natural opponent, the independent witch. Among the aboriginal tribes of India any disappointment in the aid which they are entitled to expect from their gods, to avoid the ravages of disease or famine, throws the people on the scent of witchcraft. It is too discreditable that the idol or demon spirit, after all that has been done for him in attentions, and even adulation, should have so broken down and abandoned his worshippers, as to let the cholera rage damnably, to keep wives obstinately barren, to permit the rinderpest, or to afflict people with chronic rheumatism. But, on the part of the gods, their priest is apt to disown these untoward accidents, though he is willing carefully to absorb all blessings; and the people, usually directed by priestly advice, fall back on witchcraft as the only possible alternative. The thing which torments us (they argue) is inexplicable; the only two possessors of inexplicable powers are gods and witches, the gods can't or won't help us, *argal*, we must help ourselves by a hue and cry after the witches. This solution of the puzzle is easier than any speculation as to misfortunes being the outcome of sin, or of some omission of religious duties, or the stain of crimes done in a previous state, or than ascribing them to the anger of some strange divinity; and it is the more popular because it suggests a remedy, as all solid diagnoses of disorder ought to do. If the misfortune were the work of a god who declined to be propitiated, one could only lie flat and adore Setebos who cannot be resisted or punished; but if it is the wicked invention of a magician the sufferer can proceed at once to counteract it by torturing the inventor. Observe that the witches have themselves created the dilemma, upon one horn of which they are thus impaled, by assuming powers independent of the gods; for when a man cannot get what he wants out of a god he is wont to consult a witch, who usually undertakes to do his bidding, and never confesses that he does not feel equal to dealing with a case. But in proportion to the popular faith in the witch as an ally must be of course the fear of him as an enemy.

Now it is worth noting, that, although among fetichists the simple reason why a witch is persecuted is that he is doing mischief, for otherwise there is no abstract theological objection to him, yet even in Fetichism the measures employed against him have a flavour of religion; the gods are called in to act as detectives and judges. It is public opinion that at first indicates the direction in which suspicious scrutiny should be made; the *vox populi* usually names some old woman with a smattering of simples who has attempted to work cures. That particular combination of skill and helplessness presented by a cunning old woman seems to have always suggested some underhand mystery to the untutored mind of the poor Indian, as of the English peasant; and besides, as has been already remarked, a woman who can cure toothache can produce it, for aught the savage can tell. In individual cases the patient himself, being sick, usually pitches upon his magic persecutor; and in any instance conjecture is generally justified by consulting the professional witch-finder, who will listen to your evidence and give his authoritative opinion on your case. Prescriptions thus made up are administered by the mob. The accused is seized and subjected to experiments which appear partly intended to make him or her confess, and partly aimed at forcing the witch to break the malignant charm by incessant counter-irritation, until the evil ceases or the evil-doer dies. There is as yet no exorcism in the proper sense of the word, but these operations are conducted by the light of whatever glimpses of the supernatural may have been vouchsafed to the tribe; the use of sacred weapons against witches is already indispensable. Such weapons are indeed used by primitive man to combat troubles of every sort, and the particular reason for mentioning the fact here is that it partially explains what at first puzzles an investigator into the witch-finding and witch-punishing business in India—the close resemblance of the practice and methods there in use to those formerly approved by mediæval Europe. The ordeal by water is universal among the barbarous Non-Aryan tribes of Central India, from the Bheels in the west country to the wild men in the almost unexplored jungles of Bustar and the far east, towards the Bay of Bengal. Here is a description of one water test, taken a few years ago from the mouth of an expert witch-finder among the Bheels, who got into a scrape for applying it to an old woman.

"A bamboo is stuck up in the middle of any piece of water. The accused is taken to it, lays hold of it, and by it descends to the bottom. In the meantime one of the villagers shoots an arrow from his bow, and another runs to pick it up and bring it back to the place whence it was shot. If the woman is able to remain under water until this is done, she is declared innocent, but if she comes up to breathe before the arrow is returned into the bowman's hand, she is a true witch and must be swung as such."

In the case from which this account is taken the woman failed in the test, and was accordingly swung to and fro, roped up to a tree, with a bandage of red pepper on her eyes; but it is obvious that this kind of ordeal, like almost all primitive ordeals, is contrived so as to depend for its effect much upon the manner in which it is conducted, whereby the operator's favour becomes worth gaining.* A skilful archer will shoot

* Another mode of trial is by sewing the suspected one in a sack, which is let down into water about three feet deep. If the person inside the sack

just as far as he chooses. Ordeal by water is the question ordinary, which may probably be construed as an inquiry whether the water Fetich or water spirit will accept or reject the witch, whether he is on her side or against her: and this seems the best general explanation of a world-wide custom. Another ordeal is by heat, as for instance, the picking of a coin out of burning oil. But the question extraordinary is by swinging on a sacred tree, or by flogging with switches of a particular wood. Swinging before an idol, with a hook through the muscles of the back, is the well-known rite by which a Hindu devotes himself to the god; and flogging with rods from a sacred tree manifestly adds superhuman virtue to the ordinary effect of a vigorous laying on. In 1865, a woman, suspected of bringing cholera into the village, was deliberately beaten to death with rods of the castor-oil tree, which is excellent for purging witchcraft. It is usual also to knock out the front teeth of a notorious witch; the practice appears to be connected with the belief, well known in all countries, that witches assume animal shapes; for in India they are supposed occasionally to transform themselves into wild beasts, a superstition analogous to our European lycanthropy. A good many years ago, there was an old man practising as a physician near Srinagar in the Himalayas, who was notorious as a sorcerer, insomuch that his reputation of having devoured many persons under the form of a tiger cost him most of his teeth, which were extracted by the Rajah who then held that country, so as to render him less formidable during his constant metamorphoses. Shaving the heads of female witches is very common among the tribes much infested by sorcerers; it is employed as an antidote, not merely as a degrading punishment, so that one is tempted to trace its origin to some recondite notion of power residing in the hair; and thus even back towards Samson, to Circe with the beautiful locks, and

can get his head above water he is a witch. An English officer once saved a witch in India from ducking to death, by insisting that the witch-finder and the accusers generally should go through precisely the same ordeal which they had prescribed. This idea hit off the crowd's notion of fair play, and the trial was adjourned *sine die* by consent.

to the familiar devils of early Christian times, who are said to have had a peculiar attachment for women with fine tresses.

Thus the frightful cruelties inflicted on witches by the wild tribes of Central India are prompted by the conviction that the power which is causing some exasperating calamity lies in the witch himself, and proceeds out of that human creature, not out of any fetich or intangible demon. And as the evil is not from a god, therefore they use holy gear to extirpate it: but the idea of vindicating the insulted majesty of deities is as yet far off, for the witch is simply a mischievous animal whom you knock on the head as you would a tiger, whenever you have hunted him down. Nor is sorcery yet regarded in the light of treason, for though the votaries of the gods are indeed its ill wishers, yet this is mainly because they have to account for the prevalence of sore afflictions, and for the incompetence of their gods to apply cure after due supplication. It is therefore convenient to resolve such problems by reference to witchcraft, when all that the gods need do is to disown the accused, or to lend a hand in detecting him; for which objects and reasons the ordeals have been instituted. Sorcery is at this stage not so much an illicit irreligious trade as a wily and sinister art whereby honest men are plagued; being thus esteemed very much as law and lawyer are received by the unlearned vulgar in England and elsewhere. This is, however, its malevolent and uncanny form; on its brighter side witchcraft embodies the primitive mysteries of the art of healing, combining spells with quack medicines, the spell being what the patient mainly relies on. And as the aboriginal Indian patient expects the incantation to have a precise immediate effect, like a strong drug, so we may perceive the same conception inverted still moving among the peasantry of England, who talk of a dose acting "like a charm," that is, in a novel and unaccountable manner, while the Indian employs a charm to act like a dose. Neither in England nor in India is there yet any large class of the population which has finally and firmly grasped the conclusion that a dose will act by itself, and that it cannot be in the least aided by any sort of charm or invocation whatsoever.

But just as the heavy mist which at dawn covers a primeval forest or waste fen land may be seen gradually to rise, spread out into lighter haze, and wreath itself into various fantastic shapes, so in India the dense low-lying aboriginal Fetichism expands and tapers into higher forms. Polytheism then draws closer the broad hem of its sacerdotal phylactery, and shrinks from witchcraft with increasing antipathy. Not yet does the priest abhor or assail the witch; his prejudices carry him little beyond carefully disowning such low practitioners, and relegating sorcery outside the bounds of decent spiritualism, as a college of physicians might separate themselves from a quack. The business manifestly dispenses with the intervention of the great traditional deities, with their embodiments, ministers, rites, and scriptures; it is therefore indefensible upon any orthodox scheme of religion, and is also condemned as in effect disreputable. Moreover, as the religion of a country develops, so also does its witchcraft become modified from its earliest structure, and suffer a change of character. Its essential materialism, always unconscious and hap-hazard, easily accepts a supernatural impression; and among the Hindus proper the tricks of the primitive art or trade get incrusted over by the alluvial deposits of superstitions extinct or discarded by the predominant castes and races. Prevailing popular delusions affect even the sorcerer, so to keep up with the times he also must pretend to some backstairs interest with deities; if he is a Hindu he is often patronised by (or patronises) some obscure, ill-conditioned god of the rudest type, who has lost all fashion under the improvement of general religious culture. His craft becomes complicated with the earlier and more discreditable rites of depressed races and superseded liturgies; so that he is less easily distinguishable than at a more simple stage. No ordinary Hindu, however, has any doubt that there is a wide gulf between a witch and a devout person who has imbibed thaumaturgic power, though it is very difficult to hit off the popular definition; and, on the whole, it appears that one must judge of wonder-workers by their fruits, whether they be good or evil. So long as a man possessing inscrutable secrets restricts himself to useful employment of them, to the department of detecting thieves and discovering lost property, he is respected as a kind of preternatural private inquiry office and cloak-room for friends or chattels. When, however, the wise man's art takes a dark hue, and his ways are harmful, then he is at once stigmatised as a witch, and usually with accurate justice, for the sorcerer will too often be found to have stepped into all the scandalous business which a general advance in religious ethics may prove the gods to have abandoned. So far as he relies on any rites at all, they are connected with the worship of those Helot, or outcast tribes, which are excluded from the Brahmanical temples; but his whole system escapes the control exercised in practice by public opinion over every openly-professed religion. For these reasons the witch deteriorates rapidly, and descends as polytheism rises. He is not seriously persecuted by the mob or by the learned; but he holds with all classes a position which a quack of the baser sort still holds in the department of medicine. You go to such an one because he is familiar, and gives himself no airs, does not trouble himself about orthodox forms, or about the morality of means or ends, will do your work cheaply, though perchance dirtily, and will undertake operations that no respectable priest or shrine would agree to bring about by the favour of divinity He is to be found in the back slums and alleys of superstition and of elementary physics; he dabbles largely in poisons and love philtres; he can bind or loosen the *aiguillette* in a parlous manner; and throughout he mixes up miracles with medicine after a fashion that ends later on by getting him into trouble with both camps. When his simples will not always kill or cure, he ekes them out with hideous mummery; and when that resource has failed, he has been known to perform a contract to rid a man of his enemy by mere carnal assassination. He is more prone than ever to ascribe the credit of his successful cures, not to what he really knows or has done, but to his portentous gifts or to his familiar demons; whereby any rudimentary conceptions of true science are greatly hindered, for every sudden death or skilful cure is instantly set down to magic by the vulgar. The majority of witches are, it must be owned, mere cheats and swindlers; nevertheless, they appear to be the unworthy depositaries of whatever small hoard of natural magic may have been painfully secreted during long ages of soul-destroying misrule. They know some optical tricks; and the action of emotions upon the bodily organism, as in mesmerism, has been perceived and practised from very ancient times. In the East mesmerism is pure magic; in the West it is suspicious charlatanry. Its whole history offers a good illustration of the manner in which a natural phenomenon which is obscure, uncommon, and isolated, may first be condemned as sorcery, and afterwards be repudiated as incredible; may be rejected by orthodox science as well as by orthodox religion. It may be conjectured that the reputation of insensibility to pain possessed by witches in India as well as in Europe is connected with the well-known anæsthesia produced by the mesmeric trance.

It is difficult to explain, except upon the assumption that ignorant and simple imaginations all range with a very short tether over similar ground, why we find in India the identical old English sorcerer's device of moulding an image of his doomed victim and afflicting it with pins; or wasting it in flame, in mere faith that the person imaged will bleed or pine away simultaneously. But early in this century the life of the Nizam of the Dekhan was attempted by this diabolical invention; and, as the ladies of the harem were said to be at the bottom of the plot, a scandal was caused not unlike that for which the Duchess of Gloucester had to do penance, after conspiring with sorcerers to remove Henry VI. by this very trick of an infernal doll shaped in the likeness of majesty. Not long ago, one partner in a respectable commercial firm in one of the great Indian cities applied to a reputed sorcerer for his aid in removing another partner; but the sorcerer, who was merely an honest leech, preferred to collude with the threatened partner to cheat the would-be murderer out of heavy fees, the conjurer performing the wax-doll rites, while the victim pretended mysterious ailments and a general sense of vital exhaustion.

The Banjâras of Central India, who formerly carried all the grain traffic of the country on vast droves of bullocks, are terribly vexed by witchcraft, to which their wandering and precarious existence especially exposes them in the shape of fever, rheumatism, and dysentery. Solemn inquiries are still held in the wild jungles where these people camp out like gipsies, and many an unlucky hag has been strangled by sentence of their secret tribunals. In difficult cases they consult the most eminent of their spiritual advisers or holy men, who may be within reach; but it is usual, as a proper precaution against mistakes which even learned divines may commit, to buy some trifling article on the road to the consultation, and to try the diviner's faculty by making him guess what it was, before proceeding to matters of life or death. The saint works himself into a state of demoniac possession, and gasps out some woman's name; she is killed by her nearest relative, or allowed to commit suicide, unless indeed her family are able to make it worth the diviner's while to have another fit, and to detect some one else. It is to be remarked, that though the witch and the witch-finder are in these transactions both on precisely the same level of darkest and deepest superstition, yet that the two professions are entirely distinct and mutually opposed. The Banjâras are in no sense an aboriginal tribe.

The conclusion here suggested is, therefore, that witchcraft has always been a separate art and calling side by side with the stewardship of divine systems, but apart from it. Also, that the most primitive witchcraft looks very like medicine in an embryonic state; but as no one will give the aboriginal physician any credit for cures or chemical effects produced by simple human knowledge, he is soon forced back into occult and mystic devices which belong neither to religion nor to destiny, but are a ridiculous mixture of both, whence the ordinary kind of witchcraft is generated. Now its progressive degradation as a science may be measured by the gradual elevation of its two original ingredients, of the religious sentiment, and (much later) of real experimental knowledge. In polytheism it is the relative upward growth of morality and of popular conceptions of the divine nature, which depress witchcraft to a lower level of public esteem. A higher idea of the functions of divinity usually coincides with a more restricted idea of their employment; and the notion is soon developed of gods interfering mainly on the side of virtue (except where their own majesty or privileges are concerned), and even then only on important occasions. So soon as men come to presume gods to be incapable of gross injustice, of unprovoked cruelty, or of wanton malice, they impute to the witch every sudden misfortune, like apoplexy or paralysis, that befalls a blameless man or beast. In an earlier intellectual state, vicious cruelty is not incompatible with the character of a revengeful or malignant deity who may have been introduced to Hinduism by Brahmanised fetich worshippers; but with the milder polytheism of Hindus proper, the practice of using mighty power to do evil ceases to be approved as a godlike characteristic, and thus becomes discreditable; while even to do good the great deities are reluctant to interpose, save when the knot is worthy to be loosed by divine fingers. *De minimis non curant;* they will bestow a victory or a pestilence, but for petty blessing or cursing there is a tendency towards the Epicurean theosophy. Nevertheless, since the peculiar need of the primitive mind is to insist upon a religious or supernatural causation for all queer, unaccountable facts, insomuch that to such minds the miraculous explanation is, as Grote remarks, the rational one; therefore, the vulgar polytheists still cling obstinately to witchcraft as their easiest interpretation of phenomena for which their inferior gods decline to be responsible, as their readiest source for the remedies which Heaven will no longer undertake to provide, and man has not yet tried to discover. The great plagues, like cholera or smallpox, still belong to the gods, who personally inflict and can therefore remove them; but as the nobler Hindu deities rise higher towards the clouds above, and gradually melt away into abstractions, they deign less and less to trouble themselves with trivial grievances or animosities, or to bow down their ear to the lamentation and ancient tale of wrong which comes ever steaming up from the much-enduring tillers of Indian soil. The consequence is that all dirty squabbles, and the criminal side of miraculous business generally, are gradually made over to witches; and the earlier habit of attributing malignant, monkey-like tricks to a god, or of expecting trifling services from him, is discouraged and disowned by the priests as inconsistent with the dignity of their cultus. A man cannot expect a great incarnation of Vishnu to cure his cow, or find his lost purse; nor will public opinion tolerate his going to any respectable temple or shrine with a petition that his neighbour's wife, his ox, or his ass may be smitten with some sore disease. A respectable minister will not be found to take an offering or to use his influence in such silly and scandalous jobs with any saint or deity who values his self-respect.

It must be remembered, also, that the upper sort of polytheistic priest very rapidly hardens down into a mechanical master of ceremonies, the rigid expounder of accredited traditional religion; and that under this process of change he is apt to transfer even his mantic office, the expounding of occasional marvels, to astrologers, soothsayers, convulsionists, and the like—a class which in all its branches must be distinguished, in India, from the magicians proper. Astrologers, fortune-tellers by sortilege, and interpreters by dreams or omens, all swarm throughout India, but all these watch nature in order to ascertain the will and intention of the gods: whereas we may define a witch to be one who works independently of them. The witch has originally, I imagine, nothing at all to do with the Mantis; though it is easy to see how they came to be confounded during the first centuries of the Christian era in Europe.

It must not be supposed that even the uppermost gods of Hinduism have retired behind mere ceremonial altars, like constitutional monarchs; on the contrary, all still take active interest in the well-being of their worshippers, some working by laws as loftily as any mortal Indian executive, and are therefore as well worth propitiation. But there seem to be many grades of accessibility among them, from Brahma—who since he created the world has taken no further trouble about it, and is naturally rewarded by possessing only one or two out of the million temples to Hindu gods—down to the lowest pettifogging deity to whom nothing comes amiss by way of a *douceur*. One of this last sort may often be stumbled upon enshrined in deep jungle by some lonely cross-road or choked-up well; a low caste illiterate hedge-priest presides, who with rough and ready ritual immolates a young pig before a clay image daubed with red paint. The man is a scandal to Brahmanism, and only distinct from fetichism because the image probably represents some utterly obscure saint or hero of the spot; but he is not a witch. This hedge-priest serves his god or devil, whereas a witch makes the familiar demon, if one is kept, serve *him*. Now polytheism is so tolerant that it allows a man to apply at discretion to any of its deities, and perhaps he may begin with his suit to the highest class of them, on the principle of always dealing, where possible, with the heads of departments. But if a man does not get his remedy there, he obviously goes elsewhere. He will generally try some god of local reputation and fair fame; failing these he will resort to miraculous shrines and far-famed places of pilgrimage. Thence he may come down for relief to living men, to ecstatics, ascetics, and saints marvellously gifted or afflicted; or he may take a step even lower, and consult inspired Shâmanists who inhale the divine afflatus, and deliver their reply in a frenzy;* but here he is arriving at the last stage of legitimate research into the supernatural. Beyond this line a moral man will not venture in pursuit of his object, if it is one of which he is not ashamed; for if he proceeds further he has left the region of divinity, and has got among the witches. He will only do this if his need be very trifling, such as the cure of a beast or the finding of a coin, or if it be evil and criminal—saving only the exceptional case when he, being himself manifestly vexed by a witch, is justified, according to common opinion, in seeking to employ the *lex talionis*. Here begins the black art proper, of which if we may judge by study of its practices from real life in India, we must own that our ancestors may have had very good reasons for persecuting it, though they proceeded on

* These professional convulsionists used to be notorious for oracular powers upon the Malabar coast, where their custom was to work themselves into violent hysterics, when they thundered out curses or prophecies, as the occasion required.

grounds widely mistaken, and very often against the wrong persons. In any decent condition of society the sorcerers have subsided for the most part to level of knaves and cheats, religious and medical. Obviously the wide-spread popular detestation of witchcraft was against its evil ways, and a great part of its ill-fame was quite separate from the theologic prejudices against black and white magic indiscriminately, which all Christian communities have very consistently entertained.

It is among the Mahomedans that we find, as might be expected, the first distinct expression of religious condemnation of all magic as a sin, because it is treason against God. Sorcery of all kinds is known and incessantly practised. Much business is done in amulets, charms, spells, exorcism, magic mirrors, cabalistic figures, divination, sortilege, and the like; nor do the common people curse a magician unless his dealings or deeds be wicked. The magician of Islam is he who hath power over the genii, or over fairies, and who will cast out devils by magic circles and incantations not known to the orthodox rubric for that end provided, and who is also acquainted with talismans for causing a devil to enter into possession of a man's body. Then there is the minor sorcerer, who helps to captivate women, to discover thieves, or to find out what absent friends are about by the aid of the magic mirror. The magic mirror, so famous in the mediæval romance of western Europe, whereby an honest crusader often caught most discomforting glimpses of his domestic interior, may have been imported from the East in those ages. It will be remembered that Lane, in his "Modern Egyptians," gives a minute description of this kind of magical feat, and that in "Eöthen," Mr. Kinglake relates a ludicrous failure by the conjuror whom he desired to summon Dr. Keats, late of Eton. In India the conjuror polishes with some black oily paste a child's hand; charms are muttered while the child stares steadily at the bright surface, and describes the visions which successively pass across it. It is worth noting that the image of a broom sweeping the ground, which, according to Lane, frightened a young Englishwoman who allowed the mirror to be prepared in her hand, appears to be in India also the apparition which the mirror-holder ordinarily begins by describing. There may be something in Lane's remark that the whole process reminds him of animal magnetism.

But all these arts are denounced by rigid Mahomedan divines, especially by the Wahâbi sect, whose distinctive theologic note is great jealousy of any encroachment upon the centralised unity of Divinity. Magic, say the more liberal doctors, is a concealed power, which is given to some men for profession and use, just as a sword is a visible instrument which some get hold of and learn to use; and, as with arms, so with magic, the only question should be whether it is employed for good or for ill. If a man devotes himself to the study of these abstruse and powerful arts, he may acquire the thaumaturgic faculty, and may extort obedience from genii; but he must wield his authority for right ends. He may succeed in commanding the evil genii to do him all kinds of wicked service, but then he is practising black, or Satanic magic. The story of one Shâh Dârval is famous in Central India; indeed it belongs to a kind famous throughout the world,—the legend of a man who has obtained possession, usually by chance or trick, of a power which is too strong for him to manage. Shâh Dârval was groom to a great magician of the Michael Scott type, who, lying on his death-bed, felt himself passing away at an hour when all his disciples were absent. The only person who heard the magician's call was this poor horse-boy, who brought him water, so to him did the wizard impart the secret spell, which bound two genii to serve him. But Shâh Dârval could handle his magic no better than the dwarf in the "Lay of the Last Minstrel;" some say he did some awful crime, others that he broke the vow of chastity on which his power depended; anyhow his genii soon tore him to pieces, and he is a wandering demon to this day.* Of course the ordinary moral lesson against abuse of great gifts may be pointed by

* A similar legend, widely spread over a vast tract of country, is that of Hemar Punt, by some identified with Hemâdri, an authentic physician of the ninth century. He, too, found himself obliged to keep his demons employed, and he set them to build temples with huge stones, without mortar. The demons finished them all in one night, and their ruins, called by the profane ancient Hindoo architecture, are to be seen all over the Dekhan to this day.

this legend; but it might also be imagined to be a faint and far distant reverberation of the despairing voice of some ancient seeker after knowledge, who has caught just a glimpse of what will be known after his time dying in the dark ages, surrounded by fanatics and poor fools like Shâh Dârval, with the miserable certainty that his few discoveries must perish with him, and that his name will be lost among a crowd of barbarous conjurors.

The stricter doctrines of Islam approach Christianity in their entire condemnation of all curious arts. According to them magic is designated by a word which literally means partnership, and secondarily a sort of polytheism. As applied to magic, the term may imply the admission of other supernatural beings into partnership with the miraculous powers that are God's attribute; or with the rigid unitarians it would mean that the magician himself becomes an apostate and a renegade, by arming himself rebelliously with weapons that belong by prerogative to God alone. And in this latter definition we find again the idea which is the spinal column of witchcraft; for the essence of magic, as distinguished from miracles, is in Islam that it is performed without calling on God's name and without ascribing to him glory for the deed, which, if the deed be evil or foolish, cannot of course be done. And so we come round again to our aboriginal definition of witchcraft, that it is a marvellous art independent of popular theology, and therefore disowned by it in every stage of religious belief. Nevertheless not even among Mahomedans is sorcery really laid under such uncompromising proscription as was imposed upon it by the stern persecution of the old Catholic Church in Europe, which laid so strict an interdict upon all unauthorised wonder-working that even scientific discoveries and harmless tricks were put down as a breach of it.* On the contrary, the respectable Indian world in general is of Ralpho's opinion in Hudibras, that "the Saints have freedom to go to sorcerers if they need 'em," and that by "subtle stratagem" to make use of

* Tavernier, who visited India in the 17th century, relates how, being at an English settlement, he saw that celebrated trick of the Indian jugglers—the causing of a mango-tree to grow from a slip in half an hour. He says that an English minister, who was present, declared that he would refuse the communion to any man who looked on at such devilry, and so broke up the gathering.

the devil for innocent ends is no sin at all. In mediæval Europe the ban of the Church was laid unsparingly upon all secret acts and occult practices, as being connected with demon worship and otherwise contraband. But no one, not even the soundest Mahomedan divine, is bound, for conscience' sake, to molest a witch who has not meddled with him or his.

It is probable that in no other time or country has witchcraft ever been so comfortably practised as it is now in India under British rule. In Europe it has always been either persecuted or ridiculed; and its worst sufferings must have been during that period when the Church insisted that belief in witchcraft was an essential dogma, and stamping it out a primary duty. To disbelieve in its preternatural existence was almost as bad as to practise it, wherefore between the two millstones of hard-set credulity and implacable condemnation the witch was brayed as in a mortar. Now though in India everyone believes in witchcraft as a fact, yet there is here no church convinced that scepticism as to such a dangerous moral disease is not only in itself dangerous, but may also be, as Glanvil logically calls it, an insidious sapping of all belief in the supernatural. Thus his countrymen are not bound to prosecute the Indian sorcerer on religious grounds; while he lives under laws which, instead of condemning him, interfere actively to protect him from molestation, and are much more prone to hang witch-finders than witches. Of course the witch is punished when he takes to poisoning or pure swindling; but so long as his methods are simply magical, that is, so long as he pretends to work evil in a way not admitted to be physically possible, by sticking pins in a wax figure, brewing in a cauldron, burying a fowl head downwards, howling out incantations, and the like, it is not easy for an English judge to punish the man because he can make his neighbours believe that these operations affect the climate, the cattle, or the health of anyone against whom they are directed. The Penal Code does indeed contain one section that might reach witches; * a section

* Section 508. It punishes the causing a person to do or omit anything, by inducing him to believe that he will be rendered, by some act of the offender, an object of divine displeasure.

which, it may be remarked, merely continues the ancient oriental distinction between black and white magic; for while it forbids the threatening of evil, it does not prohibit the promise of good, though one can be no more an imposture than the other. In every village of Central India they keep a hereditary servant, whose profession is to ward off impending hailstorms by incantations, by consulting the motion of water in certain pots, and by dancing about with a sword. If he threatened to bring down the hail, he would be dealt with as a witch by the public, and imprisoned as an intimidator by the magistrate; but as his intentions are beneficent, he is encouraged and supported. In short, witches in British India are exposed to little professional risk except when they are really mischievous; and they are under this special disadvantage only, that the law need not treat them with any of the caution and deference to popular feeling which protect those who claim to practise religious observances, however irrational or indefensible. For while we concede that to menace bodily harm or material mischief by the most absurd devices is clearly punishable, yet we find it more difficult to settle how far we are to take legal notice of threats of divine displeasure issued in the name of recognized divinities, although it may nevertheless show itself, like smallpox, in very substantial form.

Witchcraft is, however, a much more manageable subject for modern governments than other superstitions, because the delusion is more gross and palpable. So long as a witch keeps to white, or even to grayish magic, it would be unfair that an impartial magistracy should prosecute him hastily because he is a bit of an impostor. It should be remembered that even the most grotesque and ridiculous operations of witchcraft, the method of divining the course of a hailstorm by looking at water in a row of pots, for instance, may possibly contain the germ or hidden kernel of some real observation. At any rate, the practice seems more likely to stimulate the spirit of observation and induction than the mere watching of signs and omens, or sacrifices to gods; though Comte believes that these things stimulated early physical inquiry. Chance and strangeness are the very essence of an omen; whereas sorcery pretends to be in some sort an exact science. And from this point of view it might possibly be affirmed that even the poor aboriginal witch of the jungles, with all his sins and disreputable hocus-pocus, is in his time and generation persecuted, like Paracelsus and Cornelius Agrippa, in some slight degree on account of his singularity and of his superior ingenuity, or at least curiosity. He may be making a first step, however stumbling and unconscious, upon a road which may lead him away from abject prostration before the idols and phantasms which overawe his world; or, if he has a devil, it is his own familiar, rather his servant than his master, not the tyrannous hobgoblin that overawes the crowd. He is just touching, though he may only touch and let go, a line of thought which points, albeit vaguely and most crookedly, towards something like mental independence; whereas the worshippers of stocks and stones, of ghosts and demons, are only just setting forth into that interminable labyrinth of speculation as to invisible and supernatural personalities which at last threatens to lead modern Hindus—after ages of wandering over the waste ocean of their theology, in vain pursuit of phantoms and meteors—back again to that despised materialism of which witchcraft may be only the first dim and rudimentary expression.

# CHAPTER V.

## MISSIONARY AND NON-MISSIONARY RELIGIONS.

Professor Max Müller's Lecture in Westminster Abbey, December, 1873—His classification of religious systems as Missionary and Non-missionary—Remarks on the classification of Brahmanism as non-missionary, not upon the view that, as a proselytising religion, it is dying or dead—Brahmanism still proselytises in the sense of accepting and admitting members from the outside—Its spread among Non-Aryan tribes; examples and illustrations—Its vitality as shown by reforming and purifying movements from within; and as an indigenous religion and social system—Question as to the future of Brahmanism—Whether it can transmute and raise itself in accordance with rising standards of intelligence and morality—Extensive changes will probably be gradual—Present state of Indian polytheism compared with Gibbon's sketch of religion in the Roman Empire—Possible difficulties and hazards of a transitional period of general decay of traditional beliefs.

In the Lecture delivered by Professor Max Müller in Westminster Abbey on the day of intercession for missions in December, 1873, he counted eight real historical religions of mankind. And the Lecturer went on to say that by study, by critical examination of the sacred books upon which all these religions professed to be founded, they could be classified and compared scientifically. . . . . . A classification of these systems into non-missionary and missionary religions was directly interesting on that day of intercession for missions, and was also not based on an unimportant or accidental characteristic, but rested on what was the very heart-blood in every system of human faith. Judaism, Brahmanism, and Zoroastrianism were opposed to all missionary enterprise; Buddhism, Mahomedanism, and Christianity were missionary religions from their beginning. . . . . The Brahmans never attempted to proselytize those who did not by birth belong to the spiritual aristocracy of their country; their wish was rather to repel intruders, and they even punished those of other creeds who happened to be near enough to hear their prayers or to see their sacrifices. The Lecturer then compared those religions which had missionary spirit with those "in which any attempt to convince others by argument, to save souls, to bear witness to the truth, is treated with pity and scorn." The former were, he said, alive, the latter were dying or dead. The religion of the Parsees was fast dwindling, Judaism might not so rapidly vanish; but Brahmanism, although still professed by 110 millions, was dying or dead, because it could not stand the light of day. The worship of Siva, of Vishnu, and of the other popular deities, was of the same character as, sometimes more barbarous than, that of Jupiter or Apollo. It might live on, but when a religion had ceased to produce champions, prophets, and martyrs, it had ceased to live, in the true sense of the word; and the decisive battle for the dominion of the world would have to be fought out among the three missionary religions which are alive, Buddhism, Mahomedanism, and Christianity.

It is with great deference that I venture to demur not only to this scientific classification, but also to the conclusions which appear to be mainly drawn from it. It will be allowed that inferences as to the nature and tendency of various existing religions which are drawn from study and exegetic comparison of their scriptures, must be qualified by actual observation of these religions in their popular form and working effects. And if we look steadily at what is going on around us in Europe and Asia, we may collect numerous facts and symptoms of which the Lecture does not seem to me to have taken sufficient account. To Professor Max Müller himself the popular side of these religions is of course well known; but his Lecture, taken alone, seems to encourage the error of presenting an Asiatic religion as a mysterious thing, to be seen only through its ancient books, as through a glass, darkly; and to confirm the inveterate modern habit of assuming all great historic names to represent something definite, symmetrical, and organized—as if Asiatic institutions were capable of being circumscribed by rules or formal definitions. Now in these days it is so important for us to understand the way of growth and the constitution of a great antique religion; there are so many practical questions connected with beliefs and the historic method of inquiry which become clearer when examined by the light of Eastern experiences; and the reflex action of India upon England is so likely to make itself soon felt—that a few words may be worth saying upon those parts of the Lecture by which people in England are, in my judgment, liable to be misled.

Brahmanism is enormously the most important of the religions classified in the Lecture as non-missionary; the other two have ceased to influence the world; they are now no more than survivals of ancient faiths still preserved by scattered and expatriated races. And the Lecturer, while admitting that millions still worship the Hindu deities, considers that the national religion in India is in a state of living death, and that for the purpose of "gaining an idea of the issue of the great religious struggle of the future, Brahmanism is dead and gone." Now it is certain that Brahmanism, being a great polytheism, differs in origin, nature, and mode of growth from a religion that has arisen out of the teaching of its founder or his disciples; the former has spread naturally and unconsciously, like a huge tree, while the latter makes its way by conscious design and systematic exertion, like the higher physical organisms. It is also to be expected that a polytheism, being the most antique existing species of full-grown religions, will in these days be the first to decay and subside. But taking things as they are now, and looking upon the actual state and movement of religions in India, an eye-witness would still be justified in affirming that this religion, although powerfully affected by social and political changes so strong and sudden that they would try the constitution of any national creed, is nevertheless not yet dead, nor dying, nor even dangerously ill; and, moreover, that so far from it being a non-missionary religion in the sense of a religion that admits no proselytes, one might safely aver that more persons in India become every year Brahmanists than all the converts to all the other religions in India put together. The description in the Lecture, of Brahmanism as a moribund non-missionary religion, like the faith of the Jews or the Parsees, cannot fail to raise in England an impression quite at variance with the truth. For it must fix in the minds of an English audience the popular notion of an inflexible stationary creed, confined, like a stagnant pool inside a stone basin, within a set of beliefs and customs into which certain Indians are born by the accident that their parents were born in it and practised the ritual duly, but into which no one has for generations entered or is now allowed to enter who was not thus born within the pale. But this as a definition of Brahmanism would be only part of the whole truth, and not the part which concerns our present discussion. If by Brahmanism we understand that religion of the Hindus which refers for its orthodoxy to Brahmanic scriptures and tradition, which adores the Brahmanic gods and their incarnations, venerates the cow, observes certain rules of intermarriage and the sharing of food, and which regards the Brahman's presence as necessary to all essential rites, then this religion can hardly be called non-missionary in the sense of stagnation and exclusive immobility, because it still proselytizes in two very effective modes.

The first of these modes is the gradual Brahmanizing of the aboriginal, non-Aryan, or casteless tribes. The clans and races which inhabit the hill tracts, the outlying uplands, and the uncleared jungle districts of India, are melting into Hinduism all over India by a process much more rapid and effective than individual conversions. Among all these aboriginal or non-Aryan communities a continued social change is going on; they alter their modes of life to suit improved conditions of existence; their languages decay, and they gradually go over to the dominant Aryan rituals. They pass into Brahmanists by a natural upward transition, which leads them to adopt the religion of the castes immediately above them in the social scale of the composite population among which they settle down. And we may reasonably guess that this process has been working for centuries; though it is likely to have been much more rapid than ever under British rule. The "ethnical frontier" described in the Annals of Rural Bengal is an ever-breaking shore of primitive beliefs which tumble constantly into the ocean of Brahmanism; and when Mr. W. W. Hunter, in his Dissertation on the non-Aryan languages of India, describes the gradations by which the acknowledged non-Aryans of the highlands slide into low-caste Hindus of the plain, he describes a transmutation that is going on all over India. In Central India it has certainly gone very far, with a speed that seems to increase. In the interior of the Eastern Himalayas the Buddhists dispute with the Brahmans over the mountain clans and the sparse families that live in the habitable glens; but on the Southern slopes and in the jungles that fringe the bases of the hills the Brahmans are prevailing unopposed. For all these tribes, by becoming Hindu, come under the Brahmans; and wherever they have succeeded so far as to found a State, as the Goorkhas founded Nepal, they have established the predominancy of caste and creed as a State religion. The number of converts thus added to Brahmanism in the last few generations, especially in this century, must be immense; and if the word proselyte may be used in the sense of one who has come, and who has been readily admitted, not necessarily being one that has been invited or persuaded to come, then Brahmanism might lay claim to be by far the most successful proselytizing religion of modern times in India.

Thus Brahmanism is all over India a necessary first stage for the outlying tribes towards Indian civilization, or admission to the citizenship of the great Hindu community; it very rarely implies any ethical change, or even a formal abandonment of one ritual for another, it is usually a rapid sliding into Hindu customs and an attempt at social assimilation. But the complete process does necessitate a considerable change of worship and ways of life; for perhaps the surest sign of a family's reception into Brahmanism is that whereas the Brahman formerly was never called in, he is latterly found officiating at domestic epochs and ceremonies, of birth, marriage, or death. This implies conformity to Brahmanic rules of eating, inter-marriages, and the like, and the evolution of a caste or sub-caste. If the converted family are of standing among their own people, the Brahman, for a consideration proportionate to the emergency or complexity of the case, will usually discover for them a decent Hindu pedigree, or (what is much easier) a miraculous incident, which proves a half savage chief or rich outcaste to be really allied to one of the recognized castes. We know how readily the gods have always intervened to explain away awkward incidents of birth, and to provide a great man of humble origin with a parentage better suited to his success in after-life. Thus the Gond chiefs of the Central India highlands all now claim Rajpút ancestry, and have ranked themselves in the soldier caste. In aspiration they are now Hindus of the Hindus, some of them carrying ceremonial refinement to the highest pitch of purism; but nevertheless they are really no better than recent parvenus from the clans which still run almost wild in adjacent hills and forests, and which care nothing for Brahmans or caste prejudices. It is calculated that the Bheels, a tribe widely spread over Central India, must have been passing over in large numbers to Brahmanism during the present century. There is a tribe near Ajmere, of whom half were forcibly made Musalmáns, while the other half held its own non-Hindu customs, and until very lately intermarried with its Musalmán kindred; but now this last mentioned half has Brahmanized, and would no more marry with Musalmáns than the Raja of Benares. Sir George Campbell, in his Report upon his government of Bengal in 1871-72, wrote—"It is a great mistake to suppose that the Hindu religion is not proselytizing; the system of castes gives room for the introduction of any number of outsiders; so long as people do not interfere with existing castes, they may form a new caste and call themselves Hindus; and the Brahmans are always ready to receive all who will submit to them and pay them. The process of manufacturing Rajpúts from ambitious aborigines goes on before our eyes." This is one recently recorded observation (noticed in the Lecture), out of many that might be quoted, of the operation of that process which I have called the first mode of Brahmanic propagation. Almost the whole of the great province of Assam in the North-East of Bengal, conquered and settled by people from across the Eastern frontiers of India, supposed to be akin to the Siamese, is said to have become Brahmanized during the last two centuries. It may be granted that people who come in after this fashion do not fulfil the meaning with which the term proselyte is used in describing the operations of a professedly missionary faith, and that Professor Max Müller in his Lecture clearly used the term in this, the ordinary European, meaning. Nevertheless, when we undertake to estimate the vitality of a religion, and its capacity for future adaptation and development (without which no religion can endure long), we must consider and take account of growth by agglomeration, as well as of extension by missionary zeal. And it is fair to argue that a religion which still possesses so much power of extension and assimilation as Brahmanism, which has constantly produced reformers and revivalists, cannot safely be set out of all calculation in forecasting the religious future of Asia, a problem still so prodigiously complex and obscure.

The foregoing extracts and illustrations might be amplified considerably, but they serve to show that the views put forward in this chapter are founded on realities of actual life around us in India. The main consequence of the pacification and settling down of these non-Aryans under British rule has been to encourage their absorption into the Brahmanic ritual; and they are also directly invited to enter in by the Brahmans, to whom come great profit and repute by these additions to the crowd to whom their religious ministry is indispensable. The proselytes are now permitted, by the great favour of the divinity, to enter temple courts formerly tabooed to them, and to make offerings which would previously have been rejected with scorn. Their wives consult holy men who would once have disdained to receive them, and are admitted to the full honour of private interviews; they elect a spiritual director from among the orthodox, and are enrolled among his disciples. They may even bring over their humble deities, and get them properly Brahmanized as incarnations. It should be explained that the spiritual director is often a personage very different from and morally superior to the priest of a temple or the holy guardian of a shrine, dealing with religious questions and the consolation of troubled minds much less entirely in the concrete. All these privileges uplift the hearts of simple folk, and draw them into the great flock of those whose only systematic belief is practically laid down for them by Brahmans.

This is the first of the two modes by which Brahmanism may be said to proselytize; an acceptance of the worship of the outer tribes, invitation to them to come in and conform, assumption of their liturgic and spiritual direction; in short, holding open to them the gates of admission into Brahmanic caste and creed. It might be argued, indeed, that Brahmanism is no clear-cut religion at all, in the scientific sense with which the word is applied to the elaborated theologies of Christianity, of Islam, and even of Buddhism, which have each their founder and central doctrines, are fenced round and staked out dogmatically, with proper gates for lawful entry. And thus it might be contended that no real analogy exists between the spiritual enthusiastic conversions to the Cross or the Crescent, and this natural melting down in the crucible of Brahmanism of masses of men as they emerge, intellectually aimless and wandering, out of a half-savage state. It might also be said that a religion which thus, half involuntarily, enlarges its borders, is in no strict sense a missionary religion; and when Professor Max Müller's lecture is carefully read, it becomes evident that he admits within the class of missionary religions only those which make proselytism an essential and a sacred duty. On the other hand, it seems quite conceivable that an ordinary audience might not have caught this distinction, while no one, I venture to remark, would have inferred from the Lecture that Brahmanism has still life and growth, much less that it is spreading, and internally undergoing active changes that may prolong its existence under other forms. And this brings me to the second mode of Brahmanic proselytism, if the word may be used in the sense of admitting and welcoming adherents, who are not actually summoned and urged to join an association.

The second mode by which I should affirm that Brahmanism proselytizes is by the working of the devotees and spiritual leaders who found new sects, and set up new lights in divine matters. In a former chapter I have tried to describe upon a small scale how these personages have constantly appeared, and still appear, among the Hindus, to assert new inspirations, to insist on a peculiar way of life, to work wonders, and to enroll a body of disciples who gradually convince themselves that their master was a personification of some god. These movements are now going on all over India; some of them increase and take root, others wither and disappear; but it is impossible to describe as non-missionary a religion which permits and largely adopts all this wonderful diversity and intensity of religious propagation. For the Brahmans do not usually reject these sectaries, or disown them, unless their principle is hostility to Brahmanism; on the contrary, the movement is generally adopted and absorbed into Brahmanism. Nor would it be correct to say that these are merely interior variations or changes within Brahmanism itself, and therefore quite different from the spirit of proselytism going forth beyond its own religion to call in the outer gentiles. Many of these teachers address themselves to every one without distinction of caste or of creed; they preach to low-caste men and to the aboriginal tribes who are just emerging, out of a nomad state into a settled low-caste element; in fact, they succeed largely in those ranks of the population which would lean towards Christianity and Mahomedanism if they were not drawn into Brahmanism by some local saint or devotee. I do not assert these religious reforms or revivals are essentially Brahmanic; on the contrary, I think that their aim and first impulse are usually against orthodoxy, monopolies of inspiration, and priestly abuses generally; but this is the origin of every fresh development which any great religion has ever taken; and in surveying the general condition of such a religion one must give it credit for all its vigorous developments, heretical or otherwise. Most of these movements which I am describing in India have issued out of Brahmanism; and hitherto they have almost all ended in it; the leaders are mystics or devout ascetics who spiritualize the idolatry and rude superstition of the vulgar; but they very rarely, except in the famous instances of Buddhism and the Jaina doctrines, carry any large section of the people into any communion permanently separate from Brahmanism. Almost invariably they end by a new Brahmanic caste or sect, with peculiar doctrines and divinities that elevate the low-caste disciple, and satisfy in his spiritual nature just those needs which Christianity or Islam might otherwise have been called in to satisfy. And thus the Brahmanic revivalists at the very least occupy the ground which the more distinctly and consciously proselytizing creeds from abroad could otherwise annex; and make wholesale conversions among those classes with whom only are wholesale conversions in these days possible.

For specimens of the second mode we may take the accounts of the Kookas in the Punjab, whose outbreak was rather sternly repressed in 1872, and of kindred manifestations. The Punjab report for that year, which in this part of it reads like the letter of some legate addressed to the Emperor from one of the Asiatic provinces of imperial Rome, sets forth how "Ram Singh, the leader of the sect, a man of considerable ability, was the son of a carpenter, who gradually acquired a reputation of extreme sanctity, and even for the possession of miraculous powers. As his influence and the number of his followers increased, the tendency of his teaching became more political," * &c. &c.; but what first brought this sect into collision with the British Government was their fanatical horror at the slaughter of kine, which led them to murder the butchers; a very fair proof of the strong Brahmanic colouring which pervaded this otherwise spiritual movement. Then we have Hakeem Singh, who listened to the missionaries until he not only accepted the whole Christian dogma, but has conceived himself to be the second embodiment, has proclaimed himself as such, and has summoned the missionaries to acknowledge this latest dispensation. He works miracles, preaches pure morality, but still venerates the cow. In the remote Eastern districts of the Central Provinces, which are

* Punjab Administration Report, 1871-72, page 214.

governed from Nagpore, we may collect minute information regarding the life of one Ghási Dás, an inspired prophet, who sojourned in the wilderness for six months, and then issued forth preaching to the poor and ignorant the creed of the True Name (*Satnám*). He gathered about half a million people together before he died in 1850. He borrowed his doctrines from the well known Hindu sect of *Satnámís;* and though he denounced Brahmanic abuses he instituted caste rules of his own, and his successor was murdered, not for heresy, but because he aped the Brahmanic insignia and privileges, which is of course a very different thing, according to sacerdotal views, from merely adopting the rules and tenets prescribed by Brahmans. There can be little doubt that this community, if left alone, will relapse into a modified Brahmanism. If it be still contended that these movements are really anti-Brahmanic in their direction and impulse, we have only to point to the Sikhs, who began in just the same manner two or three centuries ago, and whose numbers, after rapidly increasing, are now beginning to diminish. As the Sikhs rise in the political and social world, they are less inclined to separate themselves from the general body of Hindus, though they conform to all rituals in the rough elastic fashion of warlike men who, like Hector of Troy, cannot be hampered by priests and augurs when there is work to be done. Other illustrations might be given from the history of Hindu schisms; and it might be even affirmed that the only great impulse of religious improvement which carried its followers fairly beyond Brahmanic caste and ritual, is Buddhism and its satellite Jainism. The other sects have merely formed separate castes, and have otherwise conformed to the general outline of the Brahmanic system.

Thus, if the word Brahmanism may be taken as the broad denomination of what is recognised by all Hindus as the supreme theological Faculty, and the comprehensive scheme of authoritative tradition to which all minor beliefs are referred for sanction and to be placed properly, we may affirm that this religion, so far from being dead, has increased very considerably within times of which we know. It has drawn in and gathered up the wild tribes and the helots of India; while all the minor sectarian off-shoots have hitherto been gradually bent backward by popular prejudice to conform to it, or else have been obliged to leave India. And while Brahmanism has spread out during the last 100 years, so far as we can guess, it is probable that on the same ground Islam and Christianity have contracted, yielding to unfavourable political circumstance. By sheer force, by its predominant political influence, and also of course by its intrinsic superiority over the indigenous superstitions, Islam made many converts in India up to the middle of the 18th century; but its extension has naturally slackened with the rapid decline and dilapidation of the political power with which the faith was so closely bound up. It has had now to bear the disadvantage of too near identity with rulership, which forces Islam to stake the authenticity and practical proof of its claim to divine favour upon the success of unstable human institutions. Of course the misfortunes of a Musalmán dynasty ruling over unbelievers must affect the proselytizing influence of the doctrines which are held to justify the dominion. With regard to Christianity, its case is in some respects the converse to that of Islam: for there is reason to believe that Christianity has suffered, as to its propagation in India, by the strange success of the Christian conquerors. For a century or more the English have consistently and sincerely disowned all connection between their politics and their religion. Colonel Dow, in his Enquiry into the State of Bengal (1770), observes that persecution for religion is not on the list of the Company's misdeeds, and "he that will consent to part with his property may carry his opinions away with freedom." But no degree of energetic asseveration by a powerful government in India has until very lately been supposed by its subjects to afford any clue to the real intentions of the governors; and so Christianity for many years got all the discredit and jealousy which accompanies support given by the State to a foreign proselytizing religion, without getting any of the support. In the days when Christianity was actually propagated and pushed forward by the whole influence of an European power in India, it did succeed very perceptibly. When Francis Xavier could and did bring the Inquisition to bear upon lukewarm Portuguese Viceroys at Goa, and when whole tribes submitted to conversion on condition of being protected by the Portuguese from the vengeance of their native princes against whom they had rebelled—in those days Christianity flourished and took root in India; but the English never have resorted to such thorough measures, and of course never will. Thus Christianity was much aided by strong political support: and it also did very well on its own merits when it had neither political support nor connection; but it has not advanced in India since it has made political connections without gaining their support. And on the whole we may conclude generally that of the three great religions of India Brahmanism alone has during the last 100 years added materially to its numbers; though whether such numerical additions as it has made are or are not deceptive symptoms of strength and endurance may be a different question. At any rate they are good evidence of actual vitality, quite sufficient to warn us against consigning Brahmanism prematurely to the cemetery of dead religions.

But it is not hard to understand why this should be, and why Brahmanism in India is likely to take an unconscionably long time in dying out utterly, instead of being, as might be supposed from a cursory glance at the Lecture, already dead. For, first, Brahmanism is indigenous to India; whereas the other two religions are exotics. Secondly, Brahmanism is a religion of the præ-Christian old-world type, being neither a State institution like Islam, nor a great Church or else a congregation of worshippers having a common creed, like Christianity. It is a way of life in itself, a scheme of living so interwoven into the whole existence and society of those whom it concerns, and placing every natural habit or duty so entirely upon the religious basis as the immediate reason and object of it, that to distinguish in Brahmanism between matters known to us as sacred and profane is almost impossible. This appears to be the earliest form of a religion; and so far as religion becomes marked off and eliminated out from ordinary civil life as a thing different in use and nature, as a department concerned mainly with immaterial needs and interests, and with a future existence, by so far may we trace the development (or deterioration as some might say) of the original religious idea. The terms layman and ecclesiastic, with all the distinctions thereby implied, indelibility of orders, monopoly of sacred ministry, Church and State existing as independent authorities—are all things which no Brahmanist understands in our European meaning of the words. Professions and privileges are hereditary in Brahmanism, whether they be sacred or profane, but a man's religion means his customary rule of everyday life, whatever that may be. A man is not a Hindu because he inhabits India, or belongs to any particular race or State, but because he is a Brahmanist. His whole status and social identity, the signs by which he may be known and described, belong to his religion.

When, therefore, we say of a religion cast in this type that it is non-missionary, we mean only that it cannot be communicated or entered without changing one's whole manner of life and habitual rules of society. And because we in England have long ago lost the notion that religion has anything to do with the food we eat, the clothes we wear, or the things we touch; we suppose that a religion thus bound up with a peculiar set of social rules, and resting not upon doctrine, but on custom, birth, and status, must be incommunicable beyond the society into the web of which it is thus woven. That is true, but the society itself extends and absorbs, the peculiar rites and theology following in second place. A tribe or individual becomes Brahmanized by adopting what are held to be the respectable high-bred manners and prejudices of Brahmanism, and afterward by desire to propitiate gods of a more refined and aristocratic stamp, as well as more powerful, than their rough-hewn jungle deities. Thus a very recent report upon certain wild tracts in Northern Madras which are gradually becoming cultivated and settled, mentions that the aboriginal tribes are taking to infant marriages, and to burning their dead instead of burying. This latter change is a sure sign of Hinduizing, more sure than a mere change of gods, for the proselyte is very apt to bring in his gods with him; the

Brahman polishes up both gods and worshippers, and introduces them into decent society.

A third reason why Brahmanism is still paramount and spreading in a country like India, particularly among the wild and ignorant, is of a sort too obvious to have been noticed, if Brahmanism had not been declared to be dead. It is quite certain that the people of India are, as a mass, still far from reaching that intellectual stage when a revelation or prophetic message may, or must, be thrown back into earlier ages and unfamiliar scenes; wherefore this religion, which is continually and copiously sustained by perpetual miraculous intervention, and which still keeps open its gates to any quantity of new prodigies and new deities, must necessarily prevail for a long time against more spiritual faiths. /It is impossible in India to make voluntary conversion of any number perceptible in so vast a population without miraculous gifts, rarely claimed by, but always imputed to, a new teacher or saint. Devotion and asceticism impress because they are found to connote influence with heaven, rather than as ethical examples/ Francis Xavier, the one successful modern missionary of multitudinous Christian conversions in India, was both an ascetic and worker of miracles. He knew well, as Lacordaire says, the main source of success by missionaries to be that strong certitude in their cause which is only attested to simple folk by vigorous self-devotion and incredible labour for no visible reward. It would never have occurred to him that evangelization could be attempted by any force weaker than spontaneous enthusiasm and emotional power. And it is yet to be seen whether the most conscientious efforts of salaried preachers to do their duty can avail much; or whether a decent middle-class education, such as is now given in the Scotch Mission Schools, will prepare heathen folk for embracing the Gospel. Xavier "usually went on foot and without shoes, living only on roasted rice, which he begged as he went on; and slept on the ground with a stone under his head;" * in fact, he lived in India like an Indian ascetic; and being also an extraordinary character, he soon acquired the fame of wonder-working. He raised a

* Life and Letters of S. Francis Xavier, Volume I. page 161. Coleridge.

youth from the dead at Travancore, when on the spot a large number were converted; the act was selected with other miracles by the Auditors of the Rota upon whose report the Bull of canonization was issued, as resting upon incontrovertible evidence, formally tested and judicially examined.

Therefore, to recapitulate what has just been said, Brahmanism still lives and is propagated in India faster than any other religion, for these three principal reasons, namely :—

That it is indigenous, the produce of the soil and of an environment that still exists.

That it is a social system, and a very elastic one; while the people in India as a body still need a religion which, like Brahmanism, provides them with social rules, with laws of custom as well as of conduct.

That it encourages and is nourished by a constant miraculous agency working at full pressure, and by relays of divine embodiments; while in the present intellectual state of the population in India no religion will be widely embraced without visible miraculous credentials.

And it may be fairly conjectured that these three characteristics are likely to keep Brahmanism alive in India for several generations to come. No one need doubt that it is gradually becoming purged and refined, but this is a process through which all popular religions pass; and they are not always extinguished by it. The more cruel and indecent rites of Brahmanism have hitherto owed their reformation principally to ordinances of the English police, who have suppressed suicide, self-mutilation, and other unsightly or immodest spectacles. But because Brahmanism has been purged by human statute, it by no means follows that the religion is dying or even dangerously ill from what is sometimes thought healthy medicine; and no religion ever possessed greater elements of elasticity or alterative capacities. The worship of Siva and Vishnu is said, and truly, in the Lecture, to be still in many cases of a more degraded character than the worship of Jupiter, Apollo, and Minerva. No one knows better than Professor Max Müller the multiform changes which the worship and attributes of the Hindu triad have undergone, or the endless variety of conceptions and personifications under which they have been already adored. And remembering that Vishnu and Siva are only different refractions of the idea of divinity seen through the prism of popular imagination, there appears no reason why they should not go on changing toward a higher evolution, as the people emerge out of abject idolatrous terror of their gods. Supposing India to have been left to work out its own destiny as an Asiatic country unconquered by Europe, the process might have been a very long one indeed, starting from the point at which Brahmanism now stands. Under European stimulants it will probably be very much abridged; but there is the religion still flourishing before our eyes like a green bay tree, and one cannot positively affirm that it is likely soon to vanish and be no more seen. That it may altogether melt away and dissolve in the course of time may be conjectured to be its not improbable destiny. On the other hand it is not impossible that Brahmanism may be able gradually to spiritualize and centralize its Pantheon, reduce its theology to a compact system, soften down its marvels by symbolisms and interpretations, discard "dogmatic extremes," and generally to bring itself into accordance with improved standards of science and intelligence. There is hardly a religion which does not go through this process, or which maintains without revision the uncompromising commands or mystic utterances of its founders. And it is a matter of surprise that scientific observers should have recognized the long course of development which other religions undergo, should admit that the religion of Zoroaster and Judaism are still alive, after so many centuries, and such tremendous calamities, and yet should also declare Brahmanism, which provides rites and beliefs to 150 millions, to be dead because its earlier forms (what are sometimes called the coarser conceptions of popular religion) are sloughing off.

"When a religion," said the Lecturer, "has ceased to produce defenders of the faith, prophets, champions, and martyrs, it has ceased to live." This is a bold and far-reaching sentence, which must have sounded through the long-drawn Gothic aisles of Westminster Abbey with a strange echo in the minds of many hearers among the crowd who were assured that, judged by this infallible criterion, Brahmanism was dead, and who may have asked themselves how many religions could stand such a test of vitality. Brahmanism, at any rate, has at this moment many prophets and champions; it has no martyrs because the British Government not only refuses obstinately to persecute any one, or to let any one persecute his neighbour, but absolutely puts down self-immolation as a public nuisance. Our police drag people from under Jagannâth's car, and fine the whole township if a man kills or mutilates himself. Human sacrifices are still perpetrated under the cloaks of mysterious unaccountable murders; and there would be plenty of martyrdom if the Magistrates would wink at it, but they do not. As for champions, the Kookas belong to our own day and have sealed their testimony; and there are thousands of tall Rajpúts who would like nothing better than to take up sword and buckler in defence of their patron divinity if exposed to insult, or of any other sacred institution. The prophets and inspired teachers of purified Brahmanism are very numerous; the saints and semi-divine personages still appear; so that, although orthodox Brahmanism may not deserve credit for all these movements, yet any one who surveys India must acknowledge that Brahmanism, tried by this criterion, is decidedly alive.

Now I have thought that it might be worth while thus to enlarge upon what seems to me to be the very premature interment of Brahmanism in Westminster Abbey; because there is no country in the world which can bear comparison with India for the study of that science of religion which the Lecturer announced. No other country contains three great historic religions (of which two are on a vast scale), and has propagated a fourth, the largest of all. Therefore it is probable that on the plains of India, if anywhere in Asia, will be fought out that decisive battle of creeds for the dominion of the world which the Lecture predicts. When, therefore, we are told that Brahmanism, which holds these plains in force and strong array, is dead, and that the decisive struggle lies between "the three missionary religions, Buddhism, Mahomedanism, and

Christianity," I own some surprise at this rendering of the actual situation, and at this forecast of the religious future. From the view-point of missionary enterprise it seems a miscalculation of the power and position of the enemy. If, indeed, the victory is to be gained by that kind of missionary activity which is explained to consist in persuading people to abandon small theologic feuds, to drop the galling chains of creeds and distinct formulas, and to rely upon gradual intellectual expansion into the pure morality which the Lecture proposes as the real end in view of all reasonable missions, then it might be agreed that Brahmanism is likely to accommodate itself to this operation more easily than sharp-set dogmatic systems. How this end can be consistent with the professed aim of missionary work is not quite plain; nor can one easily perceive how the missionary, who is by his calling a prophet, champion, or martyr (else is his religion dead) can be instructed to go about making himself acceptable to every decent heathen moralizer whom he meets, cheerfully discovering points of agreement, good-naturedly sinking little points of doctrinal difference which breed strife, and keeping somewhat in the background the positive articles of Christian faith. It may be conjectured that the more earnest missionaries will even yet hardly agree with the Lecture that the essentials of their religion are not in the creeds but in Love; because missionaries are sent forth to propound scriptures which say clearly that what we believe or disbelieve is literally a burning question. But admitting the pacific solution to be probable, then it will affect all religions equally, and the decisive battle will never be fought at all. On the other hand, if there is to be a great Armegeddon of jarring creeds, no battle-field is so likely as India; and those who go to war there must for many a day take Brahmanism into their strategic calculations.

The purport of this essay, therefore, is not to take any share in such a vast speculation as would be the attempt to trace the future course of Asiatic religions, but merely to remonstrate against a scientific forecast which begins by striking Brahmanism out of the calculation. There is nothing in the structure or present state of Brahmanism which need bring final dissolution upon this religion with fatal rapidity, or that need prevent its undergoing the same modifications, mystifications, and spiritual quickening which have preserved other Asiatic religions. Qualified observers have thought that we might at any time witness a great Brahmanic reforming revival in India, if some really gifted and singularly powerful prophet were to arise among the Hindus. Certainly the reform must come soon, for extraordinary political and social changes must always shake violently the fabric of a religion belonging to other times and circumstances. And it is most unsafe to venture even a conjecture as to the form or direction which the inevitable changes in Indian ideas must take, because the situation is so unprecedented; for the effect of suddenly bringing India into full *rapport* with the foremost of European nations cannot be estimated by this generation. We cannot say what may be the result of letting loose upon the country all the ideas and levelling forces which are engendered by a democratic European nation, and which at present tend to substitute a rather cynical utilitarianism for the traditional prestige of capricious kings and priests, and of the gods whom they made in their own image. To these forces Buddhism and Mahomedanism, the religions called missionary, are quite as much exposed as Brahmanism; nor can one perceive why Northern Buddhism should not be as much affected externally by observation and experience as the Brahmanic doctrines; while Islam has dangers of its own. Brahmanism must undoubtedly make haste to change its outward features, economise its lavish wonder-working, and concentrate its divine essences; but one would imagine that no religion was ever better qualified for protecting itself by various transformations, or better fitted with the necessary machinery. Whenever the modern forces come into widely-effective play upon Asia, what chance will Buddhism and Islam have of withstanding them, which Brahmanism may not have also? Or what prospect will there be of any great arena being left in which the dominion of the world can be staked as the prize of a tournament among religions clad in the armour and using the weapons of our ancestors? The state and movement of religion in India have always widely influenced the whole of Eastern Asia; and, so far as India is concerned, such a tournament is not likely to come off while the country forms part of the British empire, and continues to learn English. It is far more probable that the masses will for generations remain in a kind of simplified Brahmanism, which will accommodate itself to altered material circumstance and to higher moral notions. The educated and reflective classes can hardly be expected to enter any dogmatic system of faith. Brahmoism, as propagated by its latest expounders, seems to be Unitarianism of an European type, and, so far as one can understand its argument, appears to have no logical stability or *locus standi* between revelation and pure rationalism; it propounds either too much or too little to its hearers. Looking back at the history of such religions, and looking round at the present situation of India, we may well doubt whether for centuries to come any beliefs or deities hostile to Brahmanism will prevail among the masses which inhabit the vast inland provinces, the pagan multitudes that always are so slow to quit their indigenous superstitions, so reluctant to drive forth the parting genius from haunted spring and tangled thicket, and to make "Peor and Baalim forsake their temples dim." That these superstitions will be perpetually toning down and becoming civilized with the general civilization of India is a matter of course; but whether they will be replaced by a complete adoption of any other religion is very questionable, though the great precedent of Christianity in the Roman Empire cannot be disregarded, despite the wide divergencies of ages and circumstances of every kind. The use of historic analogies as a guide to the interpretation of current affairs requires great caution; and Burke says truly that one must avoid treating history as a repertory of cases and precedents for a lawyer. Nevertheless resemblances—political, social, and religious—between the Roman Empire and British India are incessantly catching the fancy of Anglo-Indians at the present day. The sketch given in Gibbon's second Chapter of the state of religion in the Empire during the second century of the Christian era might be adopted to describe in rapid outline the state of Hinduism at the present day. The tolerant superstition of the people "not confined by the claims of any speculative system;" the "devout polytheist, whom fear, gratitude, and curiosity, a dream or an omen, a singular disorder, or a distant journey, perpetually disposed to multiply the articles of his belief, and to enlarge the list of his protectors;" the "ingenuous youth alike instructed in every school to reject and despise the religion of the multitude;" the philosophic class who "look with indulgence on the errors of the vulgar, diligently practise the ceremonies of their fathers, and devoutly frequent the temples of their gods;" the "magistrates who know and value the advantages of religion as it is connected with civil government"—all these scenes and feelings are represented in India at this moment, though by no means in all parts of India. Seventeen centuries ago the outcome and conclusion of all these things in Europe and Asia Minor was Christianity, which absorbed all the nations of the Empire as they "insensibly melted away into the Roman name and people;"* though even in the heart of the Empire paganism took five or six centuries to disappear. But history does not repeat itself on so vast a scale; the seasons, and the intellectual condition of the modern world, are unfavourable to religious flood-tides; it is incredible that Islam or Buddhism should ever again invade or occupy a great country, possessing any civilization, and the mind of Europe is turning to other things more exciting in these days than religious proselytism. It may be even doubted whether Brahmanism has to fear destruction at the hands of the three great missionary religions of the Lecture, though it is quite possible that more difficult and dangerous experiences than wholesale religious conversion are before India. Little penetration is needed to anticipate the intellectual and moral effects of a state of transition, whenever the traditional forms of religious belief shall come to have fallen into universal discredit with the reflective and influential classes, who may have found nothing to substitute for these beliefs but a superficial instruction; while at the same time

* Gibbon, Volume I., Chapter II.

the rapid advance of prosperity, and the opening of a new world of material needs and allurements, shall have made men restless and discontented. These things may be still far distant in India, where European ideas have as yet touched only the outskirts of our dominion, and are only appreciated in a kind of second-hand unreal way by the artificial classes which are politically bound up with the English rule to which they owe their existence. Nevertheless our successors may one day be reminded of the picture drawn in the forcible passage which here follows, and which brings this chapter to its conclusion :

"But epochs sometimes occur, in the course of the existence of a nation, at which the ancient customs of a people are changed, religious belief disturbed, and the spell of tradition broken; while the diffusion of knowledge is yet imperfect, and the civil rights of the community are ill secured, or confined within very narrow limits. The country then assumes a dim and dubious shape in the eyes of the citizens; they no longer behold it in the soil which they inhabit, for that soil is to them a dull inanimate clod; nor in the usages of their forefathers, which they have been taught to look upon as a debasing yoke; nor in religion, for of that they doubt; nor in the laws, which do not originate in their own authority . . . They entrench themselves within the dull precincts of a narrow egotism. They are emancipated from prejudice, without having acknowledged the empire of reason; they are animated neither by instinctive patriotism nor by thinking patriotism . . . but they have stopped half-way between the two in the midst of confusion and distress." *

* Democracy in America, De Tocqueville (Reeve's translation), Volume I., Chapter XIV.

# CHAPTER VI.

## ON THE RELATIONS BETWEEN THE STATE AND RELIGION IN CHINA.

Difference between earliest and latest ideas on relations between Religion and the State—Controversies in Europe over the question—Separation between religion and civil government is becoming a recognized principle in Europe, while the contrary is still the rule in Asia—Islamitic institutions—Position of the Chinese government, and its method of dealing with the three official religions of China—Confucian, Buddhist, Taouist, all independently established as separate creeds—Public worship of the Chinese, rites performed by Emperor—The contents of the Pekin Gazette illustrate the attitude of the Government toward religion, and explain its influence—Posthumous honours and titles bestowed on deceased persons, their deification by order of Government—Titles and rewards given to divinities for public services, instances quoted—Control exercised by the State over Buddhist incarnations, cases cited from Gazette—Intellectual condition of a people which sees no clear distinction between the unseen and the visible world, between gods and men—Danger of too close connection between Religion and the State.

One important difference between the earlier and the latest principles of government is marked by the changes which have taken place in men's ideas on the subject of the proper relations between the ruler and the priesthood, the State and the Church, the civil government and the ecclesiastical bodies. In times when all authority necessarily claimed to derive from a divine mandate, when laws were supernaturally delivered, and when crimes might be most effectively treated as sins against the gods, it was natural that the ruler should assume religious as well as civil supremacy; that he should take on himself, wherever he could, the visible headship of the external worship; and that he should employ his power to obtain command of spiritual forms and institutions. We know that the Roman Emperors long kept in their own hands the chief pontifical office, until the sacred or hierophantic functions of the sovereign vanished, in Europe, with paganism. Then, in the Middle Ages, came the long struggle between the ecclesiastical and the civil powers; when the Papacy had concentrated and brought into focus all the independent spiritual authority of Western Christendom, and declared absolute separation between the dominions of the Church and of the State. But between spiritual and temporal matters, as they affect the daily life and conduct of the people, the distinction is in practice hard to draw, and harder to maintain. The attempt to partition off such things into two provinces, and to place each province under an independent and co-ordinate authority, was inevitably followed by incessant and fervent discussion and contest over the right and recognisable border that should divide two complicated and very ill-defined jurisdictions. The course and development of this conflict, which prevailed throughout Europe in various forms, have been very different in different countries: the English Reformation, which restored the Church as a national institution, is a notable instance of the manner in which some of the nations which broke away from Roman Catholicism recurred to the earlier principle of giving supremacy to the State's ruler. It may perhaps be said that from the time when the Church attempted to mark off her share in the government of mankind into a separate and independent department, the controversy over the precise range and limits of that department has never ceased. And the general result, in the most civilized countries, is that while the ecclesiastical power has in these latter days been disarmed, and can no longer uphold any pretensions to concurrent authority within the domain of civil administration, on the other hand the civil power is rapidly withdrawing from its ancient claims to headship and overlordship in matters religious or ecclesiastical. The civil government interferes very reluctantly indeed in questions of doctrine; it still maintains, under such laws as may be existing, what M. Paul Bert, the French Minister, has recently termed a general police of worship; but the tendency is towards repealing any laws which throw this duty upon the administration. The ruling power no longer looks to the religious bodies, as such, for support; but on the contrary is anxious rather to disown than to rely upon an alliance with any particular form of religion. The view now predominant is that which was set forth in Macaulay's essay on Mr. Gladstone's book on Church and State, where the reviewer argues that a government in its public and collective capacity has no more to do with religion than a railway company, and that if, as was maintained in the book, "the statesman must be a worshipping man," it would be equally reasonable and expedient to attach the same condition to the chairmanship of the railway direction. In short, politics and theology, finding that they cannot work together, have agreed to stand apart, desiring to have as little to do with each other as may be possible; and upon some compromise of this kind peace is now generally concluded, in the most advanced societies, except between the extreme and irreconcilable partizans in either camp. There may still be found in Europe a Church party that would break in the State to the Church's harness, and a political party that would give no quarter to ecclesiasticism; but on the whole it is now becoming an established principle in Western Europe, that a complete and formal separation between religion and civil rulership is essential to any rational administration either of the State or of the Church. The temporal sovereigns decline, so far as they can, interposition in spiritual affairs: the only spiritual potentate who still maintains pertinaciously his right to intervene in the temporal government of Christians, has, chiefly for this very reason, been recently deprived of his own temporalities; and the main current of modern opinion sets towards disestablishment, disendowment, suppressing *budgets des cultes*, cutting the States clear of their connection with Churches, and taking up an attitude, in regard to religious institutions, of irresponsibility and more or less respectful unconcern. So that the earlier ideas on this subject are now not only rejected, but reversed; to the principle of union between the secular and spiritual authorities is succeeding the principle of divorce.

But if it is true that European ideas on the relations between Church and State are reaching this climax, this makes it very well worth while to bear in mind that in the non-Christian world the earlier notions on this subject predominate, and materially influence societies. Three out of the great Governments of Europe—England, France, and Russia—rule over large numbers of non-Christian people, and are in constant relation with non-Christian States; and some of the many and strange difficulties besetting this position are connected with the incident that in Asia and Mahomedan Africa the temporal ruler is generally expected to do what in Western Europe he is generally denounced for doing, to assume, that is, a direct and practical authority over the administration of religious affairs; while the statesman is undoubtedly expected to be a worshipping man. Moreover, these difficulties, where Islam is concerned, have not missed appreciation at Constantinople; for the Sultan has lately been disclosing some anxiety about the spiritual unity of Islam, and is showing a disposition to employ his claims to the Kaliphate as a means of taking upon himself the functions left vacant by the disabilities of a non-Mahomedan ruler in Mahomedan countries. And the mere fact that the Turkish Sultans, with no pretensions to sacred character or descent, have for some centuries been able to impose themselves as Kaliphs upon a very large part of the Mahomedan world, proves how closely the spiritual headship is bound up, outside Europe, with temporal dominion. It is, and must be, the policy of a native Asiatic ruler to secure and maintain this union of forces; since, so long as he stands outside and disconnected from the spiritualities, he is in a dangerously imperfect condition; he leaves in other hands a lever that may be used to upset him, and he is cut off from the control and direction of an active, never-resting machinery, always at work among his people. Of course an Asiatic sovereign may and does govern people of various creeds, as in India; and it may happen, though the case is rare, that he himself professes exclusively the creed of a minority. But in this latter case (which almost always indicates recent and incomplete conquest) the position of a native ruler is unstable; while, on the other hand, the more effectually he can combine with his secular sovereignty an acknowledged authority over and control over the religious organization, the stronger and more solid is his dominion. The most obvious and well-known illustration of this principle is to be seen in the rapid rise and the complete predominance for centuries of Mahomedanism as a ruling power throughout the greater part of Asia. For it is manifest that the early successes of Islam were due to the sudden appearance, in a part of the world divided by great schisms or petty local creeds, of a series of leaders who impersonated the full idea of a theocracy, and who united more completely and effectively than ever before or since in the world's history, the two momentous forces of military and religious enthusiasm.

But the institutions of Islam are, after all, barbarous through their very simplicity; while its intolerant monotheism is a peculiar production of Western Asia. It may be more interesting to look much further eastward, and to examine the relations of the civil government to religion in a country where creeds and rituals still preserve their primitive multiformity, where they all have, nevertheless, free play, and where the ruler finds it possible and advantageous to preside over all of them. Nowhere is this better seen than in that Empire which has not only attained, as a government, the highest level yet reached by purely Asiatic civilization, but is at once the oldest of Asiatic empires, and the most likely to outlast all others now existing—the Empire of China.

The Chinese Government is singular in Asia as representing a kind of modern Conservatism. No other great Asiatic State ever got beyond the simplest forms of arbitrary sovereignty; whereas in China the governing class has for centuries been endeavouring to stand still at a remarkably forward stage of administrative organization long ago attained; and this is not the immobility of mere superstition and ignorance, as in the case of the nations around, but it is apparently due to a deliberate mistrust of progress beyond the point already reached. This feeling is probably much more justifiable in Asia than in Europe; for until the incoherent groups of different races and religions which make up the population of an Asiatic Empire become moulded into some sort of national conglomerate, they form a very shifty foundation for elaborate political buildings. A well-knit and long-established European nation may play fast and loose with its institutions, and amuse itself with new economical principles and experiments in governing; may allow chronic revolt to run on in a province, on the chance of its wearing itself out, and may be indifferent to the general weakening of the executive power, and to the relaxing of the bonds of empire which may ensue. But Asiatic constitutions cannot stand such treatment, and rulers are obliged to be much more cautious in handling rough conglomerate masses of tribes and sects. Nor can it be denied that civilization, whatever be its benefits to Asia, acts as a disintegrating force among the first principles which lie at the base of all Asiatic governments, where the corner-stone is usually the divine right of kings. However this may be, the Chinese have certainly succeeded in organizing scientific methods of administration without disturbing primitive ideas; an experiment of great interest to the English, who have before them a problem not altogether dissimilar. China has had, moreover, the good fortune of lying beyond the full sweep of the destructive waves of Mahomedan invasion, which spent their force on her extreme frontier; so she escaped the deluge which has separated all Western Asia into two distinct periods, and has operated, wherever it spread, a complete interruption of political continuity. And while her religions have thus retained their natural variety, and have escaped being crushed out or overlaid by the dead levelling power of Islam, China has attained this superiority over India, that she succeeded centuries ago in bringing her religious doctrines and worships into practical co-operation with her secular organization. It would seem as if the lavish fertility with which Indian soil produces religious ideas and forms has hindered them from being turned to account and built up into any great religious system; or else that India has never had a native government large and strong enough to organize Brahmanism as a foundation and support of its authority, as the Chinese have enlisted their ancient Pantheon into the State's service; while it does not appear that Indian religions have ever been pressed into the service of morality. The only great State religion and organized Church which ever throve in India was Buddhism; and it is precisely this religion which, after its mysterious break-up in India, found a permanent home and an immense though distorted development as the greatest established religion of China. Yet Buddhism is only one among others, for the Chinese Government seems, perhaps alone among civilized States, to have solved the problem of maintaining simultaneous relations, close and sympathetic, with several established official religions. In European States, wherever uniformity of belief can no longer be preserved, the State usually finds it impossible to identify itself with several rival creeds, and very inconvenient to remain on good terms with one particular creed, whereupon it withdraws as much as possible from connection with any of them. In Mahomedan countries this difficulty is forestalled by diligently stamping out all creeds but one, wherever this is possible. But in China, so far as can be judged from written accounts, the peculiarity is that the State is not only tolerant and fairly impartial to a multiplicity of creeds and worships (for that is seen everywhere in Asia beyond the pale of Islam), but that at least three established religions are fostered and sedulously patronised by the Government according to their specialities and respective values in use, for the great purposes of the orderly administration of the Empire, and the upholding of the national traditions of conduct and morality. Nowhere is the principle of adapting the motive power of religion to the machinery of administration carried out so scientifically as it appears to be in China. The vast area and the immense population of the Empire afford ample room for several religions; the system of government finds employment and a congenial atmosphere for them all. The tradition of the Imperial Court is to keep the Emperor's person in august and majestic seclusion; the practice is to set out all their administrative proceedings and acts of State under imposing formularies and high-sounding moral ordinances, keeping the inner mechanism of the State secret and mysterious. All this system harmonizes with and favours the policy of associating religion with every department of the public service, and of identifying the laws of the Government with the decrees of Heaven. The State interposes itself as much as possible between the people and their gods, the

Emperor claims to be the authorised *chargé d'affaires* or chief agent and intercessor for his country with the Supreme Powers. And the Chinese Government has this advantage, that although its dynasty is to some degree foreign, it is nevertheless not so far ahead of or apart from the prevailing intellectual standard among its subjects that it cannot recognize or treat with religions of low or incongruous types without offending the public opinion of some influential body among its subjects. A Christian or Mahomedan Government can at most accord unwilling recognition to creeds of a totally different species. But the Chinese Imperial Government seems able to work with and to derive support from at least three great religions of very diverse character: the Confucian system, the Buddhist Church with its Orders, and the Taouist worship of innumerable magical genii and Nature gods.

All accounts of China agree generally in describing these three forms of religion as existing separately and independently, although they have influenced and coloured one another. And if this be their condition (although no one can feel sure of understanding religions who has not been among the people who practise them) it seems certainly remarkable that in China, which possesses an ancient and comparatively uninterrupted civilization, and a highly centralized government, the various beliefs and worships should not have coalesced, in the course of many centuries, into some comprehensive national religion. Even in India, where the whole country has never fallen under complete political centralization, and where everything has aided to prevent the regular growth of one religion, all the indigenous rituals and theologic ideas are more or less grouped under the ample canopy of Brahmanism, which has an easy pantheistic method of accommodating all comers. And in other countries some sort of general religion almost invariably develops itself according to circumstances; it selects, rejects, improves, and combines the elements of the various creeds and worships which it gradually supersedes; and the more it predominates, the faster it annexes or absorbs. There may remain formidable schisms or parties, worshipping different gods, or widely at variance on points of doctrine, yet one broad band of religious affinity usually brings them all together under some primary denomination. But in China this process does not seem to have taken place; the State is uniform and highly centralized, while there are three principal religions, distinct in character and origin, all living in concord together and in intimate association with the Empire. The different religious ideas and doctrines that have from time to time sprung up in China, or have been transplanted thither, have not become assimilated, but remain apart in separate formations. The philosophic Confucianism, embodying the teachings of a great moralist and statesman, the magnificent hierarchy of Northern Buddhism, with its church, its orders, its deified abstractions, and its metaphysical doctrines; and Taouism, with its adoration of stars and spirits presiding over natural phenomena, of personified attributes, divine heroes, local genii, and the whole apparatus of anthropomorphism—all these expressions of deep moral feeling, religious speculation, and superstitious wonder, jumbled together like everything in Asia without regard to inconsistencies or absurdities, seem to prevail and flourish simultaneously in China. Mr. Edkins, in his book on religion in China,* tells us that we have there these three great national systems working together in harmony. Three modes of worship, he says, and three philosophies, have for ages been interacting on each other. They are found side by side not only in the same locality, but in the belief of the same individuals, for it is a common thing that the same person should conform to all three modes of worship; and the Government willingly follows the same impartial practice. In a country of such ancient civilization one would have expected that what has taken place in other countries during the last two thousand years would have happened to the religions of China—that they would have undergone some process of fusion, and would have been run into the mould of some general type, however loose and incoherent. Of the great historical religions that have arisen in the world, each has annexed several countries; very rarely, if ever,

* Religion in China, by Joseph Edkins, D.D. 1878.

do we find two of them established on equal terms in the same country. It is only in China that we find two mighty religious potentates such as Confucius and Buddha reigning with co-ordinate authority over one nation, and their ritual mingled with the adoration of the miscellaneous primitive divinities, who have elsewhere been usually extirpated, subdued, or refined and educated up to the level of the higher and paramount religious conceptions. For, although the Chinese religions seem to have modified each other externally, and to have interchanged some colouring ideas, no kind of amalgamation into one spiritual kingdom appears to have ensued; it is at most a federation of independent faiths united under the secular empire. Whereas in other countries the chief religion is one, but the interpretations of it are many, so that the faith is a moral system, a mysterious revelation, or a simple form of propitiating the supernatural, according to each man's feelings or habits of thought: in China a man may go to different religions for specialties of various sides or phases of belief. Confucianism gives the high intellectual morality, fortified by retrospective adoration of the great and wise teachers of mankind, and based on family affections and duties, but offering no promises to be fulfilled after death, except the hope of posthumous memorial veneration. Buddhism gives metaphysical religion of infinite depth, with its moral precepts enforced by the doctrine of reward or punishment, according to merits or demerits, acting upon the immaterial soul in its passage through numberless stages of existence. It contributes imposing ceremonial observances, the institution of monasticism, and a grand array of images and personified attributes for worship by simple folk who have immediate material needs or grievances. Buddha himself, having passed beyond the circle of sensation, is inaccessible to prayer, yet out of pity for men he has left within the universe certain disciples who, albeit qualified for Nirvana, have consented to delay for a time their vanishing into nothingness, in order that they may still advise and aid struggling humanity. Both Confucius and Buddha seem rather to have despised than denied the ordinary popular deities, and to have refrained, out of pity for weaker brethren, from open iconoclasm. Taouism has rewarded both these great teachers by apotheosis, into a pantheon which appears to be filled by every imaginable device, by personifications of everything that profits or plagues humanity, of natural phenomena, of human inventions, of war, literature, and commerce, and by the deification of dead heroes and sages, of eminent persons at large, and of every object or recollection that touches men's emotions or passes their understanding. It is worth notice that the three persons who founded these three separate and widely divergent religions appear all to have lived about the same time, in or near the sixth century B.C. And the impartial veneration accorded to them by the Chinese is shown by their being worshipped together, as the Trinity of the Sages.

Let us for a moment see by what means the Chinese Government identifies these religions with the State's administration and with the reigning dynasty. If the Government is of any one particular religion more than another, it is, we are told, Confucianist; since the literary and intellectual sympathies of the official classes are preferentially with a system of moral philosophy and practical wisdom. Nevertheless the public worship of Taouist spirits is elaborate and carefully regulated. There are three regular State services during the year, in the spring and at the solstices; while special functions take place upon any great public event, the accession of a new Emperor, and victory, or a calamitous visitation. All this is analogous to the religious customs of other countries, with the difference that in China the national prayers and sacrifices are offered up, not by chief priests or ecclesiastics, but by the Emperor himself, who also performs by deputy, through his civil subordinates, similar offices throughout the kingdom. The powers of the air, the great spirits of earth and heaven, are invoked by the State's ruler to administer the elementary forces for the general benefit of the country, precisely as the meanest of his subjects implores some obscure deity to bless or save him individually. The Emperor's style of address to the spirits of Earth and Heaven is lofty. To these two spirits alone he styles himself "subject;" and in making sacrifices to the Earth he offers the following prayer:—"I, your subject, son of Heaven by imperial succession, dare to announce to the imperial Spirit of the Earth that the time of the summer solstice has arrived, that all things living enjoy the blessing of sustenance, and depend upon it for your efficient aid. You are ranked with imperial Heaven in the sacrifices now presented." Not less important than the oblation to spirits is the worship of ancestors (prescribed by the injunction of Confucius, but probably an immemorial usage) which the Emperor celebrates with due solemnity, setting forth an example of filial piety, and at the same time claiming for the dynasty all the reverence due to the hereditary father of his people. Three of the greatest of preceding emperors are included, as a special distinction, in the sacrifices to earth and heaven; the rest are annually adored in the imperial Temple of Ancestors. "I dare (the Emperor is made to say, after reciting his pure descent) to announce to my ancestors that I have with care, in this first month of spring, provided sacrificial animals as a testimony of unforgetting thoughtfulness;" and the prayer contains the titles of all the deceased sovereigns addressed. The tablets of all the deceased emperors and empresses are set out in pairs, hymns are sung, and viands and rich garments are offered. There are also minor rituals for the imperial worship of the gods of land and grain, with whom are included, as honoured guests, the deifications of two statesmen celebrated in past times for the promotion of Chinese agriculture. It is manifest that these stately official liturgies, giving elevated expression to popular superstitions, and presenting the sovereign as high steward of the mysteries, must exercise great influence over the devout multitude, and must give the State large control over the religions themselves. But here again the peculiarity is that we see the primitive ideas preserved, exalted, and utilized by a cultivated and enlightened Government; not a barbarous or backward Oriental State, but one that makes treaties with Europe, sends out ambassadors, and conducts its affairs upon perfectly equal terms with all civilized nations, according to very distinct and serious policy of its own.

If we desire to understand how, and to what extent, the

Chinese Government uses its religious position and influence, and brings what may be called its spiritual supremacy to bear upon regular administration, we cannot have better evidence than is contained in the *Peking Gazette*, which has for some years been officially translated into English. This gazette is, to quote from a preface to the volume for 1874, "the daily record of Imperial decrees and rescripts, and of reports or memorials to the throne, together with a brief notice of Imperial and official movements, to which the name of Peking Gazette is given by Europeans;" it has an official status, and is circulated to all provincial administrations. If such an institution as a Gazette were found in any other Asiatic country, one could hardly be wrong in taking it to be a very recent importation from Europe; but the Chinese, we are told, were publishing their Gazette (styled Micellaneous, or Court, Announcements) many centuries ago. The Peking Gazette announces all acts of State, regulations, decrees, orders on important cases, and ceremonial proceedings of the Imperial Government; and it is certainly unique among *Moniteurs* and official publications of that kind in its incessant and impressive illustration of the relations of the Chinese State with the established religions. The grand functions of Imperial worship are of course all formally ordained and reported for general information by edicts, and by orders of the Board of Sacrifices; and the Gazette contains many orders allotting to the princes and other high officials the different temples at which they are to do duty. But the strange and interesting phenomenon is to find, in such a modern-sounding publication as a Government Gazette and Court Circular, the deities figuring, not occasionally but very frequently, in every department of official business, and treated much as if they were highly respectable functionaries of a superior order, promoted to some kind of upper house, whose abilities and influence were nevertheless still at the service of the State. Those who hold the first rank, with very extensive departments specially connected with the general administration, are recognized as State Gods, such gods as those of war, literature, or instruction having pre-eminent position. There is also, it is understood, a distinction between the gods who are occupied with the material or physical concerns of the country, and those who preside over intellectual and moral needs. But beside and below these chief office-bearing deities, there are evidently very numerous gods of the counties and boroughs, to whom the Imperial edicts secure regular and proper worship, whereby their influence is enlisted upon the side of Government; while the provincial officers are expected regularly to visit all those registered as State Gods, much after the fashion in which European prefects are supposed to pay attention to persons of local influence. All these deities seem to be rewarded, decorated, promoted, or publicly thanked by the Supreme Government according to their works, with due gravity and impartiality. The God of War, whose department may have increased in importance in these days of great armaments, was judiciously raised, by a decree of the last Emperor but one, to the same rank with Confucius, who had before occupied the first place in the State Pantheon. Constant reference is made in the Gazettes to the performances of the minor deities, and they seem to be all co-operating with the prefects or the magistracy in grappling with administrative difficulties; insomuch that local government appears to consist of a coalition between local deities and provincial officers, who divide the responsibility, and share praise or blame. Whatever may be the position of the more privileged and aristocratic class of governing divinities, the minor Chinese deity is not allowed to sit with his hands folded, like Buddha, or to indulge, like the gods of later Hinduism, in grotesque amusements or disreputable caprices, or to decline responsibility for storms and earthquakes, on the plea that such casualties are part of some plan beyond man's present understanding, which will all come right in the end. On the contrary, the condition on which the Chinese Government patronises the Pantheon is evidently that it shall make for morality, support the cause of order, and assist, promptly and efficaciously, in preventing or combating such calamities as floods, famine, or pestilence. And since in China the State deities, at any rate those who represent outlying places and provinces, are not sent to the

Pantheon by popular election, as elsewhere throughout Asia, but are appointed by the Government, it is obvious that they must be in some degree under ministerial influence. A remarkable personage, whether he be eminent for bravery, virtue, public charity, or any other notable characteristic, may be honoured after death by deification at the hands of the Imperial Court; whereby the State rewards a distinguished public servant or private benefactor, and at the same time retains his interest and goodwill in "another place," and in a higher and broader sphere of usefulness.

To begin with the ordinary and numerous decrees acknowledging the good services of deities. "The Governor-General of the Yellow River (says the Gazette of November, 1878) requests that a tablet may be put up in honour of the river god. He states that during the transmission of relief rice to Honan, whenever difficulties were encountered through shallows, wind, or rain, the river god interposed in the most unmistakable manner, so that the transport of grain went on without hindrance. Order: Let the proper office prepare a tablet for the temple of the river god."

"A memorial board is granted," says the Gazette of April, 1880, "to two temples in honour of the god of locusts. On the last appearance of locusts in that province last summer, prayers were offered to this deity with marked success."

February, 1880. A decree ordering the Imperial College of Inscriptions to prepare a tablet to be reverently suspended in the temple of the Sea Dragon at Hoyang, which has manifested its divine interposition in a marked manner in response to prayers for rain. In another Gazette the Director-General of Grain Transports prays that a distinction be granted to the god of winds, who protected the dykes of the Grand Canal; whereupon the Board of Rites is called upon for a report. Also the river god is recommended for protecting a fleet carrying tribute rice; and the god of water gets a new temple by special rescript. In fact, decrees of this kind, which merely convey public recognition of services rendered by the State gods, appear in almost every issue of the Gazette.

The following decrees refer to the process of qualification for divine rank:—

"The Governor of Anwhei forwards (November, 1878) a petition from the gentry of Ying Chow, praying that sacrifices may be offered to the late Famine Commissioner in Honan, in the temple already erected to the memory of his father. The father had been Superintendent of the Grain Transport, and had greatly distinguished himself in operations against some rebels. The son had also done excellent service, and the local gentry had heard of his death with great grief. They earnestly pray that sacrifices may be offered to him as well as to his father. Granted."

"A decree issued (May, 1878) sanctioning the recommendation that a temple to Fuh Tsung, a statesman of the Ming dynasty, may be placed on the list of those at which the officials are to offer periodical libations. The spirit of the deceased statesman has manifested itself effectively on several occasions, when rebels have threatened the district town, and has more than once interposed when prayers have been offered for rain."

The Gazette of June, 1880, expresses the Imperial regrets at the death of the Commander-in-Chief in Chihli, and gives him an obituary notice.

"He was indeed a brave, loyal, and distinguished officer. During the time he served as Commander-in-Chief he displayed a high capacity for military reorganization. We have heard the news of his death with profound commiseration; and we command that the posthumous honours assigned by law to a Commander-in-Chief be bestowed on him; that a posthumous title be given him, and that the history of his career be recorded in the State Historiographer's office. We sanction the erection of temples in his honour at his home in Hunan, and at the scenes of his exploits."

"October 27th. A decree sanctioning the erection of a special temple to a late Commandant of the Forces, who was killed at Tarbajatai."

These last quoted decrees, selected out of many similar ones, throw much light upon the process of the evolution of deities, under State supervision in China. We know that in other countries, notably in India, the army of deities is constantly recruited by the canonization and apotheosis of great and notorious men; but in other parts of Asia this is usually done by the priests or the people. In China a paternal bureaucracy superintends and manages the distribution of posthumous honours, beginning with honours of much the same kind as those given in Europe to celebrities, and gradually rising through the scale of ancestral worship, sacrifices, temples, and celebration by the public liturgies, to the full honours of recognised and successful divinity. It is easy to perceive how the formal bestowal of posthumous honours, in their first stage not unlike our State funerals and monuments, with memorial tablets, mausolea, and titular distinctions of a sacred character, must attract the religious feelings of the multitude, and stimulate the world-wide propensity towards adoration of the dead. The Government has therefore no difficulty in promoting the spirits of deceased notables to the superior grades of divinity, whenever this may seem expedient; and has only to anticipate and direct public opinion by a judicious selection of qualified personages. In this way the Emperor, himself a sacred and semi-divine personage, seems to have gradually acquired something like a monopoly of deification, which he uses as a constitutional prerogative, like the right of creating peers. And the special value in China of posthumous honours is that they have a natural tendency to qualify the recipients for this higher promotion to the grade of divinity.

The system of posthumous distinctions is not confined to the recognition of eminent services rendered officially, or in a private capacity, to the public. The State in China occupies itself directly with morality as well as with religion; and any person whose conduct has been meritorious or exemplary may be reported, after death, to the proper board or college, which decrees appropriate marks of approbation. Cases of filial and conjugal devotion are constantly reported by the provincial authorities; also instances of devoted widowhood; there is one example of reward sanctioned to a young lady who died of grief at the death of her betrothed; and another *fiancée* who starved herself to death for the same reason gets posthumous approbation. In all these instances the virtuous deeds of the persons mentioned are solemnly rehearsed by the Gazettes; while on the other hand, the neglect of filial duties is properly stigmatized. In April, 1878, the Censor reports an individual who, besides wearing a button to which he was not entitled, "continued to perform his official duties after his mother's death, and wore no mourning for her." A distinguished spirit may often obtain further advancement by diligent wonder-working. A decree of 1878 deals with a petition that a girl who died many years earlier may now be formally deified, upon the ground that whenever rain has failed, prayers offered up at the shrine of the girl angel have usually been successful. Whereupon an official inquiry is made into the earthly history of this lady; and the report shows that "during her childhood she lived an exemplary life, was guiltless of a smile or any kind of levity, but on the contrary spent the livelong day in doing her duty," refused to marry, and addicted herself to religious exercises. On her death the people built her a temple, and found her very efficacious in seasons of drought. The memorial urges that she has now earned a fair claim to be included in the calendar, and to enjoy the spring and autumn sacrifices. And the Board of Ceremonies, after due deliberation, records this official status.

But the Government not only bestows on deceased persons its marks of posthumous approbation and rank in the State Heaven; it also decorates them with titles. The Gazette of May, 1878, contains—

> "A decree conferring a great title upon the dragon spirit of Han Tan Hien, in whose temple is the well in which the iron tablet is deposited. This spirit has from time to time manifested itself in answer to prayer, and has been repeatedly invested with titles of honour. In consequence of this year's drought . . . . prayers were again offered up, and the provinces (mentioned) have been visited with sufficient rain. Our gratitude is indeed profound, and we ordain that the Dragon Spirit shall be invested with the additional title of 'the Dragon Spirit of the Sacred Well.'"

Another spirit had already obtained the title of "Moisture-diffusing, beneficial-aid-affording, universal-support-vouchsafing Prince;" and receives additional titles in a Gazette of 1877. And a decree of an earlier date refers to a request submitted by a provincial governor, recommending that in consequence of aid given in maintaining certain river embankments by the canonized spirit of a former Governor-General, he be included for worship in the temple of the Four Great Golden Dragon Princes, and that a title of honour be conferred by the Emperor upon this divinity. Apparently the Board of Ceremonies, carefully hoarding its resources for the encouragement of divinities, had admitted the Governor-General's spirit to the Dragon Temple, but had reserved the title "pending further manifestations of divine response." The spirit, thus put on his mettle, acquitted himself so well during the next flood time, that his case was again laid before the Emperor in a fresh report, which gave in detail repeated proofs of the spirit's interposition when the banks were in peril. The case is referred to the Board of Ceremonies "for consideration," December 7th, 1874.

It may be worth while to repeat that in all this system the remarkable feature is not that notoriety in life-time should lead to posthumous worship and divination, or that a deity should continue to increase in reputation in proportion as prayers to his temple are successful. The point is that the Government should have thus successfully laid hands on and systematized the immense power which is given by the direction and control of that deep-rooted sentiment toward the dead which leads to their adoration—a power that has elsewhere almost invariably passed from the earliest mystery men to the superior priesthoods, and which the priesthood has usually been able to make its own. If, as Mr. Edkins tells us, the common people believe that the Emperor has the power to appoint the souls of the dead to posts of authority in the invisible world, just as he does in the visible empire, it is manifest that such a prerogative confers illimitable range upon the Imperial authority. Thus the system of posthumous honours and appointments not only harmonizes with and satisfies the deepest feelings of the people, but it gives to the Government a hold upon them through their beliefs not altogether unlike the influence which the doctrine of purgatory may have given the Church in the darkest of the middle ages. Moreover, the system has this advantage over the European custom of giving peerages and distinctions during life, that it is more prudent and economical. In Europe we honour and reward the posterity of an eminent person; in China they not only honour the man himself after death, but it is well known that they also honour his ancestors, who require no hereditary pensions, and can never discredit their posterity.

In December, 1878, we find a provincial governor proposing that in recognition of the conspicuous charity during a famine displayed by Brigadier-General Chen Ling, he and his ancestors for two generations may have the first rank bestowed on them. Also that memorial arches may be put up to two old ladies, the mothers of high military officers, who have been generous in a similar way. "Granted by rescript. Let the Board take note."

We can understand how it may have been comparatively easy for the State to manipulate and utilise in this way the simple and common superstitions of popular Taouism, giving the humble deities the benefits of official patronage, and honouring the higher deities according to their rank and prestige in the country. Whether seriously or cynically, the Government evidently thinks fit to fall in with and humour the anthropomorphic fancies of its subjects; and the policy is probably a very good one for keeping the gods in hand, and for preventing their concentration into some too powerful a divinity by fostering diversities of worship. The system of civil administration in China is very broadly based upon the principle that the honours and emoluments of the governing body are open to all classes of the people according to merit; and the same principle of *la carrière ouverte aux talents* seems to be applied to the honours obtainable after death. To adapt and utilise for State purposes the worship of ancestors, and the deification of famous men which developed out of this commemoration of ancestral spirits, was no arduous task for a government of literati and philosophers, ruling over a people to whom the difference between life and death, between the phenomenal and the spiritual existence, is far less clear and striking than to modern minds, and is in fact merely shaded off as in the foreground and background of a picture.* But it might have been expected that Buddhism, one of the three organized religions of the world, with set doctrines and traditions, with its monastic orders and successive embodiments of spiritual chiefs, would have held even the Chinese Govern-

* "The sleeping and the dead
Are but as pictures."—*Macbeth.*

ment at arm's length. The visible Church of Buddhism undoubtedly enjoys much independence in China; in Mongolia the Lamas have great political influence, in Tibet itself the Imperial Government allows the Grand Lama to do much as he likes, and the provincial administration is in his hands. There are many instances in the Gazettes of the sedulous care taken by the central Government at Pekin that its political residents at Lhassa shall pay due reverence to Lamaism, that is, to the priesthood representing the dogma of emanations from Buddha, which become incarnate by spiritual succession in the Dalai Lama and other chiefs of the Buddhist hierarchy. A Gazette of 1874 publishes a despatch from an Imperial Resident in Tibet, reporting his arrangements for proceeding in person, with guard of honour and escorts, to escort the primate of Mongolian Buddhism, who has recently succeeded to his office by embodiment, from Lhassa, where he had appeared in the flesh, to his post at Urga near the Russian frontier, a great distance. And it might well be supposed that an established and richly endowed hierarchy, under a sacred chief who has also large governing powers in his own province, would decline to submit its spiritual operations to the revision and censorship of the State. Yet we find that in the matter of the incarnations, the central mystery and essential dogma of Northern Buddhism, which furnishes the process by which all successions to the chief spiritual offices are managed, the Imperial Government interferes authoritatively, calls for reports, and issues the most peremptory orders. The Gazettes of 1876 contain three decrees illustrating the attitude of the State towards the lords spiritual of Lamaism, who, it should be understood, are also very powerful officials. The published papers begin with abstracts of an official letter from the Resident, or political *chargé d'affaires* on the part of the Empire at Lhassa, the capital of the province which enjoys, as has been said, home rule under the hierarchic administration of the Grand Lama. A report had been received by the Tibetan Council that the Dharma Raja, or chief of religious law, had reappeared by metempsychosis in a certain person at a place in Mongolia, where he had been discovered and identified in due form—this being the accepted method by which the priests make their selections for such offices, and maintain the spiritual succession by transmigration of souls. The Tibetan Council reports, after proper inquiry, that this new birth turns out to be the reappearance of a religious chief who had in a former life behaved very badly indeed, and had been degraded for scandalous misconduct. Nevertheless the Council certifies that the present embodiment is perfectly authentic, and they earnestly implore the Emperor to sanction it, one of the reasons being that in his penultimate life, that is, in the existence preceding the life which he had led so badly, this very person had done good service to the State. They promise that he shall henceforward confine himself to religious practices, and shall not again meddle with worldly affairs.

For the State to deal with such metaphysical processes as these would seem to European administrators a somewhat formidable assumption of authority over things spiritual, involving delicate and somewhat mysterious problems of government. However, on the Tibetan petition there is only a brief order, "Let the Department consider and report to Us." The second decree sets out the report of the Mongolian superintendency, stating that the re-embodiment is perfectly authentic, but showing cause why, for this very reason, it should not be allowed; and repeating that the person who has ventured to come to life again is no other than one Awang, who was degraded and punished for a heinous offence in the year 1845, banished from Tibet, subjected to rigorous surveillance, and placed on the official list of those "from whom the privilege of successive births into the world is withdrawn for ever." His conduct, it appears, had been so intolerably disgraceful that it was ordered that "on his decease, whether this should occur at his place of banishment or at home, he should be for ever forbidden to reappear on earth in human form, as a warning to those who bring disgrace upon the Yellow Church;" and in 1854 he died while under surveillance. Lastly, we have the final orders on the case pronounced by Imperial rescript, upholding the previous sentence, and deciding authoritatively that the re-embodiment is not to be permitted. Obviously the Government has no notion of allowing an offender of this degree to elude surveillance by a temporary retirement into incorporeal existence, or to whitewash himself by the simple subterfuge of a fresh birth. The case seems to have been important, and the decision must have caused some excitement in Lhassa, for vague rumours of trouble caused by an unauthorised incarnation spread as far as India, through the Buddhist monasteries on the Indian slopes of the Himalayan range separating Tibet from Bengal.

It seems, indeed, that prohibition to reappear is not an uncommon exercise of control by the Government over disorderly Lamas; for in another case, where a spiritual dignitary had been dismissed and transmigration interdicted, a lenient view is taken, and the sentence is rescinded on petition of appeal, after the appellant's death (be it noted) at Pekin. "We decree that, as is besought of us, search may be made to discover the child in whose body the soul of the deceased Hucheng has been reborn, and that he be allowed to resume the government of his proper Lamasery." All these proceedings afford evidence of the extraordinary rigour with which the Imperial Government seems to exercise its supremacy over all matters spiritual; and they are curious as illustrating the little deference paid to religious susceptibilities whenever the public service, or the police of the Empire, or morality generally, is concerned. The Chinese Government surrounds itself with fictions and formulas; it seems to encourage every possible development of superstition, and to let the people be priest-ridden and spirit-ridden to any extent, on the understanding that the State is always master, whether of priests, spirits, or deities. There is nothing unnatural in a despotic ruler wishing to hold this attitude; although it is very rare that he succeeds in doing so, or that, as seems to be the case in China, the people and even the priests acquiesce thoroughly in the arrangement. But all these things are to be explained by the peculiar religious atmosphere of Asia (as once of the whole primitive world), in which forms and fictions are real and yet unreal, familiar and yet mysterious, and where the gods are mixed up with actual everyday life, not separated off from the world of humanity by vast distances of space, or known through traditions of what happened long ago. Where infinite and various supernatural agencies are incessantly abroad upon earth and at work, it becomes obvious to the practical sense of mankind that unless they submit to some kind of regulation society can hardly go on; and thus the civil ruler, who is after all immediately responsible for keeping things in order, is allowed some reasonable and reverent latitude in dealing with the national divinities. Some compromise or concordat is almost always discovered, whereby a *modus vivendi* is arranged between the spiritual and temporal powers; although, as has been said already, in China it is very striking that the predominance should be so much on the temporal side. But in order to appreciate properly the patronizing or (if necessary) unceremonious ways of the Chinese Government towards spiritual or divine manifestations, we have to recollect that a belief or doctrine such as that of transmigration does not usually harden into the consistency of a mysterious dogma, or become the exclusive property of theology, until it has passed far beyond the range of everyday popular experience. So long as these ideas about the gods, or about the re-embodiment of souls, are being actually applied to account for or to conceal events and actions that go on all round us, they are subject to the wear and tear of practical life; and they can be, and are, constantly modified to suit varying circumstances and emergencies. While they are in this loose, flexible stage, a strong and shrewd Government can seize the occasion of shaping them to its own purposes. It is clear, indeed, that unless some such control were insisted upon, a Government would be exposed to all kinds of trickery and imposture, such as probably underlies the system of Lamaist embodiments; and could be met at every turn by pretensions to immunity from administrative discipline, based on claims to divine or sacred character. To deny such a character, or to uncover and prosecute the impostors would shake the whole edifice, and might drag the civil power into controversy between the police and the priests as to the identity of a reappearance, wherein the police would lose all *locus standi*, being manifestly incompetent to distinguish between true or false divinity; while the position of the priest would be impregnable. So the Chinese prefer to act as if the spiritual or divine character of a *mauvais sujet* should make no difference to the authorities; and the people would probably think much less of a ruler who should take a religion of this kind too seriously, when they themselves are by no means blind to its practical working. Various reverential fictions are occasionally invented to save the reputation of deities or spiritual personages whenever their privileges are being pushed so far that to yield implicit deference to supernatural manifestations would be clean against plain reason and common sense. Of course any considerable *coup d'état* against factious or obstructive divinities must be a stroke needing great resolution and an eye for the situation, but it can be done, as the Chinese example shows, by a consistently devout and religious Government, when necessary for the preservation of order, and the proper conduct of public business.

To modern habits of thought, which conceive a great gulf set, or a blank wall standing, between life and death, between the body and the spirit, the human and the divine, this grotesque intermixture of religion with municipal government, of miracles with police regulations, must appear strange and bewildering. The epigram that was supposed to have been written up over the place in Paris where the convulsionist miracles were suppressed by royal ordinance—

> "De par le roi, défense à Dieu
> De faire miracle en ce lieu—"

reads in European history as a very profane jest, but apparently, it might be accepted in earnest, as emanating from proper and uncontested authority, if it were issued on a similar occasion by the Board of Worship or of Ceremonies in China. The fact seems to be that the mass of the Chinese are still in that intellectual period when, in regard to the conditions of their existence, and to the nature of the agencies and influences which surround them, men's ideas are altogether hazy and indefinite. The Emperor lives far away at Pekin, shrouded in semi-divine mystery, making himself heard at intervals by his majestic ordinances, or seen occasionally at high altars in the performance of some stately ceremonial. Between him and his ministers on the one hand, and the gods of heaven and earth on the other hand, there can be to the multitude little or no difference of kind, and not much of degree. Such doctrines as those of transmigration and re-embodiment obviously tend to deepen the cloudy confusion which hangs over the frontier separating the phenomenal from the unseen world. That world is not a bourne whence no traveller returns, but only a stage in the circle of existence, a place where you change forms as costumes are changed behind scenes, and whence you may come forward again to play a different part in a different character or mode of being, or in a subsequent act of the same drama. And beneath all this stage play of the natural imagination there probably lies the Pantheistic feeling that perceives the substantial identity of divinity with every act and phase of nature with men and spirits indifferently. One can comprehend how a highly-organised State could take firm grasp of all these shifting and anarchic ideas, and retain command over them as a natural incident of supreme rulership, without giving offence to its subjects, indeed with their full approbation. It may be supposed that this position must add immensely to the moral authority of the reigning dynasty; and that, for example, the strange power of veto exercised over re-embodiments must be very useful in a country where ambitious and turbulent characters set up as revivals of precedent gods, or heroes, or prophets. In different forms, indeed, the practice is universal throughout Asia; in Mahomedan countries it constantly shows itself in the expectation of coming prophets or Imams; in India there are continually circulating papers which proclaim the advent of some miraculous personage, with a mission to revive some creed by forming a new and purified government. Nor indeed would any ordinary revolt or disturbance go far unless its leader assumed a religious character, mission, or motive. Even in British India a new embodiment can still give some little trouble, as we have seen very recently from a newspaper account of an attack made by a new sect upon the Jugunâth temple. In India the matter was simply one for the police; and the Courts will have kept carefully clear of any opinion as to the spiritual status or antecedents of the sect's leader; whereas in China the authorities would probably have pronounced the embodiment not false or counterfeit, but simply contraband, and they would have ordered him out of the world back into antenatal gloom, as if he had been a convict returned from beyond seas without proper permission.

Whether the Chinese nation is naturally, or by reason of the teachings of Confucius and the higher Buddhism, more inclined to connect religion with morals than elsewhere in Eastern Asia, or whether the Chinese Government, which has undoubtedly realized the enormous value of outward morality to an administration, has really succeeded, by persistent supervision, in maintaining in all external worships a general show of morality and propriety, it is hardly safe to conjecture. But all observers appear to agree that in China the public practices and the acknowledged principles of religion are decent and ethically tolerable, which is more than can be said for all rites and doctrines in adjacent countries. And it is not difficult to see how the Buddhist dogma of promotion by merit through various stages of existence must have worked in with the system of open competition for official employ, which in China binds up all classes of the people so closely with the State's administration. So also the systems of re-embodiment and deification serve to keep up the prestige and dignity of the Great Pure dynasty, for the Emperors of previous dynasties are not only worshipped as gods, but they may reappear and reign again, occasionally, in the person of later sovereigns, thus attesting the divine right and the true succession of the present family. On the other hand, all these devices for identifying the Government with the prevailing religion have one weak side: a religion may fall, and by its fall may drag down the dynasty. How dangerous to the Empire may be a religious uprising founded on a principle that escapes from or rejects the traditional State control, has been proved to the present generation by the

Taiping insurrection, which is stated by all accounts to have derived it religious character and fervour from the misunderstood teachings of Christian missionaries. The enthusiasm of the new sect at once took a political form, and the leader, as usual, credited himself with a divine mission to seize temporal dominion, according to the invariable law of such movements in Asia, whereby the conqueror always claims religious authority, and the religious enthusiast declares himself ordained for political conquest. The whole atmosphere became rapidly charged with fanatic energy of a type more characteristic of Western than of Eastern Asia. Tai Ping, the leader, denounced idolatry, condemned the Taouist and Buddhist superstitions, and proclaimed fire and sword not only against the creeds, but against the dynasties that encouraged them. Probably nothing is more perilous to a Government that has incorporated the elder and milder religions into its system, and has soothed them and lulled them into tame and subordinate officialism, than an assault upon those very religions by a wild and ardent faith suddenly blazing up in the midst of them. The fabric of conservative government is threatened at its base; the more it has leant upon the old creeds the greater its risk of falling; and this is evidently the vulnerable point of the whole principle of using religion as bulwarks to the State. A great ruler, like Constantine, may have the address and foresight to save his government by going over to the winning side in time, but this has been rare in all ages and countries; while in Asia strong religious upheavals still shatter dynasties and subvert empires.

# CHAPTER VII.

## ON THE FORMATION OF SOME CLANS AND CASTES IN INDIA.

Early history of nations runs back to a tribal period—Reference to this period in European history—The Native States of Central India, which have been left outside the great empires of India, are still in the state of tribal formation—Description of this state of society, no nationalities, the people are classed in clans and sects, by kinship or worship—Examples of grouping by consanguinity and by religion—Description of the structure and development of a consanguineous group—Circles of affinity—Connection between lowest and highest groups, non-Aryan tribes, predatory tribes, half blood and pure blood clans—Influence on a clan of the original founder or leader—Effect upon social formations of religious ideas, rise of sects, and their transition into castes—Narrowing of circle of affinity—Possible connection of these early phases of society with latest European forms.

THE accounts of the origin of nations generally run back to a period, either of authentic history or accepted tradition, when the people of a country appear to have been grouped and ranked in tribes. The precise constitution of these tribes at the time when history opens has of course varied much in different countries; but almost everywhere the original source and explanation, if not always of the tribe, yet of the interior groups which make up the tribe, is assumed to have been kinship among all the members. The superstructure that is gradually built up on this foundation is shaped by political and social circumstances; the cement of the building is usually religion. Of the best-known tribal periods the general aspect is very similar in all ages and countries; the prevailing feature is a great diversity of forms and usages; and a piecemeal and patchwork distribution of mankind into political and social compartments. These pieces and patches gradually amalgamate and are fused into larger masses of people and better-defined territories; very slowly when they are left to themselves, often very rapidly under the violent compression and levelling forces of great conquests. Rome, itself formed out of a conflux of tribes, was of course the great consolidator of tribal atoms in Europe and Western Asia; and when Rome had declined and fallen, her Western provinces relapsed for a time into their primitive confusion. Their condition is described by Guizot in his Lectures on the Civilisation of France, where he sketches the period before Karl the Great attempted, and for his time accomplished, the task of restoring Imperial unity in the West. Nothing appears settled, nothing definite or uniform according to modern notions; territorial frontiers are constantly shifting and changing; distinct nations, in the proper sense of the word, exist nowhere; but instead there is a jumble of tribes, races, conquering bands, heaven-born chiefs —of languages, customs, and rites. Out of this confusion Guizot undertakes to extract and exhibit the elements which have been gradually fused into the two or three supreme political ideas and institutions which divide modern civilisation, and one important element is found in tribal manners and usages.

Now, when one passes from those parts of India which have long been under great centralizing governments, down into the midland countries which have never been fairly conquered by Moghals, Marathas, or Englishmen, the transition is probably very much the same as the change would have been from a well-ordered province of Imperial Rome into lands still under the occupation and dominion of powerful barbarian tribes. In these regions of India—so often invaded and thrown into disorder, but never subdued—the population has remained in a much more elementary and incoherent stage than in the great fertile plains and river-basins of Mahomedan India, where empires and kingdoms have been set up on a large scale, and powerful religious communities have been organised. In fact, the tribal period has here survived, and has preserved some of its very earliest social characteristics, while it still mainly influences the political formation. The surface of the country is marked off into a number of greater and lesser divisions, which we English call Native States, some of these very ancient, others quite modern; most of them mixed up and interlaced in territorial patchwork and irregularity of frontiers, very much as they were left fifty years ago at the end of the stormy time which followed the dissolution of the Moghal Empire. Geographical boundaries, however, have no correspondence at all with distinctive institutions or grouping of the people, and have comparatively slight political significance. Little is gained toward knowing who and what a man is by ascertaining the State he obeys or the territory he dwells in, these being things which of themselves denote no difference of race, institutions, or manners. Even from the point of view of political allegiance, the government under which a man may be living is an accidental arrangement, which the British Viceroy or some other distant irresistible power decided upon yesterday and may alter to-morrow. Nor would such a change be grievous unless it divorced him from a ruler of his own tribe or his own faith; in other respects there is little to choose among governments in central India, which are simple organisms without the complicated functions of later development, being mainly adapted for absorbing revenue by suction. The European observer—accustomed to the massing of people in great territorial groups, and to the ideas (now immemorial in the West) contained in such expressions as fatherland, mother-country, patriotism, domicile, and the like—has here to realise the novelty of finding himself in a strange part of the world, where political citizenship is as yet quite unknown, and territorial sovereignty or even feudalism only just appearing. For a parallel in the history of Western Europe he must go back as far as the Merovingian period, when chiefs of barbaric tribes or bands were converting themselves into kings or counts; or, perhaps, he should carry his retrospect much further, and conceive himself to be looking at some country of Asia Minor lying within the influence of Rome at its zenith, but just outside its jurisdiction. He gradually discerns the population of central India to be distributed, not into great governments, or nationalities, or religious denominations, not even into widespread races such as those which are still contending for political supremacy in Eastern Europe; but into various and manifold denominations of tribes, clans, septs, castes and sub-castes, religious orders, and devotional brotherhoods. And the peculiarity is that these distinctions are not, as in later forms of society, subordinated to the primary relations of a man to his fatherland, his nation, or his State; but are still maintained as the first and most important facts which unite and isolate the people. We have here a good opportunity of investigating what is obviously the survival of a very rudimentary stage of society, which has existed more or less throughout the world, and which may possibly be turned to account for illustrations of the obscurest and most remote parts of the history of nations.

In attempting to give some very concise and yet tolerably intelligible description of this remarkable stratification of society among the clans and sects of central India, we may say that the whole is traversed by two ideas in unbroken continuity, and that all the predominant institutions arrange themselves upon two lines. The essential characteristics of a man's state of life and position among his people, those which settle who he is and where he belongs, are his kinship and his religion; the one or the other, sometimes both. Of these two words, the former varies wonderfully (as we shall see hereafter) in its scope. It may sometimes include the whole of a very numerous clan widely dispersed, and sometimes it may mean no more than three or four degrees of agnatic consanguinity. The latter word should always be taken in its primary sense of a tie of common belief or worship, which binds together a set of people; expressing the fact of such a union rather than the reason or devotional sentiment of it. If, now, having laid hold of these two facts, we look around us in central India and try to perceive how they have been worked out, we shall find the simplest and earliest expression of them in two institutions—the pure clan by descent and the religious order; the brotherhood by blood and the spiritual brotherhood; those to whom a common ancestry, and those to whom a common rite or doctrine, is everything. The best examples of the class first named may be found among the petty Rajpút chiefs who live down in the far western states upon the confines of the great salt and sandy plains that stretch from the Aravalli Hills towards the Indus. One of these may come to visit the camp of an English officer, girt with sword and shield, having the usual tail of clansmen with their whiskers knotted over the top of their heads. The first greeting may probably be made in Homeric style, by inquiring after his name, parentage, and people; when he will proceed at once to answer after the same fashion, naming his clan, the branch to which he belongs, his family, and lineage, and being as particular about his eponymous ancestor as if he were a Dorian Herakleid. If he be interrogated, according to incongruous modern notions, as to the State which claims him as subject, he will indeed admit that he dwells within the territorial authority of a dominant ruler, whose orders he obeys when there is no help for it. But this ruler is only a powerful chief, who has reached the stage of territorial sovereignty: and if our friend is of the ruler's clan, he may go on to explain that his eponym was elder brother of the chief's eponym, many centuries ago; whence it is obvious that he himself, coming from the elder stock, owes no proper allegiance to a younger branch of the family. Or he may be of a different clan, or his forefathers came in by an earlier tribal invasion: all these being good primitive reasons for asserting, in theory, a kind of privilege against the pretensions of territorial administration, of revenue demands, and meddlesome officials generally. For leagues around the soil is possessed by his brothers, of the same stock with his own, to whom the ultimate source of all ideas upon things political, social, and even religious is that same eponymous heroic ancestor, who is talked of with a certitude that would have impressed Niebuhr. Here, in the head of the main stock of a pure-blooded clan, we have the primeval aristocrat, fairly representing, perhaps, the earliest ancestors of long-haired Merovingian kings: or even the remote forefathers of Highland chiefs now become Scottish dukes, of ancient Armorican nobles in Brittany, and Spanish grandees with Gothic blood in their veins; the founders of that peculiar institution, the noblesse of blood, inheriting rank and formal privileges by a title as good as their sovereign's hereditary right to reign.

Secondly, we may take, as the simplest expression of spiritual brotherhood, a specimen of persons who claim no kindred at all. A boy may be noticed, sitting by the roadside, who can be known at once to belong to a religious order by the large trident painted in a special fashion on his forehead, having for vestments only a light martingale of yellow cloth around the loins. Being questioned as to his circumstances, he explains that he has forgotten his people and his father's house, that his parents both died of cholera a year or so back, whereupon his uncle sold his sister into a respectable family, and presented the boy to a mystic who had had a new revelation, and was developing a religious fraternity thereupon. To that fraternity he now belongs, and all other ties of blood or caste have dropped away from him. Or if one questions in like manner any strange pilgrim that comes wandering across central India from the shrines upon the Indian Ocean towards the head-waters of the Ganges in the Himalayas, he may describe himself simply as the disciple of some earlier saints or sage, who showed the Way; the path by which one may best hope to seek out a higher spiritual life, or absorption, or release in some shape from this unintelligible world. The point to be remarked is that he undertakes no other definition of himself whatever, and declines all other connections or responsibilities.

It is thus that the exceedingly primitive state of things still surviving in the middle regions of India may enable us to observe and register in their simplest forms two institutions which play a great part in all archaic societies—the grouping of men by their folk and their faith, by kinship and worship. As these institutions are certainly the roots from which society has grown up all over India, we have here the means of tracing up from very low down in their growth the course which they have followed in that country, whereby we may come to understand better how the combination and crossing of two predominant ideas have worked out in India perhaps the most singularly complicated pattern of society that exists anywhere. The inquiry may also have some bearings upon the processes by which, all over the world, the primitive groups of men have been formed, dissolved, or absorbed into larger civilisations.

Taking first, then, kinship or consanguinity, we find that among the Rajpút clans of central India the sentiment still maintains its widest, and what is probably its most primitive, development; for the feeling of kindred evidently dwindles and contracts, through obvious causes, as civilisation brings other ties. In the combination of modern European society it is of little importance even within the narrow sphere of families, and throughout the greater part of India it is merely an important social element; but among the clans it is the supreme consideration. It must be remembered that in all pure Hindu society the law which regulates the degrees within which marriage is interdicted, proceeds upon the theory that between agnatic relatives *connubium* is impossible. And as by an equally universal law no legitimate marriage can take place between members of two entirely different castes or tribes, we have thus each member of Hindu society ranged by the law of intermarriage, first, as belonging to an outer group within which he *must* marry; and secondly, as belonging to an inner group of agnatic kinsfolk among whom he must *not* marry. This is the normal and typical structure of Hindu society; it is distributed primarily into tribes or castes, and secondarily into clans or families. It is with these last-mentioned secondary groups that we are now concerned, since they clearly embody the idea of kinship; and their shape and composition may best be explained by calling each group a circle of affinity, described by the radius of descent from the central point of one common ancestor, real or reputed, so that all persons swept within this circumference are barred from intermarriage. Now of course this formation is of itself no way abnormal, since every table of prohibited degrees places persons within a similar ring-fence and interdict; but we begin to appreciate the immense influence of the idea of kinship on primitive minds when we perceive that widespread and numerous clans in central India are nothing else but great circles of affinity, including, perhaps, a hundred thousand persons who cannot lawfully intermarry. It becomes worth while to look round and try to make out how these very curious groups formed themselves, and what is their place in the general order of the society to which they belong, what is their connection and relation with other stages of growth.

As to the formation, the accounts preserved among the clans of how they conquered and settled in the lands follow a well-known course of tradition; and their narratives resemble precisely what has been handed down of tribal migrations and expeditions under kings and heroes in the early history of Europe, or in the Old Testament. All that can be gathered regarding the way in which these central Indian clans originated, and the source from which they spread, corroborates the abundant evidence which we already possess upon the beginning and development of such communities. Whereas in modern times great men of action found dynasties or noble families, which transmit the founder's name down along the chain of direct lineage, so in prehistoric ages men of the same calibre founded clans or septs, in which not only the founder's actual kinsfolk who followed his fortunes were enrolled under his name, but also all those who had any share in his enterprises, who took service with him, or got lands by joining his company. Thus was established in central India the stock group of a clan, that organised and maintained itself as a circle of affinity which has gone on widening or contracting under various fortunes, until we find it at its present dimensions. Now although this phenomenon of a whole community associated upon the reputed basis of a common descent is of itself not peculiar, being indeed almost universal among ancient societies, yet the instances of a tribe or clan preserving in full working order a pure genealogic structure are rare in all history, and especially rare is a specimen which has survived in the midst of later formations. It is even more uncommon to find a clan, among which common ancestry actually operates as an impassable bar to intermarriage, realising this kinship of all its members with a strength that withstands political separation. For there is evidence that in other countries and ages separation from the authority of the patriarchal chief dissolved the bond of kinship, as union under one chief had originally produced it. Yet a clan of pure Rajpúts is often scattered abroad under half-a-dozen different rulers, of its own tribe or of alien race, but nevertheless continues to hold marriage between any two persons of the clan to be incest. Moreover, each pure-blooded Rajpút clan now acts strictly upon its assumption of affinity, and employs none of the devices which must necessarily have been allowed in the earlier stages of its growth for recruiting its body from outside. It is impossible to suppose that all the members of a large clan are really descended from one stock; but whatever fictions were formerly permitted in order to keep up the strength, none are now tolerated, and the clan relies for reproduction entirely upon the marriage of males with the women of cognate clans, never bringing in or adopting any one that has not been actually born within the circle. On the other hand, a certain depletion goes on through the occasional cutting off of blemished families or individuals, who have not kept up their pedigree without flaw, who contract irregular marriages, or who in any way suffer a custom to creep in which is condemned by the strict law of the clan. For example, the custom of marrying a deceased brother's wife, which is a recognized duty among some Indian tribes or castes, but is contrary to the law of the clans, has crept in among one at least of them; and the effect has been to detach a sept from the rest of its brotherhood.

Here, then, in the pure genealogic clans of central India, we have a very perfect specimen of the circle of affinity in large type, containing a whole multitude of people tightly bound together as brethren by the tradition of lineage. We may assume this to be a very early phase of the tribal institution, since almost all the tribes of which history gives any particulars appear to have taken actual kinship and a common descent as the basis for their superstructure, religious or political, and all tradition recurs to this as the original type. Nevertheless a little reflection upon and observation of the constitution of the pure clan will convince one that it is by no means the most primitive form. These rigid rules of kinship and intermarriage are excellent for preserving a clan's purity when it has reached its grand climacteric, and is on the road towards transmuting itself into a patrician *gens*, or into an aristocracy. But they are far too stiff and cramping to be endured while the group is struggling for predominance and territory; they would certainly hinder more than help; nor, as has been said above, is it possible to believe any great clan to have really and literally descended from a few families. What, then, were the actual forces and circumstances which produced the pure clan as it now exists? If we are to search for traces of the process of the gathering together of the group before it becomes a clan of descent, we must examine the still more primitive societies which exist below and around the clans in the same region.

Let us move our camp from the north-western plains, where we met our Herakleid, toward the low hill-tracts and endless jungles of scrubby woodland which run for hundreds of miles across the centre of India, on the south of the more open country settled by the great Aryan clans. Here is the place of meeting of what is called a Border *Punchàyat*, which means a meeting of arbitrators, under the presidency of one or two English officers, upon the marches of two or three native States to inquire into and settle cases of raids, and to award compensation for injuries and losses, among the half-savage tribes along these borders. The tract is mainly peopled by the aboriginal tribe of Bheels, and the headman of a Bheel village is being examined touching a recent foray. A very black little man, with a wisp of cloth around his long ragged hair, stands forth, bow and quiver in hand, swears by the dog, and speaks out sturdily: "Here is the herd we lifted; we render back all but three cows, of which two we roasted and eat on the spot after harrying the village, and the third we sold for a keg of liquor to wash down the flesh. As for the Brahman we shot in the scuffle, we will pay the proper blood-money." A slight shudder runs through the high-caste Hindu officials who record this candid statement; a sympathetic grin flits across the face of a huge Affghan, who has come wandering down for service or gang robbery into these jungles, where he is to the Bheels as a shark among small pike;

and it is clear that we have got into a stratum of society far below Aryan or Brahmanic prejudices. The pure clansman, the descendant of heroes and demigods, now looks down with patrician disgust upon the wild Bheel, who is very rough in his practical views upon the subject of marriage, food, and ritual generally; yet there still exists in this outlying country the clue, elsewhere entirely lost, of a remote connection between the two societies. If we analyse the population of the wilder tracts in central India, we discover that it is largely composed of an intricate medley of tribal groups, all strongly dashed with a strain of non-Aryan blood, and perceptibly differentiated in their form or stage of growth. These differences appear to be due mainly to the variety of the needs and distractions of predatory life among the wolds, where cultivation is scarce and communication difficult; but they also imply distinctions of descent and origin, though something may also be ascribed to the peculiarities naturally produced by segregation among separate hill ranges. All these tribes subdivide into manifold sections, and even the lowest have a loose formation of clan; but the chief whom the pure Bheel really acknowledges is merely the most powerful person in his neighbourhood, whether the headman of a strong village or a petty territorial lord of many villages. The Bheels proper are the aborigines, that is, the earliest known inhabitants, the relics of tribes who undoubtedly held all this country before the migrations into central India of the Aryan Rajpúts. They represent the lowest and oldest stratum of the population, and may be taken to represent generally the barbarian type before the earliest civilisations had brought in ideas and prejudices about food, worship, and *connubium.* So far as can be ascertained, the Bheels are all subdivided into a variety of distinct groups, a few based on a reputed common descent, but most of them apparently muddled together by simple contiguity of habitation, or the natural banding together of the number necessary for maintaining and defending themselves. Next above these in the social scale come the tribes of the half-blood, claiming paternal descent, more or less regular and distant, from the Aryan clans, and having their society framed on a rather less indistinct outline of the real clan; and again above the half-bloods come predatory clans, of a very mixed and obscure origin by descent, which rank in the order by which they gradually approximate more and more to the customs and ritual of the pure clan. So that we might make out roughly, in central India, a graduated social scale, starting from the simple aboriginal horde at the bottom, and culminating with the pure Aryan clan at the top; nor would it be difficult to show that all these classes are really connected, and have something of a common origin. The most valuable, to the observer, of the intermediate communities are groups of which it is not easy to say whether they are degradations from the upper ranks or promotions from the lower ranks. They usually assert themselves to be fallen patricians, but they are probably derived from both sources. A very little observation will show that such degradations and promotions still go on constantly. If a lower group multiplies and acquires wealth, it begins at once to ape the fashions of the group immediately above it, precisely after the manner of English society; if a family belonging to the higher groups has ill-luck, or shocks public opinion irremediably, it subsides perforce and herds with its inferiors. Now these composite groups are very useful as links in the chain of sociologic evolution. They appear to be formed out of the fortuitous association of people banded together under the combining effects of various accidents and interests—of some common misfortune, peculiar object, custom, or pressing necessity—and their mode of life is usually predatory; they are the roving species, not yet extirpated in half-civilised countries, which prey upon their settled and peaceable fellow-creatures.

If we place one of these groups under analysis, we find that it has already attained the normal formation of very numerous inner circles of affinity within a tribal circle. But these inner circles, which at a later stage have hardened into the clear-cut ring of pure clanship, are in their intermediate state such loose coalitions that the progress of building the separate cells of the social honeycomb under the outer hive of a tribal designation can be actually watched going on. One of the most widespread and formidable of these impure groups in central India is that of the Meenas, who are famous robbers and caterans; and an opportunity has been taken of examining it closely. This name represents four great sections of one tribe, which inhabit four different and distant tracts, and are evidently fast separating off into alien clans by reason of distinct habitation. Each section is of course distributed off into manifold circles of affinity, and these circles being in various phases of growth and consistency, can mostly be traced back by the clue of their names or other characteristics to their real distinction of origin. In one section alone there are said to be 146 *gôts* or different stock families, of whom some claim descent from a cross between Meenas and Brahmans, others for the most part from a cross with pure Rajpúts. Some of them preserve the name of the higher clan or caste from which the founder of the circle emigrated and joined the Meenas, some names denote only the founder's original habitation, while other circles bear the names of notorious ancestors. We can perceive plainly that the whole tribe is nothing else but a cave of Adullam which has stood open for centuries, and has sheltered generation after generation of adventurers, outlaws, outcasts, and refugees generally. It is well known from history, and on a small scale from experience of the present day, how famines, wide desolating invasions, pestilences, and all great social catastrophes, shatter to pieces the framework of Oriental societies, and disperse the fragments abroad like seeds, to take root elsewhere. Not only have these robber tribes received bands of recruits during such periods of confusion, so common in Indian history, but there goes on a steady enlistment of individuals or families whom a variety of accidents or offences, public opinion or private feuds, drives out of the pale of settled life, and beyond their orthodox circles. Upon this dissolute collection of masterless men the idea of kinship begins immediately to operate afresh, and to rearrange them systematically into groups. Each new immigrant becomes one of the Meena tribe, but he nevertheless adheres so far to his origin and his custom as to insist on setting up a separate circle under the name of his lost clan, caste, family, or lands. Where an Englishman, settling perforce at Botany Bay or spontaneously in Western America, kept up familiar local associations by naming his homestead after the county town in his old country, a Rajpút driven into the jungles tries to perpetuate the more primitive recollection of race. Several fresh groups have been formed by the Meenas within the last few years, under stress of the frightful famine which desolated Rajputána in 1868, when starving families were compelled to abandon scruples of caste and honesty, to steal cattle and to eat them.

Another fact worth notice is that the state of the wife-market and the facilities for the supply of brides have a direct influence upon the rate at which the circles of affinity, thus formed upon the basis of origin, again subdivide and reunite within the tribe-circle. This phenomenon was expounded with much candour to the present writer by a leading Meena. In times of misrule, when the country-side is disordered, women are easily captured by the robber clans. From what caste or class a girl may have been ravished is of no consequence at all to a clan of this sort (though to a Rajpút this would make all the difference), for she is solemnly put through a form of adoption into one circle of affinity in order that she may be lawfully married into another—a fiction that would now be quite inadmissible among the pure clans, though it is good enough law for the Meenas, who split heads more neatly than hairs. Nevertheless this fiction looks very like the survival of a custom that may once have been universal among all clans at a more elastic stage of their growth, for it enables the circles of affinity within a tribe to increase and multiply their numbers without a break, while at the same time it satisfies the conditions of lawful intermarriage. But in these latter days of orderly government in central India under British supervision the raiding grounds of the Meenas have been sadly curtailed, and women are not so easily captured or retained after capture. Hence the Meenas are being forced back upon the resources of their own tribe for the supply of wives; and as one circle may have too many girls while another has too few, the theologians of the tribe are called in to discover orthodox reasons why two members of the same circle may intermarry. The device, however, by which this is effected is always by breaking up one circle of affinity upon some plausible ground of distinct ancestry, and re-forming it into two separate circles, with pedigrees properly disjoined, whereby is contrived a more convenient and productive distribution of marriageable females.

The present writer has carefully examined the ingredients and composition, in different parts of India, of several of these irregular tribes, which are neither pure clans of descent nor castes, but seem to be in a state of transition. There is a tribe in South West Rajputána called the Grassias, separate from the Bheels, and ranking next above them in social order, which is obviously of artificial and composite formation. The word Grassia means a chief who has the right to collect dues, originally of the nature of black-mail, from certain villages or upon certain lands or roads; and with this sense the name is still in common use in certain parts of India. But here, in Rajputána and the adjacent hills, it means a group of people, who have their internal circles of affinity upon the model of a regular clan; and the Grassia is probably of mixed Rajpút blood, possibly in some cases he may be a pure Rajpút stock detached and isolated in the backwoods. We may conjecture the designation to have been extended to the original Grassia chief's kinsfolk and retainers, perhaps also to the people who settled on his land and became attached to him in various ways; so that after this manner it became applied to a separate set or association of men living apart with the same habits and interests. Other half-blood tribes, somewhat higher in the social scale, are the Meos and the Mers; the former are now Mahomedan, but still keep up their circles of affinity; the latter claim Rajpút lineage. There is also a widely spread tribe of professional thieves which is evidently by origin nothing more than an association for the purpose of habitual robbery; but even these people pretend to a remote descent from Rajpúts, and shape their internal society upon the pattern of the clan. And the Bungáras, a clan which does all the carrying trade in the wild parts of India, are made up by contingents from various other castes and tribes, which have at different times joined the profession. So that it may be affirmed generally that all these intermediate groups have the same character of aggregation from miscellaneous stocks, with inner circles of affinity more or less numerous and orthodox. Upon the evidence gathered it may not be too rash to hazard the theory that in the conflux and consolidation of these groups we can trace the working of the regular processes by which tribes and clans are first formed, and of the circumstances which favour and oppose growth. Let any cause drive together a collection of stray families which have been cut off from different stocks, the law of attraction groups them into a tribe, banded together by force of circumstances, by living in the same place and in the same way; while the law of exogamy, or marriage outside kinship, immediately begins to work each family into a separate circle of affinity, and at the same time strings together all these circles upon the tribal band of union, like rings on a curtain-rod. If one of these circles has a great run of success, if the group happens to produce a man of remarkable luck and capacity, it may widen and develop to any extent, and may become a clan. The prestige of a famous leader, especially if he be a broken man out of a patrician clan of descent, brings to his standard all the roving blades of the country; his kinsmen may leave their villages to join him upon the rumours of his success; and the hardy Bheel, ambitious to shine in the company of a noble Aryan captain, invaluable as a scout and a guide in the forests, attaches himself to the association. David, son of Jesse, in his cave, a valiant man of the pure clans, with his gathering of men in debt and distress, and his hard-fighting kinsmen, the sons of Zeruiah, is the type of the personages who first create a group, and then push forward their particular circle of affinity until it expands into a clan. We know that David did become an eponymous ancestor of the first order, supplanting to a great degree the original tribal founder; but he did not develop a group of his own because he fought his way back to the chiefship of his own tribe; and the Semitic clan of descent is, accurately speaking, of a different variety from that which is now being described. From companionship in war and venture the band soon closes up into the idea of kinship, assuming the name and entering the circle of its leader, who after death becomes the eponymous ancestor, while his repute keeps the circle together by preserving a common name and pride of descent. So long as these advantages give predominance in war this circle commands the market for wives, and is less tempted to split up into sections or otherwise to break the strict rule which prohibits marriage within itself. And, lastly, its prosperity soon brings it under the patronage of Brahmans and of the strict canon law, whereby it gradually acquires the dignity of orthodox prejudices, and its loose customs are stereotyped by divine sanction. Thus in the incessant struggle for existence among barbarous races certain conditions of origin and environment have favoured the predominance of selected groups; so that the perfect clan may represent the great oak of a forest, which is the fortunate survivor of a thousand acorns, saplings, and trees, which have succumbed to various misfortunes at various stages of growth. A vast number of rudimentary clans must have been cut off or disqualified early in their formation by one or another of the innumerable calamities which beset primitive mankind, or by some impediment or accident which broke the circle of affinity or fatally reduced its strength. War, famine, and pestilence are great disintegrating powers; the blood is corrupted, the genealogy is lost, the brethren are scattered abroad to take to new habits of life and unauthorised means of subsistence, to strange gods and maimed rites. These broken groups re-form again like a fissiparous species; the leading emigrant, exile, or outcast may become the starting point for a fresh circle of affinity; but they are lost to the clan, and lose way in the struggle. And as the great majority of these circles fade away in outline, or break up again into atoms before they can consolidate, there goes on a constant decomposition and reproduction of groups at different stages, whence we get at the extraordinary multitude of circles of affinity, all alike in type and structure, but differing widely as to their radius of prohibited degrees, which make up the miscellany of Indian society. Within the outer circle of castes, as distinguished from tribes, all the affinity circles are necessarily smaller, for reasons that will be touched upon presently.

It must be explained that this theory of the growth and decay of clans is drawn from a good deal of actual minute observation of what is still going on in the wilder regions of India. There is, of course, good historic evidence for believing that some of the Aryan clans were full-grown when they first entered India, though the fact is hardly demonstrable; but the theory is supposed to apply to the beginning of a clan anywhere. What can be still noted of this process of aggregation of diverse families into circles of affinity does at any rate throw some light upon a question which is raised both by Maine in his "Ancient Law," and by Mr. McLennan in his "Primitive Marriage." How, it is asked, has it come to pass that in those primitive societies which assume as their basis a common descent from one original stock one so constantly finds traces of alien descent? How came a variety of alien groups to coalesce into a local tribe? The fiction of male adoption is suggested as the answer, but such adoption from alien stocks is quite unknown throughout India, where the adoption of a son is always made within the circle of affinity, ordinarily from the nearest kindred. The real explanation may, perhaps, be indicated by what we see in the hills and wolds of central India, where the different stocks congregate by force of circumstances, and tend to form a tribe, and clans within a tribe, under the name and prevailing influence of the most successful groups.

It has already been suggested that a group in its earlier stages pushes itself forward among and above other groups by the great advantage of possessing a vigorous leader who becomes a famous ancestor. So great is this advantage, that there is probability in the surmise that all the pure clans now existing in central India have been formed around the nucleus of a successful chief. Certainly that is the source to which all the clans themselves attribute their rise; and this view fits with an analogy that runs through all ancient tradition and authentic history of the first gathering and amalgamation, whether of men into a tribe, or of tribes into a kingdom or empire. To borrow Carlyle's words, the perplexed jungle of primitive society springs out of many roots, but the hero is the tap-root from which in a great degree all the rest were nourished and grown. In Europe, where the landmarks of nationalities are fixed, and the fabric of civilisation firmly entrenched, people are often inclined to treat as legendary the enormous part in the foundation of their race or their institutions attributed by primitive races to their heroic ancestor. Yet it may be difficult to overrate the impression that must have been produced by daring and successful exploits upon the primitive world, where the free impulsive play of a great man's forces is little controlled by artificial barriers or solid breakwaters, and the earth in its youth lies spread out before him, where to choose. In such times, whether a group which is formed upon the open surface of society shall spread out into a clan or a tribe, or break up prematurely, seems to depend very much on the strength and energy of its founder. It is like throwing stones into a lake, which make small or great circles according to the stone's size. Throw in a big stone, and you start a vigorous widening circle with sharp outline, just as the splash made in the early world by a mighty man of valour created a powerful expanding circle of affinity. Throw in a pebble, and you have a circle faintly outlined and soon exhausted, like the kinship of an obscure ancestor. Then we can conceive how disruption and combination would both be constantly at work. Half-a-dozen minor groups or circles of affinity might be quietly developing into tribes or clans, when a big boulder like Cyrus, or Alexander, or Jinghiz Khan comes crushing into the middle of the lake, overwhelming or absorbing all of them, only to be formed again when these high waves of world-conquest shall have again begun to subside. The captivities of the Jews are examples of the way in which many a tribe of descent must have been shattered. Ezra on his return to Jerusalem mourns over the unlawful intermarriages of the people of Israel, the priests, and even the Levites, with the alien tribes, "so that the holy seed have mingled themselves with the people of those lands;" and the genealogies of those who came up out of the captivity were carefully overhauled. Certain families could not show their father's house, and their seed, whether they were of Israel; these were probably the children of the captivity, born in exile, and they seem to have been excluded from the brotherhood; while in other cases the true Israelites were readmitted into the tribes on promising to put away their strange wives. This careful inquiry into the genealogy of a clansman whose family has been long settled at a distance is constantly practised among the Rajpúts; though if the Patháu emperors had transported a clan into central Asia it is doubtful if any would have ever got back into their circle of affinity after an absence of nearly a century. But a tribe of Israel intermarried within its own circle, and could therefore settle its own marriage questions; whereas a Rajpút has to satisfy the genealogic scruples of a different clan. Ten of the tribes of Israel thus disappeared for ever, unless we place faith in the tradition, of itself not improbable, that they are the ancestors of the Afghans; and in the same manner there are traces all over India of tribes lost or extinct, some of them cut off within historic times by the pitiless sweep of some Pathán invader's scimitar. But then again, in the confusion and anarchy of the dilapidation of these huge top-heavy Asiatic empires, some daring chief of just such a loose predatory tribe as we now see gathered in the central Indian hills, issues out with his kindred band and gets a name and a territory; so that in the incessant flux and change of Asiatic institutions the whole history of the ascent from the cave of Adullam to the chiefship of a clan, to the rulership over tribes, and sometimes to empire over a great territory, is constantly repeating itself.

I have said already that the strict rules of intermarriage which distinguish the pure central Indian clan of descent are too rigid for a good working institution; and indeed they seem to have been modified, on social or political grounds, all over the world by the clans which have developed further. The Israelites clearly modified some custom of marriage beyond the clan, and permitted intermarriage with the clan, in order that the inheritance of daughters should not go out of the clan by exogamy.* The Rajpút never gives lands with his daughters, except possibly a life interest in the revenue; and he adheres to his genealogies with a stringency that is politically and socially unhealthy. Looking to the actual condition and relative strength at this moment of the pure and impure clans, some good judges are inclined to believe the pure Rajpúts to be an exhausted tribe which is reaching its term, and that impure clans like the Meenas, which up to very lately were adding to their number and strength by enlisting all the hardy outlaws and venturous men of the country, would, if the tribes were left to fight it out among themselves, gradually push forward and subdue or expel the Rajpúts, who are now dominant over the Meenas. The impure clans are rough and unscrupulous; the pure clans are shackled by all kinds of jealousies and punctilio, by luxurious vices and the pride of race. These things not only touch the spirit and physique of a clan; they tend directly to diminish its number. The very poor clansmen cannot marry their daughters; while the rich clansmen have too many wives, being incessantly importuned to take a portionless daughter, if only for the name of the thing, off the hands of a poor and proud neighbour. Hence the deplorable rarity of heirs among the leading Rajpút families, and the direct encouragement to two ruinous social practices, female infanticide and polygamy. There is probably a natural tendency in the pure clan of descent, as in the exclusive aristocracies, to become enervated after passing its grand climacteric, when the tie of blood which united the early conquering bands becomes too tight for the free spread of a settled community, until it is overthrown and superseded by a more vigorous group in its earlier and therefore more elastic stages, with prejudices and prohibitions not yet stereotyped. If some such revolution were even now to bring an impure clan into predominance in central India, it is pretty certain that the new lords of the dominion would at once proceed to set up as patricians, to cluster

* See Numbers xxxvi. The divisions of the Israelites appear to have belonged to the species of genealogic clans, though in compliance with usage they are sometimes called tribes in this paper.

round eponyms, to lay down the straitest rules about purity of blood, and to settle down under Brahmanic direction on the lines of a pure-blooded race. For the predilection of all these rough clans towards becoming particular and orthodox as they rise in the Indian world is very marked; being due, of course, to the increasing pressure of the Brahmanic atmosphere as they ascend.

After this manner, in prehistoric days, the impure clan may have been constantly developing into the pure clan, drawing closer the lines of patrician kinship and of religion as it worked its way upward; while again the pure clan, having reached its full as an institution, begins to decline and give place to younger groups under more capable leaders than the effete descendants of ancient heroes. But the time for such tribal revolutions has gone by in India, because the surrounding world has advanced too far ahead of these primitive peoples cooped up in the central regions. The only political speculation now worth making regarding the clans, is how these antique groups will manage to melt themselves down in the crucible of civilisation, and to join the general association of modern India. At the beginning of the eighteenth century the clans showed symptoms of feudalising, under the influence of events similar to those which transformed Europe during the break-up of the Carlovingian Empire. At the end of that century the Rana of Oodipoor, whose ancestor had the leadership of all the clans, was reduced to the condition of the last of the Merovingians. All the clans would have been broken up politically if the English had not interfered; and it is now very hard to guess whether the ruling chiefs will preserve separate political States, when the clan may merge into an aristocracy of the general population; or whether the great old families will filter through the Fergus McIvor phase of cultured chieftainship into an hereditary nobility of the empire.

Thus far we have been tracing the development and the operation upon primitive society of the unmixed idea of kinship. Undoubtedly, as has been suggested already, kinship as an institution in India has been fostered and cemented by the influence of a powerful religion. Perhaps only in India have the religious notions common to all early polytheisms been concentrated in the hands of a great Levitic tribe, the Brahmans, who have for centuries undertaken to interpret the divine rules and provide the sanctions upon which every Asiatic society necessarily rests. And as the marriage law lies at the foundation of society, this of course has fallen specially under Brahmanic jurisdiction, so that the prevailing customs and sentiments of a tribe, which may have been originally formed according to practical needs and experiments at a level below the Brahmanic atmosphere, become hardened into sacred laws as they emerge into orthodox latitudes. Yet Brahmanism chiefly registers and confirms; being itself an inorganic sort of religion, it has never attempted any sweeping reforms of the rude tribal customs, such as are introduced everywhere by Christianity or Islam. It is remarkable how completely, from Bosnia to Rajputána, religious antipathy exterminates the sympathy of race, whenever the two principles come into collision. And Islam in India has a very distinctive effect upon early institutions—it crushes out the innumerable sects and rituals of heathendom, and abolishes among its proselytes their Gentile marriage laws. Some of the half-blood tribes of central India, which were converted by the Musalmán emperors, have struggled hard against this process; and up to this day they have clung in a most curious way to their ideas of kinship, though they are now being rapidly absorbed under one uniform canon.

But although Brahmanism, so far as it is systematically administered, operates as a cement to the rude edifice of primitive kinship, yet the working of religious ideas among the population is a mighty agent in what Sir H. Maine has called the "trituration" of Hindu society. We know that the word Hindu denotes no common religious denomination, but comprises a vast multitude of Indians who have for ages been absorbed, beyond all other people upon earth, in attempting to decipher the way of the gods with mankind and the tokens of divinity; and who still continue, everywhere

"Errare, atque viam palantes quaerere vitae."

While the higher intellects, like Buddha, are disgusted equally with the ways of gods and of men, and only desire to escape out of sensation into the silence, the crowd still stands gazing at the heavens. Among a people with this turn of mind new worships and new sects have incessantly arisen. Now it appears that a religious body with some distinctive object of worship or singular rule of devotion has usually (though not invariably) come to split off into a separate group, which, though based upon a common religion, constructs itself upon the plan of a tribe. The common faith or worship forms the outer circle, which has gradually shut off a sect not only from intermarriage but even from eating with outsiders; while inside this circumference the regular circles of affinity have established themselves independently, just as families settle and expand within the pale of a half-grown tribe. Each body of proselytes from different tribes and castes has preserved its identity as a distinct stock; keeping up the fundamental prohibition against marriage within the particular group of common descent. But with some other group of the sect it is essential to marry; and thus in the course of time has been reproduced upon a basis of common belief or worship the original circle of a tribe, beyond which it is impossible to contract a legitimate marriage. Where the sect has hardened into a caste, it is quite impossible for any one to marry beyond it; but where the sect is of recent formation, difference of religious belief is not so absolute a bar; and under the jurisdiction of English law there is a growing tendency toward disregarding the impediment, at any rate the courts are inclined to discourage it. It seems certain, for example, that two or three generations ago the Sikhs, who are a religious sect by origin, only intermarried with Sikhs; but they are now known to marry often with others who, though not of their rite, are of their original tribe. And a man can now adopt or relinquish any special form of Brahmanic worship, or even Jainism, without prejudice to his status; although in the case of a great banker who imported from South India a very unusual ritual, the question was undoubtedly raised. On the other hand, several instances could be given of sects having gradually rounded themselves off into complete castes, neither eating nor marrying with any beyond the pale.

We can thus make out an analogy between the process of the formation of a tribe and that of some of the religious castes. It has been already said that a wild tribe seems to grow out of a collection of recruits from the settled communities, who either from necessity or a love of adventure join together under some notable leader. So likewise in the spiritual world a sect often begins with a gathering of venturesome thinkers or enthusiasts, who leave the trodden paths of religion and set up for themselves with a few followers; to whom sometimes repair outcasts, persons excommunicate, publicans and sinners, and other such who have good reasons for quitting the caste-circle in which they were born. In Northern India there are several of these purely sectarian castes whose origin can be historically traced back to a famous personage, often a good fighter as well as preacher, who is now the semi-divine head-centre of the caste. Within at least one of these castes the idea of affinity has woven during the last three or four centuries a wonderful network of separate groups, deriving from the various clans, castes, or families of the proselytes who at sundry times and in divers places have joined the sect. These perfect specimens of the development of a caste from a sect are not common; there are many petty sects which, although more or less insulated by their peculiar doctrine, never attain the scale of a caste, and which seem to owe their low development to the obscurity of their founder, probably some casual outcaste. It will be understood that a Hindu who, having broken the rules of his caste, is dismissed beyond the rim of his outer circle, finds himself altogether at sea, with no social anchorage whatever. He has neither nationality, tribe, clan, caste, nor family; he is literally in an indescribable condition. The best resource for a religious outsider of this sort, who does not take to "the hills of the robbers," is to start a religion of his own, and to get others to join him. If he be of the mystic turn of mind, he can have a call, and can turn the flank of orthodoxy by opening out direct intercourse with a god; he can show a new light which in the dim religious twilight of India attracts restless souls as a lantern brings moths out of the summer darkness. If, as often happens, he is rather crazy and fanatic, he may do precisely what mad Thom did fifty years ago in the Kentish woods within sight of Canterbury Cathedral—proclaim himself an incarnation, lead a body of wild rustics into some brawl, and get himself killed. He may then become a local saint, with a petty group of distinctive worshippers. But it needs a great enthusiast or *illuminé* to found a caste; a very great one may go near to founding a nationality, as is shown by the example of the Sikhs; and the greatest of all these Indian spiritualists, Sakya Gotama, changed the religion of Eastern Asia.

It will be understood that this paper only touches upon the subject of castes which seem to originate out of peculiarities of worship and belief, and has nothing to say about that very large class of castes which are formed out of association in professions, trades, or crafts. One thing worth noticing, however, is that the Brahmans, whom most people would assume to be a religious caste *par excellence*, betray symptoms of being by origin a caste by profession or calling. For though the Brahman caste is now a vast circle inclosing a number of separate Levitic tribes, which again are subdivided into numberless family groups, yet several of these tribes appear to have developed out of literary and sacerdotal guilds. Indeed, one distinctive tenet of the Hindu Broad Church, which rests (I am told) upon passages quoted from the Vedas, affirms that Brahmanism does not properly come by caste or descent, but by learning and devotional exercises. This is now laid down as an ethical truth; it was probably at first a simple fact. There is fair evidence that several of these Brahmanic tribes have at different periods been promoted into the caste circle by virtue of having acquired in some outlying province or kingdom (where Brahmans proper could not be had) a monopoly of the study and interpretation of the sacred books; and having devoted themselves for generations to this profession, at last graduated as full Brahmans, though of a different tribe from the earlier schools. Some glimpse of the very lowest rudimentary stage of a Levitic caste (that is, a caste with a speciality for ritual and interpretation of the sacred books) may still be obtained in the most backward parts of India. The Meena tribe, which has already been mentioned, is as to its religion in the ordinary state of slow transition toward Brahmanism; the superior section, which lives northward toward Delhi, being under the ministry of accommodating Brahmans, while the clans of the remote south-west are beef-eating and utterly excommunicate. These last-mentioned clans have got attached to them a Levitic tribe of their own, as Robin Hood had his Friar Tuck, who perform the essential social rites and expound the caprices of divinity. The story of this tribe's origin, according to the Meenas, is that most of these families are descended from pure Brahmans who have from time to time been persuaded or forced by some wild chief or captain of the pure clans to officiate in a human sacrifice; and that, having thereby quite forfeited their pure caste, they became degraded, and were driven forth to minister into the tribes beyond the pale. This story must not hastily be set aside as improbable, for the tradition of human sacrifice is still so powerful in that part of India, that within the last two years a whole tribe of Bheels has fled to the hills upon the rumour that a Rajpút chief intended to celebrate his accession as ruler by sacrificing one of them; and human sacrifice was undoubtedly practised in the backwoods of India up to the end of the last century by others beside the aboriginal tribes. These Meena Levites appear to be a collection of all kinds of waifs and cuttings from the upper religious castes; they may possibly rise in respectability as their clients get on in the world; and one might almost hazard the speculation, though it will be received with horror in certain quarters, that they are something like a Brahmanic tribe in faint embryo.

The attempt has now been made to describe what may be observed, by looking at Indian society in a very primitive and unsophisticated state, of two processes of social growth—the formation of tribes and clans under the working of the simple idea of kinship, and the formation of sectarian castes, with interior kindred groups, under the more complicated working of the ideas of kinship and religion combined. It would seem to be a reasonable theory that the caste, as an institution, is of a later formation than the tribe. For, so far as the actual course of things can be watched, in early and wild times a tribe or clan regularly throws off another tribe or clan after its own kind, as swarms come out of a wild bees' nest, the state of the world being favourable to the existence of such groups. But there comes a later period when the pressure of powerful dynasties and the rise of industrial bodies render tribal formations no longer possible, driving men into peaceful pursuits, and swallowing up petty warlike independencies. In the western world these agencies rapidly obliterated the tribes, and gradually produced the modern populations, pounded up and measured out into nationalities, with their circles of affinity narrowed down to the immediate family. In India religion seems to have stepped in as the tribal institutions dissolved, and to have strung all the kindred groups upon the circle which we call caste. Within a caste the inner circles of affinity survive, but in a stunted condition as compared with a clan within a tribe, it being obviously impossible that in this altered phase of society the kindred groups should continue to hold together by descent from a common stock. The folk take to various occupations, inhabit different places, contract strange marriages, worship other gods; the ups and downs of a more complicated life break short the pedigree, sever the kinship, and rub off the patronymic; the distant branches of a family fall out of sight, and the long genealogies of the clan give place to the comparatively narrow tables of prohibited degrees which prevail among castes. Then the trade, or the profession, or the common ritual becomes the bond of union instead of descent or political association; and thus the mixed population of India may have rearranged itself into castes, propelled into those grooves by the archaic and inveterate exclusiveness of primitive Asiatics regarding marriage and food. You must not marry one of your own blood, but neither must you marry a stranger of unknown descent and foreign habits; your caste means those with whom you may safely intermarry and share food, without risk of incurring some unlucky taint which may give you much trouble in this existence and the next.

Whether the new ideas encouraged (if not generated) everywhere by English rule in India are not dissolving, in their turn, the castes as well as the tribes, may be a remote speculation worth hinting at. The spread of what we may call mysticism in certain parts of India has been much noticed by the natives themselves, and by very competent observers among the missionaries. One of these last (Mr. Shoolbred, of Ajmere) writes, in a valuable paper upon religious and social movements, that "the surface-drifting of the semi-Hinduized classes toward orthodoxy is nothing in comparison with the current which is setting in among the people toward sects and secret societies that disown caste prejudices about bodily purity and distinctive ceremonial." This tendency of religious enthusiasm to shake off the restraints of traditional external forms, and to prefer the vague disorderly suggestions of spiritual freemasonry and inward grace, is a known symptom of the decline of priestly influence, and of the rise of a kind of democracy in religion, which, if it spreads, will soon disintegrate the Indian caste.

This very condensed account of the condition and tendencies of social matters in an outlying part of India may possibly be useful to those who are working by the comparative method at the foundations of history and sociology generally. It may have some bearings upon much that has recently been written about early institutions in Europe. Here in India, for instance, can still be seen primitive sets of people who never came under the arbitrary despotism of a single man, and among whom no written law has ever been made since the making of the world. Yet these people are not loose incoherent assemblages of savages, but are very ancient societies, restrained and stringently directed by custom and usage, by rules and rites irresistible. "The Greeks," writes Mr. Freeman, "were the first people who made free commonwealths, and who put the power of the law instead of mere force and the arbitrary will of a single man;" and whatever impression this passage might convey to the students for which it was written, others might hastily infer from it that in the ancient world men were all lawless or under despotisms until the Greeks invented free institutions. Perhaps it may be suggested that what the Greeks did invent is political citizenship and rules of conduct under State sanction. Between the clans and the commonwealths the difference is not so much between lawlessness and free institutions, as between the primitive man, whose social and political customs are as much part of his species as the inherited habits of an animal, and the highly civilised man, who consciously chooses his own laws and form of government according to expediency and logic. Politically speaking, the extremes of two systems may be seen by contrasting those tribal States of Central India which are presided over each by a chief of the eldest family of the oldest stock in the clan, with the United States of America, founded upon and held together by a written constitution setting forth abstract rights. In the Indian State we have the rigid circle of affinity hedging in the political privileges of a dominant clan, and resting upon close marriage rules; in the American State we see citizenship open to any foreigner who applies for it, absolute equality before a written code, and often a most liberal law of divorce. Whether across the wide interval which separates the earliest and latest phases of Aryan institutions may still be traced any connected filiation of ideas is a speculation not to be entered upon here; possibly the theory that the peculiar demise of the French kingship followed a rule of the law of inheritance among the Salian tribe, is the most notable European instance of the distorted survival of a tribal custom.

"The forms of the Juden Gesse, rousing the sense of union with what is remote, set him musing on the two elements of our historic life which that sense raises into the same region of poetry—the faint beginnings of ancient faiths and institutions, and their obscure lingering decay." This is what was suggested to Daniel Deronda by the scene in the synagogue at Frankfort; and the passage touches the way of thought into which Englishmen are led in India, by looking around them at the actual institutions and worships of a primitive people, and endeavouring to see clearly among what manner of men they find themselves. One seems to be catching at the beginnings of

European nations, and to discern a little less dimly what the ancient generations of one's own folk were thinking about in the foretime, and what motives or conceptions, now extinct in Western Europe, presided over the infancy of some of the ideas and institutions which lie at the roots of European society.

# CHAPTER VIII.

## THE RAJPÚT STATES OF INDIA.

Political institutions of Rajputána preserved by the English—Description of the country called Rajputána, its boundaries, and the States which it includes—Origin and development of Rajpút States and the dominant clans—Brief retrospect of their history during the time of the Moghal empire; connection of the ruling families with the Emperors—Effect on Rajputána of period of anarchy during 18th century when the empire collapsed—The States rescued from destruction by the English Government—Extinction of predatory rights by Lord Hastings, and his establishment of permanent peace—Examination of the constitution of a Rajpút State and of the nature of its organization: the Chief is the head of a clan, and the descendant of the State's founder—Rules of succession to chiefship and customary practice of selection; the hereditary right subject to condition of fitness—Policy of English Government in disputed cases—Subordinate chiefs and landholders, their rights and obligations—Tenures not feudal, but according to tribal usages and privileges of kinship—Primogeniture—Marriage customs—Religious movements—Fosterage—Remarks on the character and durability of these institutions.

One of the popular notions in England and Europe regarding the establishment of the English empire in India is that our conquests absorbed nationalities, displaced long-seated dynasties, and levelled ancient nobilities. These are some of the self-accusations by which the average home-keeping Englishman justifies to himself the indulgence of sitting down and casting dust on his head whenever he looks back upon the exploits of his countrymen in India—an attitude which is observed by foreigners with suspicion or impatience according to their insight into English character. Yet it would be easy to prove that one important reason why the English so rapidly conquered India was this, that the countries which fell into our hands had no nationalities, no long-seated ruling dynatsies, or ancient aristocracies, that they had, in fact, no solid or permanent organization of the kind, but were politically treasure trove, and at the disposal of the first who, having found, could keep. The best proof that in these countries the English destroyed no organized political institutions is the historical fact that in the countries which they annexed none such had been left for them to destroy. On the other hand, where indigenous political institutions of long standing do still exist, it is the English who have saved them from destruction; and this may best be illustrated by giving some description of the only considerable region of India in which such institutions still practically survive, having resisted for centuries the incessant attacks of Mahomedan invaders, and the crushing weight of the Moghal empire. That these institutions did not at last topple over and disappear toward the end of that long storm of anarchy which swept the length and breadth of India for a hundred years after the death of the Emperor Aurungzeb in 1707, is mainly due to their protection at the last moment by the English, who may thus claim at least the credit of having rescued the only ancient political structures in Northern India which their predecessors had been unable to demolish.

The region to which we refer is that which is now called, in the administrative nomenclature of the Indian empire, Rajputána; and, by the natives of India, Rajasthán, or the country of the Chiefs. It is the region within which the pure-blooded Rajpút clans have maintained their independence under their own chieftains, and have in some instances kept together their primitive societies, ever since the dominion of the Rajpúts over the great plains of North-Western India was cast down and broken to pieces seven centuries ago by the Musalmán irruptions from Central Asia. The first Musalmán invasions found Rajpút dynasties ruling in all the chief cities of the North and over the rich Gangetic plains Eastward to the confines of modern Bengal—at Lahore, Delhi, Kanauj and Ayodhya. Out of these great cities and fertile lands the Rajpút Chiefs were driven forth Southward and Westward into the central regions of India, where a more difficult country gave them a second line of defence against the foreigners. And this line they have held not unsuccessfully up to the present day. The boundaries of their actual territory are not easily defined without a map, though no boundaries of political territory in India have varied so little in historic times. After the earliest Mahomedan conquests the Rajpút country seems to have extended (speaking roughly) from the Indus and the Sutlej on the West and North-West, right across the Indian continent Eastward up to the vicinity of the Jumna River at Agra and Delhi, and Southward until it touched the Vindhya range of mountains. This great central region had for its natural barriers on the West and North-West the desert, on the East the rocky broken tracts which run along West of the Jumna, and on the South the passes and woodlands of the Vindhya mountains. And though in many parts of this country, to the South and South-East especially, the dominion of the Rajpúts has been overlaid by Mahomedan or Maratha usurpations, yet everywhere Rajpút septs or petty chiefships may still be found existing in various degrees of independence. And there are, of course, Rajpút Chiefs outside Rajputána altogether, though none of political importance. But Rajputána proper, the country still under the independent rule of the most ancient families of the purest clans, may now be understood generally to mean the great tract that would be crossed by two lines, of which one should be drawn on the map of India from the frontier of Sind Eastward to the gates of Agra; and the other from the Southern border of the Punjab Government near the Sutlej Southward and South-Eastward until it meets the broad belt of Maratha States under the Guicowar, Holkar, and Sindia, which runs across India from Baroda to Gwalior. This territory is divided into nineteen States, of which sixteen are possessed by Rajpút clans, and the Chief of the clan or sept is the State's ruler. To the Sesodia clan, the oldest and purest blood in India, belong the States of Oodipoor, Banswarra, Pertábgarh and Shahpura; to the Rathore clan, the States of Jodhpoor and Bikanír; Jeypoor and Ulwar to the Kuchwáha, and so on.

Of these States the highest in rank and the most important politically are the States of Oodipoor, Jodhpoor and Jeypoor.

The ancestors of the family which now rules in Oodipoor were hereditary leaders of the clan which has held from time immemorial, from a date before the earliest Mahomedan invasion, the country which now forms the territory of their Chief; the Chiefs of Jodhpoor and Jeypoor are the descendants of families who gave princes to the tribes that were dominant in Upper India before the Musalmáns came. In fact, all these States have very much the same territorial origin; they are the lands which a clan, or a sept, or a family, has seized and settled upon, and have managed to hold fast through centuries of warfare. And what we know of the manner in which these States were founded gives a very fair sample of the movements and changes of the primitive world. When the dominant Rajpút families lost their dominion in the rich Gangetic plains, one part of their clan seems to have remained in the conquered country, having submitted to the foreigner, cultivating in strong communities of villages and federations of villages, and paying such land tax as the ruler could extract. These communities still exist and flourish in British India, where there are very many more Rajpúts than in Rajputána. Another part of the clan, probably the near kinsmen of the defeated Chief, followed his family into exile, and helped him to carve out another, but a much poorer, dominion. They discovered a tract just productive enough to yield them food, and wild enough to shelter them from the great armies of the foreigner. Here the Chief built himself a fort upon a hill; his clansmen slew or subdued the tribes they found in possession of the soil, and the lands were all parcelled off among the Chief's kinsfolk, the indigenous proprietors being subjected to payment of a land tax, but not otherwise degraded. Having thus made a settlement and a city of refuge, the Chief and his Rajpúts started upon an interminable career of feuds and forays, striving eternally to enlarge their borders at the cost of their neighbours. When the land grew too strait for the support of the Chief's family, or of the sept, that is, when there were no vacant allotments, a landless son of the Chief would assemble a band and set forth to make room for himself elsewhere. If he was lucky, he found his room; if not, the family was rid of his company; in either event he was provided for. In this way the whole country of Rajputána was occupied by the clans and septs which we now find there; and their territories are now called by us States; but these States are constitutionally quite unlike any others in India. For while everything else in the political order of India has changed, the Rajpút States have managed to preserve unaltered much of their original structure, built up out of the needs and circumstances of primitive life. The strain of incessant warfare in which these tribal sovereignties were engaged from their foundation centuries ago until the English peace of 1818, has served to keep tight the bonds which held them together, without being violent enough to break them asunder. Of course the original type has undergone some modifications; towns have grown up round the ancient forts; the lands of each sept have gradually, and by constant friction, rounded themselves off into distinct territories; and the Chiefs have in some instances succeeded in modernizing their status toward the likeness of territorial sovereignty. But on the whole there are probably few or no political fabrics having any pretence to be called States, in any part of historic Asia, which have suffered so little essential change between the eleventh and nineteenth centuries, a period which for Rajputána was one long war-time, from the first inroads of the Ghaznevi kings to the final pacification of Central India by the military and political measures of the English Governor-General, Lord Hastings.

During these seven centuries or so the Rajpút clans had various fortunes. The kings of the early Musalmán dynasties in Northern India pierced their country from end to end by rapid rushing invasions, plundering and ravishing, breaking the idols, and razing the beautifully sculptured temples, Buddhist and Brahmanic. But so long as the object of these incursions was mere booty or fanatical slaughter, there was not much to be got out of the interior of Rajputána. The Chiefs retired to their fortresses, great circumvallations of the broad tops of scarped hills, with three or four lines of defence, strongholds which cost the enemy a siege of some twelve or eighteen months, with the grand finale of a desperate sally *en masse* upon your lines by the garrison, without hope or fear, dressed in saffron garments, drunk with opium and with the blood of their own womankind. The victor in obstinate and dangerous conflicts of this kind found himself paying rather dear for a warlike triumph; and as for conquest in the sense of establishing permanent dominion, the country was not worth the trouble of holding it against the clans and their faithful allies, the aboriginal non-Aryan tribes of the jungle. So early as the end of the twelfth century, nevertheless, the Mahomedans had discovered the great importance, as a *point d'appui* in the middle of the Rajpút country, of Ajmere, a city lying at the foot of an almost impregnable hill fort, well watered for these arid tracts, in a situation at once strong, central, and most picturesque. The fort was taken by the Afghan King Shaháb-ud-din at the end of the twelfth century, and on the crest of the hill the traveller is still shown a graveyard thick with mounds, where are said to lie the bones of the faithful Islamites who fell in the storm,* or in the massacre by which the Rajpúts celebrated the fort's recapture a few years later. Since then Ajmere has been lost and won several times; its possession being the symbol of political predominance in Rajputána; for it is a Castle Dangerous which no government could hold in the midst of the clans without powerful supports and the prestige of military superiority. The Moghal Emperors made it an imperial residence in the seventeenth century; in the confusion of the eighteenth century the Rajpúts got it again for a while, but soon had to yield it to the Maratha chief Sindia, then at the height of his fortunes. By him it was ceded, with the lands adjoining, to the British in 1818; and thus for six centuries or more, with a few intervals, Ajmere has contained the garrison by which the masters of India have enforced their paramount jurisdiction over the unruly clans of Rajputána.

But if we except this important occupation of Ajmere, the

* It is called the *Ganj Shahid*, or granary of martyrs (*semen fidei*); but we are bound to add that this edifying memorial is shown in every Mahomedan fortress of ancient renown that is properly fitted out for the satisfaction of devout pilgrims.

Mahomedan inroads made little lasting impression upon the Rajpút countries up to the end of the fourteenth century. The capture of even the chief stronghold of a clan, as of Chitor, the citadel of the Sesodias, was only one of the more famous incidents, marked by unusual carnage, of constant war. When, however, the empire of the Toghlak dynasty at Delhi went to pieces, about the close of the fourteenth century, two Musalmán kingdoms were set up, independent of Delhi, in the Southern Provinces of Gúzerat and of Malwa. These powers wrested from the Rajpúts their most fertile dominions in the South and South-West, and thus confined the free clans still more closely within their natural barrier of hills, wood-land, or waste. Henceforward the territory which they have permanently possessed has been mainly defined by one or both of two conditions—comparative poverty of production, or difficulty of access. For a short interval of the sixteenth century, indeed, the talents and valour of the famous Rana Sanga of Oodipoor, the Chief of the Sesodia clan, once more enlarged the borders of the Rajpúts; and obtained for them predominance throughout Central India. This was the leader who in 1527, at the head of all the cavalry of the united clans (said to have numbered 100,000 horsemen), encountered the Emperor Baber near Agra on the Eastern frontier of Rajputána, and was defeated after a furious conflict. Baber's victory established the empire of the Moghals, as it is popularly called in India as well as in England. After his death the struggle for empire between Baber's family and the Afghan Sher Shah, which lasted up to the accession of the Great Akbar in 1560, allowed the rival clans of the Sesodias and the Rathores, under their Chiefs at Oodipoor and Jodhpoor, to rise successively to predominance among the Rajpúts, and to obtain greater political power than has ever since been held by any Chief. But the Emperor Akbar represented the power of the Moghal empire at the full, wielded by one man of singular ability both in civil and military affairs. He undertook to subdue and settle Rajputána systematically; he recovered Ajmere; Chitor, the citadel of the premier Chief of the eldest clan, was again besieged and taken with the usual desperate sortie and massacre of the defenders; the other chiefs were overawed and conciliated. Akbar took to wife the daughters of two great Rajpút families; he gave their sons high rank in his army, and succeeded in enlisting the Rajpúts (except only the proud Sesodia clan) not only as tributaries but as adherents. After him Jehángír made Ajmere his headquarters;* the Rajpút princesses became the wives and mothers of Moghal Emperors; the Chiefs entered the imperial service as governors and generals; they sent their regular contingents to join the army, and the headlong charges of their Rajpút cavalry became famous in the wars of the empire. The Emperors Jehángír and Sháh Jehán were both sons of Rajpút mothers; their kinship with the clans helped them powerfully in the contest which every Emperor had to pass through before he could succeed to the throne, while the strain of Hindu blood softened their fanaticism and mitigated their foreign contempt for the natives of India. But Aurungzeb, the son of Sháh Jehán, was a Mahomedan by full parentage, and a bigoted Islamite by temper; the Rajpúts had fought hard on the side of his elder brother Dára against his usurpation, and the Sesodia Chief had actually intercepted a daughter of the Rathore family who had been betrothed to Aurungzeb. So he made bitter war, though very unsuccessfully, on the Sesodias and in Rajputána generally, whereby he had thoroughly alienated the clans before he died. It was his policy to employ the chiefs on distant wars; and during his reign one Rajpút Chief governed the province of Kábul for the empire, and another commanded an army in the Dekhan; but Aurungzeb is said to have had them both poisoned.

The whole period of 151 years, from Akbar's accession to Aurungzeb's death, is occupied by the reigns of only four Emperors; and the fact that every one of these four was much superior to the average standard of Asiatic despots, is a good argument on behalf of competitive trials for high office, since each of these had to fight hard for his place. Moreover, they all had large families; indeed it will be found that, in contrast

* It was here that he received Sir Thomas Roe, sent by James I. in 1607.

to the Fredericks and Napoleons of Europe, most of the great rulers of Asia have been prolific; and the prince who wins life and crown from a death struggle with half-a-dozen brothers is the product of natural selection out of a naturally vigorous family. In the East a long reign means a strong reign; and for a century and a half the Moghal was fairly India's master.* The political effect upon Rajputána was that, whereas up to the reign of Akbar the Rajpút clans had maintained a warlike independence, from the beginning of the seventeenth century we may regard their Chiefs as having become feudatories of the empire, which was their natural and honourable relation to the paramount power whose territory encircled them, and with whose military calibre they had no pretence to compete.† And this relation was undoubtedly acknowledged as the political status of the Chiefs, until the sinking Moghal empire got hopelessly among the breakers, and was finally wrecked by Maratha freebooters. After Aurungzeb's death in 1707 came the ruinous downfall of an overgrown centralised empire, whose spoils were fought over by Affghans, Jâts, Sikhs, revolting Viceroys, rebellious governors, and military adventurers at large. The Rajpút Chiefs took advantage of the usual free fight among competitors for the vacant throne to cut adrift from the Mahomedans, and to attempt the formation of an independent league for the defence of Rajputána, and they renewed the attempt later when Nádir Shah invaded India.‡ But these clans and septs, with their barbarous feuds and jealousies about primitive punctilio, have never been able

* We may compare three periods (of which two almost exactly synchronize) in the history of three famous dynasties and kingdoms, in which the reigns of four successive Kings covered 150 years or more :

| | Years. |
|---|---|
| Four Moghal Emperors [1556 to 1707 A.D.] . . . . | 151 |
| Four Spanish Kings [1555 to 1700 A.D.] . . . . | 145 |
| Four French Kings [1610 to 1792] . . . . | 182 |

It is a coincidence that after the end of each of these periods came a change of dynasty, a disruption of dominions, and a great war.

† When Nádir Shah's invasion of India was impending, Raja Jai Singh (of Jeypoor) said to the emperor : "You must keep your eye on the Moghal nobles, who will probably be treacherous ; as for us Rajpúts, we are ready to join the royal standards."

‡ Nádir Shah heard of this league, and feeling himself bound, after his

to achieve any solid union, and the federation soon parted. Moreover, this was not the ordinary interlude of confusion between two long and strong reigns, as heretofore in the annals of Moghal empire; it was the beginning of the empire's end. Aurungzeb's imprudent greed for extensive conquests had ruined the vast fabric so firmly built up by his great-grandfather. He made the fatal political error of attacking and subverting the Mahomedan kingdoms in the far South of India, which had kept in subjection the Hindus of the peninsula; and he thus let loose upon himself the Marathas of the Dekhan, who ruined his dynasty. It could not be expected that a fifth Emperor should arise, capable of coping with a state of public affairs much more complicated and dangerous than any which his four predecessors had faced; and so the Moghal empire went to wreck; it was literally pulled asunder by wild horsemen. During the century which followed the death of Aurungzeb, from 1707 to 1807, all the dynasties and principalities now existing in India, except only the Rajpút States and several which no longer exist, were set up.* It was an era of chaos unprecedented even in the annals of Asiatic history, such an era as only follows the break up of a wide spreading despotic empire which has so carefully knocked out and cut away all internal or local stays and ties that its fall, when it comes, is a ruinous crash, and leaves a vast territory in a state of complete political dissolution. The Moghal empire had made a clean sweep of indigenous political institutions within its sway; and in their turn the Marathas, aided in the work of destruction by Nádir Shah, by the Afghans, Sikhs, Játs, by rebels and commanders of free companies generally, made a clean sweep of the Moghal empire. At

awful sack of Delhi, to do something for the ruined and prostrate Moghal Emperor before leaving India, he wrote to the Rajpúts a letter desiring them to "walk in the paths of submission and obedience to our dear brother" (the prostrate Moghal aforesaid). The letter ends thus characteristically—"God forbid it, but if accounts of your rebellion reach our ears, we will blot you out of the pages of the book of creation."

* We may perhaps except the State of Travancore, in the extreme corner of the peninsula. But this had been half swallowed up by Tippoo of Mysore, when we made him disgorge. As for Mysore itself the present rulership is of British creation, dating from the year 1867.

the end of the last century very few indeed of the reigning families in India could boast more than twenty-five years of independent and definite political existence; while the Rajpút chieftainships, the only ancient political groups left in India, were threatened with imminent obliteration.

From destruction these States were rescued only by seeking shelter at last within the sphere of the political system of the English. We owe the present constitution of our empire over the whole of India to three Governors General—to Lord Wellesley, Lord Hastings, and Lord Dalhousie—who at different epochs pushed forward the broad policy of establishing British supremacy, and the recognition of the British guarantee for order and territorial possessions, by treaties, alliances, and subsidies, throughout all India. When, in 1803, war broke out with the Maratha powers, Sindia and Holkar were deliberately ruining Rajputána, lacerating it by violent incursions, or bleeding it scientifically by a horde of relentless tax-gatherers; Ameer Khan, the Patháu filibuster, was living at free quarters in the heart of the country; the clans had been exhausted, and their lands desolated by thirty years' incessant war within their own territories. In 1803 the three principal States of Oodipoor, Jodhpoor, and Jeypoor were in the utmost distress, and the whole group of chieftainships was close upon collapse, when Lord Wellesley struck in. By the sharp fighting which ensued Sindia was politically disabled for life, and Holkar, after hunting poor Colonel Monson right across Rajputána, was himself driven off by Lord Lake, who smote him blow upon blow. But upon Lord Wellesley's departure our policy changed; we drew back from what seemed to Lord Cornwallis and Sir George Barlow a dangerous network of new ties and responsibilities, and we attempted to contract the sphere of British influence; that is to say, we left all Central India, including Rajputána, to take care of itself. The consequence was that which in India has always followed a retrograde movement, whether in the cabinet or in the field, the situation became much more dangerous; the great predatory leaders of Central India enriched themselves with the spoils of the country which we had abandoned to them, and became seriously arrogant and aggressive toward ourselves. These backward steps by the English in India, being always inevitably followed by an advance far beyond the original halting place, have come to be regarded by native politicians as a retreat *pour mieux sauter*, and have much helped to build up our popular reputation for deep perfidious calculations. In the present instance the attitude of "masterly inactivity" lasted nearly ten years, an unusually long term for India. Rajputána was being desolated during this interval. General Arthur Wellesley, the soundest of Indian politicians, had long before pointed out how the cessation of arms enforced over one large portion of India must for the time aggravate disorder in that other portion with which the pacifying authority refuses to interfere. Large bodies of disbanded troops go from the pacified or protected countries to become banditti too strong for the weak police of the States left by us to their own resources; while round these unlucky States the British Government establishes a cordon of rigid irresistible order which shuts up all the brigands of India within a ringfence. These were the conditions under which roving bands had increased and multiplied in Central India into Pindaree hordes, until, in 1814, Ameer Khan was living upon Rajputána with a compact army of at least 30,000 horse and foot and a strong artillery. That a regular army of this calibre should have been moving at large among the Rajpút States, entirely disconnected with any recognisable government or nationality, and absolutely free from the trammels of any political or civil responsibility, is a strong illustration of the condition of the country. The Rajpút chieftainships of Jodhpoor and Jeypoor had brought themselves to the verge of extinction by the famous war between the two ruling Chiefs for the hand of the princess Kishen Konwar, of Oodipoor. The story is well known and perfectly authentic (though it is precisely the kind which some future mythologist will prove to be an obvious solar myth); and the fact that these two States, surrounded by mortal enemies and in the direst political peril, should have engaged in a furious blood feud over a dubious point of honour, shows at once that the Rajpúts were a people quite apart from the rest of India, and strikes the primitive note in their political character. The plundering Marathas and Patháns, to whom such a *casus belli* must have appeared supremely absurd, encouraged and strenuously aided the two Chiefs to destroy each other, until the dispute was compromised upon the basis of poisoning the princess, a termination which very fairly illustrates the real nature of barbaric chivalry. The Marquis of Hastings thought it high time to interpose before Sindia and the Pindaree captains should have eaten up all the minor principalities and set themselves up as formidable fighting powers in their stead. He determined to extinguish the predatory system, to stop the annexations of the Maratha Chiefs, and to extend over Rajputána British supremacy and its correlative, protection and territorial guarantee. This was done by the treaties of 1818 and by the Pindaree war: the free companies were driven out; Ameer Khan and the Marathas were partly bribed to let go the Rajpút territories, and partly choked off by threats; there was a great restoration of plundered districts and rehabilitation of boundaries; the Chiefs acknowledged the British government as supreme political arbiter; and from that year internal peace has succeeded the war which, with one brief interval, had been chronic in and round Rajputána from time immemorial.

Thus it has come to pass that, as we began by saying, the only ancient political institutions now surviving upon any considerable scale in India have been saved by the English. There can be no manner of doubt that the Rajpút States would have been broken up in a few years had the English not interposed; their primitive constitution rendered them quite unfit to resist the professional armies of Marathas or Patháns, which included *corps d'élite* under European officers. The clans would have dissolved and become mixed with the great composite multitude of India, which is made up out of innumerable tribal dispersions; leaving only a few insignificant septs in the highlands of Central India, and some strong cultivating communities in the plains. The fortunate escape of these States has rescued out of the flood of ordinary Asiatic despotism what are perhaps the best specimens of early institutions that can now be found within the purview of comparatively settled civilization. But peace and prosperity are as disintegrating to primitive societies as war and rapine, though in a different way; nor is it likely that these institutions will remain many years without radical changes. And therefore some account of the more striking peculiarities of the Rajpút chieftainships has at least the interest that attaches to a photograph of things that are passing away, and that are sure not to re-appear in the world, when their day has closed and they have once left it.

There are, moreover, few things more important to the English, in their dealings with India, than a right understanding of the real constitution and historic growth of the Native States; for upon this subject misleading analogies and most fallacious misnomers have for at least a century influenced public opinion generally upon Indian affairs. The main source of these misconceptions may probably be traced back to the great Indian orations of Burke, who was never wearied of denouncing the oppressors of Indian nationalities, the degraders of ancient nobility, and the dethroners of sovereign princes. When, in 1784, he compared our possessions in India with the empire of Germany as "the nearest parallel"* he could find —likening the Nawab of Oudh to the King of Prussia, Cheyte Singh of Benares to the Prince of Hesse, the Nawab of Arcot to the Elector of Saxony, and classing the northern zemindars and the polygars of Madras with Counts and Bishops of the empire—he committed one of the most notable political solecisms on record. This may be called, literally as well as by Eastern metaphor, the great grandfather of all the false analogies that have since been current; and at the present day even the recollection of it must be still exceedingly painful to such sensitive historic nerves as those which vibrate at the slightest breath of a blunder regarding the Holy Roman Empire. The famous story of Warren Hastings' sale of the "whole nation of the Rohillas" is discoloured throughout by a similar abuse of the word nation, which has darkened the reality of the case up to our own day. Macaulay knew India much more closely than Burke; but he did not care to spoil

* Speech on Mr. Fox's East India Bill.

the rhetorical effects of his famous Indian essays by too minute accuracy. And one consequence has been that the best known writings about Indian politics have rather confirmed than dislodged the popular notion, drawn from very modern analogies in Western Europe, that a State under a distinct political designation denotes in Asia a territory occupied by a people of one nation under a king or ruler of their own nationality, as in France, England, or Spain at the present day.* It follows logically, from this conception of nationalities in Asia, that when the governing class in a State is known to be distinct in race and religion from the mass of its subjects, that State is vaguely supposed to be under foreign rule. But it cannot be too clearly understood that the unwilling subjection of one nationality to another, which in Europe is always supposed to constitute an oppression and a legitimate grievance, is a political condition absolutely different in kind from that forcible domination of one clan or family over other races or tribes which we so constantly find in Asia. It may be said broadly that from China to Constantinople the great States of Asia consist of heterogeneous populations under dynasties of foreign race. This may be called foreign rule, if we keep in mind exactly what the words, thus used, mean; but the meaning is not always quite clear even when the term is used by experts. Colonel Malleson, for instance, in his very useful book on the

* The history of modern India forcibly illustrates what is pointed out in Maine's Ancient Law that during a very long period of history no such conception has been entertained as that of territorial sovereignty. In India territorial political titles are extremely rare; if any exist, the English are almost sure to have had a hand in inventing them. Nothing can better mark the distinctive ideas of sovereignty which are described in "Ancient Law," than a comparison of the inscription on the coin of the Moghal Emperor in A.D. 1700, with that on the coin of the contemporary Chief of the Germanic Empire. On the former we read only that it was issued by Shah Aurungzeb Alamgir, with some religious titles on the reverse; on the latter we have all the great provinces of the house of Hapsburg claimed by different feudal or hereditary tenures. In Rajputána the State takes its name from its capital, the residence and citadel of its Chief; and the town itself almost always takes its name from the ancient Chief who founded it. This nomenclature is a peculiar sign of a præ-feudalic origin, if it is true that in feudalised countries the family always takes its name from the place, when the two names correspond.

Native States of India, says that the period of Mahomedan empire in India, from 1206 to 1707 A.D., is one of the longest periods of *foreign rule* which any country has ever witnessed. Even if Colonel Malleson here meant rule by an alien dominant race, the dominion of the Arabs in Spain was much longer; but he can only mean that the imperial throne was for five hundred years occupied in India by dynasties of foreign extraction, and since almost every Asiatic empire is or has been in a like condition, the casual reader would hardly have guessed him to mean so little. That these dynasties maintained themselves by force, is only an incident common to all tenures of extensive rule in Asia.

The first step, therefore, toward understanding the constitution of Native States in India is to keep in mind clearly that they are in no sense nationalities. The second step is to master the great difference in structure between different groups of these States. Colonel Malleson's sketch of the Native States (already cited) divides them into six geographical groups. His work deals mainly with the history of the reigning families, and with their external relations with the British Government, not with the internal economy of the States themselves. So that no ordinary reader would suspect a radical difference of constitution between the Maratha group and the Rajpút group, between the State ruled by Maharaja Sindia, for instance, and the conterminous State of Jeypoor or Oodipoor. Any difference existing between the two States would probably be assumed in England to mean this, that the Maratha Prince ruled over Marathas, and the Rajpút Chief over Rajpúts. But this would be all wrong; for there are very few Marathas in the dominion of Sindia, the Maratha Prince; while he probably has more Rajpút subjects than the Rajpút Chief of Oodipoor, the oldest Rajpút territory. The real difference is that Sindia is the representative of the single family of a successful captain of armies who annexed in the last century all the territory he could lay hands on, and whose son finally encamped so long in one place that his camp grew into his capital some sixty years ago; while the Rajpút Chief is the head of a clan which has for many centuries been lords of the soil which now makes up the Oodipoor State's territory. And this distinction of origin represents a vast distinction in the whole constitution and political classification of the two States. Sindia is a despot of the ordinary Asiatic species; ruling absolutely the lands which his ancestor seized by the power of a mercenary army; but the Rajpút chieftain is a very different personage, of a much rarer and more instructive type politically and socially; insomuch that some accurate description of this type may be useful and interesting even to general readers in England.

The word Rajputána, then, does not mean the country of the Rajpúts in the sense in which France now means the country of the French, but in that much earlier sense according to which Lombardy once denoted the country taken by the Lombards, and France the country occupied by the Western Franks. And a Rajpút State, where its genuine form has been least modified, denotes the territory over which a particular clan, or division of a clan, claims dominion for its chief and possession for itself by right of conquest and settlement. In the Western States the conquering clans are still very much in the position which they took up on first entry upon the lands. They have not driven out, slain, or absolutely enslaved the anterior occupants, or divided off the soil among groups of their own cultivating families, after the manner of the children of Israel entering Palestine, and of many another invading tribe in Asia. Their system of settlement was rather that of the Gothic tribes after their invasion of the Danubian provinces of the Roman empire, who "never formed the bulk of the population in the lands which they occupied, but were only lords of the soil, principally occupied in war and hunting."* In a Rajpút State of the best preserved original type we still find all the territory (with a few exceptions in favour of particular grantees) partitioned out among the Rajpúts, in whose hands is the whole political and military organization, though the mere officials, or agents in the internal administration, form on

* Finlay, Greece under the Romans.

influential class apart. Under the Rajpúts are the cultivating classes, mainly belonging to castes or clans whom the Rajpúts overcame when they took possession, and who now pay land rent to the lords or their families, living in village communities with very few rights and privileges, and being too often no more than rack-rented peasantry. Where either non-Aryan tribes, or tribes of the half blood (descended from irregular Rajpút marriages) exist, these hold together as subordinate tribal groups, and pay tribute. With these may be classed several peculiar clans inhabiting the outlying tracts, where they carry on just enough cultivation to disguise thereby their real profession, which is gang-robbery. In the towns are, of course, the usual mercantile and miscellaneous castes; a few of undoubted Rajpút origin, but disintegrated into separate castes by difference of occupation or of worship. And below all are the ordinary servile and menial castes, with the wandering casteless gipsies and others who, according to the Indian phrase, carry their house on their back.

Authentic history, as well as all tradition, points to the first band of successful adventurers as the nucleus out of which has grown directly the existing separate Rajpút State. A sept, or the offshoot from a sept, of a particular clan, sets out on an expedition, takes as much land as it can hold, and builds the forts which are still the palaces or strongholds of the ruling family. The case of Bikanír, a State in the desert on the North-West border of Rajputána, is a fair illustration. It was founded at the end of the fifteenth century by Bika, who was the sixth son of Jodha, Chief of the Rathore clan, which then, as now, possessed the lands that constitute the modern State of Jodhpoor. Jodha had twelve sons, and as the land available for their proper maintenance had become hard to find, he gave his sons a broad hint to do something for themselves. So Bika set off to win new lands, with five uncles, three brothers, and six hundred kinsmen. The expedition was also accompanied by men of the mercantile and writing castes; the land was gradually conquered, and to this day the territory of the Bikanír State is divided among the descendants of the original adventurers, the chieftainship belonging to the stock of Bika, while the posterity of the merchants and writers claim hereditary office. The whole story of this adventure is a counterpart of the episode of the Danites in the Book of Judges; when that tribe sought them an inheritance to dwell in, and six hundred men, "well appointed with weapons of war," emigrated to Laish, where they smote the people with the edge of the sword, built a city, and dwelt therein, while the sons of the Levite whom they carried off on their road remained hereditary priests of the sept. It should be observed, however, that the Rajpút immigrants are never stated to have exterminated those whom they found in possession of the land, as the Israelites seem usually to have done, but were quite content to remain the dominant minority. Of the 300,000 people who now inhabit Bikanír about 12,000 only are Rajpúts. The fact that the Rajpúts of Rajputána never settled down to cultivate the land which they divided off "among the tribes according to their families" (to use the words of the Book of Joshua), and that some of their clans have retained for so many centuries that earliest form of a conquering tribal settlement in which the victors merely distribute themselves as lords of the soil, is the prominent peculiarity of their history and existing political status. Elsewhere in India the Rajpúts form great cultivating communities; but this is where their Chiefs have long lost tribal sovereignty, and where the land, being very fertile, is very valuable. In the barren regions of North-West Rajputána where, as they say, there are more spears than spear-grass heads, and where blades of steel grow better than blades of corn, in such regions war and foray are more profitable than tillage, and this state of constant fighting kept the dominant clan together like a standing army.

Such being the origin and way of growth of a Rajpút State, the governing authority is, of course, in the hands of the hereditary Chief of the dominant clan. Mr. (now Sir Henry) Maine, when discussing in his Ancient Law the origin of primogeniture, observed that in India the succession to public office or political power forms an exception to the principle of equal distribution of property, being almost universally according to the rules of primogeniture.

"There seems, in truth," he wrote, "to be a form of family dependency still more archaic than any of those which we know from the primitive records of organized civil societies. The agnatic union of the kindred in ancient Roman Law, and a multitude of similar indications point to a period at which all the ramifying branches of the family tree held together in one organic whole; and it is no presumptuous conjecture that, when the corporation thus formed by the kindred was in itself an independent society, *it was governed by the eldest male of the oldest line.* It is true we have no actual knowledge of any such society."

This extract is taken from the third edition of Ancient Law published in 1866, and it is curious to remember that about that very time the author must have been occasionally in the company, at Simla or elsewhere in India, of Chiefs who hold precisely the position here described conjecturally at the head of societies of the very kind for which Mr. Maine was then searching. The passage is a fine example of successful deduction; since the conclusion that such an organization must have existed appears to have been reasoned out from the indication and structural characteristics of later forms, without any knowledge that the earlier species could actually be observed in existence. In Rajputána the Chief is supposed to be the nearest legitimate descendant in direct line from the founder of the State according to the genealogy of the tribe; and the heads of the branches from this main stock are the leading Rajpút nobles, the pillars of his State. And here it may be remarked, by the way, that it does not follow, because a tribe claims its descent from a god, that the divine founder is a personage entirely mythical, as certain comparative mythologers do vainly imagine. He is quite as likely to be a real hero deified, for the founder of at least one Rajpút State, who is authentic as any historic personage can be in India, is freely worshipped by his clan to this day. The Chief, therefore, must belong to certain families of the founder's kin; and among sons the succession now always goes by primogeniture, though the rule has by no means been observed from time immemorial. There are several good precedents showing that an eldest son has been passed over for another more worthy, though the reason for such a step must be extraordinary, and almost always the choice had to stand the test of appeal to the sword. But the characteristic of every important rule (political, religious, or social) in India is that, whereas it is always assumed in theory to be inflexible, it is nevertheless always readily flexible in practice. And it seems probable that primogeniture as the rule in theory of the demise of tribal sovereignty has prevailed ever since the first successful leader founded the State. If a Chief has no issue to his body, he can of course adopt a son in his lifetime from one of the founder's kin; but he has usually very sound reasons against giving some ambitious or impatient youth, or family, an interest in his death; and the same feeling has at the present moment much to do with the constant default of legitimate male issue from the marriages of the reigning Chief. In Lord Canning's viceroyalty, the British Government formally recognised the power of a childless Chief to adopt a successor. It was supposed that this would be regarded as a most valuable privilege, of which the Chiefs would avail themselves eagerly; but as a matter of fact they use it very seldom, leaving the choice of the successor to be arranged after their death. Thus a Chief too often dies childless, and then the successor must be chosen from among the branches of the founder's original stock, which are represented by the families aforesaid. Here again the nearest in degree to the deceased has a *primâ facie* right, though one by no means indefeasible; for the selection virtually lies, when there is any doubt at all, with the heads of the great agnatic branch-families, subject to a sort of wider appeal to the whole of the leading families of the clan. It is true that when the Chief dies without an heir, either by blood or adoption, the recognised form is that the widows shall adopt; but the person to be adopted is usually settled in concert among the widows and the leading families, and if the widows adopt without the concurrence of the kinsfolk, there is dissension, and a storm begins to gather. It has sometimes happened that the chief widow has been instigated by a cabal to adopt one whom the families do not desire for a ruler over them, or whose legal claim seems inferior; thence comes a rift which has often widened into civil war. The families are almost always in the right; they usually look first to birth-right, and secondly to capacity, requiring a fair combination of both; but the widow's choice is apt to be the result of some backstairs intrigue of which the object is to gain the regency for herself during a long minority with some favourite official of the Mazarin or Godoy type as prime minister. One or two families of the clan may join her, she gains over her mercenary forces, summons her own kinsfolk (it will be remembered that a Rajpút never marries into *his own* clan), and perhaps seizes the capital. Then the heads of the families retire to their own estates, muster their septs, declare the chief whom they have chosen, and fierce struggles have ensued between the two factions in days before the English arbitration had been thoroughly acknowledged. John Stuart Mill, in his Subjection of Women, made the striking general assertion that whenever any intervals of good government are recorded in the annals of native Indian States, it will be always found that a woman was concerned in them. Unluckily the same might be predicated of almost all violent paroxysms of misrule in India; so that upon a complete survey of experiences we begin to perceive that Mill's observation is only part of the wider popular generalization as to a woman being at the bottom of all strange or eccentric combinations of human circumstance. In regard to the influence of women on public affairs in India, all that the candid observer can fairly say is that, for good or for evil, princesses with a taste for politics have usually employed amazing energy toward gaining their ends, and have shown a remarkable aptitude for short and sharp methods with adversaries. In Rajputána an ambitious widow has at her peculiar command one resource for creating political dilemmas, that of declaring herself *enciente* immediately after the death of her husband, and of demanding adjournment of the question of a successor. But as to abide the result of this declaration would be to give ample time for spreading a complicated net of fraud and intrigue, with a long minority as the most favourable upshot possible, the nobles are apt to receive the announcement with disloyal scepticism, and sometimes to disregard it utterly. What they want is a man at the head of their clan, which is just what the palace or court party does not want.

Indeed, before the English stopped free fighting over debateable vacancies, and insisted on the establishment of some peaceable and fairly consistent practice of succession, even the eldest son, or whoever might be indisputably nearest of kin, was liable to disqualification on the ground of incapacity. There have been recent cases in which the clan simply chose the fittest kinsman of full age, though of course such an election raised issues to be tried by hard blows; but the political faction interested in a Chief's weakness or imbecility has usually been a minority, and the idea of divine right has not reached that phase when it is concentrated upon an individual. Divine right in Rajputána exists only in the primitive sense of right by descent from a divinised ancestor, and this divinity does not yet hedge a king only, but includes whole families within its aureole. Under English arbitration this scrambling custom of succession is being steadily though very cautiously moulded, by the natural bias of pacific influences toward consistency, into some less easily variable law of inheritance. Here, as elsewhere in India, the English found native institutions at the stage in which they are forms to which the facts usually, but not at all necessarily, correspond; the people obeying facts while they make immense show of respect for forms, and being only moderately distressed by glaring inconsistencies between the two. The English cannot, if they would, help compressing facts into correspondence with the forms they have recognized, being compelled to do so partly by the modern spirit which abhors inaccuracy, partly by our unlucky habit of purging by positive statutes the loose customs of the general weal, and partly because, according to our notions, there is no political continuity or regularity until forms and facts of this kind do correspond. For Rajputána, as for all other Native States, the imperial policy is to abstain from directing successions, and to let the natural guardians of the State settle doubtful cases. But when doubt warms into dispute, every one looks to the paramount power for a decision;

and the English, as we have said, cannot help deciding according to some consistent rule. And thus the practice of succession must tend gradually more and more to conform to a strict principle of indefeasible hereditary right. Now even in Europe this principle, as distinguished from the earlier practice which admitted also the claims of superior strength and fitness, has never been very successful in supplying decent kings, so long as kings were expected to govern as well as reign. The rule seems to answer well only in highly civilized kingdoms, where the competency or incompetency for actual government of the hereditary prince is a matter of indifference and the only thing essential is a stable principle. But Asia has never been able to develop any principle except that of personal government, in which the competency of the monarch is of the first and last importance. And in Asia hereditary succession actually means the succession to each vacancy of the ablest and most popular of the ruling dynasty or tribal family, the incompetent being rapidly eliminated as failures after short and sharp experiment. When no able man turns up for a dynastic vacancy, the dynasty collapses; but the tribal sovereignty stands on a much broader foundation, because the choice may range among half a dozen families, and the chance of finding a fit man is proportionately greater. If the unanimous voice of the elders of the tribe does not name the right man, he would have been identified in earlier times by the process of diligent fighting. But the English are being slowly compelled, by the necessities of orderly administration, to abolish this effective test of capacity to rule; and it is becoming very questionable whether any equally serviceable method of furnishing the protected Native States with tolerable rulers can be substituted. A strict law of hereditary succession to petty Asiatic despotisms is not a very promising political innovation; it renders the Chief independent of personal qualifications, and makes him reckless of offending any one except only the British Government. Meanwhile his people care little for him, having assured themselves that according to the present policy of the British Government, misrule does not involve annexation of the

State (the only consequence dreaded by the leaders of the community) but merely a change of rulers, which is often welcome, like a change of ministry in Europe. For the paramount power, having arrested the operation of the natural law by which the fittest ruler prevails, is compelled itself to maintain a kind of providential selection, and sometimes to depose incapable Chiefs. In Rajputána, however, the tribal institutions which still limit the personal government of the Chief, render interference by the supreme authority less necessary than elsewhere; and accordingly it is among these States that the new system has the best chance of working.

The condition, then, of hereditary sovereignty in a Rajpút State may be shortly described thus: The primary right to a vacancy is by primogeniture, and the sovereign is also the Chief of the clan, who is understood to represent the oldest and purest blood of the political group which traces back its consanguinity to the vanishing point of a far distant common ancestor. But even primogeniture must qualify up to a low standard of competency; and when direct heirs fail the Chief may be chosen from any branch of the common stock, the choice sometimes going from one branch to another, according to critical needs and circumstances, the electors being the heads of the branch families and the elders of the tribe generally. The constant default of direct heirs keeps alive this elective machinery, which would fall into disuse and decay under a powerful and prolific dynasty, as it has done elsewhere. A standard case in the matter of succession to Rajpút suzerainty is that of Kerowlie, a small territory on the eastern border of Rajputána belonging to a very ancient sept of the bluest blood. In 1852 its Chief died, aged fifteen years only, having adopted on his deathbed an infant descended through half a dozen generations from the third son of a common ancestor. Lord Dalhousie, *more suo*, raised the ominous question whether the Supreme Government was bound to recognize this adoption as conveying a right to succeed; and he appears to have been at first quite unconscious that there could be any rightful heir to a Rajpút chieftainship after the extinction of all lineal descendants of the Chief to whose heirs and successors the English had guaranteed the succession of Kerowlie in 1817. He held that the distant kinsman adopted was no natural heir at all, and that the adoption was an act which the Supreme Government might or might not sanction, as seemed expedient. It is curious, as showing the absence of exact knowledge, to find Lord Dalhousie minuting that the circumstances of Kerowlie resembled in all essential particulars those of the Maratha State of Sattára, whereas it was in all essential particulars that the two States differed. The question, whether this adoption made by the deceased Chief should be sanctioned, was referred to England for decision; but in the meantime the heads of the branch families (some thirty-eight in all) entitled to decide disputed successions to the Kerowlie chieftainship, had met, and they set aside altogether the adoption, electing instead a man of full age, descended from another son of the ancestor common to the late Chief and to the infant whom he had adopted. The widows went through the form of adopting this candidate, and the tribal elders then informed the British Government that this was their Chief, and that they would have no other. Probably they had got an inkling of the danger which overshadowed their little State, and thought that this was one of the critical conjunctures in the affairs of a clan when a man at their head is more useful than a child. "This is the reason," said one of their leaders, "for adopting a grown-up person, the splendour and government of the State are preserved; but by adopting a child injury and evil come upon the State." And in reply to a suggestion of some legal axiom (elaborated by an English officer) that only a child could be adopted, the Rajpút answered broadly that if any grown-up heir (*i.e.*, person of founder's kin) can be found, a child cannot be adopted, "because injury to the State is apparent from a child's reigning." This may or may not have been correct; but the two different views contrast very curiously two widely distant stages in the formation of a rule of hereditary succession. In the primitive stage the birthright is primarily subordinate to practical expediency, and infancy is a disqualification; in the latest and purely legal phase the rule disregards practical expediency altogether, and the adoption of a child is assumed to be in accordance with some law of nature. The Kerowlie Rajpúts adhered so steadily to their view and to their election, which was backed by unanimous public opinion throughout Rajputána, that the Government of India very wisely confirmed their choice. In the present day the feudal notion of a Rajpút State escheating in default of lineal descendants has vanished below the political horizon; but the foregoing example proves how important is accurate knowledge of the multiform societies with which an Indian Government has to deal, and how unsafe it is to follow imperfect European analogies. In the Kerowlie papers the words escheat, fief, suzerainty, and feudal superior, constantly recur. The analogy of feudalism so completely filled the mind of even our best writers upon Rajputána, that it is no wonder if Lord Dalhousie to some extent adopted it, though perhaps only as a convenient formula to aid his real convictions as to the right policy with Native States. He was much too great a statesman to be the servant of a formula; he may have intended to make the formula serve him.

But it was the interior constitution of a complete Rajpút State that most forcibly suggested the analogy of feudalism. A Rajpút State where its peculiar structure has been least modified, means the territory over which a particular clan, or division of a clan, claims dominion for its chief, and political predominance for itself, by right of occupation and conquest. A Rajpút chief is the hereditary head of a clan whose members have for centuries been lords of the soil, or of the greater part of it, within the State's limits. In the Western States, where the original type is best preserved, the dominant clans are still much in the position which they first took up on entry upon the lands. The whole territory is understood (for there are exceptions to every rule in Asia) to be divided off and inherited among the branch families of the dominant clan and their offshoots. The Chief himself possesses the largest portion, though not always a larger portion than the aggregate holdings of other families; and apportions very large grants to his nearest agnatic kinsfolk, providing of course for his wives and his predecessor's widows, and sometimes for their relatives. A few estates are owned by families of a clan different from the ruling clan, these being usually relics of a clan whose anterior dominion upon that part of the soil has been superseded; though this is comparatively an inferior tenure, except where these families have intermarried with the chief branches of the dominant clan. The proportion of territory under the direct administration of the Chief of the State varies widely in different States; where the clan organization is strongest and most coherent the Chief's dominion is smallest, and largest where the Chief is, or has lately been, a strong, energetic, and therefore acquisitive ruler. Large tracts of land are possessed by the hereditary heads of the branch septs which have spread out from the main stock, and by the kindred families which are as boughs to the great branches. Sometimes these branches have ramified into a numerous sept; sometimes they are represented only by a family; they take greater or lesser rank and power according to birth, possessions, and number. The family chief also apportions out his land among his nearest brethren; in fact he is the State Chief in miniature, and his group is a sub-group. The relations of these minor chiefs to the Chief of the State vary in different States; in some of the Eastern States they are little more than grantees of land or of rents assigned to them who pay some sort of fee to their suzerain, have a right to maintenance as the Chief's kinsmen, but have no political power. In the best preserved States of the West, as in Oodipoor or Jodhpoor, they exercise almost complete jurisdiction within their own domain, though not over all the domains of their family; and their obedience to the State Chief depends mainly upon his power to meddle with them. They pay him certain duties, regulated according to immemorial custom; they are bound to render military service against the foreigner or against rebels; and their lands are usually rated at so many horsemen to be furnished for the ordinary public service. At every succession to their States the heir is bound to do homage to the Chief, and to pay into the State treasury a fine of some value—these acts being essential to his entry into legal possession of his inheritance—he also pays some other customary dues of a feudal nature. In the States of the West, belonging to the Rathore and Sesodia clans, the domains of all the subordinate chiefs are rated at a certain valuation of annual rent-roll; and for every thousand rupees a certain number of armed horsemen and footmen must be provided for the State's service. The attempt has often been made by the rulers to commute this militia service for cash payment; but the great landholders have always resisted any such attempts with united obstinacy. They know well enough that to fill their Chief's treasury with hard cash instead of providing him with a rabble of their own retainers would be to transfer all real strength from their side to his. And their jealousy of his power never sleeps. Disobedience to a lawful summons or refusal to do homage involves sequestration of the lands, if the Chief can enforce it, *bien entendu;* and if the Chief has not got right on his side in a quarrel over the homage to be done or the fine to be paid, he will usually not find it easy to enforce his decree. On such occasions the lesser chief holds out in the ancestral fort as long as he can, and if the fort is made too hot for him, he may take to the wolds with a select band of brethren, where he is joined by the wild Bheels with their bows and arrows, by any professional banditti that may be prowling about, and by swashbucklers and landless loons generally. Here he sets up, like the injured Earl of Huntingdon in Peacock's Maid Marian, in the combined character of patriotic outlaw and generous reiver; his hand being against the commercial public generally —for young men must live, as Falstaff said at Gadshill, and gorbellied knaves with long purses are fair game—but specially against all officials, and very particularly against the officers sent to seize and administer his vacant estate. Usually these proceedings bring on compromise and a reconciliation; but at the worst the estate is only made over to another near kinsman of the outlaw; for it is very rarely indeed that an estate is ever confiscated outright and permanently annexed to the fisc by the suzerain. The whole federation of kindred families would combine against such an absorption if there were any practical alternative.

Around and below the chief of each family are his kinsfolk, which claim to belong to his sept, and hold land of greater and less extent, some independently of him, others on a sort of grant from him. Where the Rajpút himself cultivates he hardly ever pays any rent; his freehold has its original signification of the holding of a free man, as distinguished from the holdings of other castes and classes, which are assessed to land rents according to the soil, as elsewhere in India. Very commonly the petty Rajpút holds his fields on condition of service, of protecting the village or the roads, or of attending in arms on certain occasions; or it may be a special grant to compensate bloodshed, to settle a feud, or to reward acts of valour in the field. Sometimes these tenures represent the possessions of the remnants of an earlier Rajpút clan, which has kept its freehold rights to the soil. Excepting some special grants, all the lands either pay rent immediately to the ruling Chief, who must of necessity be a Rajpút, or to some minor chief within whose lordship they fall; or else they are held by septs and cultivating groups of Rajpúts, who pay a fixed quit rent to some overlord. And as in all these lands the lordship cannot, in the still surviving phase of society, pass permanently out of Rajpút hands by which they are held on a sort of noble tenure, it may be said that in the best preserved States the territorial dominion of the clan still survives unbroken. There are grants of land, mainly terminable, made by the ruling Chief to favourites and wives, while in the Eastern States there are some non-Rajpút beneficiaries; but all over the West it would be difficult to find a single important estate not held by a Rajpút. Then there are of course assignments of lands to temples and religious bodies, some of whom give nearly as much trouble to Rajpút Chiefs as ever churches and monastic orders did to mediæval European princes. It is difficult to deal with a holy man whose disciples are ready to bury themselves alive if the government puts pressure on their master for land taxes, and thus to bring down a curse upon the whole administration. This is the Hindu method of excommunication, very effective still in Rajputána, and not to be faced with impunity by the most powerful Chief. The best known remedy is to negotiate a private arrangement with some influential Balaam, whereby curses are suddenly turned into blessings. And, lastly, there are long stretches of wild and hilly tracts occupied by the aboriginal tribes, who pay tribute to the dominant Rajpúts and are nominally under the Chief's rule, though they swarm out like wild bees if he sends his police into their country. These are mostly in the South-Western regions of Rajputána.

But this is not the place for a complete and detailed description of the interior organization of a Rajpút State, or of the land tenures. Sufficient has been said to explain why the organization of Rajpút society has been almost always said to be feudal; and indeed the resemblance to feudal society is at the first sight striking enough. Even Colonel Tod, whose intimate knowledge of Rajputána has been never equalled, and whose work is perhaps the most valuable and exhaustive special study of Indian history and manners that has ever been produced, has been so far misled by the likeness as to miss the radical distinction between the two forms of society, tribal and feudal. Although he clearly understands the connection of those whom he calls 'vassals' with their suzerain to be affinity of blood, still he insists that the working system of Rajputána is feudal. He devotes several chapters to proving the extraordinary identity of the feudal incidents of the European system with that which he found at the beginning of this century in Rajputána; and it is he who is chiefly responsible for the introduction into writings about Rajputána of all those mediæval terms [escuage, reliefs, Knights' fees, subinfeudation, &c., &c.], which were seized upon as convenient phrases by others who had not Tod's intimate qualifying acquaintance with the facts. Now in these days the difficulty of eradicating a convenient theory is enormous, because the habit of general reading disseminates it so widely, and because even men who could collect and examine their own facts find it so much easier to go to the standard books of reference, where they can find some ready-made theory which helps them to arrange their facts; in short, because over-indulgence in book-reading and too implicit reliance on authorities produce an atrophy of the observing faculty. Colonel Tod, however, gathered all his materials at first hand; and perhaps we should not blame him for failing to see that his Rajpút feudalism was not the basis of the society, but an incomplete superstructure, and that Rajputána, as he surveyed it, was a group of tribal suzerainties rapidly passing into the feudal stage, which we now know to have been largely built up in Europe over the tribal foundations. He saw that a chain of reciprocal authority and subordination ran from the Chief downward by gradations to the possessor of one or more villages. The lands held by the head of a branch family in a clan he therefore persists in calling fiefs held of the Chief as of a feudal sovereign, and he quotes Hallam to show how the feudal structure was based immediately upon the necessity of mutual preservation—a compact between lord and vassal for exchange of service and protection. This identical compact he discovers in Rajputána; and yet the invaluable documents which he has cited might have shown him that the cement of the system was something much stronger than feudalism. The subordinate Chiefs of the Jodhpoor State had been driven from their lands by the oppression of their Maharaja, the head of their clan and the ruler of their State. They write thus (1821 A.D.) to Colonel Tod: "The Maharaja and ourselves are of one stock, all Rathores. His forefathers have reigned for generations, our forefathers were their ministers and advisers, and whatever was performed was by the collective wisdom of the council of our Chiefs. Whenever Marwar (the Jodhpoor country) was concerned, there our fathers were to be found, and with their lives preserved the land . . . . *When our services are acceptable, then he is our lord; when not, we are again his brothers and kindred, claimants and laying claim to the land.*" Again, we find the kinsmen in Oodipoor of the chief of Deogurh [called by Tod sub-vassals], himself a branch from the main stock of the Chief of the Sesodia clan, who rules Oodipoor, thus remonstrating against the head of their family: "When Deogurh was established, at the same time were our allotments; as is his patrimony, so is ours." These protests take their stand on rights far beyond the feudal conception; and indeed it is universally assumed in every clan of Rajputána that the Chief and Ruler of the State is only *primus inter pares.*

It is of course easy, for those who write after reading the History of Early Institutions, to prove that a society of this nature is by origin primitive and præfeudalic. Sir Henry Maine's remarkable power of insight into the real meaning and connections of archaic customs so alien to modern ideas as to be ordinarily incomprehensible, and his luminous generalizations upon the materials found scattered over these obscure fields of research, have greatly influenced local inquiries in India. He surveys and marks out the whole line of penetration into difficult and entangled subjects, and workers in the field are constantly verifying the extraordinary precision of their chief engineer's rapid alignments. In the actual condition, for example, of the Rajpút clan-society, with its tribal Chief at the head of a cluster of families and sub-families, each having a separate representative, we find a living illustration of that set of ideas to which Sir H. Maine points as the true origin of some European aristocracies, the conception of an aristocracy deriving from blood alone, the families being noble according to the degree of nearness of their consanguinity with the pure stock of their Chief, and nobility depending entirely upon a man's position in his own clan, while outside of all the clans there is no nobility at all. There are in most States a few noble families belonging to a clan different from that of the territorial Chief; but we can usually trace them back to the group upon which the clan now ruling imposed its supremacy by conquest, and with these the test of nobility is intermarriage with the ruling tribe. If they intermarry, they also are of good Rajpút blood, though the clan is alien. Land tenure is not the base of this noblesse, but their pure blood is the origin of their land tenure; from the vast estates of a sub-Chief who lives in independence almost complete at the head of a branch family which has multiplied into a sept, down to the single free-holding Rajpút who is bound to follow his kinsmen to the field. We have thus the starting point for a wide survey of the filiation of historic institutions. Let us imagine Bernier, who travelled from Paris to Delhi toward the end of the seventeenth century, surveying the whole line of connection between the Rajpút noblesse and the noblesse of Versailles. At one end of the range he might have seen, in India, a primitive stratification of society, having its superior and subordinate layers divided by kinship, its tenures of land (excepting religious tenures) corresponding to distinctions of birth, its hereditary officials forming a separate caste, and the mass of its commercial and cultivating population ranked in classes altogether apart from the 'upper ten thousand,' as the Rajpúts might be literally called in more than one State. At the other end he would have seen Louis XIV. of France, absolute as an Asiatic despot throughout his dominions, having reduced his nobles to political nonentity while he admits a Montmorenci to be a better gentleman by descent than himself. At Ajmere as at Versailles the noblesse of blood is predominant and rigidly exclusive; but in Rajputána the noblesse are the clan, and the clan is the State. Whereas the French nobility has passed clean through and beyond the feudal phase, and has not only lost its political independence or influence, but for the most part even its hold on the land, yet it still hangs together as a separate caste by the archaic tie of blood. The wear and tear of a thousand restless years has hollowed out the primitive organism into a thin shell, which breaks at the first serious social pressure.

Side by side with these two extreme forms of true aristocratic institutions we have in the history of Asia, as of Europe, specimens of societies in which the primitive forms have been utterly crushed out and obliterated. "The only man noble in my dominions," said the Emperor Paul of Russia in reply to a question as to the status of Russian nobility, "is the man to whom I speak for the time I am speaking to him;" and Sir H. Maine observes* how such a pretension would have been resented in Bourbon France, by the Duc de St. Simon (we may add) for example. The Russian answer is just what might have come out of the mouth of a Moghal Emperor of India in the seventeenth century, speaking of his own courtiers and high officers; while the resentment of a Rajpút Chief

* Early Institutions, pp. 137 and 138.

at the bare notion of such a status would have been ten times as great as a French noble's. The Rajpút is most punctilious on points of etiquette, knowing the value of forms in keeping up substantial rights* when one has to do with princes; and the tradition of common ancestry has preserved among them the feeling which encourages a poor Rajpút yeoman to hold himself as good a *gentilhomme* as his Chief, and immeasurably superior to a high official of the professional class. Yet, as was said at the beginning of this chapter, there is no more favourite commonplace about our English rule in India than that it has levelled the native aristocracy; though it is impossible to do much levelling upon a dead flat, such as had been prepared for us by the steam-roller of Mahomedan despotism and its satrapies. The only ancient aristocracy which the Mahomedan Emperors spared in Upper India survives still among the tribes which they could not subdue or break up, and the only aristocracy which they set up consisted of a few lucky individuals who managed to hold and transmit for a few generations the grants of land obtained as rewards for service,†

* "Le goût des formes, choses ennemies de la servitude."—Tocqueville, Ancien Régime.

† The following extract from Bernier's Travels in the Moghal Empire may give some people a new view of the status of grandees at the imperial court:

"It must not be imagined that the omrahs or lords of the Mogul's court are members of ancient families, as our nobility in France. The king being proprietor of all the lands in the empire, there can exist neither dukedoms nor marquisates; nor can any family be found possessed of wealth arising from a domain and living upon its own patrimony. The courtiers are often not even descendants of omrahs, because the king being heir of all their possessions, no family can long maintain its distinction, but, after the omrah's death, is soon extinguished, and the sons, or at least the grandsons, reduced generally to a state bordering on mendicity, and compelled to enlist as common men in the cavalry of some omrah. The king, however, usually bestows a small pension on the widow, and often on the family; and if the omrah's life be sufficiently prolonged, he may obtain the advancement of his children by royal favour, particularly if their persons be well formed, and their complexions sufficiently fair to enable them to pass for genuine Moguls. But this advancement through special favour proceeds slowly, for it is an almost invariable custom to pass gradually from small salaries and inconsiderable offices to situations of greater trust and emolument. The omrahs, therefore, mostly consist of adventurers from different nations, who entice one another to the court, and are generally persons of low descent, some having been originally slaves, and the majority being destitute of education. The Mogul raises them to dignities, or degrades them to obscurity, according to his own pleasure and caprice."

often as bigots, lackeys, or panders. It is worth noting that the Emperors were never able to reduce the Rajpút Chiefs even to the status of beneficiaries, or to pass them into the feudal stage proper, for the plain reason that even if the Chiefs were willing their kinsmen were not; and the ruling Chiefs had never sufficient power to have their own way in a matter of this sort.

It must not be inferred from what has been written above that the political organism of the ruling clan prevails with equal integrity in all the Rajpút States. It is least damaged in the Western and North-Western States, which are held by the clans of the Kuchwáhas, the Rathores, and the Sesodias; but even in these States the organism is, as we have shown, much overlaid by feudal growth, the state of incessant war having prominently developed the obligations of military service. Nowhere, however, has the system become entirely feudal; that is, nowhere has military tenure obliterated altogether the original tenure by blood and birth-right of the clan. There are a few real beneficiaries, but their tenure is acknowledged to be special and inferior; and as the tribal Chief is kept in order by his powerful kinsmen, so the powerful kinsman has to reckon with his brotherhood. The only class that can be taxed or bullied in real feudal fashion is the non-Rajpút peasantry; but even here the cultivator is so valuable that he must not be driven away. In the Eastern Rajpút States, which were most exposed to the disintegrating ravages of the Moghal and Maratha, the tribal organization has been much effaced politically, and the Chief has centralized his power and acquired almost complete jurisdiction over the whole of his territory. So that whereas in the North and West a ruling Chief could not break through the compact front which his clansmen would at once oppose to any serious political encroachment, and has a dubious jurisdiction within the domains of his leading kinsmen, in the South a Chief rules a State more or less under his own administrative orders, and a population of which his own clansmen form but a small part. In these States, indeed, the chief families are decaying into a French noblesse, living on the rents and fees of estates assigned to them for maintenance, a distinct class with right to appear on all State occasions and to be provided for upon the lands, but having no independent strength or separate following, while the ruler is gradually centralizing all power. It is manifest that these Eastern States have long been rapidly sliding into the normal type of ordinary oriental government, irresponsible personal despotism; and these are precisely the States which were nearest to the brink of destruction when the English interposed in 1817. In this stage of the decay of the tribal system, when a Rajpút Chief has managed to cut away all round himself the power and independence of his kinsmen, the State topples over at the first vigorous push like any other ephemeral Asiatic principality. It is a sound political as well as a mechanical truth that you can have no real support without resistance, or the capacity to resist.

We may conjecture that primogeniture, as a rule of political succession, was born out of a combination between expediency and the right of blood. To have any settled political existence a tribe wants a leader, but as that leader must be of the purest blood of the founder of the tribal dominion, the choice is restricted to founder's kin. Among these the candidate most likely to unite the two desiderata, purity of blood and influence in the society, is the eldest son of the last ruler; and thus may come to be formed the rule of primogeniture, always conditional upon qualification for the office, which has governed succession to tribal States in Rajputána. The advantage of primogeniture as the first step toward political amalgamation may be measured by observing that in one or two very peculiar tracts of Rajputána, where the rule has never got established, the septs have never been able to build up any political system at all. On the Western border of Rajputána is a tract called Mullánee, nominally within the territory of the Chief of Jodhpoor. It is possessed by a sept which claims descent, every man of them, from the divinized ancestor of the whole Rathore clan; by a line earlier and more direct than that of the Jodhpoor Chief himself, the acknowledged political head of the Rathore clan. According to primitive ideas this superior lineage gives a clear right to demur at discretion to the Jodhpoor

Chief's authority, and the sept being wild borderers, fond of feuds and forays, any good pretext for demurring to established authority is heartily welcome. But the peculiarity of this sept is that though it descends from one stock, it has no chief of its own; it is made up of a number of distinct family groups, each separate and independent under its head. And the land is not only parcelled off among these groups, but there goes on a constant struggle between the ordinary rule of Hindu succession to property, which divides off the land among the sons at each succession, and the rule of political expediency which inclines toward primogeniture. The ordinary outcome of this struggle is a sort of inchoate primogeniture, allotting a larger portion of the family lands and superior authority to the elder heir of the chief family in a group. But the blood feuds, family and faction fights, and general anarchy caused by these chronic quarrels over the land are incessant, and have totally prevented any political consolidation of the sept into a State. The whole tract would long ago have been incorporated quietly into the Jodhpoor State, to which it does nominally belong, had it not been an outlying country, full of hardy caterans not easily tamed. There is at the North-East of Rajputána another tract in a very similar condition, peopled by the Kuchwáha clan, of whom the head is the Jeypoor Chief, to whom this sept owes an allegiance that is very unpunctually paid. Here again this sept consists of the descendants of a son of an ancient Chief of the main stock of the Kuchwáhas who went forth and conquered this tract on his own score and private venture. They have never formed a State under one tribal leader, and they still continue in the molecular condition of an uncertain federation of family groups of different magnitudes, usually dividing and subdividing the land down to the point consistent with some kind of cohesion for self-protection and the recognition of a head to each family. These groups seem to represent the fluid unconsolidated stage of tribal aggregations, before they have begun to crystallize round an acknowledged head, and to harden into political shape. And latterly the consolidation of these septs has been greatly hindered by the policy of the Chiefs of Jodhpoor and Jeypoor, who being unable to control these unruly communities became alarmed lest they should unite under one head and become formidable independent rivals. With much the same motive as that which, according to Sir H. Maine, induced the English to gavel the lands of the Irish Papists and make them descendible to all the children alike, the Jeypoor Chiefs used all influence to push forward among the refractory sept the custom of equal division of the land among males on each succession; using it as a wedge to split up the groups as they began to form. Under this impetus each field has in some villages been repeatedly parcelled off into lots of heritage; and as no real central authority has been imposed in this tract, the interminable blood-letting over these landmarks has effectively kept down the strength of the sept, and prevented political amalgamation.

Marriage plays so important a part both in the political and social systems of the Rajpúts that some brief description of it is essential. The invariable custom is, to use the term introduced by Mr. J. F. McLennan, that of exogamy, or the custom which prohibits intermarriage within the clan, so that every clan depends, for wives, upon the other clans; for of course no Rajpút can take a wife elsewhere than from Rajpúts. Thus a Rathore clansman, for instance, could never wed a woman from the most distant sept that bears the Rathore name; if he does, the children are certainly not pure Rathores, whatever else they may become. The custom is very widespread and well known all over Asia; but the Mahomedan law (of which the peculiar effect is to break up the archaic tables of prohibited degrees) has very largely obliterated it, and now it could hardly be better exemplified than in Rajputána, where we can trace it directly and palpably back to its source in the assumption that the whole of a great clan scattered over many distant parts of a large country are kinsfolk. Here, as wherever exogamy prevails, marriage by abduction of the bride flourishes universally in form, however it may have decayed in fact; and the ceremony may be witnessed in great perfection at any marriage in high life, when the bridegroom arrives with his wedding band of armed kinsmen, who clash their arms and rush in with a shout upon the bride's party. It can be easily understood that exogamy has always operated to stimulate jealousies and heart-burnings between clans, and to make the taking of a wife a still more troublesome and perilous business than even in civilized life. For it leaves the supply of wives in the hands of a neighbouring clan, always jealous, and often at open feud, who may suddenly refuse to give their daughters, as in the famous story of the war between Israel and Benjamin. Disputes over brides and betrothals have been important in Rajpút history. Socially the custom makes marriage difficult by narrowing the field of selection, for neither can a man go very far among strange tribes to seek his wife, nor a father to seek a husband for his daughter; so that a poor man often does not marry at all, while a rich man of high birth is besieged with applications for his hand, in order that the stigma of an unmarried daughter may at least be formally removed. And if there were space here, we might give some curious facts to show how this difficulty of marriage has been one cause of that constant *morcellement*, or splitting up into isolated groups, the larger group into smaller ones, which is a radical law of the dynamics which govern the construction of primitive societies. In the old war times many companies of Rajpúts took service with the Emperors in their distant expeditions to the frontiers, and were placed under their own leader in charge of the distant border forts. They settled on the lands close round these forts; became the hereditary garrison; and their descendants may be found occupying the ruined inclosure to this day. But as these military colonists could not, by reason of distance and the dangers of travel, obtain wives from the legitimate clans, they sometimes took wives in the country of their adoption, and sometimes intermarried among themselves. In the former case they unwillingly founded a new sub-caste; in the latter they cut themselves off from the parent clan, and became a separate impure clan, with numerous internal subdivisions. Then again the disintegrating effect of sectarianism among the Rajpúts must at one time have been great; for there are in Rajputána some distinct castes who appear to be of pure Rajpút origin, but to have been detached many generations ago by following a peculiar religious movement. When a Rajpút turns aside after the new light shown by one of the spiritual teachers who are incessantly arising in Hinduism, and completely adopts a new way of life, he exchanges a tribe for a caste. And it appears (though the subject is very obscure) that whereas his tribal bond of consanguinity extended round his whole clan, in the caste his kinship is at once narrowed down to that section of the great caste group which was originally Rajpút. The most famous sect in Rajputána holds within its pale no less than 1,444 distinct groups; all apparently formed by this process of partial accretion, intermarrying one with another, but never *within* themselves. In this instance, so far as can be learnt, all this spreading reticulation of spiritual relationship has grown out of the teaching of a single revivalist who appeared only four centuries ago. There is also in Rajputána a very curious fraternity of warlike devotees claiming to be founded by a Rajpút who seems to have been a kind of fighting ascetic, disdaining any other garments save shield and sword belt; and these men, being vowed to strict celibacy, recruit their ranks by adoption, purchase, or abduction of children. The orphanage of old-fashioned India for males is a religious order. But irregular marriages are in Rajpútána the commonest source of a fresh group formation.

The institution of fosterage of course flourishes among communities so distinctively of the primitive Aryan type as the Rajpúts. And though the foster-family of a Chief is never of the Rajpút clan, but belongs almost always to some particular family of a well-known pastoral tribe, yet the foster brothers often attain much influence and position at his court; and the family has a recognized hereditary status of "kinship by the milk."

After this manner, therefore, does the cross of blood, the change of faith, or other variation from ancestral custom, continually operate to cut off the diverging family from the parent species, which is kept pure through this careful pruning away of unsound offshoots. And thus the pure Rajpút clans are those great kindred groups which have kept immaculate the rules and conditions of exogamic connubium throughout the genealogy of their tribal tree in all its branches, every family showing its pedigree leading back to some branch, however insignificant, which springs out of the original stem and root of the tribe. This is the real aristocracy of India, with which every Hindu dynasty and family of influence or new wealth (except Brahmans) tries to find, beg, or buy a connection, from the petty non-Aryan Chief of the Central Indian woodlands to the greatest Maratha ruler, the kings of Nepal, and the half Chinese princes on the far North-Eastern frontiers of India and Burma.

We have left ourselves no space to describe any class of the population of Rajputána beside the Rajpúts, or much might have been said of the enterprising commercial and banking class who made their head-quarters in the fenced cities of Jodhpoor and Bikánir, oases in the desert which marauding bands could not reach, and who conducted exchange operations all over India in the midst of the anarchy of the eighteenth century. There is much vague talk about the English rule in India being the paradise of money-makers; but the great bankers of Upper India with one accord look back regretfully from these levelling times of railway and telegraph to the golden days of immense profits upon daring ventures, when swift runners brought early secret news of a decisive battle,* or a great military leader offered any terms for a loan which would pay his mutinous troops. In those times a man whose bills were duly cashed in every camp and court of the Northern Provinces had often to remit specie at all hazards, and the best swords of Rajputána were at the service of the longest purse. A tremendous insurance policy was paid to some petty chief or captain of banditti, who

* One of the few picturesque touches in Grant Duff's History of the Marathas is where he tells how Bájee Rao, the great Peshwa, lay in camp on the bank of the Nerbudda, waiting anxiously for news of the grand army which he had sent to conquer North India. He could hear nothing until his scouts brought in a runner they had stopped, who had undertaken to run in nine days across India from beyond Delhi to Aurungabad in the Deccan, with a cipher message to some bankers from their correspondents in the North that the Maratha army had been routed with vast slaughter on the plains of Paneeput.

undertook by hook or crook to cut his way across country and deposit the treasure at its appointed place, and who almost always discharged his contract with great daring and fidelity. Something might also have been said of the curious religious sects and divinities of Rajputána, and much of the non-Aryan tribes. But this must be merely a sketch of institutions that are interesting not more by their past history, than by the speculations which are suggested as to the transmutations which await them. Change these institutions must, and rapidly; for under the weighty pressure of the English empire everywhere we see the old order changing, giving place to new, because the English rule is itself such an entire alteration of political circumstances in India. The future of these States is a question well worth the deepest consideration of those who guide the policy of our empire, because, as we began by saying, these States contain the only ancient institutions in India which have shown stability, and are worthy of free men. Every other indigenous experiment at political development in India has broken down; during the last eight centuries there have been none except ephemeral tyrannies, a hopelessly sterile species. The Rajpút States, in spite of all their defects, stand out in marked contrast against the native despotisms which we overturned, or those which we still protect and endeavour to improve in India, or against the Moghal empire at its best. Our modern notions are apt to make us too readily disgusted or disheartened with turbulent nobles, a weak central administration, a bad police, and a general indifference to the great civilizing watchwords of order and progress. And each ruling Chief, in proportion to his dexterity or ambition, attempts to enlist these notions on his own side against his nobles. Now that he no longer needs the support of his powerful kinsfolk against external enemies, he feels their restraint upon his internal authority. They help him neither in the field nor in the cabinet, for there is no such usage as would necessitate an assembly of the notables; and the minor chiefs often live apart in their forts, hating and hated by the supple ministers who advise their ruler, who are of another caste altogether, and whose interests are on the side of centralized and absolute power. It is easy to see that the tendency of modern officialism would be to strengthen the sovereign against the nobles. We have the same feeling of impatience with these troublesome half-barbarous communities that prompted, and still prompts, many able men to rejoice at the crushing out of the Polish kingdom, with its quarrelsome Diet and unreasonable assemblage of tumultuous nobles; which contained nevertheless more life and promise of free development than the dull immovable bureaucracy, Russian or Austrian, that has succeeded it. Military rulers in Europe, and experienced European officials in India, declare that order and a strong centralized government is the one thing needful. So it is; but if plants are to be hardy, we must give them time to grow. It is certain that these Rajpút societies, held together by all the cumbrous bonds and stays of a primitive organism, present far more promising elements of future development than powerful and well-ordered despotisms of the normal Asiatic type, where a mixed multitude are directly under the sway of one ruler, however able, who degrades or dignifies at his will. Let any one contrast the account which we have here given of Rajpút institutions with the descriptions which Bernier (an excellent observer, and a subject of Louis Quatorze) gives of society under the Moghal empire in the seventeenth century, a period when it was still flourishing like a green bay tree.* Nor is there much ground for hoping that we are likely soon to see in any native Indian State a race of princes so able as the descendants of the Emperor Baber, or that European education and tutorial

* Take this passage as a sample—"Instead of men of this description" (opulent, educated and well born) "the Great Moghal is surrounded by slaves ignorant and brutal; by parasites raised from the dregs of society; strangers to loyalty and patriotism; full of insufferable pride, and destitute of courage, of honour and of decency. The country is ruined by the necessity of defraying the enormous charges required to maintain the splendour of a numerous court, and to pay a large army maintained for the purpose of keeping the people in subjection. No adequate idea can be conveyed of the sufferings of that people. The cane and the whip compel them to incessant labour for the benefit of others, and driven to despair by every kind of cruel treatment, their revolt or their flight is only prevented by the presence of a military force."

superintendence by English officers will rear up generations of wise and benevolent Rajahs and Nawabs. The reigning families of India have to guard themselves against rapid deterioration under the listless security produced by our protection, by the absence of personal danger, and above all by relief from the fear of serious internal revolts, of foreign invasion, or general tumults and commotion. In the present condition of political security, bringing general ease and prosperity, the surroundings are too strong for artificial training; when a youth is set up and propped up safely as a golden image of wealth and power he becomes careless, and is apt to go wrong as a ruler, if there is nothing to stop him but the English government, which is always averse to frequent interference with the internal affairs of a State. In Rajputána alone there do actually exist the natural institutions which, in various forms and stages, have checked and graduated the power of sovereigns all over the world. The incessant bickering and contests between encroaching Chief and jealous kinsmen; the weak central power; the divided jurisdictions; the obstinacy with which a man of high birth insists on the proper punctilio to be reciprocated between himself and his Chief—all these are the tokens of free society in the rough. To make haste to help the Chief to break the power of his turbulent and reactionary nobles, in order that he may establish police and uniform administration over his whole territory, is to an Englishman at first sight an obvious duty, at the second look a dubious and shortsighted policy. If these rough hewn obstructions to helpless equality under the orders of a central government are once smoothed away they will assuredly never be built up again; and as there is nothing that could take their place, the tribal chieftain will have converted himself into a petty autocrat, responsible for his doings only to the paramount power which sustains him. Now the protected autocrat in a native Indian State has not as yet turned out such a success that the English nation can feel proud of having brought him out upon the political stage. So it will be wise to have patience with the wild ways of Rajputána as long as we can, to abstain as much as possible from interference, and to maintain, so far as we do interfere, the equilibrium of weight between Chief and nobles, until it can be adjusted by the light of improved intelligence and education on both sides.

Whether such a time will ever arrive, is an open question with some who, like the Comte Gobineau,* affirms that the civilization of Europe never has taken, and never will take, root among the old races of Asia. And, looking to the present social condition of the Rajpút clans, it is much to be feared that they are declining fast in vigour and in numbers. It may be possible, indeed, that throughout Asia the warlike tribes are decaying under the spread of European dominion, which seems to be favourable mainly to the prosperity of the industrial races, the soft weak populations which swarm in the tropical low lying regions. But these races have no real political future, and only damage free institutions by burlesques that we shall some day become tired and ashamed of bringing out under the patronage of Her Majesty the Queen. If it be true, therefore, that a more polished and reasonable despotism is the only political improvement that Europeans are likely to introduce into India, then no sacrifice of modern notions of uniformity is too great for the object of preserving as long as possible in the Rajpút countries these last relics of institutions which have elsewhere proved fruitful in their development of some real advantages to political well-being. It must be confessed that the tribal system appears occasionally to stand right in the path of reforms which to an European appear of prime and peremptory necessity. The system would fall in a few years before an efficient State army, or even a strong police, in the hands of an able Chief; it would be ground to atoms under the regular mechanism of effective law courts after the Anglo-Indian model. The chicane of half civilized *avocasserie*, that bane of all British India, would make short work of all these vague customs and unwritten privileges. And when we have confessed that these primitive institutions are at present incompatible with the machinery of civilized law and police, many persons will reply that they stand self-condemned.

*"Trois ans dans l'Asie."

Nevertheless, it will be a pity if these institutions, which have survived such perilous ages, and have resisted so many despotic dynasties, should now under the dominion of a free people succumb prematurely to the cankers of a calm world, before it is clearly understood how the void which they will leave can be filled up.

# CHAPTER IX.

## ISLAM IN INDIA.*

[(*Theological Review*, 1872.)

Dr. Hunter's literary skill and success as a writer on India—Reference to Mahomedan grievances as stated by Dr. Hunter in his "Indian Musalmàns," and by Colonel Lees in a pamphlet—Remarks and criticisms upon these statements, and upon the real position and feelings of Indian Mahomedans—Brief historical retrospect of our relations with the Mahomedans, and of the cause of events leading up to the existing situation, in which the English have succeeded to the political supremacy over India relinquished by the Mahomedans—Question whether religious texts or rulings have much practical effect on the acts or attitude of Mahomedans—Observations upon the inevitable anomalies and difficulties surrounding English Government in India—Some discontent and disappointment among Mahomedans unavoidable—Syud Ahmed's polemical controversy with Sir William Muir—Unpopularity of Wahábis among Mahomedans—The educational policy of the Indian Government, how far it actually deserves the imputation of formidable errors and grievances—Examination of specific charges; nature and effect often exaggerated—Explanation of our general policy; the substantial complaints against it mainly founded on incidents inseparable from the situation; to be remedied by time, goodwill, steady and impartial administration, and the general spread of our civilizing influences.

Dr. Hunter's book on "Our Indian Musalmàns" was read with much interest, and even with anxiety, by all persons to whom secular and religious politics are a matter of serious concern. The author is very well known in England as a writer on Indian topics: indeed, it is now some years since he reached a grade of literary reputation perhaps never before so fully attained by an Anglo-Indian official. Any book which Mr. Hunter sends from India for publication at

* 1. *Our Indian Musalmàns. Are they bound in Conscience to rebel against the Queen?* By W. W. Hunter, LL.D. 1871.

2. *Indian Musalmàns. Being Three Letters reprinted from the Times, with Four Articles on Education, and an Appendix containing Lord Macaulay's Minute.* By W. Nassau Lees, Fellow of the Calcutta University, late Principal of the Mahomedan College at Calcutta, &c.

3. *Essays on the Life of Mahomed.* By Syud Ahmed Khan Bahàdur, C.S.I. [Published in India, 1870.]

home, is widely read by the public at large and carefully considered by the best judges. Hitherto those who have acquired special personal knowledge of India, have very rarely possessed also the gift of imparting it in the style and shape demanded by the high standard of even popular literature in these days; and of the few good writers who have intimate practical acquaintance with Indian administration, hardly one has succeeded so well as Dr. Hunter in drawing immediate general attention to Indian affairs. Macaulay is, of course, a signal exception: his famous essays actually created the public opinion almost universally held to this day upon the great political strokes by which certain resolute Englishmen towards the end of the last century carved out and consolidated our empire in Asia. Those great historical cartoons of the exploits of Warren Hastings and of Clive have stamped their impressions ineradicably upon the mind of ordinary readers, insomuch that if the average Englishman knows anything of such things, he implicitly believes Macaulay's version of them; and it would be vain to protest that, though this historical oil-painting (as Carlyle calls such works) is magnificent, it is not always history. But so strong and enduring is the influence of trenchant phrase and picturesque language, that many of the mistakes and over-coloured statements contained in Macaulay's sketches of thirty years ago, have been vigorously reproduced by Mr. W. M. Torrens, in a book named "Empire in Asia," which he published in 1872.

The motive and reason of Dr. Hunter's treatise are explained in one of his earliest pages, where he says that "the Musalmans of India are, and have been for years, a source of chronic danger to the British power in India." This danger is caused by "the spirit of unrest," which Dr. Hunter proceeds to exhibit in its threefold form: in the formation of a Rebel Colony on our North-western frontier, which has involved us in constant disasters; in the treasonable organization of Musalmans within our interior districts; and in the legal discussions that have arisen upon the question which Dr. Hunter has chosen for the title of his work—"Are the Indian Musalmáns bound in Conscience to rebel against the Queen?" He goes on further to examine the grievances of the Mahomedans under English rule, and to point out means of remedying them. In short, he inquires into the sources, historical, political and social, whence has flowed the disaffection, which Dr. Hunter holds to be deep-seated, wide-spread and imminently perilous to our government. In accordance with this programme, the opening chapters of the book are allotted to a brief and animated description of the foundation and fortunes in Arabia of the sect called *Wahábis;* of their establishment on our North-western border by a famous saint and martyr; of the rapid spread of the Wahábi doctrines throughout India by fanatic missionaries; and of the constant petty wars and internal seditions which have been traced entirely to this Wahábi propaganda. I shall not follow Dr. Hunter along his narrative of these events, which should nevertheless be known to all readers who desire to comprehend whence came Wahábism into India, and how it has fared there. I am bound, however, to observe that there are certain peculiarities in the style and manner of this spirited historical sketch (and indeed more or less throughout all this book) which must be taken into account by home-keeping Englishmen who desire to draw accurate and safe conclusions upon the subject which Dr. Hunter has handled so skilfully and attractively.

Dr. Hunter is before all things vigorous, clear and definite; he rejoices in strong lights, in highly-finished episodes, and in full-length portraits of personages. He excels in the art of lively scenic representations of Indian history by artistic and effective use of European metaphors and phrases for Asiatic events and institutions, whereby his ideas and allusions are made to appear quite luminous and suggestive to educated Englishmen who begin with this work their study of an unfamiliar topic. But it is impossible that the original facts and local peculiarities should not suffer even by the most skilful paraphrase or travesty; for Indian figures cannot be dressed up in European costume without some damage to their native character and complexion. So that the similes and historical illustrations in which Dr. Hunter luxuriates are often more striking than exact; they have not in Asia, where he applies them, the same connotation that they have in Europe, whence he borrows them; they convey some notion of the truth, but not the whole truth; and, moreover, the author is at times sorely vexed by an hyperbolic fiend which he would do well to cast out. With these premonitory observations, the book may be commended to all persons seeking in England to gather evidence and frame a judgment upon some of the complications and contrasts which are incessantly growing out of that extraordinary political accident, the English dominion in India.

The pamphlet by Colonel Nassau Lees is a reprint of three letters in the *Times*, which were called forth in 1871 by Dr. Hunter's book, and of four articles on Education which originally appeared in Indian journals. He has appended to them a Minute written in 1835 by Macaulay, when he was in India, upon the system of higher State education to be adopted in that country. Colonel Lees was Principal of the Mahomedan College at Calcutta, and is altogether entitled to a respectful hearing upon the condition and feelings of Mahomedans in Lower Bengal: his argument, which we shall examine at length farther on, is mainly directed towards exposing the mistakes of our educational policy in India, and the fallacies contained in Macaulay's Minute, which had immense effect at the time; and toward attempting to demonstrate how the system of instruction which has hitherto been employed has had the grave consequence of depressing the social and political status of our Mahomedan fellow-subjects.

Now as this paper is intended to give some account of what may be termed the "Mahomedan question" in India, and as Dr. Hunter and Colonel Lees both put the case on the Mahomedan side quite as strongly as it can fairly be made out, it may be convenient to take from these authorities a precise statement of the main grievances which the Indian Mahomedans are said to allege. I remark, with all other critics on Dr. Hunter's book, that he draws his facts very largely from the province of Lower Bengal, and applies his inferences to all India, a process somewhat defective in logical fairness. However, here is his chief indictment against the British Government, drawn up in sentences composed after the style of Macaulay, though this is no necessary imputation on the substance:

"There is no use shutting our ears to the fact that the Indian Musalmans arraign us on a list of charges as serious as have ever been brought against a Government. They accuse us of having closed every honourable walk of life to professors of their creed. They accuse us of having introduced a system of education which leaves their whole community unprovided for, and which has landed it in contempt and beggary. They accuse us of having brought misery into thousands of families by abolishing their Law Officers, who gave the sanction of religion to the marriage tie. . . . They accuse us of imperilling their souls by denying them the means of performing the duties of their faith. They charge us with deliberate malversation of their religious foundations, with misappropriation of their educational funds. They declare that we have shewn no pity in the time of our triumph, and with the insolence of upstarts have trodden our former masters into the mire. They . . . arraign us for want of sympathy, want of magnanimity, mean malversation . . . and for great public wrong spread over a period of one hundred years." *

These are the accusations with which I propose to deal hereafter in some detail; they make up the gravamen of the plaint stated for Mahomedans by their able and somewhat impassioned advocate; and the matter cannot be debated without joining issues on these points. But I must first say that I doubt whether these sharp-set sentences really present to us the actual feelings and utterances of the general body of Mahomedans; I am more inclined to affirm that they derive their force and weight principally from the rhetorical power and the imagination of the writer, who is evidently determined that his case shall not lose by any over caution about stating it. The words quoted are the language of a Pole under the Russian régime; of a Greek under Turkish despotism fifty years ago; of an Irish Papist under the furious penal laws of the last century; of some crushed nationality, or of some people vindictively oppressed and ground exceeding small in the mills of political tyranny. Stronger expressions could not have been employed if we Christians had done unto the Indian Mahomedans as Mahomedans have elsewhere done so often to Christians; if we had persecuted them as Aurungzeb persecuted Hindus, or treated them with the hatred and savage cruelty shewn to unbelievers by Hyder Ali or Tippu of Mysore.

* Indian Musalmans, p. 145.

Whereas the Mahomedans of India in the present day are (excepting the lowest classes) very good Oriental politicians, with fair knowledge of the world and of Asiatic history, and with some traditional experience of what bad governments really are; they know much better than Dr. Hunter the real meaning of the strong words which he so lightly puts into their mouths; they could not possibly so misunderstand our antecedents and their own, and their present circumstances, as to regard themselves as persecuted, or as reduced, the whole community, to contempt and beggary; they judge us, fairly enough, by the Oriental standard of *fas* and *nefas* as applied to rulers, and they appreciate the situation not incorrectly. They may still take some umbrage at our supremacy; they dislike some parts of our levelling administrative system; most of them are prejudiced against all Christians by the religious rivalry of a thousand years, and against English residents in India by violent contrasts in the habits and manners of East and West. But many of the charges alleged by Dr. Hunter seem too profoundly unreasonable and far-fetched to be entertained, even as popular delusions, by the mass of Mahomedans; while the words, "want of sympathy, want of magnanimity, mean malversation of funds," and "great public wrongs spread over a century," appear to me to convey only ideas and expressions selected by an English orator as likely to have a striking effect upon an English audience, if it can be persuaded that this is how the natives of India actually think and speak.

Colonel Nassau Lees writes in a cooler tone, and regrets that Dr. Hunter should have "out-Heroded Herod" in the fervency of his pleading for Mahomedans; but Colonel Lees also supplies a list of specific counts upon which the British administration is arraigned—the more important of them being our treatment of the education and the endowment of Musalmans. Both authors admit that above and around these particulars grievances there are other sources of dissatisfaction and disloyalty which were inevitable, and flowed naturally from the facts of Indian history; yet both of them appear to be led by a propensity and a desire to connect every kind of discontent with those blunders and faults for which the English can be directly blamed. Dr. Hunter, especially, seems to confound the essential with the accidental, to attribute to local and temporary causes symptoms which are inherent in and inseparable from our relations with the Mahomedans, and to interpret their indistinct regrets and uneasy murmurs by the notions and literary conceptions of a highly cultivated European bred in a totally differing environment. The consequence has been, that he views, and makes his readers view, many things through a false perspective, and estimates the weight of his facts in a deceptive balance. Or where he preserves a truer eye and hand for dealing with such phenomena, his sense of proportion tempts him to exaggerate and over-colour English shortcomings and errors, in order to present adequate causes for the extreme results which his line of argument attributes to them. Now it cannot and need not be denied that some disaffection still survives among certain classes of the Mahomedans in India: we all know that the colony of outlaw Wahábis founded beyond our North-western frontier among the wild hill tribes, must obviously be as bitterly hostile to the English in the Punjab as it was to the Sikh government which preceded us; while Mr. W. Palgrave* has told us long ago, that throughout Asia the spirit of Wahábism is a spirit of uncompromising fanaticism, which seeks by all means, secret or overt, to upset any rule, whether of Turk or Englishman, that restrains bigoted and furious intolerance. It is true also that these Wahábis at one time formed secret conspiracies of a serious kind in the province of Bengal, and that their plotting was connived at or willingly ignored by a crowd of non-Wahábi Mahomedans, who would naturally prefer the predominance of their religion, and have no objection to allow the Wahábis to try their hands at pulling the chestnuts out of the fire. It is certain that the Indian Mahomedans have not altogether grown out of the sore feelings and the heart-burning which accompany everywhere the fall from high position, the loss of power, and the descent of a despotically dominant class to fair equality with all others before a firm law. But unpleasant reverses of this

* Travels into Eastern Arabia.

kind occur constantly in the history of societies as of individuals; they are inseparable from the competition and struggles for mastery which have hitherto been the conditions of all progress in this world; and the Mahomedans, a high-spirited community which has had its share of political adventure and triumph, are not incapable of accepting with dignity such changes of fortune. It may be questioned whether the termination of a period of supremacy and the succession of a foreign government are changes as acutely felt by a community which is bound together with the tie of a common faith, as they are by a tribe or by a modern nation; and whether nationality, which is a bond quite unknown to Indian Mahomedans, be not much the more sensitive constitution. Yet undoubtedly all these things make up for the Mahomedans of India a case which requires delicate and forbearing treatment by their successors in chief sovereignty, although it was not England that pulled down the rule of Islam in India, which had fallen to pieces before we began to build up an empire; and we may concede that the English Government, with all its good intentions and high integrity for the last sixty years, has often failed to treat such difficult and complicated disorders with skill and tenderness. We are not famous, if Mr. Matthew Arnold reads us aright, for sweetness and sympathy in our dealings with subject peoples; we are too much inclined to rely upon the force of material interests for our work of fusion; to fancy that personal liberty and comfort will compensate for the wounds which our success must necessarily inflict on the pride and the prejudices of those whom we follow in political supremacy: we reckon too much on the interests of men, and too little on their passions. It may be owned that we are not always very light-handed ministers to the Oriental mind diseased. But this is a very different matter from confessing that we are responsible for the disease itself, or that it exhibits any peculiar symptoms or mysterious virulence that could only be accounted for by our reckless neglect and ignorance, or by sheer malignity.

We may at once assume that our conquest of India has been distasteful to the Mahomedans, and that their hostility may be, in certain contingencies, a matter of great concern to ourselves.

For the present we cannot help this; all that we can do is to inquire how far these unavoidable resentments can be allayed; whether the specific grievances that exist are just and reasonable; and if we have unwittingly wronged the Mahomedans by our acts, we must do them right. But nothing can be more vain or more impolitic than to foster in their minds the notion that we English are chiefly responsible, as administrators, for the condition in which the Indian Mahomedans now find themselves, or to encourage them to mistake natural sentiments of disappointment, of depression and of wounded religious pride, for the just indignation of an oppressed people or a persecuted sect.

To obtain a clear view of the situation now before us in India, we must go a few steps back. Politics and religion are with the Mahomedans (as Mr. W. G. Palgrave has lately said) two sides of the same medal; it is impossible even to approach the religious side of the Mahomedan position in India, without surveying first its political aspect.

The rule of the English in India so immediately followed the fall of the Mahomedan suzerainty, and has been so widely built up on the ruins of their great empire, that the popular mind naturally imputes to us all the misfortunes of the Mahomedans. But all readers of history know that the Moghal Empire had been severed piecemeal and dilapidated by the middle of the eighteenth century, and that province after province fell into our hands because the imperial government was rotten to the heart and paralyzed in every limb; while we alone were able to drive off the Maratha vultures which were tearing the moribund carcase. When we had driven the Maratha out of Agra and Delhi, the defenceless capitals of extinct Mahomedan dominion; when we had secured the Moghal emperor from affronts and captivity, we found all the Punjab, the land where Mahomedans had been strongest, in the hands of the Sikhs. Every one knows what it cost us to break that formidable fighting power, which had completely subdued the Mahomedans, and had even driven the Affghans out of the Trans-Indus country, and had confined them to their hills. In the south we had, at the end of the last century, saved from imminent certain destruction the Nizam, the greatest Mahomedan prince then, as now, in India; we supported and even set up again some minor kinglets, who from being viceroys had made themselves independent; others we pulled down and pensioned off: our policy was governed by the currents and chances of a long and perilous struggle. Of course the benefits we conferred have long been forgotten, while the injuries remain ever fresh. That the pensioned descendants of usurpers or of puppets should now be regarded by their fellow-religionists as the ill-used heirs of legitimate dynasties, is comprehensible enough; that acts of State which were moderate and by comparison merciful in the old days of war and tumult, should now be condemned as unscrupulous and greedy, is to be expected. But it is a curious thing to find Englishmen ready to sit down and weep with the Mahomedans, and to employ their literary skill in denouncing as oppressors the men whose hardihood and endurance in winning for England an empire were equalled only by the general justice and patience with which they pacified and administered it. There is something like a false note in these remorseful palinodes, something like the inclination to abandon in quiet times those who served us well and unreservedly in days of war and tumult. We all know what sort of legacy David bequeathed to the sons of Zeruiah, whose ready swords cleared away rivals and rebels from his path to the throne; and England seems occasionally to display a liking for that same kind of pious atonement. Those who resolutely uphold an empire recently founded, who are determined to bequeath to their children the great heritage they hold in trust from their fathers, must bear the brunt of such odiums and qualms of conscience; but the ancient smouldering resentments will die away as the edifice settles down. At this moment, however, when England is almost too ready to do penance for the high-handed misdeeds of those who won India for her, when the Mahomedans have neither wholly forgotten the old order of things, nor have become properly reconciled to the new, it is unfortunate that many causes combine to bring home rather closely to Indian Mahomedans the natural consequences of their political downfall. So long as the old fighting times lasted in India, we heard little of widespread grievances. The Mahomedan in that country was an adventurer by descent and by profession; he or his fathers (I except here the tribes of converted Hindus) had always entered the country from Western Asia in search of military or civil employment; he was very rarely a colonist or a merchant; he was usually a soldier of fortune. During our long Northern wars, the Madomedans enlisted willingly in our armies, and followed our victorious standards against Goorkhas, Sikhs and Marathas; they marched with us to Kabul and Kandahar, cities of the Muslim; and to this day they fight for us most gallantly against the wild tribes on the debatable frontier lands between India and Affghanistan. Dr. Hunter makes much of the fanatic Mahomedan hatred which provoked us into the Umbeyla campaign of 1863 against certain independent tribes in the hills just across our North-west frontier; and he traces the causes of this expedition back to the malevolence of our own subjects; but he might have mentioned how, when in that short but hard fought campaign a famous outpost of our position was lost and re-taken by the British Indian troops after a bloody struggle, a Mahomedan was one of the two officers who then led the storming party against the best and most fanatic fighting men of the frontier, charging sword in hand uphill under a shower of rifle bullets.* Thus in active military service the Mahomedans have always been loyal enough; and they held office under us contentedly, so long as we kept up the native system of civil administration, in days when surveillance was lax, the standard of education low, and officials more powerful than ever because they represented an irresistible government.

* Dr. Hunter alludes (page 12, Indian Musalmàns), to "the descendants of the Rohillas, for whose *extermination* we had venally lent our troops . . . and whose sad history forms one of the ineffaceable blots on Warren Hastings' career. Their posterity," he says, "have taken an undying revenge, and still recruit the Rebel Colony on our frontier with its bravest swordsmen." It is not true that we lent our swords for the extermination of the Rohillas; at any rate it is clear they were not exterminated, as they left a numerous posterity; but who would have guessed, from this passage, that their posterity at the present time recruit the British army in large numbers with some of its bravest and most loyal swordsmen?

But the second Punjab campaign of 1848 laid all India at our feet; the great wars of conquest were finished, and after them came "the cankers of a calm world and a long peace:" at home the reins of civil and military discipline were tightened, so that not much wealth was to be gained rapidly under our administration by the pen and still less by the sword; while we gradually annexed Nagpore, Jhansi and Oudh, thus abolishing courts and camps which still afforded some chances for the irregular ambition of a lucky captain or an adroit courtier. Long ago, General Arthur Wellesley had pointed out in his Despatches how the discontent of the adventurous classes in India, of the men who live by an unscrupulous head or hand, must become more and more exasperated by the constant spread of our arms and authority; by the imperious régime which maintains the peace of India, which insists upon universal order and truce among allied states as well as in subject territory. And all this process of transition from the old immemorial way of life to the new pressed with peculiar stringency upon the Mahomedans, to whom, from the warlike chiefs of gathered clans like Nadir Shah and Ahmed the Abdallee, down to the poorest highlander who followed their standards from Central Asia, India had for centuries been the Eldorado where stirring times brought speedy fortunes. All this spirit of unrest (to use Dr. Hunter's phrase) was brooding over India when the great mutiny broke out among our Hindu Sepoys. In Delhi, Lucknow, and other centres of disaffection the Mahomedans at once caught the contagion of rebellion, and almost immediately seized the lead of it, using the wild, aimless fury of the soldiery for their own compact and straight-pointed political designs. The consequence was, as all can recollect who were in Northern India in 1857-8, that the English turned fiercely on the Mahomedans as upon their real enemies and most dangerous rivals; so that the failure of the revolt was much more disastrous to them than to the Hindus. The Mahomedans lost almost all their remaining prestige of traditionary superiority over Hindus; they forfeited for the time the confidence of their foreign rulers; and it is from this period that must be dated the loss of their numerical majority in the higher subordinate ranks of the civil and military services. Before the Mutiny they largely outnumbered the Hindus in all the best offices which could be held by a native in Northern India; after that period they fell to a minority, and although they are no way responsible, as a body, for the misconduct of certain sections of their community in 1857, yet in certain provinces they have naturally had some hard work to recover the ground which was cut from under them when they made that last desperate spring after the shadow of a lost empire.

This brief historical retrospect was necessary, because the present religious temper of the Mahomedans is the reflection of their political and social misfortunes. It is easy to understand how these misfortunes must have stirred up fanaticism in certain sections of a community bound together and circumscribed into one pale, not by nationality, but by their faith; to whom the dissolution at the end of the last century of their Indian supremacy was a direct catastrophe for the religion which enjoins them to set up and pull down kingdoms in its name. As Colonel Lees observes, the laws of the Koran were framed for conquerors; and though texts can always be found to warrant prudence and the tactics of common sense, yet such interpretations conflict inevitably against the whole tone of their Prophet's message, and jar upon the whole framework of his system. Much learning and logic have been expended by Mahomedan schoolmen of late upon the nice sharp quillets of the law of Islam, to inquire whether it permits submission to an infidel yoke, or absolutely enjoins resistance even when resistance is not politic and the yoke easy. And Dr. Hunter writes,* almost as if he verily believed it, that "the obligations of the Indian Musalmàns to rebel or not rebel hung for some months on the deliberations of three Suni priests in the Holy City of Arabia" (he refers to the fact that the doctors of Mecca were consulted as to whether Mahomedans might lawfully yield us quiet allegiance); and he devotes a whole

* Our Indian Musalmàns, p. 11.

chapter to balancing the import of various expositions by different schools of the texts which bear on this point. He seems rather to enjoy alarming home-bred English readers by inclining the weight of authorities towards the conclusion that a war of extermination is a necessary act of faith. But, on the other hand, Syud Ahmed, in a series of letters published in India in 1872, undertook to demonstrate that the duty of *Jihád*, or religious war, is not at all imposed on Mahomedans by their actual relations with the English in India, and that Dr. Hunter's inferences from the Koran and its commentaries are overstrained and even quite unwarranted. He maintains, moreover, that the *Futwas*, or authoritative decisions which declare that Indian Musalmans are in no way bound to rebel, were not elicited by the anxiety of the Musalmans to relieve tender consciences or doubts as to their duty, but by the constant suggestions and nervous fancies of the English, who pressed the point upon them, until they were obliged to set themselves right before the world. And we see how this explanation becomes probable, when we find Colonel Lees telling us in one of his *Times* Letters * how he argued the case of the Indian Muslim in solemn earnest with the *Sheikh-ul-Islam* at Cairo, each disputant brandishing his own text; one being, " Kill them wherever you find them ; " the other, " Ye are in no wise bound to rush upon your own destruction." Of course the result of setting flat against each other a negative and a positive command like these was to produce a dead-lock, a logical stalemate ; but such games have no influence on the real business of the world. Fanaticism is the steel point of the spear-head, but cool and wary people take care how they brandish the weapon ; and no one risks his life on a text, unless it fits in generally with his own views and calculations, and justifies what is otherwise convenient and opportune. All the debaters admit that in practice no body of Mahomedans is likely to be driven into hopeless revolt by an ecclesiastical decision, as if execution followed a decree of the Sheikhs against a formidable government as necessarily as it follows a judgment of the Privy Council against heretical clerks.

* P. 7 of the pamphlet.

For the truth is, that all this painful examination of texts and authorities only illustrates what I have remarked upon before, the tendency of certain writers to attribute to special and local causes those sentiments of indisposition towards us, and of religious aversion from us, which belong naturally to the general constitution of the Mahomedan faith in its present intellectual phase and in its actual circumstances in India. These things have really very little to do with readings of the sacred books, or with the *Futwas* of Mecca. The Mahomedans, with their tenets distinctly aggressive and spiritually despotic, must always be a source of disquietude to us so long as their theologic notions are still in that uncompromising and intolerant stage when they openly encourage the natural predilection of all devout believers for the doctrine that their first duty is to prevail and, if need be, to persecute. To most Englishmen of the day, this condition of thought may appear a strange anomaly, it is only an anachronism; the unquiet spirit now abroad in India is no other than that spirit which troubled all Christian Europe for so many centuries, and which even in England has not yet been quite exorcised by the modern doctrine of toleration, or the modern affection of indifference. It is the spirit which so long upheld passive resistance to a heretic ruler to be a sin against God; because (to quote the words of Calvin*) "although obedience toward princes accords with God's service, yet if any princes usurp the authority of God, we must obey them only so far as may be done without offending God." And since the theologian claims the right to define God's jurisdiction, so that anything that touches the interests of a religion is assumed to offend the Deity, while in his service all acts are held to be justifiable, it is manifest that no merely secular government, maintaining the ordinary limits of civil jurisdiction, can hope to avoid offence. A government so placed—and the Indian Government is so placed—will always find itself exposed, whatever it may do, to great misrepresentations; to a sort of general reprobation,

* D'Aubigné. Reformation in Europe.

rather conventional and for consistency's sake perhaps than real and heartfelt, from the mass of even reasonable and easy-going religionists; and to virulent overt sedition from the extreme zealots. In India, although the thorough-going hot gospellers may be few and unpopular, as are the Wahábis; yet, like a feeble fire under a large cauldron, they serve to keep lukewarm the sentiments of the great majority, who are nevertheless very far from boiling up into dangerous explosion, or from allowing themselves to be driven by theologic fervency into following the lead of forlorn hopes against impregnable material facts. But while the Mahomedans evade by elastic glosses any conclusions which seem plainly desperate and beyond reason in practice, yet the sentiment which justifies to itself violent assertion can never be entirely dormant in an exclusive monotheistic religion, which claims as a right and duty universal spiritual despotism, while it has been levelled down by a neutral government to mere denominational equality. It would be contrary to all experience, if this sentiment did not occasionally stir up the corresponding antipathies which civilization and the considerations of sound policy have very nearly laid to sleep among Europeans. It would be rash to declare that Christians in India are yet altogether free from the old spirit which included crusading among the solemn duties of a faithful ruler; and there have not long since been English officials who would have desired nothing better than to try conclusions with the Wahábi at his own weapons on his own extreme principles, and to determine which doctrine was orthodox "by apostolic blows and knocks." Impartial Mahomedans must needs recognise the expediency of making allowance in Christians for that same tincture of sincere intolerance, and the same conscientious irreconcilability with the professors of doctrines thought to be false, which they themselves hold to be very excusable in matters theologic. But this lurking belief of the duty on both sides to contend against each other *à outrance*, this conviction that each religion is bound to destroy the other, must occasionally embitter the resentment of the party which holds secondary political rank; it may rouse and foster suspicions that the more powerful faith will use unfairly its secular predominance. In spite of all disclaimers put forth by the English Government, our ill-wishers have always raised against us the cry that we desire to compel persons to embrace our religion, and this is still widely credited by the ignorant crowd. In a volume of Travels in India, lately published by a Parsee of Bombay, the writer mentions how "strongly impressed" were certain Mahomedans, with whom he conversed, "with the belief that their rulers were now intent on making the people of this country converts to Christianity by all means in their power." Nor can we wonder that this sense of keen emulation between Christianity and Mahomedanism in the same country is stimulating, in India, that spirit of Mahomedan revivalism which is reported to be abroad throughout all the countries which profess Islam, even in those where the faith is triumphant and holds undisputed monopoly of the State's support.

Moreover, these two great rival religions have at last found in India not only a common mission field, but also a common arena and audience for polemical controversy. Hitherto the writers on either side have scarcely ever joined fair issue in argument, or opposed each on the same ground; the Christians have demolished the pretensions of Islam to Christians, at their leisure; the Mahomedans have denounced Christianity before Mahomedans; the two hostile camps were separated by different tongues and by a great interval of distance between their respective head-quarters. But now the Englishman in India is an Arabic scholar; and the Indian Mahomedan studies English works. Sir William Muir writes a Life of Mahomed, with critical examination of the canonical scriptures upon which the traditional evidences of Islam are based; and he has at once found a gainsayer in Syud Ahmed Khân Bahâdur, a distinguished officer of the government over which Sir William as Lieutenant-Governor of the North West provinces, lately presided. Although Syud Ahmed was himself born too late for acquiring that knowledge of English which would enable him to meet English critics with English writing, yet in Arabic he holds himself on a par with the accomplished author of the Life of Mahomed, whom he shows no reluctance to meet on neutral Asiatic ground with his own weapon. Instead of bigoted contempt and invective, we have now a fair literary argument and a beginning of scholarly exegesis. Syud Ahmed naturally dissents widely from the view taken of Mahomed by the Christian biographer; and the effect of Sir William Muir's work upon his mind "was to determine him to collect, after a critical examination of them, into one systematic and methodical form, all those traditions concerning the life of Mahomed that are considered by Mahomedan divines to be trustworthy."* The completion of this plan was hindered by several obstacles; but he has presented to the public twelve Essays, which constitute the first volume of his Life of Mahomed, chiefly intended (we infer) to correct and refute certain views and conclusions of Sir W. Muir. It was perhaps imprudent for the able Mahomedan champion to rely upon second-hand learning and on interpreters for his material for a critical dissertation in regard to the meaning of the Greek versions of the Christian Testament; as when he insists that in the passage which says, "It is expedient that I go, for if I go not the Comforter will not come,"—the word *παράκλητος* is a corrupt reading for *περικλυτος* = the *famous one* = Ahmed = Mahomed; and that Christ is thereby proved to have prophesied of Mahomed as the necessary successor and complement of his own divine mission.† This method of verbal disputation, which makes the acceptance or rejection of a mighty revelation to the leading races of the world depend upon a copyist's error or a monkish forgery, has fallen somewhat out of favour in modern European polemics: we want a broader basis for our theories of religious cataclysms. But Syud Ahmed is more successful when he desists from his attempt to prove the mission of Mahomed out of Christian Scriptures, and takes to retorting upon others the generalizations and philosophic reflections which have been employed to cast doubt upon the authenticity of the Mahomedan canon. Thus Syud Ahmed extracts from the life of Mahomed such passages as (for instance) these: "The habits of the early Moslems favoured

* Preface to the Essays, p. xix.

† Essay on the Prophecies.

the growth of tradition." . . . "On what topic would early Moslems descant more enthusiastically than on the acts and sayings of their Prophet?" . . . "The mind of his followers was unconsciously led on to think of him as endowed with supernatural power; here was the material out of which tradition grew luxuriantly . . . . the memory was aided by the unchecked efforts of imagination." . . . . "Superstitious reverence was the result which lapse of time would naturally have upon the . . . narratives."* And then he asks with some point whether the miraculous deeds of Moses, or the prodigious histories of other great prophets whom Christians revere, must not also be contemplated through the same medium of calm and large-minded rationalism. He claims, in short, for Mahomed the same indulgent and respectful consideration which is accorded by all zealously devout persons to the records of the words and acts of those whom they incline to hear as a preacher sent from God; or else he desires that all miraculous histories shall be subjected to the same dissolvent analysis.

But to return from this digression to the main line of my essay. I have now gone hastily over the historical conditions and consequences of our position in India, which account very sufficiently to my mind for some unavoidable unpopularity of the English Government among a large class of Mahomedans. Taking these things into account, it would, I believe, be much nearer the truth to say that the inconsiderate and uneducated mass of them are against us, than that the "best men are not on our side," as Dr. Hunter too invidiously affirms. That author appears to lay too much stress upon the significance of the spread of Wahábism in Lower Bengal, among a comparatively depressed and unwarlike Mahomedan population. Syud Ahmed, in his letters to the Indian Pioneer (1871), denies that even the Wahábis consider that their situation under the English in India justifies a holy war; and he mentions that in 1857, when the mutineers held Delhi, Bakht Khan, the rebel commander, endeavoured to compel the Moulvies of that city

* Supplement to the Essay on Traditions.

to declare lawful a *Jihâd* against the British; but was boldly withstood and opposed by two leading Wahábis. If these two learned doctors came forward spontaneously at such a time to deny the legality of the *Jihâd*, the instance is a very strong one: but if the fact was that they had been called upon by Bakht Khan, a famous mutineer, to put their signatures to such a declaration while the English were bombarding the city, it is possible that they had noticed the lines of the English batteries pushing gradually nearer, and had reflected upon that text quoted some pages back from the Koran, about true believers not being bound to rush upon destruction. But whatever may be the real convictions of Wahábism, without doubt its followers are few throughout all India, and are intensely unpopular with all other sects of Mahomedans in provinces where Mahomedan loyalty is infinitely more important to the security of our Government than in Bengal proper. In many parts of India, the appearance of a Wahábi preacher is the signal for sharp internal discord; the *odium theologicum* breaks out at once. It is some years since the Nizam's government at Hyderabad expelled the Wahábis for breeding endless strife in that great Musalman city, where it was not safe to attend religious revivals without sword and buckler; and very recently a Wahábi teacher came down to the province of Berar, in the Hyderabad country. He was an earnest reformer, and the abuses which he denounced were patent; but in a few weeks he had quarrelled with the chief Moulvies of their district over questions of theology and ecclesiastic discipline, with all the Pharisees, and with Demetrius the silversmith, upon backslidings connected with worship at shrines, and the ungodly gains made by trading upon superstitious usages. All parties virulently accused him of sedition against Cæsar, that is, against the Queen's Government. The British officials, taking a broader view of their duty than did the Roman Gallio, not only refused to interfere in a dispute about religious law, but also took measures to preserve order and prevent violence to any man, and the Wahábi was placed under the special protection of the police.

I have thus attempted to set forth my view of the causes of Mahomedan discontents with us in India, by shewing that these causes are for the most part innate and congenital with the growth of our empire there. But Dr. Hunter and Colonel Lees have brought up prominently a series of particular grievances, and these it is right to examine. Dr. Hunter, especially, devotes a whole chapter to the wrongs of the Mahomedans, which he declares to have been inflicted by blunders criminal enough to free our subjects from their obligation of allegiance.* Now many of the most important facts and figures on which he relies in this section of his work have been briskly challenged, whether successfully or otherwise cannot be positively decided; but without going into these details, I propose to look into the substance of some of the graver charges laid by him, and by Colonel Lees against the Indian administration.

Colonel Lees and Dr. Hunter both deduce very serious and wide-reaching consequences from the educational policy inaugurated in 1836 by a very characteristic Minute of Lord Macaulay, who then held office in India. The question was, how to apply the State grant toward higher education; whether the public instruction to be subsidized by public money should be English or Oriental; whether the languages, science and philosophies of the West or of the East should be encouraged by the State. Macaulay was altogether in favour of the West; and he beat down all opposition by his brilliant and impetuous attack upon Orientalism. He said that a single shelf of a good European library was worth the whole native literature of India and Arabia; that it was not decent to use the public funds for bribing the Indian youth to read books full of monstrous lies and blunders; and so on with startling antitheses as usual, securing a great triumph to the Anglicists. From that day English (to use the words of Colonel Lees †) "has been recognized as the medium of higher education in India, and the subjects taught in it have been entirely European;" and Colonel Lees declares the effect of this change was "the gradual and steady transfer of the civil government of the

* Indian Musalmans, p. 143.

† Pp. 24, 25, of the pamphlet—Letter to the *Times*.

country from Mahomedans to Hindus." Now this sweeping assertion illustrates the rhetorical practice of which complaint has been made elsewhere in this essay, of tracing back great events to slender origins of a special and narrow kind; and certainly the very contrast between minute causes and universal effects does strike the imagination of incautious readers. I myself should be inclined to demur, with all deference to authority which deserves respect, both to the manner of inference and to the fact assumed in the conclusion. But it may be agreed that the change of system, as it was carried out, was impolitic, for reasons which are just of the sort which Lord Macaulay, with all his genius, did not always feel or understand, because he lacked full sympathy with the deeper and more delicate fibres of political sensitiveness. To him all Oriental literature was almost entirely worthless, and this was quite enough for him; that a sentimental attachment for their ancient book-lore and a prejudice against superseding it in all public instruction by a foreign language and library, might exist among the people of India, did not impress him as points calling for wary consideration. This blind side of a brilliant writer on politics is very well displayed in a somewhat similar case, when it was proposed to buy certain invaluable Irish manuscripts for the British Museum. Lord Macaulay (says Mr. M. Arnold *) declared that he saw nothing in the whole collection worth purchasing, *except* the correspondence of Lord Melville on the American war. If he thought ancient Celtic literature mere rubbish, it was not likely that he should set much store by Sanskrit and Arabic treatises, which have not even an antiquarian value. So he prevailed on the Government of that day to de-Orientalize University education; and in this he carried his point too far. It would have been wiser to permit Musalmans, as Colonel Lees has since proposed, to graduate in Oriental classics; and we might have continued ample State provision for the religious education of their youth, according to the course of study approved by their customs and their religion. We are as yet hardly so firmly established

* On the Study of Celtic Literature, p. 170.

in India as to be warranted in undertaking the propagation of true science and undenominational instruction, while such things are unpalatable to important communities with sensitive prejudices; we cannot yet afford to risk political obloquy in the dissemination of those principles. If the Mahomedan still prefers his own literature, our business is not to gainsay him disagreeably, but to let him take his own course for the present. It should be explained that primary schools have never been Anglicized or made strictly secular, and that the alleged grievances were found in the system which excluded Oriental classics from the curriculum of the Presidency Universities, thus barring the affiliation of the purely Mahomedan colleges, and in the allotment of the funds of one particular Mahomedan college (at Hooghly) toward English instead of toward Oriental learning. All these thorough-going reforms, these abrupt innovations, were far too premature; we cannot hurry an ancient people of some culture so rapidly through phases of social progress which with European nations have occupied long periods; and in fact these educational grievances have since been for the most part remedied.

On the other hand, I must repeat my opinion that the direct consequences of our educational changes have been exaggerated; and that though these things may have contributed something to the discontent and discouragement of Mahomedan students in Bengal, they have had little or nothing to do with the general feelings or position of the Mahomedans of India. Moreover, while it is certain that the Government might offend Mahomedan prejudices and interests by openly pushing on English education all over the country, especially by attempting this hastily; yet, if we are to go forward at all, the movement must be in this direction, and all true intellect and real literary capacity among Mahomedans must gradually follow, though the Hindus have been permitted to take the lead of them. The Mahomedans may be inclined to hang back, and to be much dissatisfied with the supersession of their classics by modern literature; but these are difficulties and thwarting influences which were sure to cross our path; they were not created artificially or brought about by administrative mismanagement, though some mismanagement may have complicated the problem. Anyhow, we cannot now stand still, or shut out the rush of light and air which have followed our throwing open the windows of the West, because at first it chills and dazes the conservative Mahomedan. For we must recollect that he does not so much object to the influx of Western knowledge, as to the inevitable consequence that it has become a broad open channel toward official promotion and professional eminence under our régime, free to all comers; whereby the old studies and the exclusive privileges of Mahomedan learning, are more or less superseded. Now it is very hard to discover how we can help them here, since our civil government of India demands the best heads and the highest skilled training that the world can give, and by using inferior tools we should incur a peril far more serious than any that can grow out of the reactionary susceptibilities of Mahomedans. With military service, so dear to Mahomedans, the question of superior education has as yet no concern; but our *raison d'être* in India, and our motto for ruling it, must ever be *La carrière ouverte aux talents;* and the policy of the Indian Government sets steadily toward throwing open to that career an increasing proportion of the appointments in every grade of the administrative and judicial services. With all respect for the very weighty authority of Mr. W. G. Palgrave, and for his intimate acquaintance with Mahomedan countries, I am afraid that his project* of establishing separate Mahomedan law-courts for judging all social and religious questions arising between Mahomedans by one of themselves, would now hardly satisfy in India even themselves. The measure might succeed in great Mahomedan cities, as in Delhi or Patna, though even there some might prefer courts which are quite dispassionate and incorruptible, at least for the appeal; while the separate jurisdiction might tend to increase the isolation of the Mahomedans amid the rising generations of India. But all over the vast provinces of India the Mahomedans are often very thinly scattered; and in many great districts we should be much puzzled to find them capable judges.

* See Fraser's Magazine for February, 1872.

If the Mahomedans really desire, as the best of them do, to maintain in our Indian empire the high place which their remarkable qualities, their strong mental character and their high physical courage, naturally assign to them, they must in these days make up their minds to accept Western science and literature, and to join the society of nations which rule and lead the whole world. To those Mahomedans who cling to their own classics, and who adhere to the kind of training afforded by the study of Arabic theology or philosophy, every facility and even encouragement should be given. All natives, as Colonel Lees has proposed, might be free to graduate in the *literis humanioribus* of the East or of the West, as they should please; there might be an Oriental faculty as well as an English faculty of Arts in our Indian Universities, so that every one might follow his own bent and take his choice. But although we may feel ourselves bound to throw open both lines of study to our Indian subjects, and precluded from closing the ancient road merely because we think that it leads astray, yet we cannot guarantee the same results to either branch of education and learning; we cannot promise to those who may choose Oriental scholarship, that they shall find themselves abreast, in all the various high-roads of life which lead to profit and distinction, with the men who shall have devoted themselves to acquiring the knowledge which in these days is power, the intellectual treasures which make fifty years of Europe better than a cycle in Cathay, which are the sinews of peaceful empire as surely as money is the sinew of war. It is impossible but that those who hold back in modern India will find themselves left behind; wherefore we may doubt whether the Mahomedans will be much appeased by any concessions of encouragement to their special studies; because their real grievance is that these studies are no longer in fashion, that distinction and court favour can no longer be gained by proficiency in the literature and theology of Islam. This is a real and sensible grievance; but how are we to remedy it, except by patience and extreme consideration? Nor is it possible to comply with the demands of those liberal Mahomedans who have too much intelligence not to perceive the enormous advantage of European education, yet too much patriotism to abandon without reluctance the language of their country and the traditions of their faith. These gentlemen, among whom Syud Ahmed Khan is prominent, argue that all the stores of Western knowledge should not be kept under the lock and key of the English language, but that our Government ought to provide for Indians access to this rich treasure-house through the media of their own vernaculars, so that a native need not labour for years at a foreign tongue before he can work his way up into the higher atmosphere of philosophic thought or scientific practice. No doubt this necessity of first mastering a strange language is a severe obstacle, but it is one which we should hardly attempt to remove; for we cannot undertake to translate European literature for the benefit of our Indian fellow-subjects, the best of whom would already laugh at paltry abridgments and imperfect renderings. Syud Ahmed Khan's son has passed through an English University, and has qualified himself to rise to the first rank of any profession or service which he may choose after his return to India; what chance will there be against him in intellectual competition for young men who have never learnt English, or who have worked at European literature through Hindustani translations? Possibly those pioneers from the East who have first explored and occupied this literary Eldorado of the West, may devote themselves to laying out the road, as translators and expounders in the vernacular, by which the mass of their less enterprising and less affluent countrymen may follow; but this is a task which we English are compelled to leave to their patriotic energy. The English Government has constructed for all natives a good system of primary education in their own dialects; and the official inspectors very properly heed not the strong probability (if not certainty) that some sort of religious instruction is given in the State schools, which are all quasi-denominational; that is, the Musulman and Hindu schools are ordinarily separate. There is no reason why Mahomedan boys should not receive an exclusively Mahomedan education; the State will still subsidize elementary instruction of this kind, if only decent rudiments of secular knowledge are also given. But in the higher standards of education we cannot well refrain, on free-trade principles, from showing a decided bias in favour of English learning, because, though it is undeniably a foreign importation, yet it is so incomparably the best. We may silence natural complaints and appease prejudice by an impartial and even-handed distribution of the educational grants to Eastern and Western learning; and we may attempt, as Dr. Hunter wisely recommends, to connect the two branches of study; but the ultimate result may be safely left to the shrewdness and literary taste of the cleverest races in Asia. It is no new thing that learning and science should be propagated as the result of conquest; and though the Mahomedans, like other martial races, have usually taken their civilization from conquered peoples, they may be content for once to accept light and intellectual leading from a nation that has over them the advantage of European training in arts as well as in arms.

It would take up much time to examine in detail the other specific charges alleged against the British Government, which are taken to form reasonable and sufficient ground for our unpopularity among Mahomedans, by writers who trace it immediately to administrative shortcomings. The charges are very seriously worded. "Deliberate malversation of religious foundations," is, for instance, a tremendous accusation against a Christian Government of India; and it has not been proved by Dr. Hunter. All that could be really established on this indictment is that sometimes we have scrutinized with injudicious rigour the title-deeds whereby endowments were held, and that in one instance we unwisely, though in good faith, attempted to divert towards education on the European system the funds of an estate bequeathed for Mahomedan pious uses. Another count is for "abolishing the Mahomedan law officers who gave the sanction of religion to the marriage tie;" as if we had cut asunder the bonds of Mahomedan society and broken up families. Whereas all we have done is to cease to appoint Kâzis by order of State, leaving election or selection to the Mahomedan communities. This was a change, possibly an error, of which the consequences were not foreseen at the time, and it has since been set right wherever recurrence to the former state of affairs seemed possible. The truth is, that we were seeking to dissociate the State from its patronage of non-Christian religions, and we fancied that the severing of such connections would be rather agreeable than otherwise to Mahomedans and to Hindus, who might be jealous of our exercising these powers. Meanwhile, the Kâzis are still performing their ministry and holding their official allowances, which are ordinarily secured upon the land or on the land revenue; they are in no way abolished, though they are no longer officers of the Government. It is possible that all these changes may have produced some local irritation here and there, where they affected vested interests and strong prejudices; but no reasonable politician will allow that they have ever been sufficiently important or widespread in their effects to cause a general revulsion of feeling among Mahomedans all over India. By far the greater proportion of Mahomedans have probably never heard of these things; and it must be again observed that both the writers who enlarge upon them draw their personal experience mainly from the same province, Lower Bengal. It may be fairly contended, in opposition to such views, that the feeling among Mahomedans of disinclination to our rule, and the occasional seditious stirs which move India from time to time in various quarters, are the natural incidents of alien dominion over a vast unsettled population; that all we see and hear is no more than might be expected and predicted; and that the Mahomedan element is necessarily and by its nature an element of some contrariety and restlessness. The improved means of correspondence and communication, by post and telegraph, by railway and steamboat, are drawing Islam together; and whereas at the beginning of this century the Indian Mahomedans were mainly cut off from the great Mahomedan nations westward of them, and were of no great account abroad, they are now taking, by their wealth, their education, and their civilization, a very prominent place among Mahomedan societies. India is becoming the highway from Central Asia to the sea, by the railroads which connect Peshawur, and the main thoroughfares from Kabul and Kandahar, with Bombay and Kurrachee; and in the annual concourse of pilgrims to the holy cities of the Hejaz the Indians are by far the most numerous. All these circumstances give a constantly expanding importance to any question touching Islam in India, increase its intricacy, and prove the need of surveying the whole situation before attempting to describe it. Every now and then some skilful writer startles us by a vigorous picture of one side of this question, by grouping many striking facts, and by piling up into a heap all the errors and oversights which are inevitably scattered along the difficult path we have trod. But I believe that, to other nations who act as bystanders, the real wonder is that the blunders are not more, and that unpleasant premonitory symptoms of trouble or ill feeling are on the whole so slight.

I have attempted to sketch, though much too rapidly and imperfectly, the principal causes and conditions which have originated and still keep up among the Mahomedans a certain irksome dissatisfaction with our Government, and which must long postpone a complete reconciliation between us and that high-spirited but somewhat uncompromising community, because whatever is substantial in their complaints is, for the most part, either inseparable from the situation, or else the remedy lies with themselves. In so far as these grievances are part and parcel of the actual situation, we must depend on time and reason to allay them, and we must endeavour to convince the Mahomedans that they are fairly compensated for the loss of past advantages by the benefits which certainly accrue to them from living under the most just and the most enlightened government that has ever been tried in their country. In so far as they can point to wrongs which have been accidental, and the consequence of mistakes which all foreign rulers must commit more or less, we are doing our best to apply a remedy, and we see that the Mahomedans do not lack fervent advocates among the best of our own English officers. But we must work upon our own broad notions of essential justice and expediency; we cannot continually twist and modify them so as to fit in with the curves and angles of accidental and temporary prejudices, in India or elsewhere. We cannot guarantee to Mahomedans as a right what would be unfair to other Indian fellow-subjects; we will not deny civil status to any subject of the Queen, convert or pervert; nor will we put back the hands of the dial by retarding the sowing and high cultivation of European education in so splendid and so fertile a land as India. We must continue to enlist the best men into our services, whoever they may be; and we must govern the country, at any cost, on the principles of order and progress, of civil liberty and religious equality.

# CHAPTER X.

## OUR RELIGIOUS POLICY IN INDIA.

(*Fortnightly Review*, 1872.)

Difficulty of position of the British Government in India, in regard to the numerous creeds and sects; and to the widely different phases of religious opinion in Europe and in Asia—Brief sketch of the early policy of toleration adopted by the English in India, disregard shown for political reasons to native Christians; careful performance of State ceremonial towards Hindu worships—Gradual effect of missionary protests against connexion of English Government with the religions of the country; withdrawal of Government from superintendence of endowments; counter protests of natives against total withdrawal; course and tendency of legislation on the subject; effect upon it of the mutiny—Grievances of the Mahomedans as put forward by English writers; criticism of their views—Suggestions as to the proper policy to be followed.

In Great Britain the relations of the State to religion are still in a very delicate condition. Hardly any subject is so keenly discussed or so little settled even in this country, where we are a self-governing people very fairly agreed upon essential beliefs, at any rate unanimous in accepting Christianity as the religious basis of our civil society. No question of home politics ferments so rapidly under controversy among Englishmen, and for that reason nothing would more surely attract their serious attention to Indian affairs than a general impression that our Government in the East had been blundering in its dealings with the religious convictions of the people. Yet I imagine that Englishmen at home do not always realise or make allowance for the degree to which the universal problem as to the proper functions of government becomes complicated, when the points under debate are the duties and attributes of the government of India by the English; more particularly whenever we have to decide upon the attitude which Christian rulers should take up in regard to the numerous creeds and sects which abound in and constantly issue afresh out of that *officina religionum.* For it is not merely that the leading popular faiths of India differ one from another widely and positively, to the extent of setting forth opposite conceptions of primordial morality, and contradictory practical rules as to what are acts of laudable devotion, and what are outrageous public nuisances, but we have to do with the varying shapes and colours assumed by these diverse ideas and doctrines as they are viewed through different intellectual media. Besides having to arbitrate among proclaimed antagonists, we find ourselves confronted by one or another faith in its several phases simultaneously, as when it is held outwardly by people who disagree entirely in their true appreciation and practical application of it; while the behaviour of the Government in this curious situation is watched and criticised from standpoints so far apart as are England and India. Thus the Government has not only to reconcile the interests and to recognise the peculiar institutions of several powerful native creeds radically distinct in structure, and mutually hostile in temperament, but has to submit its proceedings to tribunals of religious opinion in Europe as well as in Asia, and to take account of theological prejudices in two continents. So we are continually measured by inconsistent standards and weighed in discordant balances. In India we have to give reason for our doings to rigid Brahmans and to iconoclastic Mahomedans—

> "Such as do build their faith upon
> The holy text of pike and gun;"

we have to stand well in the dim religious light of a fetich worshipper, and to satisfy the refined Deism of the Brahmo Somàj. We must at the same time reply to vigorous missionary societies who would have a Christian government testify openly to its faith by cutting off allowances to heathendom, and we must argue with Nonconformists at home who overhaul our ecclesiastical expenditure, and would give no public money from Indian revenues to Christian ministers. During late years the growth of a strong many-sided interest in Indian affairs has created in England a general half-knowledge of them, and a sort of fusion or confusion among those ideas which lie upon the border land between Eastern and Western habits of thought regarding such a universally interesting subject as religion. Half-knowledge is proverbially dangerous; nor is it more likely to be either safe or effective when it is handled as ammunition of parliamentary warfare, or used for drawing from India analogies to support party measures in England, or for producing startling effects in the political and popular literature which occupies and diverts the minds of the outer public upon the present condition of our Indian Empire. Yet each and all of these various critics require the Government to do or abstain from something, while every step which the Government takes backward or forward is usually distasteful to one or the other.

For the time is past when the Government of India could escape all this tangle of contradictory responsibilities and demands by doing nothing, and by maintaining the *status quo.* From the beginning, indeed, of our dominion in the East one of the cardinal principles upon which we administered the country has been Toleration. It was lucky for England that she got her firm footing in India at a period when religious enthusiasm was burning very low in the nation; neither within nor without the Church of the eighteenth century was there left any ardent spirit of proselytising abroad or of ecclesiastical domination at home (except over Irish Papists), and so we avoided the terrible blunders of fanaticism made by the European nations, who in the preceding centuries had gone before us Eastward and Westward, to India and to America, in the career of adventure and conquest. Moreover, toleration, meaning complete non-interference with the religions of the natives, was of such plain and profitable expediency with the East India Company in its earlier days, that not to have practised it would have been downright insanity in an association whose object was to do business with Indians; wherefore the merchants who enforced a strict monopoly of material commerce were always careful to encourage free trade and unlimited speculation in religion. So the tradition of total abstinence from any religious policy grew up, and was maintained long after the Company had ceased to depend on the favour of Indian princes or priests, and had instead become arbiter of their destinies. We continued, as a great rising Power, to survey all religions (including Christianity) with the most imperturbable and equitable indifference. We tolerated every superstitious rite or custom to the extent of carefully protecting it; any single institution or privilege of the natives that had in it a tincture of religious motive was hedged round with respect, endowments were conscientiously left untouched, ecclesiastical grants and allowances to pious persons were scrupulously continued; in fact, the Company accepted all these liabilities created by its predecessors in rule as trusts, and assumed the office of administrator general of charitable and religious legacies to every denomination. We disbursed impartially to Hindus, Musalmans, and Parsees, to heretic and orthodox, to Jagannáth's car, and to the shrine of a Mahomedan who died fighting against infidels, perhaps against ourselves. This was, on the whole, a conduct as wise and prudent as it was generally popular; for no anterior government had preserved such complete equipoise in its religious predilections; the Mahomedans had indulged in chronic outbursts of sheer persecution, while the Marathas often laid heavy taxes on Mahomedan endowments, if they did not entirely confiscate them in times of financial need. At the least every succeeding ruler provided largely and exclusively for the services of his own religion, and most rarely for any other; to do this much was not only the right of a conquering prince, but his duty, springing obviously out of the fact that he was bound to promote the spread of certain tenets or the glorification of certain divinities. On the other hand, the only tutelary deities which the Company cared to propitiate were powerful personages in the flesh at home; and in India their chief officers were so cautious to disown any political connection with Christianity, that they were occasionally reported to have no religion at all. It thus came to pass that whereas Hinduism and Islam had been well endowed and richly salaried whenever the Hindus or Mahomedans had from time to time been predominant, Christianity took nothing by the wonderful turn of fortune which at last brought Christians to the top of the wheel in India; and for the first time India saw the wealth of vast provinces dispensed by rulers who showed not the slightest inclination to allot any portion, beyond a few very moderate salaries, to the religion which they themselves professed. The consequence was a marked and striking contrast between the condition of native Christians and that of other historical religious communities, the more extraordinary and impressive because all temporal power was in the hands of those who belonged to the religion which possessed no temporalities, and because the races which had been superseded in dominion retained great religious endowments. While Christians held the highest offices of State, with irresponsible power over immense revenues, the Christian religion was as poor and as depressed as when it first struggled for existence among the pontiffs and philosophers of the Roman Empire; and about the time when the quarrels of Greek and Latin monks over their holy places in Turkey well-nigh shook the throne of the chief sovereign of Islam, in India the Christians, as a body, were left by our English Government with no more privilege nor protectorate than would have been accorded by ordinary magistrates to any insignificant group of worshippers without pretension to political importance. Toleration of this heroic self-denying kind contradicted all the precedents and prejudices of Asia.

When I speak of the Indian Christians, I must not be supposed to mean a body composed mainly of the Company's servants, or of immigrants from Europe during English rule. It is well known that a branch of the early Nestorian Church prospered for several centuries in Southern India, principally about Travancore; and though these Christian communities are said to have been much weakened by later dissensions with the Roman Catholics, yet La Croze, whose History of Christianity in India was published in 1724; says that in his day they had fifteen hundred churches and as many towns and villages within the kingdoms of Cochin and Travancore. The Abbé Dubois stated in his evidence before the House of Commons that in 1792 the number of Roman Catholic Christians in the southern peninsula of India was estimated to exceed one million, but that "the Christian religion had been visibly on the decline during these past eighty years." As for their condition at the time (1832) when M. Dubois was speaking, he goes on to suggest that "the state of the native Christians might be materially improved if, above all, their religious guides could be placed above the state of penury, or rather beggary, in which they live generally, most of them having nothing for their support but the scanty substance of distressed flocks, themselves in the greatest poverty, and the priests being thus reduced, in order to procure themselves absolute necessaries, to the sad but unavoidable necessity of making a kind of traffic of the sacraments, and otherwise debasing themselves." * He "proposed to shelter the clergy from the horrors of indigence," by giving to every bishop a salary of about six hundred rupees (£60) yearly, and to priests in due proportion. Up to the year 1831 native Christians had been placed under stringent civil disabilities by our own regulations, which formally adopted and regularly enforced the loose and intermittent usages of intolerance which they found in vogue; native Christians were excluded from practising as pleaders, and from the subordinate official departments, although no such absolute rule of exclusion had ever been set up against them by Hindus or Mahomedans; while converts to Christianity were liable to be deprived, by reason of their conversion, not only of property, but of their wives and children; and they seem to have been generally treated as unlucky outcasts with whom no one need be at the trouble of using any sort of consideration. The British Government had ordained for their own servants some ecclesiastical establishment, but it is described as having been in Western India "a disgrace to our national character"† until the constitution of the see at Calcutta in 1814. For many decades of our rule there was in the

* Parliamentary Papers, Minutes of Evidence.

† Appendix to Report from Select Committee on the affairs of the East India Company, 1832.

Bombay Presidency only the first English church which had been built at Bombay in 1714; and just one hundred years later one bishop was appointed for all Protestant India, with nineteen chaplains for the whole Bengal Presidency, and one Scotch minister to each Presidency, an economical allowance with which the numerous Scotchmen in India appear to have always been quite contented. The local governments were also rather grudgingly permitted to build a "few cheap chapels;" but it was remarked that the Roman Catholics shamed the Protestants (and saved the revenues) by building their churches without any aid from the Treasury. It is not clear that the indigenous Christian communities got any sort of aid or subsidy; in the year 1832 they were described as being in a state of "lamentable superstitious degradation," especially in Salsette Island (close to Bombay), which had been British territory since 1774. But at this time the religious institutions and rites of the Hindus and Mahomedans were treated with deferential and scrupulous observance of the position which they held under native governments. All the customary honours, civil and military, were paid to shrines and images; the district magistrates continued to press men, according to ancient use, for dragging the cars of a famous idol, and declined to exempt Christians from this general *corvée;* we administered the endowments, paying over net rentals to priests or ministers; "our interference extended over every detail of management, we regulated their funds, repaired their buildings, kept in order the cars and images, appointed their servants, and purveyed the various commodities required for use of the pagodas."* All these matters, however, were merely forms of harmless external observance which the executive might fairly recognise, just as the law courts would take cognizance of idolatrous customs and adjudicate thereupon. But there were other superstitious practices plainly condemned by the first principles of Christian morality and decency, which yet, on account of their motive, were exempted by devout opinion from the purview of the

* Parliamentary Papers, 1832.

ordinary criminal law. During a long time the Company hesitated to interfere with such practices; and this abstention was consistent with the particular stage of toleration at which our Government in India had then arrived. For so long as the laws of each separate sect or community depend upon and are derived from its religion, are personal instead of being territorial—in such a state of society governments have usually held themselves precluded from interfering with any act warranted by the creed in which a person has been born, excepting only when such an act is dangerous to the State itself; and weakness and philosophic indifference have combined to commend these principles all the world over to prudent rulers of many strong tribes or of powerful religious factions.

This rather primitive conception of the meaning of tolerant government was soon, however, found inadequate and incomplete by the European chiefs (not individually without courage or political insight) who administered India under European direction. Then arose that knotty question which in different shapes and degrees has vexed all Christianity since we abandoned the good old rule and simple plan of pure Intolerance, and which even troubled the London School Board during its earliest discussions as to principles, namely, How far are we bound to tolerate that which we firmly believe to be wrong? Those very extreme cases which Professor Huxley suggested * by way of reducing administrative nihilism to an absurdity, came as matters of fact before Indian rulers, who had to decide practically about countenancing the worship of Astarte, and about permitting other religious usages not much less barbarous than Thuggee. So early as in 1792 Mr. Grant, in his "Review of the State of Society in Asia," had asked of the Government, "Are we bound for ever to preserve all the enormities of the Hindu system? Have we become the guardians of every monstrous principle and practice which it contains?" Yet only gradually did the Government make bold to answer these appeals by a clear negative. Under

* *Fortnightly Review*, November, 1871.

Lord Wellesley the exposure of infants and aged parents to death by wild beasts or starvation in the Hooghly was declared illegal; but the practice of "driving widows into flames by a diabolical complication of force and fraud"* was tolerated until in 1829 Lord W. Bentinck outlawed it, with some qualms and many explanations. These and other similar domestic institutions (as slavery, suicide, &c.) were gradually disallowed upon the plea that such errors were so unanimously condemned by every system of secular law and morality in the world, that even genuine religious convictions must in such instances yield to the necessity of some kind of police, were it merely for a commonwealth's self-preservation. Thus far the Government could proceed on solid ground, for Christians and Mahomedans approved, while Indus (after some grumbling) acquiesced in the drawing our new line of toleration so as to exclude acts of flagrant inhumanity; though the question of meddling with shocking indecency seems to have been adjourned as rather more metaphysical and less urgent.

But the true religious difficulty was gradually closing round us, despite our laborious declarations of "perfect Neutrality." We soon began to enter upon those intricacies of navigation which have ever since beset a government that, during its whole course, is more or less under the influence of two different currents of public opinion, setting in from the East and the West simultaneously, and both flowing stronger and stronger (though in varying proportion of strength) as the voyage proceeds. The Western current, hitherto slightly felt, was gathering drift. It brought a feeling that Christianity, among other things, ought to be tolerated; that a system which allowed native Christians to be punished publicly by canes † for refusing to drag the car of Hindu idols, which taxed them for support of these idols, and which visited them with civil disabilities, was, to say the least, an excessive

* Grant, "State of Society in Asia," Parliamentary Papers. Three hundred and ten widows were burnt, within the English dominion, as it then stood, in the year 1815.

† Minutes of Evidence before Select Committee, 1832.

deference to the opinion of majorities. So in 1832 the Government went so far as to pass a law which protected all persons who should change their religion from loss of property in consequence of that change. The enactment was general, though its special aim was relief to new Christians, yet the Hindus actually protested against it as a manifest breach of the neutrality which the English had been so careful to proclaim, although it was notorious that the Mahomedans in the days of their ascendency not only bestowed upon their proselytes immunity, but reward. From this time forward, nevertheless, the counter-pressure of English religious opinion, mainly organized and directed by the growing power of missionary societies, began to have its sensible effect upon our policy of administration; the conscientious scruples of Christians, as well as of Hindus or Musalmans, were ventilated and had gained representation; and the contrarieties occasionally produced by these cross winds were curious. For instance, about 1838 the Government desired, according to the ordinary routine, to repair the *Imàmbàrah*, or place of prayer, belonging to that same religious foundation at Hooghly in the recent management of which we have incurred (according to Dr. W. W. Hunter) the charge of "deliberate malversation." * An order was sent as usual to the Board of Revenue in Calcutta to invite tenders for these repairs, whereupon one member minuted as followed :—

> "It is deeply distressing to me to receive orders from the Government which I cannot execute without grievously offending my conscience. I must respectfully but earnestly entreat that I may not be required to make myself an instrument for the maintenance and embellishment of an edifice dedicated to worship which I am conscientiously persuaded is not that of the true God. I know that the act which I am directed to perform is one of very easy execution, and that very little interference on the part of the Board is likely to be called for; but this is not a question of degree, my objection is one of principle. . . . . It is an offence, in my opinion, of the greatest magnitude to take knowingly a single step in a direction contrary to that of truth." †

This quotation serves to illustrate the difficulties of the position in which the Government found itself occasionally placed. On

* "Our Indian Musalmans," page 185.

† Parliamentary Papers on connection of the Government of India with Idolatry or with Mahomedanism.

the one side lay the hitherto acknowledged duty of respecting and maintaining, according to the use and practice of preceding governments and the expectation of the people, the principal religious endowments of the country, and the gulf of troubled water into which any open neglect of such duty was likely to bring us. On the other side an active and increasing party of earnest Christians urged that any sort of co-operation with false creeds was a compact with Satan, a crime against the true creed, and that their scruples on this head had as much claim to respect as the phantasies of a Hindu, or the violent aversions of a Mahomedan; that Christians must no longer be required, even figuratively or constructively, to draw the car of Jagannáth; that when a Christian church fell out of repair the Government sent orders to pull it down,* while professional architects were employed on mosques; and that this species of policy only appeared to the natives as if it were blanched by timidity. Out of this particular dilemma there has in modern times been only one way of escape, which is always adopted by governments when they find themselves hemmed in and headed backward and forward by rival sects—that of attempting to slip away from all connection with ecclesiastical affairs, and of seeking safe anchorage in the calm roads of exclusively secular administration. And the unendowed minority naturally desire to drive the State into this outlet, as the best bargain which they can hope to extort; they cannot consistently hope for establishments because they are sure to have been denouncing them, but they can demand disestablishment, if not disendowment; they cannot logically propose levelling up, but they can reasonably agitate for levelling down; while the very professions of neutrality and pure impartiality set up by a modern government at once lay it open to a claim that their principle shall be universally applied. Unfortunately this solution of the difficulty, which is thought to be full of hope and promise in England, is still a little premature in India, where the customs and prejudices of the people still give a somewhat unusual aspect to the principle of complete abstinence by the State from expressing

* Parliamentary Papers, Minutes of Evidence, 1832.

or supporting any particular religious opinion. The preceding governments, who framed their religious policy on the antique pattern of doing everything for their own creed and leaving other creeds alone (save for occasional outbursts of fanaticism), were at least free from this special kind of embarrassment. But here were the missionaries saying humbly to the English Government, "We don't ask you to support Christianity, but if you must be what we call atheist, be so consistently; do not act as agents and managers for any religion at all." So the Government, being moved thereto by divers reasons, did in India what every governing body thus placed must eventually do; it resolved to withdraw from all direct connection with religious institutions, expecting thereby to please all parties, and to sit apart from the turmoil of religious strife. The principle of dissociation was imposed upon the Indian administration by their Home Government, as "due alike to the character of a Christian Government and to the scruples of its Christian officers:" and in 1846 the Indian Council reported to England that the necessary measures were in progress, which the Court of Directors entirely approved.

But the business of making over to responsible trustees or guardians the enormous possessions of the various religious bodies in India, which had been perhaps for generations under the direct and powerful administration of successive governments, involved great and complicated transactions, clogged by many hitches and much delay. Many of these establishments had no recognised heads, and when heads were found they were sometimes incompetent or untrustworthy. There were numerous landed estates to be transferred, and proprietors were not easily discovered, while the rights of tenants had to be guarded. There was a large accumulation of surplus ecclesiastical funds in Government treasuries, and to hand over big lump sums of ready cash to temples or shrines would often be merely to force waste and debauchery upon pious and ascetic communities; for they had no idea of investing such money, and no legitimate objects on which it would be suddenly spent. However, the Government persevered until, by the energy and minute local knowledge of district officers all over the empire, most of the arrangements for handing over to individuals or to corporations the conduct and personal management of religious lands and money allowances had been more or less successfully agreed upon.

Nevertheless, the Government soon discovered that these measures by no means satisfied the religious sentiment of all parties, or enabled it to shake off its religious responsibilities; for certain sections of the native population, both Hindu and Mahomedan, began to complain that the English Government was abdicating one of its most essential functions by refusing any longer to superintend the religious endowments of the country, as had been the immemorial custom and obligation of native princes to do; that no other guardians or trustees both honest and capable could be found; that there was great confusion as to title, incessant quarrels as to right to use the funds or deal with the lands; and that the Government cynically, and with subtle intent to ruin non-Christian creeds by the law's delay, referred these disputes to the civil courts, instead of deciding them by its own ancient prerogative and according to its plain duty. Meanwhile the party whose opinions were represented by the Christian missionaries was pushing forward its advantage from the other side. The Government had determined to be no longer agents and officers for institutions of false religions or of heathen superstitions; but large annual grants (the donations of our predecessors) continued to be made from the Treasury toward the support of idols and idolatrous or infidel usages; so the Honourable Company was "earnestly reminded that idolatry is not only a curse to mankind, but that any approval or countenance lent to it, directly or indirectly, is represented in the Word of God as a grievous offence against Heaven."* The leading case on which both parties relied, and in which the conduct of the Government was most impartially condemned by Hindus and Christians alike, was that of the great temple of Jagannáth, which had been formally assured of the protec-

* Memorial to Honourable Court of Directors by Protestant Missionaries, 1850 (Parliamentary Papers).

tion of the British conquerors when the province of Cuttack, in which the temple is situated, was annexed; and in observance of this pledge a large sum of money was paid yearly to the Brahmans by assignment of the revenue from certain tracts. In 1845 it was proposed to commute this assignment once for all by a grant of land in perpetuity; upon which a high official in Bengal minuted that this was a mere device of Christians by profession who wanted to conciliate the Hindu, and at the same time "to secure themselves against the execration of their fellow-Christians by presenting their oblation to an idol under the cover of a perpetual endowment," instead of undergoing the annual disgrace of a money-payment.* This uncomfortable aspect of the proposal did not in the end prevail, for certain lands were conveyed to a Hereditary Superintendent in trust for the Temple; but the Court of Directors forbade the usual posting of police inside the building to keep order on great festivals; while the missionaries charged our hapless Government with encouraging "the vilest characteristics of Hindu idolatry," and with directly subsidizing "a large idolatrous establishment which tends to perpetuate intellectual and moral debasement."† Thus the High Christian party was no longer satisfied that Government had ceased to overlook the employment of religious funds; it now required that the allowances themselves should be stopped ‡ (not, however, that their estates should be confiscated); and when it was proposed to escape the scandal of periodical disbursements by a grant of land, they retorted that this was merely to perpetuate and plant an abuse which ought to be uprooted. At the same time many natives cried aloud that Government was shirking its duties, throwing their religious institutions into confusion by declining to administer them, impoverishing them by curtailing on inadequate reasons the customary grants, and confiscating them by rigorous investigations into right and title,

* Parliamentary Papers.

† Parliamentary Papers, 1852.

‡ It will be understood that only those allowances were continued which were actually being enjoyed under valid authority at the time when a province came into British hands

such as by equity and common law of the country these endowments had never been expected to sustain.

Then the question of religious disabilities brought upon the Government similarly conflicting remonstrances against a breach of perfect neutrality. Up to 1830 the native Christians had been excluded in the Madras Presidency (where they were most numerous) by law from the bar, from judicial offices, and from the army commissions; they were even left amenable in the interior provinces to Musalman law, and their civil rights were defined by no particular code at all throughout India. The religious minority ruled both in Ireland and in India; but here all likeness ends between the two cases, for while in Ireland all the ecclesiastical revenues of the country went to support the religion of the dominant race, and the disabilities were laid on the mass of the people; in India we sought to conciliate the great majority of our subjects by maintaining civil disabilities upon that part of the indigenous population which belonged to the religion of the conquerors. In 1832 was passed in Bengal a law which protected any man from losing his property by the effect of the law of a religion which he had renounced; but in 1845 the Bishop of Bombay represented that in his diocese the benefit to native Christians of the courts of justice was confined to protecting them from personal violence; a convert had no other rights under the Regulations. Upon this, after much deliberation, the Government in 1850 framed a Bill which rescinded all laws and usages throughout India inflicting upon any person forfeiture of *rights* or property by reason of his renouncing or being excluded from the communion of any religion. Against this the Hindus of Bengal and Madras at once sent up strong memorials declaring that "the measure was viewed by the whole Hindu population with the utmost horror and dismay;" that its object was evidently to sap the foundations of their religion, and to insinuate a system of indirect persecution; and the memorialists, as usual, respectfully asked "whether *this* was the Honourable Company's principle of toleration." Lord Dalhousie (who regarded strong words as a sort of inconvertible currency of his own issue, good for paying with, but not for being paid in) carried through the reform with his usual high-handed resolution; but the Government found itself no nearer than before to the haven of refuge from theologic winds and currents; and this very grievance about disabilities has by no means died away, for Colonel Nassau Lees gravely registers it among the specific wrongs over which the Mahomedans to this day brood discontentedly.*

So far, indeed, was Lord Dalhousie from having piloted his vessel into calm waters, that he left her on the edge of a cyclone. This gradual tolerance of Christianity, the progress which it made towards admission within the circle of recognised Indian religions, the bold countenance of its thoroughgoing professors, and the perceptible inclination of the State's course under the increasing ripple of Western opinion—all these things did combine to arouse jealousy among the more sensitive Hindu and Mahomedan classes and interests. They saw that their faiths were losing their old exclusive privileges, and they openly propounded the conclusion that the Government was undermining their religious constitutions with the object of proselytism. These ideas, which were abroad not long before the great eruption of mutiny and revolt in 1857, aided much to bring the native Indian mind into an inflammable condition; when the spark fell the rebels and mutineers went to the country with the cry of Religion in danger, and the cry was very widely believed. All the proclamations issued from Delhi and Lucknow contained allusions to the invidious machinations of the English against the creeds of India; while natives about to be executed would offer to embrace Christianity if they might be spared, and would be astonished at discovering that this alternative was not permitted. On the neutrality question the effect of that bloody wrestle was natural enough. The old Puritanic intolerance which still lies hid at the bottom of the hearts of so many English and Scots was ominously rekindled, as big trees at last catch fire from blazing thorns, by the aggressive display of Indian fanaticism;

* Letter to the *Times*, from Colonel N. Lees, late Principal of the Mahomedan College, October 14, 1871.

and while the natives proclaimed that a treacherous Government had been detected in entrapping them into Christianity, English laymen went about saying that we were only suffering the divine chastisement that is surely brought down upon a nation by rulers that deny and degrade their own religion. If the more violent Mahomedans had preached holy war, it must be remembered that a section of the Christian clergy exhaled a strong savour of that very same leaven which causes Mahomedan bigotry to ferment after a manner which some people appear to regard as a peculiar and portentous characteristic of Islam. For in a memorial to Government drawn up by the Bombay Missionary Conference in 1858, requiring the Government to discountenance and deprive of their customary money grants all non-Christian places of worship, the petitioners urged that "even if treaties bind us to support heathen temples, the obligation forbidding such treaty is far superior, as imposed by God Himself, which (obligation) cannot be set aside without drawing down the displeasure of the Almighty.* The missionaries were thus disturbed in conscience by precisely the same problem as that which occasionally hampers loyal but strictly pious Mahomedans—the dilemma between the manifest obligations of honesty and good faith on the one side, and the suggestion of God's displeasure on the other; and the solution proposed by the memorial to our Government is very nearly identical with what in our subjects we call treason—the subordination of allegiance to theology, the principle that we cannot keep pledge with persons of a different creed without apostasy from our own. Nor were missionaries the only Englishmen who held political doctrines of this colour during the period which immediately followed the great mutiny; for though the chief governors and councillors of India were proof against such arguments, and untouched by such passions, yet about this time there appeared in certain parts of Northern India a bias toward such combinations as the Bible and the sword, and a disposition to entertain the idea that the Government might

* Parliamentary Papers.

sever its connection with heathen endowments by the sharp knife of confiscation.

As the heats generated by the mutiny gradually cooled down, the extreme tension of the situation relaxed; but the events of those years probably intensified the desire of our Government to be rid of the connection between Churches and State in India. The Home Secretary issued a fresh despatch on the subject, and after much correspondence the Act was passed, in 1863, which relieved officers of Government from all duties which embraced the appointment to religious offices, the superintending of lands assigned for pious uses, the appropriation of religious incomes, the preservation of sacred buildings, or the management in any form of establishments belonging to the Hindu or the Mahomedan religion. Such properties and agencies were to be made over absolutely to local trustees or committees to be once for all appointed by the Government, after which the Government positively ceased to nominate or in any manner to interfere. The check on the trustees resembles that which was devised by the Archbishop of Canterbury for the English clergy in the scheme which the Upper House rejected in 1872; any person interested in any mosque or temple, or in the performance of the worship or service thereof,* may sue before the civil court the trustee, manager, or member of the committee for misfeasance, breach of trust, or neglect of duty; and the civil court may direct specific performance of any act, decree damages, or remove from office. Next followed, in 1864, the law by which Government proclaimed that it would no longer appoint the semi-ecclesiastical Mahomedan Kâzis, whereby the dissociation between the State and the religious institutions of the natives of British India was completed; all civil disabilities on account of religion had by this time been abolished,† and the Government may have been flattered with

* This may mean (says the Act) any person having a right of attendance, or having been in the habit of attending at the performance of the worship or service.

† I should perhaps except some indirect and intricate impediments to marriage or divorce, which still hampered persons who changed caste or creed. These have since been mostly removed.

the hope that it had at last attained the true equilibrium of toleration.

How far we are still, nevertheless, from any such consummation in India may be calculated by a survey of the present state of religious politics in India, and by marking the movements in different camps. Christianity has been liberated from her unfair disadvantages, and other creeds have been deprived of their unfair privileges; we have thus been brought nearer than ever before to liberty and equality in religions. But fraternity is as distant as ever, for equality stimulates rivalry; and it is in the electric religious atmosphere of India that the two great monotheistic Faiths which each claim all mankind as their due heritage by divine ordinance —Christianity and Mahomedanism—now confront each other face to face, as they have never met before throughout history, in one great neutral country of paganism. Both maintain that the heathen have been given unto them for a possession, and in their competition for proselytes the antagonists find themselves at last not unevenly matched. The Mahomedan faith has still at least a dignity, and a courageous unreasoning certitude, which in Western Christianity have been perceptibly melted down and attenuated by the disease of casuistry and by long exposure to the searching light of European rationalism; whereas the clear, unwavering formula of Islam carries one plain line straight up toward heaven like a tall obelisk pointing direct to the sky, without shadow of turning. It thus possesses a strong attraction for Hindus who are seeking an escape from the labyrinth of sensual Polytheism, but who yet require something more concrete and definite in the way of a belief than is offered by their indigenous speculations about Deism or Pantheism; while the vigour and earnestness of the high message announced so unflinchingly by Mahomed conquer the hearts of simple folk, and warm the imagination of devout truth-seekers. It is by these weapons that the Mahomedan now enlarges his borders among the Hindus, and the emulation between the two propaganda, now left entirely to their own resources by our Government, neither encouraged nor discouraged, must needs be close enough to present the unique spectacle of two powerful and enthusiastic religions, contending one against the other, and both against the greatest polytheism surviving in the world, whose gradual dissolution will necessarily throw open to the higher faiths a wide field of proselytism. When forces are thus ranged and opposed, the parties actually engaged are apt to be impatient of and to disregard the neutral flag of toleration; nor does our Government at present obtain unanimous applause for its appearance in the character (so novel on the Asiatic stage) of an impartial bystander, prejudiced only in favour of order and material prosperity. And thus it has come to pass that our neutrality has been challenged simultaneously, yet from different and indeed opposite points of view, by Hindus, Mahomedans, and various energetic partisan leaders of Christians in England.*

Of these several parties the most important in India, because the most united, are the Mahomedans, whose grievances have from time to time obtained much sympathy and vivid representations from English writers. In 1871, Dr. W. W. Hunter, published a book styled "Our Indian Musalmáns," upon the condition of the Mahomedans in India, wherein the British Government was somewhat hastily charged with deliberate misappropriation of the Mahomedan endowments; also with having abolished their law officers, the Kâzis; for as the Madras High Court has formally decreed upon a dispute between two claimants for the office that according to precise Mahomedan law a Kâzi can only be appointed by the State, it has been maintained that the State, by ceasing to appoint Kâzis, has virtually abolished an indispensable religious office. These heavy accusations were endorsed by Colonel W. Nassau Lees, in a pamphlet which brought together various articles and letters on the subject; and the following quotation exemplifies the point from which he opened fire upon that eternally besieged citadel of religious Neutrality.

* In 1860, 2,049 petitions were presented to Parliament for the admission of the Bible into all Government schools and colleges in India.

"Starting," he says,* "from our own standpoint of strictly religious neutrality, both Hindus and Mahomedans might reasonably object to a considerable sum out of the revenues raised by the sweat of their brows being devoted annually to the maintenance of an Established Church for the benefit of Christians, be they Government servants or not, while *no annual grant at all* is made for the support of Hindu and Mahomedan places of worship, or for their clergy."

Now the view here taken is avowedly that which is in accordance with English ideas on the subject; and it might have been safely declared not to be the Indian view, since there is every reason to doubt whether either Hindus or Mahomedans would of themselves have ever discovered any objection on principle against the small annual grant made to the Christian Churches in India. But the assertion that no annual grant at all is made for Hindu or Mahomedan religions is indeed the unkindest cut of all, and is enough to make our unlucky Indian Government abandon in despair its long pursuit after the true method of toleration. For generations, as has been explained above, we have been charged with apostasy because we administered and scrupulously nurtured large assignments from the revenue to Hindus and Mahomedans in every part of India; and only a few years ago the Bombay Missionary Conference pointed out to Government, with compressed indignation, that—

"According to the best information obtainable by your memorialists, the number (26,589) of idol temples and shrines in the *Bombay Presidency alone* receiving support (by payments from the Treasury and from sources under Government control) from the Government is much larger than the number of Christian churches receiving Government support in Great Britain, and scarcely, if at all, inferior to the entire number of churches of all Christian denominations whatsoever in the British Islands. If your memorialists are correctly informed . . . . . . seven lakhs (£70,000) are annually expended from the Government treasuries in the Bombay Presidency, and a still larger sum (£87,678) in the Madras Presidency."

In Madras the surplus funds lying in the treasuries to credit of religious institutions amounted in 1856 to several hundred thousand pounds; and the total annual payments up to 1859 were about £100,000. One devout person in Southern India,

* *Times*, Oct. 20, 1871.

who states in a petition that he leads a "reclusive life," claimed £25,000 due to him from the treasury in 1847. Throughout the vast Bengal Presidency and the great provinces directly administered (like Nagpore and Oudh) by the supreme Government, the allowances in money or in kind, and the endowments of land to religion, were found to be in great number; nor do even these accounts include the numerous estates set aside for the support of Hindu and Mahomedan places of worship all over British India. These estates are settled in perpetuity, free of land-tax, on the institutions to which they belong, and it is certain that such exemptions from assessment are tantamount to a direct provision measured by the amount of revenue which would have accrued to the State if the lands had not been assigned to religious services. One would suppose that in no country of the world were the great popular religions so richly endowed from the public revenue as in India; nevertheless Colonel Lees assured the readers of the *Times* that a few scattered British chaplains and priests are the only clergy for whom the toiling Indian sweats.

From the passage which I have quoted above, and from another to the same purport,* it is by no means plain what religious policy Colonel Nassau Lees would recommend.

* "Are we to take from the people of this country £47,000,000 of annual revenue for the purposes of the Government of the country, and allow not *one rupee* of those millions, the greater portion of which has been raised by the sweat of their brows, for the maintenance of their religious institutions? Are we to spend annually out of these revenues £150,000 on bishops, priests, deacons, ecclesiastical establishments, maintained solely for the spiritual welfare of a few thousand Englishmen, and leave the 150,000,000 of our Hindu and Mahomedan subjects to provide for the care of their own souls out of the pittance our Revenue collectors may leave them for their private purposes, on the plea that their religions are monstrous superstitions?" — *Extract from a pamphlet, being reprint of letters and articles by W. Nassau Lees, late Principal of Mahomedan College*, &c. 1871.

Of this sum 16,47,269 rupees (£164,726) is incurred in the Civil department, and is distributed as follows:—To the Church of England, 15,02,739 rupees (£150,273); the Church of Scotland, 1,07,704 rupees (£10,770); and the Roman Catholic Church, 36,825 rupees (£3,682). In the Military department 1,97,559 rupees (£19,755) are paid to Roman Catholic chaplains; and 22,798 rupees (£2,279) to Presbyterian chaplains. There is also an expenditure upon ecclesiastical buildings of 2,40,595 rupees (£24,059).—*Parliamentary Return.*

Would he have us enhance the present enormous revenues of the Mahomedan and Hindu establishments by an additional money grant? Or would he desire us to discontinue the allowances made to Christian ministers mainly for performing religious services to our Christian officials and soldiers? The latter alternative has probably suggested itself to an influential party in England; for returns showing the total annual expenditure on account of Christian ecclesiastical purposes have been called for by Parliament, and the English Nonconformists are naturally deliberating whether the British Government shall not be pressed to cut off all this subvention from the State to the Churches in India.

Now the expediency of paying chaplains for the British army is not likely to be questioned; and as to the general provision by the State for ministry to different Christian sects in India, this is not the place for discussing either the system of Church establishment, or that of concurrent dotation. But it is worth while to point out that if the English Parliament determines to suppress altogether (as the Comtists would say) the theologic budget in India, this affirmation of the principle involved will inevitably bring to the front, sooner or later, a much larger and more serious question; for it is not easy to see how the Christian ecclesiastic allowances can be forbidden except on the broad principle that the State has no business to recognise or support any particular religious sentiment, and that it is mere indirect persecution to tax a man for contributions toward the maintenance of liturgies from which he dissents. That principle might be logical enough, but then it hardly admits of partial application; we can hardly strain at such a gnat as this budget allotment to Christianity, and swallow such camels as the Mahomedan and Hindu endowments. It is of little use to relieve the native conscience of the burden of contributing towards a Protestant bishop, if we still leave the people paying rates and taxes indiscriminately to idols and to Islam, without the remotest connection between the creed of the individual taxpayer and the creed which his money may go to support. But a motion in England to forbid the Indian Government from disbursing public money to any religious institution would not find much favour among Indians; since the chief gravamen of recent complaints made against us by natives in India lies in allegations that we have been disestablishing these institutions and revising their endowments, that we have refused to appoint Kâzis or to retain any kind of religious patronage, and that we have either thrown up the superintendence of religious foundations or attempted to reform them.

The truth seems to be that we have got to a climax of the conflict between Eastern and Western opinion as to what are the proper functions of a neutral State. Neutrality in the West means complete secularisation of the State's functions; disestablishment is largely accepted in principle, and disendowment is a question of public utility. In the East these ideas are entirely new; and of all the various kinds of new wine which we have latterly been pouring into old bottles, none is more likely to disagree with the Indian taste and constitution. In India they have no conception of the animosity against Establishment which has been fostered in England by Acts passed to enforce unity of religious profession and uniformity of clerical teaching, by the old attempts to drive wandering sects like sheep into one fold under one official shepherd. As there has never been one nation or one religion in India, so a national Church establishment, excluding all others, has never been imagined. That the Sovereign should provide decently for his own persuasion is regarded as natural and decorous; that he should distribute revenue allotments (or continue them) to every well-defined religious community is thought liberal; that he should administer to all religious properties and interests is right and proper; that he should ignore them all and provide not even for his own faith would be a policy comprehensible only by those who had studied English polemics, and one without precedent in Asia. Lord Shaftesbury's recent declaration that he would sooner have a child brought up as a Papist than under no religion at all, would be approved; while the Nonconformist who would rather disendow all churches and schools than continue endowments or grants to institutions from whose teaching he dissented, would be thought unreasonable. The Oriental would judge our quarrel over English pauper children as Solomon judged the dispute between two women for the possession of a son. Lord Shaftesbury would be she who would give up the child rather than let it die; the Nonconformist would be the woman who would sooner it were dead than made over to a rival.

And assuredly some of the wisdom of Solomon is needed to bring the Indian Government out of its straits without running upon some rock of offence. We are like a man who should desire to set his watch so as to keep true time in two different longitudes at once. In the meridian of Greenwich establishments and State endowments belong to an obsolete system; in the meridian of Delhi disestablishment (by which is here meant disconnection of the State from the religious institutions of the country) has caused much dissatisfaction; and of course disendowment would be to rob a great many deities and religious communities. It has been said latterly, and with some reason, that the English Government acted prematurely, and upon incomplete knowledge of all the considerations involved, when it resolved to sever the ancient chain which bound the religious institutions of each province round the feet of the Government which annexed them, and when we thus, in liberating ourselves from being plagued with old-world fancies, threw away the repute and leadership which accrued to the Sovereign of India from being universally recognised as the authority whose *congé d'élire* was required, or whose arbitration was accepted, in all nominations and successions to important religious office or estate. In the Madras Presidency the superintendence of "no less than seven thousand six hundred Hindu establishments had hitherto been vested in the officers of Government; and this was more than a nominal superintendence; the people regarded the district officer as the friendly guardian of their religion. . . ."* Speaking of the aversion of the people to the abandonment by Government of the management of a famous pagoda in North Arcot, the district magistrate wrote: "No persuasion or reasoning could effect a change in the resolution they had

* Note by Under-Secretary, Madras (Parliamentary Papers).

taken; the management of this pagoda, they said, had been in the hands of the ruling power for ages back, the innovation proposed was contrary to established custom, and, if persisted in, religious worship in their temple would cease." Without doubt the people greatly exaggerated the effects of the change; but their feelings thereupon are illustrated by the foregoing quotations. Nor is it to be forgotten that religious offices and properties in India have very generally yielded to that peculiar tendency which governs the course of all rights and interests throughout the country; they have to a great extent become heritable family possessions on a service tenure; and we cannot attempt to alter the regular succession by inheritance, except on extreme necessity. Even the semi-religious duties of the Kâzi had become usually hereditary, and his appointment by the State a mere form, long before the Act of 1864, long indeed before the English took over from Mahomedans or Marathas their dominion in India. It is quite a mistake to infer that the result of ceasing to appoint Kâzis was to lay our Musalman subjects under some such interdict as in the middle ages disabled Christian priests from giving the "sanction of religion to the marriage tie;"* such a bewildering confusion of ideas cannot be seriously entertained by a writer of ability and high culture. But the form of confirming each succession or election did survive, and to abolish it was not to render the Kâzi independent of infidels, but to cast a slur upon his status, to lower his dignity, and even to render his tenure of office less absolutely incontestable. Undoubtedly these slights are felt; and it is questionable whether the motives were sufficiently grave and urgent which induced the Government to dissolve the natural and traditional tie between Church and State, as we should call it; because this formal act not only involved a loss of power, it also drew attention to the religious anomaly of a Mahomedan community under Christian rulers; it raised

* "The Mahomedans . . . accuse us of having brought misery into thousands of families by abolishing their law officers, who gave the sanction of religion to the marriage tie; they accuse us of imperilling their souls, by denying them the means of performing the duties of their faith."—*Our Indian Mussulmans*, p. 145.

precisely the points which we ought to smooth down. The very fact that we had succeeded, in some parts of the country, to Musalman sovereigns should have made us more careful to supply their exact place, and to continue their functions as nearly as possible; instead of passing a self-denying ordinance to strip off the prerogative which every Mahomedan king exercises as an attribute of his rulership. "She who doth hold the gorgeous East in fee," the English Queen, rules over more Musalmans than does the Osmanli Sultan; our policy should be to prove that we are proud of this great sovereignty, and to lift up the heads of our Muslim fellow-subjects until they also feel the pride of living under the most powerful monarch in Asia.

But to go further into this complicated discussion would require much more space than is here available. The object of this chapter has been to give some account of the oscillations during the present century of our religious policy in India, and to point out certain misunderstandings which seem to have been at the bottom of our attempts to apply very modern European principles to the adjustment of our relations with Asiatic institutions. At first we were over careful to conciliate native prejudices by showing official respect and deference to rites and ceremonies of a nature largely repugnant to European habits of thought on such matters; and we were far too anxious to prove that we had no notion of giving umbrage to powerful creeds by favouring Christianity, which had no political importance. This overshot the mark, and naturally displeased European opinion; so we gave way to a strong reaction, and at one time we borrowed from the religious politics of Great Britain to an extent which laid us open to complaints that the English Government, in its endeavour to assume an impartial and irresponsible attitude toward all religions, had not sufficiently regarded the material interests of the native creeds and rituals, or their prescriptive claims upon the ruler, whoever he may be, of their country. And if the Indian people, as a body, hold that the Indian Government should not dissociate itself entirely from the superintendence of their religious establishments and endowments, it is no consolation whatever to them that Parliament should also be prepared to forbid all State provision for Christian Liturgies.

If, as may be suspected, we have occasionally missed, in the course of these transactions, the right meaning and scope of that perfect neutrality in religious matters which is very properly announced as the keynote of our policy, probably the cause may be that we have been influenced by the reminiscences of controversies that have been going on over a very different political situation at home. In England an assurance of neutrality would probably mean that the Government had determined to have nothing whatever to do with the affairs, temporal or spiritual, of any sect or creed; in India the declaration is generally taken to convey a welcome guarantee that the Queen will not favour one religion more than another; but it is not so welcome if it is found to mean the complete renunciation by their governors of all direct authority or headship over the management of the temporal interests of their religions. Such a course of action is foreign to all historic experience of the relations between secular and ecclesiastic authorities throughout Asia. It may be the only course now open to the English in India; nevertheless another might be learned from observing the organization of all great Asiatic governments, and from the example of every ruler over divers tribes or nationalities—namely, that in certain conditions of society the immediate authority and close supervision of a monarch over the powerful religious interests with which he has to reckon at every step, is a matter of political expediency, not an affair of doctrine or opinion, but a recognised duty of the State. To relinquish this position is to let go at least one real political advantage which accrues to us from our attitude of perfect neutrality, that of enabling us to superintend and guarantee the religious administration of all sects with entire impartiality, and with the confidence of our subjects. There is no reason whatever to regret the abolition of the old *régime* under which public officers were literally agents and managers for religious institutions; that system was rightly condemned. But to cut away all the historic ties between Church and State, to free Asiatic religions from every kind of direct subordination to the executive power, would be to push the principle further in India, where it is not understood and has no advocates, than has as yet been attempted even in any country of Europe, where it is supported by a large and increasing party.

# CHAPTER XI.

## THE RELIGIOUS SITUATION IN INDIA.

(*Fortnightly Review*, 1872.)

The striking appearance presented by the religious aspect of India as a survival of the world of præ-Christian ages—Geographical and historic reasons why India has been thus preserved, whereas all Asia west of India has been levelled by Islam, which only partially established itself in India—Incoherence and confusion of religions in India, to be accounted for mainly by its political history—India has never been organized, as a whole, into one great State; and it has been dilapidated by incessant wars—The multitude of gods and rites recalls the description of polytheism in the Roman Empire, given by Eusebius—Analogy between the effect on ancient polytheism of the establishment of the Roman peace, and the possible influence upon Hinduism of the English government in India—Speculation as to the future of Hinduism under civilized influences and an ordinary government—Probable disappearance or complete transformation of existing ideas and worships—The English have only to superintend gradual moral and intellectual progress; their empire the most efficient instrument of civilization among dissociated communities.

No one examines attentively the extraordinary religious confusion that still prevails throughout the great continent of India without marking it as one very peculiar characteristic of her social condition. For whereas primitive paganism, with all its incoherency, deficient alike in organic structure and in dominant ideas, has been utterly extinguished many centuries ago in Europe and throughout Western Asia, yet, wherever and whenever we cross the border or land on the shore of India, we may find going on before our eyes the things of which we read in ancient books. We seem to step suddenly out of the modern world of formal definite creeds, back into the disorderly supernaturalism of præ-Christian ages. After making allowance for every difference of manners, creed, and climate, and for innumerable distinctions of detail, we may still fancy that in looking over India we catch a reflection of classic polytheism. There we seem to have the nearest surviving representative of a half-civilized society's religious state, as it existed before Christianity and Mahomedanism organized and centralized the beliefs of all nations, from Ireland to the Indus. To those, indeed, who collect their notions of Indian religion out of the traditional scriptures and sacerdotal ordinances, the elaborate apparatus of Brahmanic mythology and ceremonial may appear to furnish forth a comprehensive system. But closer observation discovers a whole jumble of contradictory ideas and practices, a medley of popular superstitions underlying the authoritative ritual, and that total indifference to plan or fundamental unity which is the surest symptom of religion in a rudimentary and unorganized condition.

The seclusion of India within difficult geographical frontiers will, of course, explain much of her religious eccentricities. And the contrast which she now presents, when compared with Western Asia, may be directly accounted for by the course of her known history. Political vicissitudes seem to have powerfully affected religious development, while the half-conquest of India by the Mahomedans was only able to check and disturb consolidation. The mountains and desert tracts which guard her north-western and western borders acted as breakwaters against the first flood-tides of Musalman invasion; those great waves of enthusiasm were nearly spent before they reached this far Eastern region; they could not be beaten back or kept out, but their force was stopped and scattered. Subsequent inroads of fierce Central Asian hordes gradually beat down all sustained opposition, and the political supremacy of Islam was established. But the Mahomedans gained their footing gradually, and held it precariously: they never completed the territorial conquest of India, and on the whole they made little way against the customs and creeds of Hinduism. In western countries their overpowering political preponderance had pressed down flat and crushed out the old religions of subject races; the ancient and flourishing Zoroastrian worship, for example, was utterly extinguished in Persia. In India so little real progress toward extirpating polytheism had been made, that seven hundred and fifty years after Mahmud of Ghazni destroyed the famous idol at Somnâth, Mahomedans were still fighting with idolaters on the plains of Northern

India. An eye-witness to the great battle of Pâniput, in 1761, describes how the Musalman cavalry charged with the cry of *Yâ Allah*, while the Marâthas came on with their shouts of *Hur, Hur, Mahadeo*. The two armies appealed to different gods: the divinities of India were still separated into hostile camps, as in the days of the Trojan war. In India this might be still an every-day incident; but such war-cries have not been heard for many centuries in any of the battles that have been fought on the fields of Europe or Western Asia; though men have contended fiercely enough to ascertain by ordeal of battle which revelation of the One God is true, who was his messenger, and what may be the right interpretation of the message.

But though India was never thoroughly subdued by the sword of Islam, and though the country only became partially Mahomedan, yet the whole framework of her institutions was shaken and dislocated by incessant resistance. The Mahomedans disorganized Hinduism without substituting any strong religious edifice of their own, as they managed to do elsewhere. The military adventurers, who founded dynasties in Northern India and carved out kingdoms in the Dekhan, cared little for things spiritual; most of them had, indeed, no time for proselytism being continually engaged in conquest or in civil war. They were usually rough Tartars or Moghals; themselves ill grounded in the faith of Mahomed, and untouched by the true Semitic enthusiasm which inspired the first Arab standard-bearers of Islam. The empire which they set up was purely military, and it was kept in that state by the half-success of their conquests and the comparative failure of their spiritual invasion. They were strong enough to prevent anything like religious amalgamation among the Hindus, and to check the gathering of tribes into nations; but so far were they from converting India, that among the Mahomedans themselves their own faith never acquired an entire and exclusive monopoly of the high offices of administration. They only managed to maintain for several centuries an absolute government administered by a few great officers, and surrounded by a hierarchy of captains of thousands and ten thousands, who held assign-men tsof land on service tenure at will of their sovereign. The throne itself can hardly be said to have been hereditary, so often and so successfully was the inheritance disputed, and the dynasty changed. Such an empire as this, upheld at home and abroad entirely by violence and the fortune of war, must always have been independent of spiritual influence, because the whole system detained religious growth and arrested religious assimilation. And, as a matter of fact, among Indian Mahomedans their religion was never a power in the State. That great ecclesiastic corporation of the Ulema, which formed itself in the constitution of the Turkish empire, has maintained the theocratic idea of Islam by framing laws, interpreting tradition, regulating the services and ritual of the faith, administering the endowments, and otherwise asserting itself palpably as a recognised authority, not beneath, but side by side with the temporal ruler. At one period, indeed, the Ulema overawed the throne, and their decrees could pull down or set up its occupant: their authority has always increased whenever the military activity of the sultans declined; and they are still very influential. Their chief, the *Sheikh ul Islâm*, sits in the privy council, and expounds a law which binds sovereign as well as subjects. But in India the English, on succeeding to the paramount supremacy, found no counterpart of the Ulema, and hardly a trace of any such balance of powers; nor does the purely religious element of Mahomedan supremacy seem, even at its zenith, ever to have worked out there any separate constitution or enduring influence. Their Establishment, as we might call it, was never organised or even regularly endowed by the orthodox tithe; for, although large grants were made to devotion and charity, yet at no time do we hear of a great college or connected body preserving and expounding the sacred law.

If, however, the Musalmáns were never able to settle and develop their own spiritual institutions in India as they did in countries completely subdued by them, they were at least quite strong enough to counteract and depress the authority of the indigenous priesthoods. Whatever may at one time have been the sacerdotal power of the Brahmans, it is certain that the long predominance and proselytizing success of Mahomedans must have seriously lowered the general level of their popular reputation and sacred influence. Any hope of their eventually building Hinduism up into some higher stage of belief, must have been ruined and dispersed by foreign conquest; so that the general effect of the long ruinous wars and political troubles which fill the annals of India during the Mahomedan period was to keep all religion in a dispersed and dilapidated state. The whole tradition of the empire was, for Mahomedan despotism, remarkably tinged with religious indifference. Akbar, the greatest of Indian emperors, was rationalist and tolerant to a degree which distinguishes very plainly the general tone of Mahomedanism in India from that which prevailed about the same time elsewhere. Aurungzeb was a successful Richard III. His hypocrisy served him among the Mahomedans in his intrigues for the throne, but his pious practices stirred up more fanaticism against him than on his side. When he died, in 1710, there followed the great *débâcle* and dissolution of an empire that rested upon force, with no bond of union more elastic and less liable to snap suddenly, if we except the weak and incomplete lien of Mahomedan faith. The character and consequences of the events which preceded British supremacy in India have, perhaps, been seldom adequately estimated. There intervened a period of political anarchy greater and more widespread than the Indian continent had experienced for centuries. It was a mere tearing and rending of the prostrate carcass, a free fight with little definite aim or purpose beyond plunder or annexation of land revenue. The first Maratha captains were energetic and unscrupulous guerrilla leaders. They scarcely cared more for speculative notions of caste or creed than the wild Turcomans who followed the standard of the Emperor Baber or Nadir Shah, or than the adventurers of various creeds and nationalities who were disputing the spoils of empire in Bengal or in the Dekhan. It is remarkable that in the warlike Maratha federation, which subsisted by violent inroads and plundering, the paramount power had, by the eighteenth century, fallen into the hands of a Brahman family.

Not only was the Brahman Peshwa a military chief who commanded troops in person, but his Maratha army was mainly officered by Brahmans; and as the western Brahmans are by custom and profession remarkable rather for intellectual and literary capacity than for physical energy or hardihood, this conversion of them into soldiers shows how far the military spirit of the times had prevailed over sacerdotal or Levitic tradition.

Thus at the end of the last century India was further than ever from anything like a universal or uniform religion; and as there were no nations, so was there not in any part or province of the whole continent what we in Europe call a distinct national faith. It may be assumed that the formation of nationalities aids powerfully the concentration of religious beliefs, and that when a nation has once got shaped into political existence, it soon fits itself with a creed of its own, the stronger sect gradually absorbing all weaker species. There were signs in India that nations might have been eventually generated out of the decomposition of the Moghal empire, for some of the large tribes were drawing together under one head, and fixing themselves territorially and politically; but just at this point the English intervention turned the whole course of Indian history.

In this manner the political vicissitudes which have bequeathed to us India may be admitted to explain why a country which two thousand years ago had already reared and propagated over Eastern Asia two such vast popular religions as Brahmanism and Buddhism, should still be struggling with religious anarchy, and should have failed so completely in the uniting and building up some such religious institutions as have been completed, not only in all other great Aryan countries, but throughout Western Asia? Here is India still full of the mythologies, mysteries, and metaphysical theosophies of the ancient world, not lying one below the other, as in the religious stratification in which all these fossils may still be discovered even in Europe, but mixed and crowded together without order or coherence. The Christianity which we profess at this day in England is the outcome of an immensely long upward growth; the fruit of a tree whose roots are in primitive ages; yet the distance which separates Protestant England from the scenes and manners of the Pentateuch is no unfair measure of the breadth which lies between Englishmen and Hindus along the line of religious evolution. Take, for instance, the story of Micah, in the seventeenth and eighteenth chapters of the Book of Judges; how he had a house of gods, and made silver images, and consecrated one of his sons to be his priest; how he afterwards hired a wandering Levite to be his house-priest, and how one day six hundred Danites, appointed with weapons of war, carried off the images and the Levite together. Listening while this narrative is read before a Sunday congregation, one is amazed and absorbed by looking back over the extraordinary chain of events and filiation of ideas which have brought the annals of an ancient Syrian tribe to be read periodically in the villages of Great Britain. The story thus presented could only have come down to us from a far-off country and time; just as a broad river in a hot rainless plain must have risen in mountains long distant. And as a man enjoys the sight of the snow-fed waters of the Indus flowing full in midsummer between scorching sand-banks two thousand miles from its source in Tibet, so is he filled with the sense of vast intervals of space and time, of picturesque contrast between Now and Then, and of the long winding course of history which lies between the idol chapel of Micah in Mount Ephraim and the reading of an afternoon lesson in an English Protestant church.

Now what strikes one in India is that this stream of religious development, strong and perennial as it is, never has cut for itself a clear channel in which it could gather volume and flow on; it has only spread abroad like a vast swamp under the Himalayas, a range which marks one of the main religious watersheds of the world. To Europeans the episode of Micah is apt to be puzzling; the learned commentator in Dr. Smith's Dictionary of the Bible is quite unable to reconcile the manifest inconsistencies of Micah's practice with the authorised ritual, or to explain the conduct of the Danites. "It is," he remarks, "startling to our Western minds, accustomed to associate the blessings of order with religion, to observe how religious were these lawless freebooters." We need not stop here to discuss how far the Western mind is justified historically in the habitual association of order with religion: to the writer a religion is evidently a definite code of morals, resting upon an established system of theology; and he forgets that perils and adventures are apt to stimulate devotion. But while to an European scholar this picture of Syrian life is dim with the mists of three thousand years, to anyone who has lived in a lawless part of India the picture would be striking by its familiarity, and the supposed inconsistencies would be good proof of its authenticity. The very details of the narrative would adjust themselves to an Indian scene with little essential alteration, and would cause no surprise in Rajputána, though such an incident is now hardly intelligible to students in the Western world. Not since the days of Micah has India made any clear step in the general advance of religious ideas or discipline, so as to place its whole population solidly on a higher spiritual level. During so many centuries of spiritual wandering in the wilderness the Hindus have constructed no systematic fabric, no catholic organisation of religion, no tabernacle whither all their tribes go up; whereas all other races of equal and even lower civilization, many of inferior intellect, have built for themselves some such edifice. The face of the land is covered with innumerable temples, shrines, and sanctuaries, with places of prayer and altars of sacrifice. But as out of the ruins of early Indian sanctuaries no clear procession of styles can be traced, the earlier being often the more perfect, so we can follow no plain upward series of spiritual conceptions; and the creeds and ceremonies in daily use are a mosaic of old and new superstitions. They resemble some of their temples, which we can now see built over and out of the *débris* of earlier edifices; stones carved with the emblems of one god fitted into the chapel of another, phallic symbols in a niche which once contained Buddha, and outside a Mahomedan cupola surmounting the stone lintel and pillars of ancient Hindu architecture. It is by no means to be supposed that in India no tendencies have been displayed, or no efforts made, to rise into a higher life or a purer air; on the contrary, the whole religious history of India is full of such attempts. In a preceding chapter the entire landscape of Hinduism has been described as alive with incessant movement and change, with the constant struggle for existence of a multitude of religious species, among which are many rudimentary survivals of high conceptions deformed and degenerate. Out of the host of saints and devotees whom Indian superstition generates, there has often arisen some spiritually-minded man who reveals a new light, who cries aloud for a great moral change, who creates and propels a deep movement in the hearts of people. Such teachers have left their mark on Indian society, and their sects endure, but their true impulse gradually subsides; the lamp is passed from hand to hand, but its light grows fainter and fainter in the darkness of ignorant terror; it remains as a mystic spark to a few initiated, and as a mere portent to the vulgar who live in irrational fear of malignant deities. Since the collapse of Buddhism in India no religious system has acquired such a dynamic purchase or leverage upon the minds of men as to lift a great body of the Hindus clean out of the lower depths of superstition up on to the firm ground of an organised and progressive faith.

This, then, is in many ways the most noteworthy phænomenon to one who surveys India, its religious condition. And I have ventured to suggest that this dilapidated and disorganised state of popular Hinduism may be ascribed, for its more immediate cause, to the political catastrophes of the people, to the fierce, disorderly, and precarious existence which, as societies, they have led for so many centuries; so that the military spirit long maintained untempered predominance. More especially did the continual scrambling wars of the eighteenth century scatter piecemeal the elements of religious unification, and thereby arrest religious development. When, therefore the English became lords of India, they found no well-disciplined fanatic monotheism, as was found in Egypt or Algeria, to be dealt with, no great influential priesthood to be managed; Mahomedanism had already lost its political ascendancy; while Hinduism was, if one or two powerful sects and tribal groups be excepted, in a state of much confusion and disunion.

If it is reasonable to suppose that this religious prostration of India is nearly connected with its political misfortunes through many generations, then one can hardly avoid speculating on the consequences to be anticipated from its rapid restoration to substantial order and peace under the steady irresistible administration of the British.

It has been already observed that this strange multitude of gods and variety of rites among the Hindus may be imagined to represent the panorama of classic paganism. Eusebius of Cæsarea, in his book on the Theophaneia, gives a description of the lawless supernaturalism of the civilised world before the triumph of Christianity, which might almost apply word for word to India at the present day. He recites how the heathen made gods of the fruits of the earth, of their own base passions, and of animals; also how they published of certain men that "after undergoing a common mortality they became gods and demigods; imagining that the divine essence moved about the sides of graves and among the monuments of the dead;" how they made images of man and beast, and sacrificed to invisible demons; how their rites were shameful and their offerings bloody. He goes on to denounce the philosophers, who "by mere discovery of persuasive words, making no experiment even after the truth," pretended to discover the origin of all things, and "determined Rest to be the chief good;" while others said that the sensible word was God, and others again denied the imposition of any plastic hand upon matter. There is so much in this description that applies to India at the present time that any one who could take a general survey of the country might be struck by the resemblance. He might almost imagine himself (to use a fanciful illustration) removed to one of those distant stars of which the light only reaches our earth in sixteen hundred or eighteen hundred years, so that a reflection of what passes on earth must traverse as many centuries before it can strike the retina of a gazer from the star; and where, consequently, the inhabitants, if they have vision powerful enough to discern what is going on here below, may see at this moment the whole Roman Empire spread out before them; with all the numberless temples and high places of classic heathendom. Now, says Eusebius, the wonder of the matter is, that during the prosperity of this vile polytheism "there prevailed wars, conflicts, commotions, and the reducing of cities; but with the desolation and suppression of paganism came on entire peace with every good thing without drawback." Of course the main conclusion drawn out by the Bishop of Cæsarea is that the world was pacified by Christianity, nor is anyone likely to gainsay the immense political impression which must have been made by the greatest religious and moral reformation in all history. But he also points out emphatically the way in which the Roman conquests had driven a crushing and levelling roller over all the ancient barriers that cut up the old world by isolating and imprisoning societies, had knocked down these partition walls, and let in air and light. He sees very clearly that a profound peace did of itself operate upon polytheism to its discredit, decay, and ruin. Because, he says, "human life had undergone a change to a state henceforth of peace and rest; the divine revelation was shown forth at the time which was suitable. Nor were these multitudes of Rulers, Princes, Tyrants, and Governors of the people . . . the one Empire of the Romans had extended itself over all; and the peaceless uncompromising enmity which had so long been the portion of nations came to an end. And as the knowledge of one God was, by the teaching of our Saviour, delivered to all men; so also one king was established over the whole Roman Empire, and a profound peace prevailed. . . . Two singular advantages also sprung up among mankind, the Instruction that was in righteousness and the Empire of the Romans." Anyone could send merchandise, or go himself, whithersoever he pleased—the west would come to the east, and the east to the west, without danger. In short, so great and manifest were the advantages of the Roman rule to the spread of one religion, that it was clearly fore-ordained for the dissemination of the Gospel. "Who will not confess this, when he has considered that it would not have been easy to send forth disciples, when all the nations were divided one against another? . . . But God, who is over all, had restrained the wrath of the worshippers of demons in the cities, by the fear of the great Empire."

The quotation might have been given at much greater length; for Eusebius is filled with the idea that the Roman Empire had been appointed as a great war engine to beat down and demolish the feuds and jarring antagonisms of the pagan world, to put away barbarous misrule, and the tyranny of "Satraps in every city." The rapid fading away and collapse of these immemorial superstitions before the steady maintenance of peace and law over an immense territory is one of the most wonderful phænomena of the world's history, however we may seek to account for it. Those superstitions had been engendered and fostered by ignorance and isolation; they were the shadows and phantasmagoria of human passions, and of inexplicable calamities from the earliest times—the memory of man ran not to the contrary thereof. In a few centuries the whole fabric and apparatus of polytheism had broken up and melted off the surface of the civilised nations, whose pacification and orderly government were then seen to have been the necessary forerunners and pioneers of a wide spiritual reformation.

If we may draw a broad analogy between the social and political changes worked upon the Western world by the Roman conquests, and that which is being worked upon the great continent of India by English dominion, then it may not be rash to prolong the parallel, and to speculate on the probability of some consequences following in the latter case not unlike those which ensued in the former. We are changing the whole atmosphere in which fantastic superstitions grow and flourish. We may expect that these old forms of supernaturalism will suddenly thaw and subside without any outward stroke upon them, and without long premonitory symptoms of internal dissolution; like icebergs that have at last floated into a warmer sea, which topple over at the invisible melting of their submarine base. At this moment Hinduism still overshadows the land; the intricate jungle of creeds and worships appears thick and strong as ever; yet one may conjecture that its roots are being effectually cut away. Uncertainty and insecurity prolonged what ignorance and stagnation had produced; but the old order has now changed, giving place to new. The last stand made against the new system of peace and law by the warlike and unruly elements of the population was from 1846 to 1858. Never perhaps in all the history of India has more decisive fighting been compressed into twelve years; the English scattered two formidable disciplined armies, the Sikh army and their own sepoys, and dissolved two incipient kingdoms that might have hardened into nationalities: they prevailed over the momentary fanaticism of the Hindu and the enthusiasm of the Mahomedan; they employed these two forces to each counteract and repress the other; they disarmed India, and closed for the present its military era. We have now established reasonable personal security and free communications; we are giving to the Indians leisure and education, the scientific method and the critical spirit; we are opening to them the flood-gates behind which Western knowledge is piled in far greater volume than the stream of Grecian philosophy which the Romans distributed over their empire, when they made the source accessible and its outflow easy. It is not easy to conceive any more interesting subject for historical speculation than the probable effect upon India, and consequently upon the civilisation of all Asia, of the English dominion; for though it would be most presumptuous to attempt any kind of prediction as to the nature or bent of India's religious future, yet we may look forward to a wide and rapid transformation in two or three generations, if England's rule only be as durable as it has every appearance of being. It seems possible that the old gods of Hinduism will die in these new elements of intellectual light and air as quickly as a net-full of fish lifted up out of the water; that the alteration in the religious needs of such an intellectual people as the Hindus, which will have been caused by a change in their circumstances, will make it impossible for them to find in their new world a place for their ancient deities. Their primitive forms will fade and disappear silently, as witchcraft vanished from Europe, and as all such delusions become gradually extinguished. In the movement itself there is nothing new, but in India it promises to go on with speed and intensity unprecedented; for she has been taken in tow by Europe, where we are now going forward with steam at high pressure; and herein seems to lie the peculiar interest, perhaps the danger, of the Indian situation. At certain epochs the progressive nations of the world find it necessary to readjust the intellectual equilibrium, that is to say, to establish afresh a certain harmony between what they believe and what they know. One of the earliest symptoms that knowledge and belief are falling out of balance is perceptible in what has been called the *malàise religieux*, which was seen in the Roman Empire before Christianity cured it, and which one may fancy to be visible in India already. It may possibly be that very "spirit of unrest" which Dr. W. W. Hunter has detected among Indian Mahomedans; as it is probably at the bottom of the Mahomedan revival, which Mr. W. G. Palgrave * believes to be taking place throughout all Islam. It seems certainly indicated by numerous sectarian advances among the Hindus towards a more spiritual kind of creed; toward mystical interpretations, at least, of substantial polytheism, and toward such an abstract dogma as that upon which is founded the profession of the *Brahmo Somâj*. In the North it is fermenting among various sects; and in the South it appears in the demand recently made to Government by educated Hindus for the reform of their religious endowments, a demand that will carry us and them far if we attempt to comply with it; for any serious attempt to purify the abuses of polytheism and to establish the external worship upon a decent and rational system, can hardly fail to let in views and principles that may disintegrate the very foundations of the whole edifice.

Thus there may be grounds for anticipating that a solid universal peace and the impetus given by Europe must together cause such rapid intellectual expansion that India will now be carried swiftly through phases which have occupied long stages in the lifetime of all other nations. The Hindu now makes in

* *Fraser's Magazine*, Feb. 1872.

two days a journey that occupied a month ten years ago, because the English have laid down their railways before the Indians had invented the paved road; and his mental development may advance by similar overleaping of intermediate improvements. And whereas hitherto new religious ideas have constantly sprung up in India, and have as constantly withered or been dissipated for want of protection and undisturbed culture, any such ideas that may hereafter arise will be fostered and may spread uninterruptedly, if they have the principle of persistent growth. Some great movement is likely to come about in India, if only the peace lasts; but what may be the complexion of that movement, and whither its gravitation, is a question which time only can answer. Orderly Christian rule has given to Islam in India an opportunity for becoming regenerate and for reuniting its strength, which it owes entirely to us. We have restored its communications by sea and by land; we have already felt some of the consequences of pulling down the barriers which Ranjít Singh and his Sikhs set up on our north-western frontier between the Mahomedans of India and the rest of Western Asia. Mahomedanism may yet occupy a larger space in the history of Indian rationalism; but it must make haste, or the country may drift beyond it. Some may think that Christianity will a second time in the world's history step into the vacancy created by a great territorial empire, and occupy the tracts laid open by the upheaval of a whole continent to a new intellectual and moral level. But the state of thought in Western Europe hardly encourages conjecture that India will receive from that quarter any such decisive impulse as that which overturned the decaying paganism of Greece and Rome just at the time when the Pax Romana had at last brought local beliefs into jarring collision one with another, and into contact with the profound spiritualism of Asia. The influence of Europe on India is essentially industrial and scientific; England's business in particular is to construct there some firm political system under which all other social relations may be reared and directed; but here comes in the difficulty of founding and keeping steady any such edifice without the cement of some binding idea. It is in the religious life that Asiatic communities still find the reason of their existence, and the repose of it. When the Indian has gained his intellectual freedom, there remains to be seen what he will do with it; and the solution of this problem is of incalculable importance to our successful management of the empire. The general tendencies of modern thought are toward doubt and negation; the sum total of what we call civilisation is to such a society as that in India a dissolving force: it is the pouring of new wines into old skins; the cutting away of anchors instead of hauling them up, so that in the next emergency there are none to throw out. Conquest and civilisation together must sweep away the old convictions and prejudices; and unless some great enthusiasm rushes in to fill the vacancy thus created, we may find ourselves called to preside over some sort of spiritual interregnum.

Such transitional periods are apt to be troublesome to governments. In India the English difficulty is that, whatever the religious movement may be, we cannot expect to take part in or guide it, because we are in many ways so far ahead of, or at least too far removed from, the mass of the people whom we have to manage, that our superiority begets want of sympathy, and in our desire to lead them we lose patience and discrimination. On the other hand there is already springing up among the natives of India an advanced party, of those who are easily inoculated with the Voltairean spirit, with contempt for irrational beliefs, and for institutions that seem absurd on the face of them. But all our European experiments in social science have taught us the unwisdom of demolishing old-world fabrics which no one is yet prepared to replace by anything else. Caste, for instance, looks unnecessary and burdensome, it is wildly abused by Europeans,* to whom the Brahmanic rules of behaviour seem unmeaning and unpractical; but these things will tumble quite fast enough

* "Caste is the devil's yoke. . . . . Hindu widowhood is Satan's masterpiece. . . . Juggunâth was invented by devils." See "A Plea for Indian Missions," by Alexander Forbes, 1865; a pamphlet which is not only unfair to Satan, but which betrays a curious tendency toward that very same superstitious polytheism (the belief in a multitude of evil spirits) which the writer is denouncing.

without our knocking out their keystones by premature legislation. It is hardly our interest to bring them down with a crash. We have ourselves to overcome the rather superficial contempt which an European naturally conceives for societies and habits of thoughts different from those within the range of his own ordinary experience; and also to avoid instilling too much of the destructive spirit into the mind of young India: remembering that for English and natives the paramount object is now to preserve social continuity. M. Pierre Lafitte, in his *Considérations générales sur l'ensemble de la Civilisation Chinoise*, quotes from a book* in which an English Protestant Missionary describes China as undergoing a succession of moral earthquakes, and congratulates Europe on the total ruin of "fossil prejudices," bigotry, and superstition, which these "terrible convulsions" are causing. Storms and hurricanes, Mr. Mylne had observed, purify the air. But M. Lafitte remarks that this is to welcome a state of violent agitation ending in complete anarchy; and that to talk of convulsions as the conditions of progress has a dangerous resemblance to revolutionary jargon, though the writer may not mean it. Hurricanes clear the earth as well as the air, and earthquakes are not very discriminating in their operations. It is certain, at any rate, that moral earthquakes and cyclones in the Indian climate will severely test the stability of our rule, and we are by no means concerned to encourage them. M. Lafitte, in the lecture just mentioned, points out the vague notions of progress and civilisation upon which people rely who desire to pull down a society which they do not comprehend, or whose real aim is sometimes no more than the exploitation of the East by the West. He protests, for example, against the English raising a jubilee over the remarriage of Hindu widows, and he thinks we had no business whatever to make war on the old custom by legalising breaches of it. It is possible that M. Lafitte himself may have been verging on the error of judging the East by the West, and may not have recollected that in India very many girls become widows at an age when they would still be in an European

* La Vie réelle en Chine, par le Révérend C. Mylne. 1858.

nursery. Here is good cause for interference, and there are other cases in which the action of our own law courts, in stereotyping and enforcing invariably customs that were naturally very elastic and varying, tended to check the natural modifications according to circumstances, the sloughing off of decayed forms, so that special legislation became necessary. Yet withal there is something to be said against our passing any laws to abolish social rules which do not concern us personally, and which do not openly violate morality; and there is everything to be said against being impatient with people who, belonging to a different social formation, are reluctant to give up hastily the very principles on which their society has been moulded. Such impatience is akin to the injustice with which, as has been often remarked, we are too much accustomed to treat the past, forgetting that written records tell us very little indeed of what really went on, and can still less explain how and why people felt and acted a few centuries ago. This is, indeed, the reason why an opportunity of studying closely the condition and progress of such a country as India is most valuable, because we can there look round at things which we can hardly realise by looking behind us on them. We are turning back, as it were, along the broad path of history, and by seeing with our own eyes the scenes we have often tried to look at through old books blurred with ignorance and prejudice, we get at more clear notions of and sympathy with those bygone times, when men from whom we are descended—who were of like passions with ourselves, nor inferior in intellect—yet firmly held beliefs which their posterity rejects with contempt, and conscientiously did deeds which we now read of with horror and amazement.

All that the English need do is to keep the peace and clear the way. Our vocation just now is to mount guard over India during the transitional period which may be expected to follow, much as we used to station a company of soldiers to keep order at Jagannâth's festival in the days of the East India Company. Jagannâth himself may be safely left exposed to the rising tide of that intellectual advancement which the people must certainly work out for themselves if they only keep pace and have patience. No doubt this negative attitude, this standing aloof, is an imperfect and not altogether well secured position, for a political system founded mainly upon considerations of material interests and well-being has been declared by high philosophic authority to be unstable.* We have not yet sailed out of the region of religious storms in India; and though spiritual enthusiasm may be gradually subsiding in fervour, yet it may also tend to combine and organize its forces, as polytheism melts down and concentrates. Against such impulses, among men who will still die for a rule of faith, as our forefathers did so often, material considerations must occasionally avail little. But there is, at any rate, one gospel which the English can preach and practise in India, the gospel of high political morality, which, because it is a complete novelty and new light among Asiatic rulers, should for that reason be the characteristic note of our administration; and to maintain it we may risk much misunderstanding of motive. We must even endure temporary loss of that reputation for high-handed consistency, whatever it may be worth, which is to be maintained by upholding a blunder once committed, and by stooping to the untrained public opinion which would applaud it. We cannot undertake in any way the spiritual direction of Hindus; but neither are we prepared to take lessons from them upon questions of public morality. A certain line of conduct may be congenial to the notions of native princes or people; but our governors and chief rulers go to India, not to be taught, but to teach, the duties of rulership, and to instruct the consciences of half-barbarous communities.

Finally, we may hope that all reflecting and far-sighted natives of that class which we are rapidly training up in large towns to political knowledge and social freedom will perceive that England's prime function in India is at present this, to superintend the tranquil elevation of the whole moral and intellectual standard. Those who are interested in such a change

* "Une expérience décisive a maintenant prouvé l'instabilité nécessaire de tout régime purement matériel, fondé seulement sur des intérêts, indépendamment des affections et des convictions." —COMTE, *Cours de Philosophie.*

in the ethics of their country, in broadening the realms of the known and the true, must see how ruinously premature it is to quarrel with the English Government upon details of administration, or even upon what are called constitutional questions. The peculiar crisis and conjuncture of Indian affairs at the end of the last century brought out one supremely strong government by the same pressure of circumstances which has struck out the type of all empires. A modern empire means the maintenance of order by the undisputed predominance of one all-powerful member of a federation; and where representative assemblies, in the English sense of the term, are impossible, it is the best machine for collecting public opinion over a wide area among dissociated communities. It is the most efficient instrument of comprehensive reforms in law and government, and the most powerful engine whereby one confessedly superior race can control and lead other races left without nationality or a working social organization. It breaks up the antipathies, narrowness, and exclusive antagonism which always check the growth of earlier civilizations, and which have hitherto lain like rusty fetters on India. If ever the imperial system was necessary and fitted to a time and country, it is to India as we now see it.

THE END.

BRADBURY, AGNEW, & CO., PRINTERS, WHITEFRIARS.

ALBEMARLE STREET, LONDON,
*February*, 1888.

# MR. MURRAY'S
## GENERAL LIST OF WORKS.

ALBERT MEMORIAL. A Descriptive and Illustrated Account of the National Monument at Kensington. Illustrated by numerous Engravings. With Descriptive Text. By DOYNE C. BELL. With 24 Plates. Folio. 12*l*. 12*s*.

———— HANDBOOK TO. Post 8vo. 1*s*.; or Illustrated Edition, 2*s*. 6*d*.

ABBOTT (REV. J.). Memoirs of a Church of England Missionary in the North American Colonies. Post 8vo. 2*s*.

ABERCROMBIE (JOHN). Enquiries concerning the Intellectual Powers and the Investigation of Truth. Fcap. 8vo. 3*s*. 6*d*.

ACLAND (REV. C.). The Manners and Customs of India. Post 8vo. 2*s*.

ÆSOP'S FABLES. A New Version. By REV. THOMAS JAMES. With 100 Woodcuts, by TENNIEL and WOLFE. Post 8vo. 2*s*. 6*d*.

AGRICULTURAL (ROYAL) JOURNAL. (*Published half-yearly.*)

AINGER (A. C.). [See ETON.]

ALICE (PRINCESS); GRAND DUCHESS OF HESSE. Letters to H.M. THE QUEEN. With a Memoir by H.R.H. Princess Christian Popular Edition. Portrait. Crown 8vo. 7*s*. 6*d*., or Original Edition, 12*s*.

AMBER-WITCH (THE). A most interesting Trial for Witchcraft. Translated by LADY DUFF GORDON. Post 8vo. 2*s*.

AMERICA. [See BATES, NADAILLAC, RUMBOLD.]

APOCRYPHA: With a Commentary Explanatory and Critical By Prof. Salmon, D.D, Prof. Fuller, Archdeacon Farrar, Archdeacon Gifford, Canon Rawlinson, Dr. Edersheim, Rev. J. H. Lupton, Rev. C J. Ball. Edited by HENRY WACE, D.D. 2 vols. Medium 8vo.

ARISTOTLE. [See GROTE.]

ARTHUR'S (LITTLE) History of England. By LADY CALLCOTT. *New Edition, continued to* 1878. With Woodcuts. Fcap. 8vo. 1*s*. 6*d*.

———— HISTORY OF FRANCE, from the Earliest Times to the Fall of the Second Empire. With Woodcuts. Fcp. 8vo. 2*s*. 6*d*.

AUSTIN (JOHN). GENERAL JURISPRUDENCE; or, The Philosophy of Positive Law. Edited by ROBERT CAMPBELL. 2 Vols. 8vo. 32*s*.

———— STUDENT'S EDITION, compiled from the above work, by ROBERT CAMPBELL. Post 8vo. 12*s*.

———— Analysis of. By GORDON CAMPBELL. Post 8vo. 6*s*.

BABER (E. C.) Travels in W. China. Maps. Royal 8vo. 5*s*.

BAINES (THOMAS). Greenhouse and Stove Plants, Flowering and Fine Leaved. Palms, Ferns, and Lycopodiums. With full details of the Propagation and Cultivation. 8vo. 8*s*. 6*d*.

BARCLAY (BISHOP). Extracts from the Talmud, illustrating the Teaching of the Bible. With an Introduction. 8vo. 14*s.*

BARKLEY (H. C.). Five Years among the Bulgarians and Turks between the Danube and the Black Sea. Post 8vo. 10*s.* 6*d.*

— — Bulgaria Before the War. Post 8vo. 10*s.* 6*d.*

— My Boyhood: a True Story. Woodcuts. Post 8vo. 6*s.*

BARROW (JOHN). Life of Sir F. Drake. Post 8vo. 2*s.*

BATES (H. W.). Records of a Naturalist on the Amazons during Eleven Years' Adventure and Travel. Illustrations. Post 8vo. 7*s.* 6*d*

BAX (CAPT.). Russian Tartary, Eastern Siberia, China, Japan, &c. Illustrations. Crown 8vo. 12*s.*

BEACONSFIELD'S (LORD) Letters, and "Correspondence with his Sister," 1830—1852. A New Edition with additional letters and notes. Portrait. Crown 8vo. 2*s.*
*,* A few copies of the larger editions may still be had.

BECKETT (SIR EDMUND). "Should the Revised New Testament be Authorised?" Post 8vo. 6*s.*

BELL (SIR CHAS.). Familiar Letters. Portrait. Post 8vo. 12*s.*

— (DOYNE C.). Notices of the Historic Persons buried in the Chapel of St. Peter ad Vincula, in the Tower of London. Illustrations. Crown 8vo. 14*s.*

BENJAMIN (S. G. W.). Persia and the Persians. With Illustrations. 8vo. 24*s.*

BENSON (ARCHBISHOP). The Cathedral; its necessary place in the Life and Work of the Church. Post 8vo. 6*s.*

BERKELEY (COMMDR. HASTINGS). Wealth and Welfare: an Examination of Recent Changes in the Production and Distribution of Wealth in the United Kingdom, and of the Effect of our National Trade Policy on the General Welfare of the Nation. Crown 8vo. 6*s.*

BERTRAM (JAS. G.). Harvest of the Sea: an Account of British Food Fishes, Fisheries and Fisher Folk. Illustrations. Post 8vo. 9*s.*

BIBLE COMMENTARY. THE OLD TESTAMENT. EXPLANATORY and CRITICAL. With a REVISION of the TRANSLATION. By BISHOPS and CLERGY of the ANGLICAN CHURCH. Edited by F. C. COOK, M.A., Canon of Exeter. 6 VOLS. Medium 8vo. 6*l.* 15*s.*

| | | | |
|---|---|---|---|
| Vol. I. 30*s.* | GENESIS—DEUTERONOMY. | VOL. IV. 24*s.* | JOB—SONG OF SOLOMON. |
| Vols. II. and III. 36*s.* | JOSHUA—ESTHER. | Vol. V. 20*s.* | ISAIAH, JEREMIAH. |
| | | Vol. VI. 25*s.* | EZEKIEL—MALACHI. |

THE NEW TESTAMENT. 4 VOLS. Medium 8vo. 4*l.* 14*s.*

| | | | |
|---|---|---|---|
| Vol. I. 18*s.* | INTRODUCTION, ST. MATTHEW, ST. MARK, ST. LUKE. | Vol. III. 28*s.* | ROMANS—PHILEMON. |
| Vol. II. 20*s.* | ST. JOHN. ACTS OF THE APOSTLES. | Vol. IV. 28*s.* | HEBREWS — REVELATION. |

— THE STUDENT'S EDITION. Abridged and Edited by PROFESSOR J. M. FULLER, M.A. Crown 8vo. 7*s.* 6*d.* each Volume.
THE OLD TESTAMENT. 4 Vols. THE NEW TESTAMENT. 2 Vols.

BIGG-WITHER (T. P.). Pioneering in South Brazil; Three Years of Forest and Prairie Life in the Province of Parana. Map and Illustrations. 2 vols. Crown 8vo. 21*s.*

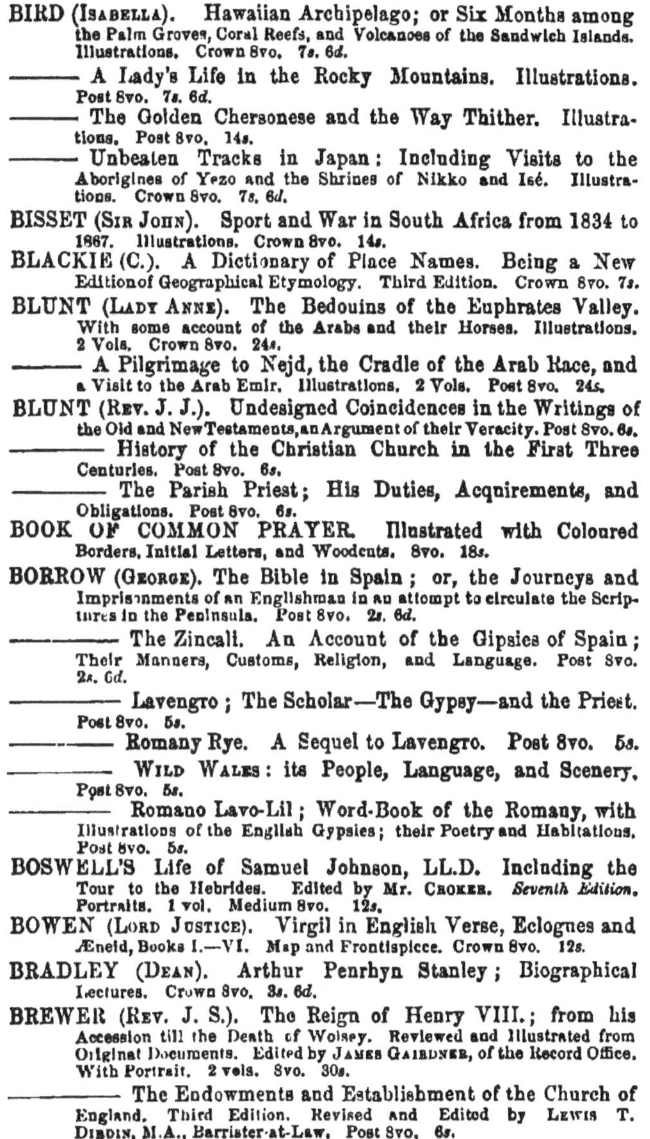

BIRD (Isabella). Hawaiian Archipelago; or Six Months among the Palm Groves, Coral Reefs, and Volcanoes of the Sandwich Islands. Illustrations. Crown 8vo. 7*s.* 6*d.*

——— A Lady's Life in the Rocky Mountains. Illustrations. Post 8vo. 7*s.* 6*d.*

——— The Golden Chersonese and the Way Thither. Illustrations. Post 8vo. 14*s.*

——— Unbeaten Tracks in Japan: Including Visits to the Aborigines of Yezo and the Shrines of Nikko and Isé. Illustrations. Crown 8vo. 7*s.* 6*d.*

BISSET (Sir John). Sport and War in South Africa from 1834 to 1867. Illustrations. Crown 8vo. 14*s.*

BLACKIE (C.). A Dictionary of Place Names. Being a New Editionof Geographical Etymology. Third Edition. Crown 8vo. 7*s.*

BLUNT (Lady Anne). The Bedouins of the Euphrates Valley. With some account of the Arabs and their Horses. Illustrations. 2 Vols. Crown 8vo. 24*s.*

——— A Pilgrimage to Nejd, the Cradle of the Arab Race, and a Visit to the Arab Emir. Illustrations. 2 Vols. Post 8vo. 24*s.*

BLUNT (Rev. J. J.). Undesigned Coincidences in the Writings of the Old and New Testaments, an Argument of their Veracity. Post 8vo. 6*s.*

——— History of the Christian Church in the First Three Centuries. Post 8vo. 6*s.*

——— The Parish Priest; His Duties, Acquirements, and Obligations. Post 8vo. 6*s.*

BOOK OF COMMON PRAYER. Illustrated with Coloured Borders, Initial Letters, and Woodcuts. 8vo. 18*s.*

BORROW (George). The Bible in Spain; or, the Journeys and Imprisonments of an Englishman in an attempt to circulate the Scriptures in the Peninsula. Post 8vo. 2*s.* 6*d.*

——— The Zincali. An Account of the Gipsies of Spain; Their Manners, Customs, Religion, and Language. Post 8vo. 2*s.* 6*d.*

——— Lavengro; The Scholar—The Gypsy—and the Priest. Post 8vo. 5*s.*

——— Romany Rye. A Sequel to Lavengro. Post 8vo. 5*s.*

——— Wild Wales: its People, Language, and Scenery. Post 8vo. 5*s.*

——— Romano Lavo-Lil; Word-Book of the Romany, with Illustrations of the English Gypsies; their Poetry and Habitations. Post 8vo. 5*s.*

BOSWELL'S Life of Samuel Johnson, LL.D. Including the Tour to the Hebrides. Edited by Mr. Croker. *Seventh Edition.* Portraits. 1 vol. Medium 8vo. 12*s.*

BOWEN (Lord Justice). Virgil in English Verse, Eclogues and Æneid, Books I.—VI. Map and Frontispiece. Crown 8vo. 12*s.*

BRADLEY (Dean). Arthur Penrhyn Stanley; Biographical Lectures. Crown 8vo. 3*s.* 6*d.*

BREWER (Rev. J. S.). The Reign of Henry VIII.; from his Accession till the Death of Wolsey. Reviewed and Illustrated from Original Documents. Edited by James Gairdner, of the Record Office. With Portrait. 2 vols. 8vo. 30*s.*

——— The Endowments and Establishment of the Church of England. Third Edition. Revised and Edited by Lewis T. Dibdin, M.A., Barrister-at-Law. Post 8vo. 6*s.*

BRIDGES (Mrs. F. D.). A Lady's Travels in Japan, Thibet, Yarkand, Kashmir, Java, the Straits of Malacca, Vancouver's Island, &c. With Map and Illustrations from Sketches by the Author. Crown 8vo. 15s.

BRITISH ASSOCIATION REPORTS. 8vo.

*** The Reports for the years 1831 to 1875 may be obtained at the Offices of the British Association.

| | | |
|---|---|---|
| Glasgow, 1876, 25s. | Swansea, 1880, 24s. | Canada, 1884, 24s. |
| Plymouth, 1877, 24s. | York, 1881, 24s. | Aberdeen, 1885, 24s. |
| Dublin, 1878, 24s. | Southampton, 1882, 24s. | Birmingham, 1886, 24s. |
| Sheffield, 1879, 24s. | Southport, 1883, 24s. | |

BROCKLEHURST (T. U.). Mexico To-day: A Country with a Great Future. With a Glance at the Prehistoric Remains and Antiquities of the Montezumas. Plates and Woodcuts. Medium 8vo. 21s.

BRUCE (Hon. W. N.). Life of Sir Charles Napier. [See Napier.]

BRUGSCH (Professor). A History of Egypt under the Pharaohs. Derived entirely from Monuments, with a Memoir on the Exodus of the Israelites. Maps. 2 Vols. 8vo. 32s.

BULGARIA. [See Barkley, Huhn, Minchin.]

BUNBURY (E. H.). A History of Ancient Geography, among the Greeks and Romans, from the Earliest Ages till the Fall of the Roman Empire. Maps. 2 Vols. 8vo. 21s.

BURBIDGE (F. W.). The Gardens of the Sun: or A Naturalist's Journal in Borneo and the Sulu Archipelago. Illustrations. Cr. 8vo. 14s.

BURCKHARDT'S Cicerone; or Art Guide to Painting in Italy. New Edition, revised by J. A. Crowe. Post 8vo. 6s.

BURGES (Sir James Bland, Bart.) Selections from his Letters and Papers, as Under-Secretary of State for Foreign Affairs. With Notices of his Life. Edited by James Hutton. 8vo. 15s.

BURGON (J. W.), Dean of Chichester. The Revision Revised: (1.) The New Greek Text; (2.) The New English Version (3.) Westcott and Hort's Textual Theory. Second Edition. 8vo. 14s.

——— Twelve Lives of Good Men. Martin J. Routh, Hugh James Rose, Chas. Marriott, Edward Hawkins, Samuel Wilberforce, Richard Lynch Cotton, Richard Gresswell, Henry Octavius Coxe, Henry Longueville Mansel, Wm. Jacobson, Chas. Page Eden, Chas. Longuet Higgins. 2 vols. Crown 8vo.

BURKE (Edmund). [See Pankhurst.]

BURN (Col.). Dictionary of Naval and Military Technical Terms, English and French—French and English. Crown 8vo. 15s.

BUTTMANN'S LEXILOGUS; a Critical Examination of the Meaning of numerous Greek Words, chiefly in Homer and Hesiod. By Rev. J. R. Fishlake. 8vo. 12s.

BUXTON (Charles). Memoirs of Sir Thomas Fowell Buxton, Bart. Portrait. 8vo. 16s. *Popular Edition.* Fcap. 8vo. 5s.

——— Notes of Thought. With a Biographical Notice by Rev. J. Llewellyn Davies, M.A. *Second Edition.* Post 8vo. 5s.

——— (Sydney C.). A Handbook to the Political Questions of the Day; with the Arguments on Either Side. Sixth Edition. 8vo. 7s. 6d.

——— Finance and Politics, an Historical Study. 8vo. [*In the Press.*

BYLES (Sir John). Foundations of Religion in the Mind and Heart of Man. Post 8vo. 6s.

BYRON'S (Lord) LIFE AND WORKS:—

Life, Letters, and Journals. By Thomas Moore. *Cabinet Edition.* Plates. 6 Vols. Fcap. 8vo. 18s.; or One Volume, Portraits. Royal 8vo. 7s. 6d.

BYRON'S (LORD) LIFE AND WORKS—*continued.*

LIFE AND POETICAL WORKS. *Popular Edition.* Portraits. 2 Vols. Royal 8vo. 15*s.*

POETICAL WORKS. *Library Edition.* Portrait. 6 Vols. 8vo. 45*s.*

POETICAL WORKS. *Cabinet Edition.* Plates. 10 Vols. 12mo. 30*s.*

POETICAL WORKS. *Pocket Ed.* 8 Vols. 16mo. In a case. 21*s.*

POETICAL WORKS. *Popular Edition.* Plates. Royal 8vo. 7*s.* 6*d.*

POETICAL WORKS. *Pearl Edition.* Crown 8vo. 2*s.* 6*d.* Sewed Cloth. 3*s.* 6*d.*

CHILDE HAROLD. With 80 Engravings. Crown 8vo. 12*s.*

CHILDE HAROLD. 16mo. 2*s.* 6*d.*

CHILDE HAROLD. Vignettes. 16mo. 1*s.*

CHILDE HAROLD. Portrait. 16mo. 6*d.*

TALES AND POEMS. 16mo. 2*s.* 6*d.*

MISCELLANEOUS. 2 Vols. 16mo. 5*s.*

DRAMAS AND PLAYS. 2 Vols. 16mo. 5*s.*

DON JUAN AND BEPPO. 2 Vols. 16mo. 5*s.*

BEAUTIES. Poetry and Prose. Portrait. Fcap. 8vo. 3*s.* 6*d.*

CAMPBELL (LORD). Life: with his Autobiography, selections from Journals, and Correspondence. By Mrs. Hardcastle. Portrait. 2 Vols. 8vo. 30*s.*

——— Lord Chancellors and Keepers of the Great Seal of England. From the Earliest Times to the Death of Lord Eldon in 1838. 10 Vols. Crown 8vo. 6*s.* each.

——— Chief Justices of England. From the Norman Conquest to the Death of Lord Tenterden. 4 Vols. Crown 8vo. 6*s.* each.

——— (THOS.) Essay on English Poetry. With Short Lives of the British Poets. Post 8vo. 3*s.* 6*d.*

CAREY (Life of). [See GEORGE SMITH.]

CARLISLE (BISHOP OF). Walks in the Regions of Science and Faith—a Series of Essays. Crown 8vo. 7*s.* 6*d.*

CARNARVON (LORD). Portugal, Gallicia, and the Basque Provinces. Post 8vo. 3*s.* 6*d.*

CARNOTA (CONDE DA). The Life and Eventful Career of F.M. the Duke of Saldanha; Soldier and Statesman. 2 Vols. 8vo. 32*s.*

CARTWRIGHT (W. C.). The Jesuits: their Constitution and Teaching. An Historical Sketch. 8vo. 9*s.*

CAVALCASELLE'S WORKS. [See CROWE.]

CESNOLA (GEN.). Cyprus; its Ancient Cities, Tombs, and Temples. With 400 Illustrations. Medium 8vo. 50*s.*

CHAMBERS (G. F.). A Practical and Conversational Pocket Dictionary of the English, French, and German Languages. Designed for Travellers and Students generally. Small 8vo. 6*s.*

CHILD-CHAPLIN (Dr.). Benedicite; or, Song of the Three Children; being Illustrations of the Power, Beneficence, and Design manifested by the Creator in his Works. Post 8vo. 6*s.*

CHISHOLM (Mrs.). Perils of the Polar Seas; True Stories of Arctic Discovery and Adventure. Illustrations. Post 8vo. 6*s.*

CHURTON (ARCHDEACON). Poetical Remains. Post 8vo. 7*s.* 6*d.*

CLASSIC PREACHERS OF THE ENGLISH CHURCH. Lectures delivered at St. James'. 2 Vols. Post 8vo. 7*s.* 6*d.* each.

CLIVE'S (LORD) Life. By REV. G. R. GLEIG. Post 8vo. 3*s.* 6*d.*

CLODE (C. M.). Military Forces of the Crown; their Administration and Government. 2 Vols. 8vo. 21*s.* each.

CLODE (C. M.). Administration of Justice under Military and Martial Law, as applicable to the Army, Navy, and Auxiliary Forces. 8vo. 12*s.*

COLEBROOKE (SIR EDWARD, BART.). Life of the Hon. Mountstuart Elphinstone. With Portrait and Plans. 2 Vols. 8vo. 26*s.*

COLERIDGE (SAMUEL TAYLOR), and the English Romantic School. By PROF. ALOIS BRANDL, of Prague. An English Edition by LADY EASTLAKE, assisted by the Author. With Portrait, Crown 8vo. 12*s.*

——— Table-Talk. Portrait. 12mo. 3*s.* 6*d.*

COLES (JOHN). Summer Travelling in Iceland. With a Chapter on Askja. BY E. D. MORGAN. Map and Illustrations. 18*s.*

COLLINS (J. CHURTON). BOLINGBROKE: an Historical Study. Three Essays to which is added an Essay on Voltaire in England. Crown 8vo. 7*s.* 6*d.*

COLONIAL LIBRARY. [See Home and Colonial Library.]

COOK (Canon F. C.). The Revised Version of the Three First Gospels, considered in its Bearings upon the Record of Our Lord's Words and Incidents in His Life. 8vo. 9*s.*

——— The Origins of Language and Religion. Considered in Five Essays. 8vo. 15*s.*

COOKE (E. W.). Leaves from my Sketch-Book. With Descriptive Text. 50 Plates. 2 Vols. Small folio. 31*s.* 6*d.* each.

——— (W. H.). Collections towards the History and Antiquities of the County of Hereford. Vol. III. In continuation of Duncumb's History. Illustrations. 4to. £2 12*s.* 6*d.*

COOKERY (MODERN DOMESTIC). Adapted for Private Families By a Lady. Woodcuts. Fcap. 8vo. 5*s.*

COURTHOPE (W. J.). The Liberal Movement in English Literature. A Series of Essays. Post 8vo. 6*s.*

CRABBE (REV. G.). Life & Works. Illustrations. Royal 8vo. 7*s.*

CRAIK (HENRY). Life of Jonathan Swift. Portrait. 8vo. 18*s.*

CRIPPS (WILFRED). Old English Plate: Ecclesiastical, Decorative, and Domestic, its Makers and Marks. New Edition. With Illustrations and 2010 facsimile Plate Marks. Medium 8vo. 21*s.*

*** Tables of the Date Letters and Marks sold separately. 5*s.*

——— Old French Plate; With Paris Date Letters, and Other Marks. With Illustrations. 8vo. 8*s.* 6*d.*

CROKER (RT. HON. J. W.). Correspondence and Diaries, comprising Letters, Memoranda, and Journals relating to the chief Political and Social Events of the first half of the present Century. Edited by LOUIS J. JENNINGS, M.P. With Portrait. 3 Vols. 8vo. 45*s.*

——— Progressive Geography for Children. 18mo. 1*s.* 6*d.*

——— Boswell's Life of Johnson. [*See* BOSWELL.]

——— Historical Essay on the Guillotine. Fcap. 8vo. 1*s.*

CROWE AND CAVALCASELLE. Lives of the Early Flemish Painters. Woodcuts. Post 8vo, 7*s.* 6*d.*; or Large Paper 8vo, 15*s.*

——— History of Painting in North Italy, from 14th to 16th Century. With Illustrations. 2 Vols. 8vo. 42*s.*

CROWE AND CAVALCASELLE—*continued.*

——— Life and Times of Titian, with some Account of his Family, chiefly from new and unpublished records. With Portrait and Illustrations. 2 Vols. 8vo. 21*s.*

——— Raphael; His Life and Works, with Particular Reference to recently discovered Records, and an exhaustive Study of Extant Drawings and Pictures. 2 Vols. 8vo. 33*s.*

CUMMING (R. GORDON). Five Years of a Hunter's Life in the Far Interior of South Africa. Woodcuts. Post 8vo. 6*s.*

CURRIE (C. L.). An Argument for the Divinity of Jesus Christ Translated from the French of the ABBÉ EM. BOUGAUD. Post 8vo. 6*s.*

CURTIUS' (PROFESSOR) Student's Greek Grammar, for the Upper Forms. Edited by DR. WM. SMITH. Post 8vo. 6*s.*

———Elucidations of the above Grammar. Translated by EVELYN ABBOT. Post 8vo. 7*s.* 6*d.*

——— Smaller Greek Grammar for the Middle and Lower Forms. Abridged from the larger work. 12mo. 3*s.* 6*d.*

——— Accidence of the Greek Language. Extracted from the above work. 12mo. 2*s.* 6*d.*

——— Principles of Greek Etymology. Translated by A. S. WILKINS and E. B. ENGLAND. New Edition. 2 Vols. 8vo. 28*s.*

——— The Greek Verb, its Structure and Development. Translated by A. S. WILKINS, and E. B. ENGLAND. 8vo. 12*s.*

CURZON (HON. ROBERT). Visits to the Monasteries of the Levant. Illustrations. Post 8vo. 7*s.* 6*d.*

CUST (GENERAL). Warriors of the 17th Century—Civil Wars of France and England. 2 Vols. 16*s.* Commanders of Fleets and Armies. 2 Vols. 18*s.*

——— Annals of the Wars—18th & 19th Century. With Maps. 9 Vols. Post 8vo. 5*s.* each.

DARWIN (CHARLES). Life and Letters, with an autobiographical Chapter. Edited by his Son, FRANCIS DARWIN, F.R.S. With Portraits and Woodcuts. 3 Vols. vo. 36*s.*

DARWIN'S (CHARLES) WORKS:—New and Cheaper Editions.

JOURNAL OF A NATURALIST DURING A VOYAGE ROUND THE WORLD. Crown 8vo. 7*s.* 6*d.*

ORIGIN OF SPECIES BY MEANS OF NATURAL SELECTION; or, the Preservation of Favoured Races in the Struggle for Life. Woodcuts Library Edition. 2 vols. Crown 8vo. 12*s.*; or popular Edition, Crown 8vo. 6*s.*

DESCENT OF MAN, AND SELECTION IN RELATION TO SEX. Woodcuts. Library Edition. 2 vols. Crown 8vo. 15*s.*; or popular Edition, Crown 8vo. 7*s.* 6*d.*

VARIATION OF ANIMALS AND PLANTS UNDER DOMESTICATION. Woodcuts. 2 Vols. Crown 8vo. 15*s.*

EXPRESSIONS OF THE EMOTIONS IN MAN AND ANIMALS. With Illustrations. Crown 8vo. [*In preparation.*

VARIOUS CONTRIVANCES BY WHICH ORCHIDS ARE FERTILIZED BY INSECTS. Woodcuts. Crown 8vo. 7*s.* 6*d.*

MOVEMENTS AND HABITS OF CLIMBING PLANTS. Woodcuts. Crown 8vo. 6*s.*

INSECTIVOROUS PLANTS. Woodcuts. Crown 8vo. 9*s.*

EFFECTS OF CROSS AND SELF-FERTILIZATION IN THE VEGETABLE KINGDOM. Crown 8vo. 9*s.*

DIFFERENT FORMS OF FLOWERS ON PLANTS OF THE SAME SPECIES. Crown 8vo. 7*s.* 6*d.*

DARWIN—*continued.*

POWER OF MOVEMENT IN PLANTS. Woodcuts. Cr. 8vo.

THE FORMATION OF VEGETABLE MOULD THROUGH THE ACTION OF WORMS. With Illustrations. Post 8vo. 6*s.*

LIFE OF ERASMUS DARWIN. With a Study of his Works by ERNEST KRAUSE. Portrait. New Edition. Crown 8vo. 7*s.* 6*d.*

FACTS AND ARGUMENTS FOR DARWIN. By FRITZ MULLER Translated by W. S. DALLAS. Woodcuts. Post 8vo. 6*s.*

DAVY (SIR HUMPHRY). Consolations in Travel; or, Last Days of a Philosopher. Woodcuts. Fcap. 8vo. 3*s.* 6*d.*

——— Salmonia; or, Days of Fly Fishing. Woodcuts. Fcap. 8vo. 3*s.* 6*d.*

DE COSSON (MAJOR E. A.). The Cradle of the Blue Nile; a Journey through Abyssinia and Soudan. Map and Illustrations. 2 Vols. Post 8vo. 21*s.*

——— Days and Nights of Service with Sir Gerald Graham's Field Force at Suakim. Plan and Illustrations. Crown 8vo. 14*s.*

DENNIS (GEORGE). The Cities and Cemeteries of Etruria. 20 Plans and 200 Illustrations. 2 Vols. Medium 8vo. 21*s.*

——— (ROBERT), Industrial Ireland. Suggestions for a Practical Policy of "Ireland for the Irish." Crown 8vo. 6*s.*

DERBY (EARL OF). Iliad of Homer rendered into English Blank Verse. With Portrait. 2 Vols. Post 8vo. 10*s.*

DERRY (BISHOP OF). Witness of the Psalms to Christ and Christianity. The Bampton Lectures for 1876. 8vo. 14*s.*

DICEY (PROF. A. V.). England's Case against Home Rule. Third Edition. Crown 8vo. 7*s.* 6*d.*

——— Why England Maintains the Union. A popular rendering of the above. By C. E. S. Fcap. 8vo. 1*s.*

DOG-BREAKING. [See HUTCHINSON.]

DRAKE'S (SIR FRANCIS) Life, Voyages, and Exploits, by Sea and Land. By JOHN BARROW. Post 8vo. 2*s.*

DRINKWATER (JOHN). History of the Siege of Gibraltar, 1779-1783. With a Description of that Garrison. Post 8vo. 2*s.*

DU CHAILLU (PAUL B.). Land of the Midnight Sun; Illustrations. 2 Vols. 8vo. 36*s.*

——— The Viking Age. The Early History, Manners, and Customs of the Ancestors of the English-speaking Nations. Illustrated from antiquities found in mounds, cairns, and bogs, as well as from the ancient Sagas and Eddas. 2 Vols. Medium 8vo. With 1,200 Illustrations. [*In the Press.*

DUFFERIN (LORD). Letters from High Latitudes; a Yacht Voyage to Iceland, Jan Mayen, and Spitzbergen. Woodcuts. Post 8vo. 7*s.* 6*d.*

——— Speeches and Addresses, Political and Literary, delivered in the House of Lords, in Canada, and elsewhere. 8vo. 12*s.*

DUNCAN (COL.) History of the Royal Artillery. Compiled from the Original Records. Portraits. 2 Vols. 8vo. 18*s.*

——— English in Spain; or, The Story of the War of Succession, 1834-1840. With Illustrations. 8vo. 16*s.*

DÜRER (ALBERT); his Life and Work. By DR. THAUSING. Translated from the German. Edited by F. A. EATON, M.A. With Portrait and Illustrations. 2 Vols. Medium 8vo. 42*s.*

EASTLAKE (SIR C.). Contributions to the Literature of the Fine Arts. With Memoir by LADY EASTLAKE. 2 Vols. 8vo. 21*s.*

EDWARDS (W. H.). Voyage up the River Amazon, including a Visit to Para. Post 8vo. 2*s*.

ELDON'S (LORD) Public and Private Life, with Selections from his Diaries, &c. By HORACE TWISS. Portrait. 2 Vols. Post 8vo. 21*s*.

ELGIN (LORD). Letters and Journals. Edited by THEODORE WALROND. With Preface by Dean Stanley. 8vo. 14*s*.

ELLESMERE (LORD). Two Sieges of Vienna by the Turks. Translated from the German. Post 8vo. 2*s*.

ELLIS (W.). Madagascar Revisited. The Persecutions and Heroic Sufferings of the Native Christians. Illustrations. 8vo. 16*s*.

——— Memoir. By HIS SON. Portrait. 8vo. 10*s*. 6*d*.

——— (ROBINSON). Poems and Fragments of Catullus. 16mo. 5*s*.

ELPHINSTONE (HON. M.). History of India—the Hindoo and Mahommedan Periods. Edited by PROFESSOR COWELL. Map. 8vo. 18*s*.

——— The Rise of the British Power in the East. A Continuation of his History of India in the Hindoo and Mahommedan Periods. Edited by SIR E. COLEBROOKE, Bart. With Maps. 8vo. 16*s*.

——— Life of. [See COLEBROOKE.]

——— (H. W.). Patterns and Instructions for Ornamental Turning. With 70 Illustrations. Small 4to. 15*s*.

ELTON (CAPT.) and H. B. COTTERILL. Adventures and Discoveries among the Lakes and Mountains of Eastern and Central Africa. With Map and Illustrations. 8vo. 21*s*.

ENGLAND. [See ARTHUR—BREWER—CROKER—HUME—MARKHAM—SMITH—and STANHOPE.]

ESSAYS ON CATHEDRALS. Edited, with an Introduction. By DEAN HOWSON. 8vo. 12*s*.

ETON LATIN GRAMMAR. Part 1.—Elementary. For use in the Lower Forms. Compiled with the sanction of the Headmaster, by A. C. AINGER, M.A., and H. G. WINTLE, M.A. Crown 8vo. 3*s*. 6*d*.

——— THE PREPARATORY ETON GRAMMAR. Abridged from the above Work. By the same Editors. Crown 8vo. 2*s*.

——— FIRST LATIN EXERCISE BOOK, adapted to the Latin Grammar. By the same Editors. Crown 8vo. 2*s*. 6*d*.

——— LATIN GRAMMAR. Part II. For use in the Fifth Form. By FRANCIS HAY RAWLINS, M.A., and WILLIAM RALPH INGE, M.A., Fellows of King's College, Cambridge, and Assistant Masters at Eton College. Crown 8vo. [*In the Press.*

——— FOURTH FORM OVID. Selections from Ovid and Tibullus. With Notes by H. G. WINTLE. Post 8vo. 2*s*. 6*d*.

——— HORACE. Part I. The Odes, Epodes, and Carmen Sæculare. With Notes. By F. W. CORNISH, M.A. Maps. Crown 8vo.

——— EXERCISES IN ALGEBRA, by E. P. ROUSE, M.A., and ARTHUR COCKSHOTT, M.A. Crown 8vo. 3*s*.

——— EXERCISES IN ARITHMETIC. By REV. T. DALTON, M.A. Crown 8vo. 3*s*.

FELTOE (REV. J. LETT). Memorials of John Flint South, twice President of the Royal College of Surgeons. Portrait. Crown 8vo. 7*s*. 6*d*.

FERGUSSON (JAMES). History of Architecture in all Countries from the Earliest Times. With 1,600 Illustrations. 4 Vols. Medium 8vo.
Vols. I. & II. Ancient and Mediæval. 63*s*.
III. Indian & Eastern. 42*s*. IV. Modern. 31*s*. 6*d*.

FITZGERALD (Bishop). Lectures on Ecclesiastical History, including the origin and progress of the English Reformation, from Wicliffe to the Great Rebellion. With a Memoir. 2 Vols. 8vo. 21*s*.

FITZPATRICK (WILLIAM J.). The Correspondence of Daniel O'Connell. the Liberator. Now first published, with a Memoir and Notes. With a Portrait. 2 Vols. 8vo.

FLEMING (PROFESSOR). Student's Manual of Moral Philosophy, With Quotations and References. Post 8vo. 7s. 6d.

FLOWER GARDEN. By REV. THOS. JAMES. Fcap. 8vo. 1s.

FORBES (CAPT.). British Burma and its People; Native Manners, Customs, and Religion. Crown 8vo. 10s. 6d.

FORD (RICHARD). Gatherings from Spain. Post 8vo. 3s. 6d.

FORSYTH (WILLIAM). Hortensius; an Historical Essay on the Office and Duties of an Advocate. Illustrations. 8vo. 7s. 6d.

FRANCE (HISTORY OF). [See ARTHUR—MARKHAM—SMITH—STUDENTS'—TOCQUEVILLE.]

FRENCH IN ALGIERS; The Soldier of the Foreign Legion—and the Prisoners of Abd-el-Kadir. Post 8vo. 2s.

FRERE (SIR BARTLE). Indian Missions. Small 8vo. 2s. 6d.

——— Missionary Labour in Eastern Africa. Crown 8vo. 5s.

——— Bengal Famine. How it will be Met and How to Prevent Future Famines in India. With Maps. Crown 8vo. 5s.

——— (MARY). Old Deccan Days, or Hindoo Fairy Legends current in Southern India, with Introduction by Sir BARTLE FRERE. With 50 Illustrations. Post 8vo. 7s. 6d.

GALTON (F.). Art of Travel; or, Hints on the Shifts and Contrivances available in Wild Countries. Woodcuts. Post 8vo. 7s. 6d.

GAMBIER PARRY (T.). The Ministry of Fine Art to the Happiness of Life. Revised Edition, with an Index. 8vo. 14s.

GEOGRAPHY. [See BUNBURY—CROKER—RICHARDSON—SMITH—STUDENTS'.]

GEOGRAPHICAL SOCIETY'S JOURNAL. (1846 to 1881.)
SUPPLEMENTARY PAPERS.
Vol. I., Part i. Travels and Researches in Western China. By E. COLBORNE BABER. Maps. Royal 8vo. 5s.
Part ii.—1. Notes on the Recent Geography of Central Asia; from Russian Sources. By E. DELMAR MORGAN. 2. Progress of Discovery on the Coasts of New Guinea. By C. R. MARKHAM. With Bibliographical Appendix, by E. C. Rye. Maps. Royal 8vo. 5s.
Part iii.—1. Report on Part of the Ghilzi Country, &c. By Lieut. J. S. BROADFOOT. 2. Journey from Shiraz to Jashk. By J. R. PREECE. Royal 8vo. 2s. 6d.
Part iv.—Geographical Education. By J. S. KELTIE. Royal 8vo. 2s 6d.
Vol. II., Part i.—1. Exploration in Southern and South-western China. By ARCHIBALD R. COLQUHOUN. 2. Bibliography and Cartography of Hispaniola. By H. LING ROTH. 3. Explorations in Zanzibar Dominions by Lieut. CHAS. STEWART SMITH, R.N. Royal 8vo. 2s. 6d.

GEORGE (ERNEST). The Mosel; Twenty Etchings. Imperial 4to. 42s.

——— Loire and South of France; Twenty Etchings. Folio. 42s.

GERMANY (HISTORY OF). [See MARKHAM.]

GIBBON'S History of the Decline and Fall of the Roman Empire. Edited with notes by MILMAN, GUIZOT, and Dr. WM. SMITH. Maps. 8 Vols. 8vo. 60s. Student's Edition. 7s. 6d. (See STUDENT'S.)

GIFFARD (EDWARD). Deeds of Naval Daring; or, Anecdotes of the British Navy. Fcap. 8vo. 3s. 6d.

GILBERT (JOSIAH). Landscape in Art: before the days of Claude and Salvator. With 150 Illustrations. Medium 8vo. 30s.

GILL (CAPT.). The River of Golden Sand. A Journey through China to Burmah. Edited by E. C. BABER. With MEMOIR by Col. YULE, C.B. Portrait, Map and Illustrations. Post 8vo. 7s. 6d.

—— (MRS.). Six Months in Ascension. An Unscientific Account of a Scientific Expedition. Map. Crown 8vo. 9s.

GLADSTONE (W. E.). Rome and the Newest Fashions in Religion. Three Tracts. 8vo. 7s. 6d.

—— Gleanings of Past Years, 1843-78. 7 Vols. Small 8vo. 2s. 6d. each. I. The Throne, the Prince Consort, the Cabinet and Constitution. II. Personal and Literary. III. Historical and Speculative. IV. Foreign. V. and VI. Ecclesiastical. VII. Miscellaneous.

GLEIG (G. R.). Campaigns of the British Army at Washington and New Orleans. Post 8vo. 2s.

—— Story of the Battle of Waterloo. Post 8vo. 3s. 6d.

—— Narrative of Sale's Brigade in Affghanistan. Post 8vo. 2s.

—— Life of Lord Clive. Post 8vo. 3s. 6d.

—— Sir Thomas Munro. Post 8vo. 3s. 6d.

GLYNNE (SIR STEPHEN). Notes on the Churches of Kent. With Preface by W. H. Gladstone, M.P. Illustrations. 8vo. 12s.

GOLDSMITH'S (OLIVER) Works. Edited with Notes by PETER CUNNINGHAM. Vignettes. 4 Vols. 8vo. 30s.

GOMM (F.M. SIR WM.). His Letters and Journals. 1799 to 1815. Edited by F. C. Carr Gomm. With Portrait. 8vo. 12s.

GORDON (SIR ALEX.). Sketches of German Life, and Scenes from the War of Liberation. Post 8vo. 3s. 6d.

—— (LADY DUFF), The Amber-Witch. Post 8vo. 2s.

—— The French in Algiers. Post 8vo. 2s.

GRAMMARS. [See CURTIUS — ETON—HALL — HUTTON—KING EDWARD—LEATHES—MAETZNER—MATTHIÆ—SMITH.]

GRANVILLE (CHARLES). Sir Hector's Watch. 2s. 6d.

GREECE (HISTORY OF). [See GROTE—SMITH—STUDENTS'.]

GREY (EARL). Ireland: the Cause of its Present Condition. and the Measures proposed for its Improvement. Crown 8vo. 3s. 6d.

GROTE'S (GEORGE) WORKS :—

HISTORY OF GREECE. From the Earliest Times to the close of the generation contemporary with the Death of Alexander the Great. *Cabinet Edition.* Portrait and Plans. 12 Vols. Post 8vo. 4s. each.

PLATO, and other Companions of Socrates. 3 Vols. 8vo. 45s.; or, a New Edition, Edited by ALEXANDER BAIN. 4 Vols. Crown 8vo. 6s. each. (*The Volumes may be had Separately*).

ARISTOTLE. 8vo. 12s.

MINOR WORKS. Portrait. 8vo. 14s.

LETTERS ON SWITZERLAND IN 1847. 6s.

PERSONAL LIFE. Portrait. 8vo. 12s.

GROTE (MRS.). A Sketch. By LADY EASTLAKE. Crown 8vo. 6s.

GUILLEMARD (F. H.), M.D. The Cruise of the Marchesa to Kamschatka and New Guinea. With Notices of Formosa and Liu-kiu and various Islands of the Malay Archipelago. With Maps and 150 Illustrations 2 vols. 8vo. 42s.

HALL'S (T. D.) School Manual of English Grammar. With Illustrations and Practical Exercises. 12mo. 3s. 6d.

——— Primary English Grammar for Elementary Schools. With numerous Exercises, and graduated Parsing Lessons. 16mo. 1s.

——— Manual of English Composition. With Copious Illustrations and Practical Exercises. 12mo. 3s. 6d.

——— Child's First Latin Book, comprising a full Practice of Nouns, Pronouns, and Adjectives, with the Verbs. 16mo. 2s.

HALLAM'S (HENRY) WORKS:—

THE CONSTITUTIONAL HISTORY OF ENGLAND, from the Accession of Henry the Seventh to the Death of George the Second. *Library Edition*, 3 Vols. 8vo. 30s. *Cabinet Edition*, 3 Vols. Post 8vo. 12s. *Student's Edition*, Post 8vo. 7s. 6d.

HISTORY OF EUROPE DURING THE MIDDLE AGES. *Library Edition*, 3 Vols. 8vo. 30s. *Cabinet Edition*, 3 Vols. Post 8vo. 12s. *Student's Edition*, Post 8vo. 7s. 6d.

LITERARY HISTORY OF EUROPE DURING THE 15TH, 16TH, AND 17TH CENTURIES. *Library Edition*, 3 Vols. 8vo. 36s. *Cabinet Edition*, 4 Vols. Post 8vo. 16s.

——— (ARTHUR) Literary Remains; in Verse and Prose. Portrait. Fcap. 8vo. 3s. 6d.

HAMILTON (ANDREW). Rheinsberg: Memorials of Frederick the Great and Prince Henry of Prussia. 2 Vols. Crown 8vo. 21s.

HART'S ARMY LIST. (*Published Quarterly and Annually.*)

HAY (SIR J. H. DRUMMOND). Western Barbary, its Wild Tribes and Savage Animals. Post 8vo. 2s.

HAYWARD (A.). Sketches of Eminent Statesmen and Writers, 2 Vols. 8vo. 28s.

——— The Art of Dining, or Gastronomy and Gastronomers. Post 8vo. 2s.

——— A Selection from the Correspondence of the late Abraham Hayward, Q C., edited with an Introductory account of Mr. Hayward's Early Life. By H. E. CARLISLE. 2 vols. Crown 8vo. 24s.

HEAD'S (SIR FRANCIS) WORKS:—

THE ROYAL ENGINEER. Illustrations. 8vo. 12s.

LIFE OF SIR JOHN BURGOYNE. Post 8vo. 1s.

RAPID JOURNEYS ACROSS THE PAMPAS. Post 8vo. 2s.

BUBBLES FROM THE BRUNNEN. Illustrations. Post 8vo. 7s. 6d.

STOKERS AND POKERS; or, the L. and N. W. R. Post 8vo. 2s.

HEBER'S (BISHOP) Journals in India. 2 Vols. Post 8vo. 7s.

——— Poetical Works. Portrait. Fcap. 8vo. 3s. 6d.

HERODOTUS. A New English Version. Edited, with Notes and Essays by CANON RAWLINSON, SIR H. RAWLINSON and SIR J. G. WILKINSON. Maps and Woodcuts. 4 Vols. 8vo. 48s.

HERRIES (RT. HON. JOHN). Memoir of his Public Life. By his Son, Edward Herries, C.B. 2 Vols. 8vo. 24s.

HERSCHEL'S (CAROLINE) Memoir and Correspondence. By MRS. JOHN HERSCHEL. With Portrait. Crown 8vo. 7s. 6d.

## FOREIGN HAND-BOOKS.

HAND-BOOK—TRAVEL-TALK. English, French, German, and Italian. New and Revised Edition. 18mo. 3s. 6d.

———— DICTIONARY: English, French, and German. Containing all the words and idiomatic phrases likely to be required by a traveller. Bound in leather. 16mo. 6s.

———— HOLLAND AND BELGIUM. Map and Plans. 6s.

———— NORTH GERMANY and THE RHINE,—The Black Forest, the Hartz, Thüringerwald, Saxon Switzerland, Rügen, the Giant Mountains, Taunus, Odenwald, Elsass, and Lothringen. Map and Plans. Post 8vo. 10s.

———— SOUTH GERMANY,—Wurtemburg, Bavaria, Austria, Styria, Salzburg, the Alps, Tyrol, Hungary, and the Danube, from Ulm to the Black Sea. Maps and Plans. Post 8vo. 10s.

———— SWITZERLAND, Alps of Savoy, and Piedmont. In Two Parts. Maps and Plans. Post 8vo. 10s.

———— FRANCE, Part I. Normandy, Brittany, the French Alps, the Loire, Seine, Garonne, and Pyrenees. Maps and Plans. 7s. 6d.

———— FRANCE, Part II. Central France, Auvergne, the Cevennes, Burgundy, the Rhone and Saone, Provence, Nimes, Arles, Marseilles, the French Alps, Alsace, Lorraine, Champagne, &c. Maps and Plans. Post 8vo. 7s. 6d.

———— MEDITERRANEAN — its Principal Islands, Cities, Seaports, Harbours, and Border Lands. For Travellers and Yachtsmen, with nearly 50 Maps and Plans. Post 8vo. 20s.

———— ALGERIA AND TUNIS. Algiers, Constantine, Oran, the Atlas Range. Maps and Plans. Post 8vo. 10s.

———— PARIS, and Environs. Maps and Plans. 3s. 6d.

———— SPAIN, Madrid, The Castiles, The Basque Provinces, Leon, The Asturias, Galicia, Estremadura, Andalusia, Ronda, Granada, Murcia, Valencia, Catalonia, Aragon, Navarre, The Balearic Islands, &c. &c. Maps and Plans. Post 8vo.

———— PORTUGAL, Lisbon, Oporto, Cintra, Mafra, Madeira, the Azores, and the Canary Islands, &c. Map and Plan. Post 8vo. 12s.

———— NORTH ITALY, Turin, Milan, Cremona, the Italian Lakes, Bergamo, Brescia, Verona, Mantua, Vicenza, Padua, Ferrara, Bologna, Ravenna, Rimini, Piacenza, Genoa, the Riviera, Venice, Parma, Modena, and Romagna. Maps and Plans. Post 8vo. 10s.

———— CENTRAL ITALY, Florence, Lucca, Tuscany, The Marshes, Umbria, &c. Maps and Plans. Post 8vo. 10s.

———— ROME AND ITS ENVIRONS. 50 Maps and Plans. 10s.

———— SOUTH ITALY, Naples, Pompeii, Herculaneum, and Vesuvius. Maps and Plans. Post 8vo. 10s.

———— NORWAY, Christiania, Bergen, Trondhjem. The Fjelds and Fjords. Maps and Plans. Post 8vo. 9s.

———— SWEDEN, Stockholm, Upsala, Gothenburg, the Shores of the Baltic, &c. Maps and Plan. Post 8vo. 6s.

———— DENMARK, Sleswig, Holstein, Copenhagen, Jutland, Iceland. Maps and Plans. Post 8vo. 6s.

———— RUSSIA, St. Petersburg, Moscow, Poland, and Finland. Maps and Plans. Post 8vo. 18s.

HAND-BOOK—GREECE, the Ionian Islands, Athens, the Peloponnesus, the Islands of the Ægean Sea, Albania, Thessaly, Macedonia. &c. In Two Parts. Maps, Plans, and Views. Post 8vo. 24*s.*

——— TURKEY IN ASIA—CONSTANTINOPLE, the Bosphorus, Dardanelles, Brousa, Plain of Troy, Crete, Cyprus, Smyrna, Ephesus, the Seven Churches, Coasts of the Black Sea, Armenia Euphrates Valley, Route to India, &c. Maps and Plans. Post 8vo. 15*s*

——— EGYPT. The Course of the Nile through Egypt and Nubia, Alexandria, Cairo, Thebes, Suez Canal, the Pyramids, Sinai, the Fyoom, &c. Maps and Plans. Post 8vo. 15*s.*

——— HOLY LAND—SYRIA, PALESTINE, Peninsula of Sinai, Edom, Syrian Deserts, Petra, Damascus; and Palmyra. Maps and Plans. Post 8vo. 20*s.*

*** Map of Palestine. In a case. 12*s.*

——— BOMBAY—Poonah, Beejapoor, Kolapoor, Goa, Jubulpoor, Indore, Surat, Baroda, Ahmedabad, Somnauth, Kurrachee, &c. Map and Plans. Post 8vo. 15*s.*

——— MADRAS—Trichinopoli, Madura, Tinnevelly, Tuticorin, Bangalore, Mysore, The Nilgiris, Wynaad, Ootacamund, Calicut, Hyderabad, Ajanta, Elura Caves, &c. Maps and Plans. Post 8vo. 15*s.*

——— BENGAL—Calcutta, Orissa, British Burmah, Rangoon, Moulmein, Mandalay, Darjiling, Dacca, Patna, Benares, N.-W. Provinces, Allahabad, Cawnpore, Lucknow, Agra, Gwalior, Naini Tal, Delhi, &c. Maps and Plans. Post 8vo. 20*s.*

——— THE PANJAB—Amraoti, Indore, Ajmir, Jaypur, Rohtak, Saharanpur, Ambala, Lodiana, Lahore, Kulu, Simla, Sialkot, Peshawar, Rawul Pindi, Attock, Karachi, Sibi, &c. Maps. 15*s.*

---

## ENGLISH HAND-BOOKS.

HAND-BOOK—ENGLAND AND WALES. An Alphabetical Hand-Book. Condensed into One Volume for the Use of Travellers. With a Map. Post 8vo.

——— LONDON. Maps and Plans. 16mo. 3*s.* 6*d.*

——— ENVIRONS OF LONDON within a circuit of 20 miles. 2 Vols. Crown 8vo. 21*s.*

——— ST. PAUL'S CATHEDRAL. 20 Woodcuts. 10*s.* 6*d.*

——— EASTERN COUNTIES, Chelmsford, Harwich, Colchester, Maldon, Cambridge, Ely, Newmarket, Bury St. Edmunds, Ipswich, Woodbridge, Felixstowe, Lowestoft, Norwich, Yarmouth, Cromer, &c. Map and Plans. Post 8vo. 12*s.*

——— CATHEDRALS of Oxford, Peterborough, Norwich, Ely, and Lincoln. With 90 Illustrations. Crown 8vo. 21*s.*

——— KENT, Canterbury, Dover, Ramsgate, Sheerness, Rochester, Chatham, Woolwich. Maps and Plans. Post 8vo. 7*s.* 6*d.*

——— SUSSEX, Brighton, Chichester, Worthing, Hastings, Lewes, Arundel, &c. Maps and Plans. Post 8vo. 6*s.*

——— SURREY AND HANTS, Kingston, Croydon, Reigate, Guildford, Dorking, Winchester, Southampton, New Forest, Portsmouth, ISLE OF WIGHT, &c. Maps and Plans. Post 8vo.

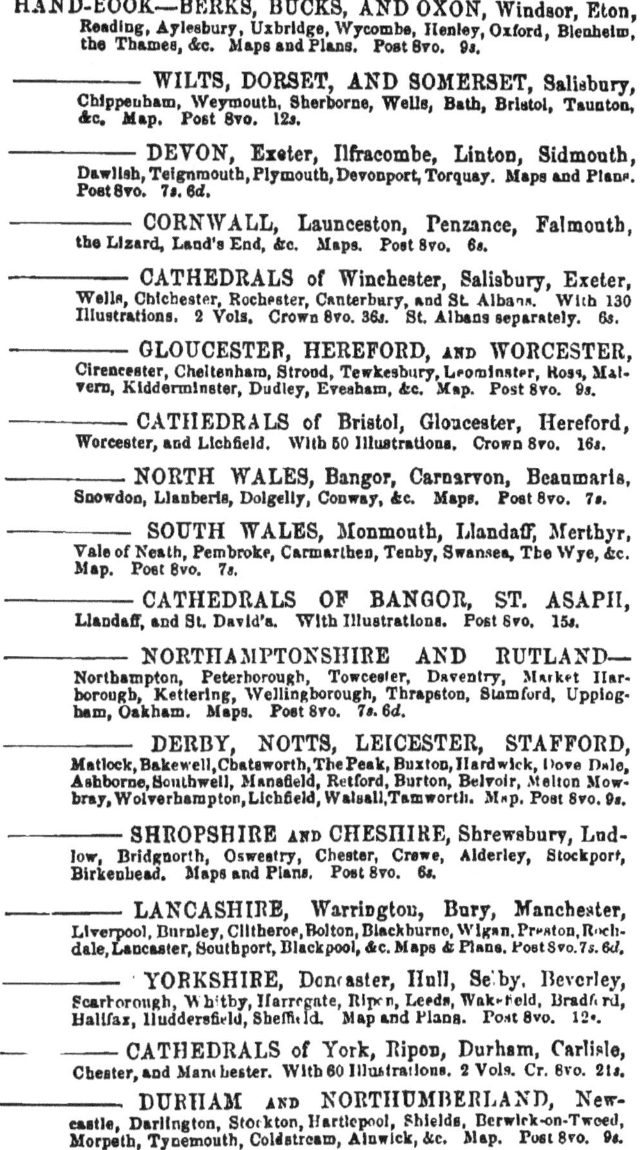

HAND-BOOK—BERKS, BUCKS, AND OXON, Windsor, Eton, Reading, Aylesbury, Uxbridge, Wycombe, Henley, Oxford, Blenheim, the Thames, &c. Maps and Plans. Post 8vo. 9s.

——— WILTS, DORSET, AND SOMERSET, Salisbury, Chippenham, Weymouth, Sherborne, Wells, Bath, Bristol, Taunton, &c. Map. Post 8vo. 12s.

——— DEVON, Exeter, Ilfracombe, Linton, Sidmouth, Dawlish, Teignmouth, Plymouth, Devonport, Torquay. Maps and Plans. Post 8vo. 7s. 6d.

——— CORNWALL, Launceston, Penzance, Falmouth, the Lizard, Land's End, &c. Maps. Post 8vo. 6s.

——— CATHEDRALS of Winchester, Salisbury, Exeter, Wells, Chichester, Rochester, Canterbury, and St. Albans. With 130 Illustrations. 2 Vols. Crown 8vo. 36s. St. Albans separately. 6s.

——— GLOUCESTER, HEREFORD, AND WORCESTER, Cirencester, Cheltenham, Stroud, Tewkesbury, Leominster, Ross, Malvern, Kidderminster, Dudley, Evesham, &c. Map. Post 8vo. 9s.

——— CATHEDRALS of Bristol, Gloucester, Hereford, Worcester, and Lichfield. With 50 Illustrations. Crown 8vo. 16s.

——— NORTH WALES, Bangor, Carnarvon, Beaumaris, Snowdon, Llanberis, Dolgelly, Conway, &c. Maps. Post 8vo. 7s.

——— SOUTH WALES, Monmouth, Llandaff, Merthyr, Vale of Neath, Pembroke, Carmarthen, Tenby, Swansea, The Wye, &c. Map. Post 8vo. 7s.

——— CATHEDRALS OF BANGOR, ST. ASAPH, Llandaff, and St. David's. With Illustrations. Post 8vo. 15s.

——— NORTHAMPTONSHIRE AND RUTLAND—Northampton, Peterborough, Towcester, Daventry, Market Harborough, Kettering, Wellingborough, Thrapston, Stamford, Uppingham, Oakham. Maps. Post 8vo. 7s. 6d.

——— DERBY, NOTTS, LEICESTER, STAFFORD, Matlock, Bakewell, Chatsworth, The Peak, Buxton, Hardwick, Dove Dale, Ashborne, Southwell, Mansfield, Retford, Burton, Belvoir, Melton Mowbray, Wolverhampton, Lichfield, Walsall, Tamworth. Map. Post 8vo. 9s.

——— SHROPSHIRE AND CHESHIRE, Shrewsbury, Ludlow, Bridgnorth, Oswestry, Chester, Crewe, Alderley, Stockport, Birkenhead. Maps and Plans. Post 8vo. 6s.

——— LANCASHIRE, Warrington, Bury, Manchester, Liverpool, Burnley, Clitheroe, Bolton, Blackburne, Wigan, Preston, Rochdale, Lancaster, Southport, Blackpool, &c. Maps & Plans. Post 8vo. 7s. 6d.

——— YORKSHIRE, Doncaster, Hull, Selby, Beverley, Scarborough, Whitby, Harrogate, Ripon, Leeds, Wakefield, Bradford, Halifax, Huddersfield, Sheffield. Map and Plans. Post 8vo. 12s.

——— CATHEDRALS of York, Ripon, Durham, Carlisle, Chester, and Manchester. With 60 Illustrations. 2 Vols. Cr. 8vo. 21s.

——— DURHAM AND NORTHUMBERLAND, Newcastle, Darlington, Stockton, Hartlepool, Shields, Berwick-on-Tweed, Morpeth, Tynemouth, Coldstream, Alnwick, &c. Map. Post 8vo. 9s.

HAND-BOOK—SCOTLAND, Edinburgh, Melrose, Kelso, Glasgow, Dumfries, Ayr, Stirling, Arran, The Clyde, Oban, Inverary, Loch Lomond, Loch Katrine and Trossachs, Caledonian Canal, Inverness, Perth, Dundee, Aberdeen, Braemar, Skye, Caithness, Ross, Sutherland, &c. Maps and Plans. Post 8vo. 9*s.*

——— IRELAND, Dublin, Belfast, the Giant's Causeway, Donegal, Galway, Wexford, Cork, Limerick, Waterford, Killarney, Bantry, Glengariff, &c. Maps and Plans. Post 8vo. 10*s.*

HOLLWAY (J. G.). A Month in Norway. Fcap. 8vo. 2*s.*

HONEY BEE. By Rev. Thomas James. Fcap. 8vo. 1*s.*

——— (Theodore) Life. By J. G. Lockhart. Fcap. 8vo. 1*s.*

HOOK (Dean). Church Dictionary. A Manual of Reference Clergymen and Students. New Edition, thoroughly revised. Edited Walter Hook, M.A., and W. R. W. Stephens, M.A. Med. 8vo. 21*s*

HOPE (A. J. Beresford). Worship in the Church of England. 8vo, 9*s.*; or, *Popular Selections from*, 8vo, 2*s.* 6*d.*

——— Worship and Order. 8vo. 9*s.*

HOPE-SCOTT (James), Memoir. [See Ornsby.]

HORACE; a New Edition of the Text. Edited by Dean Milman. With 100 Woodcuts. Crown 8vo. 7*s.* 6*d.*

——— [See Eton.]

HOSACK (John). The Rise and Growth of the Law of Nations: as established by general usage and by treaties, from the earliest times to the Treaty of Utrecht. 8vo. 12*s.*

HOUGHTON'S (Lord) Monographs, Personal and Social. With Portraits. Crown 8vo. 10*s.* 6*d.*

——— Poetical Works. *Collected Edition.* With Portrait. 2 Vols. Fcap. 8vo. 12*s.*

---

HOME AND COLONIAL LIBRARY. A Series of Works adapted for all circles and classes of Readers, having been selected for their acknowledged interest, and ability of the Authors. Post 8vo. Published at 2*s.* and 3*s.* 6*d.* each, and arranged under two distinctive heads as follows:—

### CLASS A.

### HISTORY, BIOGRAPHY, AND HISTORIC TALES.

1. SIEGE OF GIBRALTAR. By John Drinkwater. 2*s.*
2. THE AMBER-WITCH. By Lady Duff Gordon. 2*s.*
3. CROMWELL AND BUNYAN. By Robert Southey. 2*s.*
4. LIFE of Sir FRANCIS DRAKE. By John Barrow. 2*s.*
5. CAMPAIGNS AT WASHINGTON. By Rev. G. R. Gleig. 2*s.*
6. THE FRENCH IN ALGIERS. By Lady Duff Gordon 2*s.*
7. THE FALL OF THE JESUITS. 2*s.*
8. LIVONIAN TALES. 2*s.*
9. LIFE OF CONDÉ. By Lord Mahon. 3*s.* 6*d.*
10. SALE'S BRIGADE. By Rev. G. R. Gleig. 2*s.*
11. THE SIEGES OF VIENNA. By Lord Ellesmere. 2*s.*
12. THE WAYSIDE CROSS. By Capt. Milman. 2*s.*
13. SKETCHES of GERMAN LIFE. By Sir A. Gordon. 3*s.* 6*d.*
14. THE BATTLE of WATERLOO. By Rev. G. R. Gleig. 3*s.* 6*d.*
15. AUTOBIOGRAPHY OF STEFFENS. 2*s.*
16. THE BRITISH POETS. By Thomas Campbell. 3*s.* 6*d.*
17. HISTORICAL ESSAYS. By Lord Mahon. 3*s.* 6*d.*
18. LIFE OF LORD CLIVE. By Rev. G. R. Gleig. 3*s.* 6*d.*
19. NORTH-WESTERN RAILWAY. By Sir F. B. Head. 2*s.*
20. LIFE OF MUNRO. By Rev. G. R. Gleig. 3*s.* 6*d.*

## CLASS B.

## VOYAGES, TRAVELS, AND ADVENTURES.

1. BIBLE IN SPAIN. By George Borrow. 3s. 6d.
2. GYPSIES of SPAIN. By George Borrow. 3s. 6d.
3 & 4. JOURNALS IN INDIA. By Bishop Heber. 2 Vols. 7s.
5. TRAVELS in the HOLY LAND. By Irby and Mangles. 2s.
6. MOROCCO AND THE MOORS. By J. Drummond Hay. 2s.
7. LETTERS FROM the BALTIC. By A Lady. 2s.
8. NEW SOUTH WALES. By Mrs. Meredith. 2s.
9. THE WEST INDIES. By M. G. Lewis. 2s.
10 SKETCHES OF PERSIA. By Sir John Malcolm. 3s. 6d.
11. MEMOIRS OF FATHER RIPA. 2s.
12 & 13. TYPEE AND OMOO. By Hermann Melville. 2 Vols. 7s.
14. MISSIONARY LIFE IN CANADA. By Rev. J. Abbott. 2s.
15. LETTERS FROM MADRAS. By A Lady. 2s.
16. HIGHLAND SPORTS. By Charles St. John. 3s. 6d.
17. PAMPAS JOURNEYS. By F. B. Head. 2s.
18. GATHERINGS FROM SPAIN. By Richard Ford. 3s. 6d.
19. THE RIVER AMAZON. By W. H. Edwards. 2s.
20. MANNERS & CUSTOMS OF INDIA. By Rev. C. Acland. 2s.
21. ADVENTURES IN MEXICO. By G. F. Ruxton. 3s. 6d.
22. PORTUGAL AND GALICIA. By Lord Carnarvon. 3s. 6d.
23. BUSH LIFE IN AUSTRALIA. By Rev. H. W. Haygarth. 2s.
24. THE LIBYAN DESERT. By Bayle St. John. 2s.
25. SIERRA LEONE. By A Lady. 3s. 6d.

*** Each work may be had separately.

HUBNER (Baron von). A Voyage through the British Empire; South Africa, Australia, New Zealand, The Straits Settlements, India, the South Sea Islands, California, Oregon, Canada, &c. With a Map. 2 Vols. Crown 8vo. 24s.

HUHN (A. Von). The Struggle of the Bulgarians for National Independence: A History of the War between Bulgaria and Servia in 1885, under Prince Alexander. With Map. Crown 8vo. 9s.

HUME (The Student's). A History of England, from the Invasion of Julius Cæsar to the Revolution of 1688. New Edition, revised, corrected, and continued to the Treaty of Berlin, 1878. By J. S. Brewer, M.A. With 7 Coloured Maps & 70 Woodcuts. Post 8vo. 7s. 6d.
*** Sold also in 3 parts. Price 2s. 6d. each.

HUNNEWELL (James F.). England's Chronicle in Stone: Derived from Personal Observations of the Cathedrals, Churches, Abbeys, Monasteries, Castles, and Palaces, made in Journeys through the Imperial Island. With Illustrations. Medium 8vo. 24s.

HUTCHINSON (Gen.). Dog Breaking, with Odds and Ends for those who love the Dog and the Gun. With 40 Illustrations. Crown 8vo. 7s. 6d. *** A Summary of the Rules for Gamekeepers. 1s.

HUTTON (H. E.). Principia Græca; an Introduction to the Study of Greek. Comprehending Grammar, Delectus, and Exercise-book, with Vocabularies. *Sixth Edition.* 12mo. 3s. 6d.

——— (James). James and Philip van Artevelde. Two remarkable Episodes in the annals of Flanders: with a description of the state of Society in Flanders in the 14th Century. Cr. 8vo. 10s. 6d.

HYMNOLOGY, Dictionary of. [See Julian.]

ICELAND. [See Coles—Dufferin.]

INDIA. [See Elphinstone — Hand-book — Smith— Temple— Monier Williams—Lyall.]

INGE (Wm. Ralph). Society in Rome under the Cæsars. Crown 8vo. 6s.

IRBY AND MANGLES' Travels in Egypt, Nubia, Syria, and the Holy Land. Post 8vo. 2s.

IRELAND. [See Grey.]

**JAMES** (F. L.). The Wild Tribes of the Soudan: with an account of the route from Wady Halfah to Dongola and Berber. With Chapter on the Condition of the Soudan, by Sir S. Baker. Map and Illustrations. Crown 8vo. 7*s*. 6*d*.

**JAMESON** (Mrs.). Lives of the Early Italian Painters—and the Progress of Painting in Italy—Cimabue to Bassano. With 50 Portraits Post 8vo. 12*s*.

**JAPAN.** [See Bird—Mounsey—Reed.]

**JENNINGS** (Louis J.), Rambles among the Hills in the Peak of Derbyshire and on the South Downs. With sketches of people by the way. With 23 Illustrations. Crown 8vo. 12*s*.

———— Field Paths and Green Lanes: or Walks in Surrey and Sussex. Popular Edition. With Illustrations. Crown 8vo. 6*s*.

**JERVIS** (Rev. W. H.). The Gallican Church, from the Concordat of Bologna, 1516, to the Revolution. With an Introduction. Portraits. 2 Vols. 8vo. 28*s*.

**JESSE** (Edward). Gleanings in Natural History. Fcp. 8vo. 3*s*. 6*d*.

**JOHNSON'S** (Dr. Samuel) Life. [See Boswell.]

**JULIAN** (Rev. John J.). A Dictionary of Hymnology. A Companion to Existing Hymn Books. Setting forth the Origin and History of the Hymns contained in the Principal Hymnals, with Notices of their Authors. Medium 8vo. [*In the Press.*

**JUNIUS'** Handwriting Professionally investigated. Edited by the Hon. E. Twisleton. With Facsimiles, Woodcuts, &c. 4to. £3 3*s*.

**KERR** (Robt.). The Consulting Architect: Practical Notes on Administrative Difficulties. Crown 8vo. 9*s*.

**KING EDWARD VIth's** Latin Grammar. 12mo. 3*s*. 6*d*.

———— First Latin Book. 12mo. 2*s*. 6*d*.

**KIRK** (J. Foster). History of Charles the Bold, Duke of Burgundy. Portrait. 3 Vols. 8vo. 45*s*.

**KIRKES'** Handbook of Physiology. Edited by W. Morrant Baker and V. D. Harris. With 500 Illustrations. Post 8vo. 14*s*.

**KUGLER'S HANDBOOK OF PAINTING.**—The Italian Schools. A New Edition, revised, incorporating the results of all the most recent discoveries. By Sir A. Henry Layard. With 200 Illustrations. 2 vols. Crown 8vo. 30*s*.

———— The German, Flemish, and Dutch Schools. Revised. By J. A. Crowe. With 60 Illustrations. 2 Vols. Crown 8vo. 24*s*.

**LANE** (E. W.). Account of the Manners and Customs of Modern Egyptians. With Illustrations. 2 Vols. Post 8vo. 12*s*.

**LAWLESS** (Hon. Emily). Major Lawrence, F.L.S.: a Novel 3 Vols. Crown 8vo. 31*s*. 6*d*.

**LAYARD** (Sir A. H.). Nineveh and its Remains. With Illustrations. Post 8vo. 7*s*. 6*d*.

———— Nineveh and Babylon: Discoveries in the Ruins, with Travels in Armenia, Kurdistan, &c. Illustrations. Post 8vo. 7*s*. 6*d*.

———— Early Adventures in Persia, Babylonia, and Susiana, including a residence among the Bakhtiyari and other wild tribes, before the discovery of Nineveh. Portrait, Illustrations and Maps. 2 Vols. Crown 8vo. 24*s*.

**LEATHES** (Stanley). Practical Hebrew Grammar. With the Hebrew Text of Genesis i.—vi., and Psalms i.—vi. Grammatical Analysis and Vocabulary. Post 8vo. 7*s*. 6*d*.

**LENNEP** (Rev. H. J. Van). Missionary Travels in Asia Minor. With Illustrations of Biblical History and Archæology. Map and Woodcuts. 2 Vols. Post 8vo. 24*s*.

LENNEP. Modern Customs and Manners of Bible Lands, in Illustration of Scripture. Maps and Illustrations. 2 Vols. 8vo. 21*s.*

LESLIE (C. R.). Handbook for Young Painters. Illustrations. Post 8vo. 7*s.* 6*d.*

LETO (POMPONIO). Eight Months at Rome during the Vatican Council. 8vo. 12*s.*

LETTERS FROM THE BALTIC. By LADY EASTLAKE. Post 8vo. 2*s.*

——— MADRAS. By MRS. MAITLAND. Post 8vo. 2*s.*

——— SIERRA LEONE. By MRS. MELVILLE. 3*s.* 6*d.*

LEVI (LEONE). History of British Commerce; and Economic Progress of the Nation, from 1763 to 1878. 8vo. 18*s.*

——— The Wages and Earnings of the Working Classes in 1883-4. 8vo. 3*s.* 6*d.*

LEX SALICA; the Ten Texts with the Glosses and the Lex Emendata. Synoptically edited by J. H. HESSELS. With Notes on the Frankish Words in the Lex Salica by H. KERN, of Leyden. 4to. 42*s.*

LIDDELL (DEAN). Student's History of Rome, from the earliest Times to the establishment of the Empire. Woodcuts. Post 8vo. 7*s.* 6*d.*

LINDSAY (LORD). Sketches of the History of Christian Art. New Edition. 2 Vols. Crown 8vo. 24*s.*

LISPINGS from LOW LATITUDES; or, the Journal of the Hon. Impulsia Gushington. Edited by LORD DUFFERIN. With 24 Plates. 4to. 21*s.*

LIVINGSTONE (DR.). First Expedition to Africa, 1840–56. Illustrations. Post 8vo. 7*s.* 6*d.*

——— Second Expedition to Africa, 1858-64. Illustrations. Post 8vo. 7*s.* 6*d.*

——— Last Journals in Central Africa, from 1865 to his Death. Continued by a Narrative of his last moments and sufferings. By Rev. HORACE WALLER. Maps and Illustrations. 2 Vols. 8vo. 15*s.*

——— Personal Life. By Wm. G. Blaikie, D.D. With Map and Portrait. 8vo. 6*s.*

LIVINGSTONIA. Journal of Adventures in Exploring Lake Nyassa, and Establishing a Missionary Settlement there. By E. D. YOUNG, R.N. Maps. Post 8vo. 7*s.* 6*d.*

LIVONIAN TALES. By the Author of "Letters from the Baltic." Post 8vo. 2*s.*

LOCKHART (J. G.). Ancient Spanish Ballads. Historical and Romantic. Translated, with Notes. Illustrations. Crown 8vo. 5*s.*

——— Life of Theodore Hook. Fcap. 8vo. 1*s.*

LONDON: its History, Antiquarian and Modern. Founded on the work by the late Peter Cunningham, F.S.A. A new and thoroughly revised edition. By JAMES THORNE, F.S.A. and H. B. WHEATLEY. Fine library edition, on laid paper. 3 Vols. Royal 8vo.

LOUDON (MRS.). Gardening for Ladies. With Directions and Calendar of Operations for Every Month. Woodcuts. Fcap. 8vo. 3*s.* 6*d.*

LUTHER (MARTIN). The First Principles of the Reformation, or the Ninety-five Theses and Three Primary Works of Dr. Martin Luther. Portrait. 8vo. 12*s.*

LYALL (SIR ALFRED C.), K.C.B. Asiatic Studies; Religious and Social. 8vo. 12*s.*

LYELL (SIR CHARLES). Student's Elements of Geology. A new Edition, entirely revised by PROFESSOR P. M. DUNCAN, F.R.S. With 600 Illustrations. Post 8vo. 9*s.*

——— Life, Letters, and Journals. Edited by his sister-in-law, MRS. LYELL. With Portraits. 2 Vols. 8vo. 30*s.*

LYELL (K. M.). Handbook of Ferns. Post 8vo. *7s. 6d.*

LYNDHURST (LORD). [See MARTIN.]

LYTTON (LORD). A Memoir of Julian Fane. Portrait. Post 8vo. 5s.

M<sup></sup>CLINTOCK (SIR L.). Narrative of the Discovery of the Fate of Sir John Franklin and his Companions in the Arctic Seas. With Illustrations. Post 8vo. *7s. 6d.*

MACDONALD (A). Too Late for Gordon and Khartoum. The Testimony of an Independent Eye-witness of the Heroic Efforts for their Rescue and Relief. With Maps and Plans. 8vo. 12s.

MACGREGOR (J.). Rob Roy on the Jordan, Nile, Red Sea, Gennesareth, &c. A Canoe Cruise in Palestine and Egypt and the Waters of Damascus. With 70 Illustrations. Crown 8vo. *7s. 6d.*

MAETZNER'S ENGLISH GRAMMAR. A Methodical, Analytical, and Historical Treatise on the Orthography, Prosody, Inflections, and Syntax. By CLAIR J. GRECE, LL.D. 3 Vols. 8vo. *36s.*

MAHON (LORD). [See STANHOPE.]

MAINE (SIR H. SUMNER). Ancient Law: its Connection with the Early History of Society, and its Relation to Modern Ideas. 8vo. *12s.*

——— Village Communities in the East and West. 8vo. *12s.*

——— Early History of Institutions. 8vo. *12s.*

——— Dissertations on Early Law and Custom. Chiefly Selected from Lectures delivered at Oxford. 8vo. *12s.*

——— Popular Government; Four Essays. I.—Prospects of Popular Government. II.—Nature of Democracy. III.—Age of Progress. IV.—Constitution of the United States. 8vo. *12s.*

MALCOLM (SIR JOHN). Sketches of Persia. Post 8vo. *3s. 6d.*

MALLOCK (W. H.). Property and Progress: or, Facts against Fallacies. A brief Enquiry into Contemporary Social Agitation in England. Post 8vo. 6s.

MANSEL (DEAN). Letters, Lectures, and Reviews. 8vo. *12s.*

MARCO POLO. [See YULE]. Maps and Illustrations. 2 Vols. Medium 8vo. 63s.

MARKHAM (MRS.). History of England. From the First Invasion by the Romans, continued down to 1880. Woodcuts. 12mo. *3s. 6d.*

——— History of France. From the Conquest of Gaul by Julius Cæsar, continued down to 1878. Woodcuts. 12mo. *3s. 6d.*

——— History of Germany. From its Invasion by Marius, continued down to the completion of Cologne Cathedral. Woodcuts. 12mo. *3s. 6d.*

——— (CLEMENTS R.). A Popular Account of Peruvian Bark and its introduction into British India. With Maps. Post 8vo. *14s.*

MARSH (G. P.). Student's Manual of the English Language. Edited with Additions. By DR. WM. SMITH. Post 8vo. *7s. 6d.*

MARTIN (SIR THEODORE). Life of Lord Lyndhurst. With Portraits. 8vo. *16s.*

MASTERS in English Theology. Lectures by Eminent Divines. With Introduction by Canon Barry. Post 8vo. *7s. 6d.*

MATTHIÆ'S GREEK GRAMMAR. Abridged by BLOMFIELD. *Revised* by E. S. CROOKE. 12mo. *4s.*

MAUREL'S Character, Actions, and Writings of Wellington. Fcap. 8vo. *1s. 6d.*

MELVILLE (HERMANN). Marquesas and South Sea Islands. 2 Vols. Post 8vo. *7s.*

MEREDITH (MRS. CHARLES). Notes and Sketches of New South Wales. Post 8vo. *2s.*

MEXICO. [See BROCKLEHURST—RUXTON.]

MICHAEL ANGELO, Sculptor, Painter, and Architect. His Life and Works. By C. HEATH WILSON. Illustrations. 8vo. 15s.

MILLER (WM.). A Dictionary of English Names of Plants applied among English-speaking People to Plants, Trees, and Shrubs. In Two Parts. Latin-English and English-Latin. Medium 8vo. 12s.

MILMAN'S (DEAN) WORKS:—

HISTORY OF THE JEWS, from the earliest Period down to Modern Times. 3 Vols. Post 8vo. 12s.

EARLY CHRISTIANITY, from the Birth of Christ to the Abolition of Paganism in the Roman Empire. 3 Vols. Post 8vo. 12s.

LATIN CHRISTIANITY, including that of the Popes to the Pontificate of Nicholas V. 9 Vols. Post 8vo. 36s.

HANDBOOK TO ST. PAUL'S CATHEDRAL. Woodcuts. 10s. 6d.

QUINTI HORATII FLACCI OPERA. Woodcuts. Sm. 8vo. 7s. 6d.

FALL OF JERUSALEM. Fcap. 8vo. 1s.

——— (CAPT. E. A.) Wayside Cross. Post 8vo. 2s.

——— (BISHOP, D.D.,) Life. With a Selection from his Correspondence and Journals. By his Sister. Map. 8vo. 12s.

MILNE (DAVID, M.A.). A Readable Dictionary of the English Language. Crown 8vo.

MINCHIN (J. G.). The Growth of Freedom in the Balkan Peninsula. An Historical, Descriptive Account of Montenegro, Bosnia, Servia, Bulgaria, and Greece. With a Map. Crown 8vo. 10s. 6d.

MIVART (ST. GEORGE). Lessons from Nature; as manifested in Mind and Matter. 8vo. 15s.

——— The Cat. An Introduction to the Study of Backboned Animals, especially Mammals. With 200 Illustrations. Medium 8vo. 30s.

MOGGRIDGE (M. W.). Method in Almsgiving. A Handbook for Helpers. Post 8vo. 3s. 6d.

MONTEFIORE (SIR MOSES). Selections from Letters and Journals. By LUCIEN WOLF. With Portrait. Crown 8vo. 10s. 6d.

MOORE (THOMAS). Life and Letters of Lord Byron. [See BYRON.]

MOTLEY (J. L.). History of the United Netherlands: from the Death of William the Silent to the Twelve Years' Truce, 1609. Portraits. 4 Vols. Post 8vo. 6s. each.

——— Life and Death of John of Barneveld. With a View of the Primary Causes and Movements of the Thirty Years War. Illustrations. 2 Vols. Post 8vo. 12s.

MOZLEY (CANON). Treatise on the Augustinian doctrine of Predestination, with an Analysis of the Contents. Crown 8vo. 9s.

MUNRO'S (GENERAL) Life and Letters. By REV. G. R. GLEIG. Post 8vo. 3s. 6d.

MUNTHE (AXEL). Letters from a Mourning City. Naples during the Autumn of 1884. Translated by MAUDE VALERIE WHITE. With a Frontispiece. Crown 8vo. 6s.

MURCHISON (SIR RODERICK). And his Contemporaries. By ARCHIBALD GEIKIE. Portraits. 2 Vols. 8vo. 30s.

MURRAY (A. S.). A History of Greek Sculpture from the Earliest Times. With 130 Illustrations. 2 Vols. Royal 8vo. 52s.

MURRAY'S MAGAZINE. A New Home and Colonial Monthly Periodical. 1s. Vol. I, Jan.—June, 1887. Vol. II, July—December, 1887. Now ready. 8vo. 7s. 6d. each.

*** Forwarded Monthly on receipt of an annual subscription of 13s.

**MUSTERS' (CAPT.)** Patagonians; a Year's Wanderings over Untrodden Ground from the Straits of Magellan to the Rio Negro. Illustrations. Post 8vo. *7s. 6d.*

**NADAILLAC (MARQUIS DE).** Prehistoric America. Translated by N. D'ANVERS. With Illustrations. 8vo. *16s.*

**NAPIER (GENERAL SIR CHARLES).** His Life. By the Hon. WM. NAPIER BRUCE. With Portrait and Maps. Crown 8vo. *12s.*

——— (GENL. SIR GEORGE T.). Passages in his Early Military Life written by himself. Edited by his Son, GENERAL WM. C. E. NAPIER. With Portrait. Crown 8vo. *7s. 6d.*

——— (SIR WM.). English Battles and Sieges of the Peninsular War. Portrait. Post 8vo. *9s.*

**NAPOLEON AT FONTAINEBLEAU AND ELBA.** Journals. Notes of Conversations. By SIR NEIL CAMPBELL. Portrait. 8vo. *15s.*

**NASMYTH (JAMES).** An Autobiography. Edited by Samuel Smiles, LL.D., with Portrait, and 70 Illustrations. New Edition, post 8vo., 6s.; or Large Paper, 16s.

——— And JAMES CARPENTER. The Moon: Considered as a Planet, a World, and a Satellite. With 26 Plates and numerous Woodcuts. New and Cheaper Edition. Medium 8vo. *21s.*

**NEW TESTAMENT.** With Short Explanatory Commentary. By ARCHDEACON CHURTON, M.A., and the BISHOP OF ST. DAVID'S. With 110 authentic Views, &c. 2 Vols. Crown 8vo. *21s. bound.*

**NEWTH (SAMUEL).** First Book of Natural Philosophy; an Introduction to the Study of Statics, Dynamics, Hydrostatics, Light, Heat, and Sound, with numerous Examples. Small 8vo. *3s. 6d.*

——— Elements of Mechanics, including Hydrostatics, with numerous Examples. Small 8vo. *8s. 6d.*

——— Mathematical Examples. A Graduated Series of Elementary Examples in Arithmetic, Algebra, Logarithms, Trigonometry, and Mechanics. Small 8vo. *8s. 6d.*

**NIMROD,** On the Chace—Turf—and Road. With Portrait and Plates. Crown 8vo. *5s.* Or with Coloured Plates, *7s. 6d.*

**NORDHOFF (CHAS.).** Communistic Societies of the United States. With 40 Illustrations. 8vo. *15s.*

**NORTHCOTE'S (SIR JOHN)** Notebook in the Long Parliament. Containing Proceedings during its First Session, 1640. Edited, with a Memoir, by A. H. A. Hamilton. Crown 8vo. *9s.*

**O'CONNELL (DANIEL).** Correspondence of. (See FITZPATRICK.)

**ORNSBY (PROF. R.).** Memoirs of J. Hope Scott, Q.C. (of Abbotsford). With Selections from his Correspondence. 2 vols. 8vo. *24s.*

**OTTER (R. H.).** Winters Abroad: Some Information respecting Places visited by the Author on account of his Health. Intended for the Use and Guidance of Invalids. *7s. 6d.*

**OVID LESSONS.** [See ETON.]

**OWEN (LIEUT.-COL.).** Principles and Practice of Modern Artillery, including Artillery Material, Gunnery, and Organisation and Use of Artillery in Warfare. With Illustrations. 8vo. *15s.*

**OXENHAM (REV. W.).** English Notes for Latin Elegiacs; with Prefatory Rules of Composition in Elegiac Metre. 12mo. *3s. 6d.*

**PAGET (LORD GEORGE).** The Light-Cavalry Brigade in the Crimea. Map. Crown 8vo. *10s. 6d.*

**PALGRAVE (R. H. I.).** Local Taxation of Great Britain and Ireland. 8vo. *5s.*

PALLISER (MRS.). Mottoes for Monuments, or Epitaphs selected for General Use and Study. With Illustrations. Crown 8vo. 7s. 6d.

PANKHURST (E. A.). The Wisdom of Edmund Burke: Being Selections from his Speeches and Writings, chiefly bearing upon Political Questions. Fcp. 8vo. 6s.

PARIS (DR.). Philosophy in Sport made Science in Earnest; or, the First Principles of Natural Philosophy inculcated by aid of the Toys and Sports of Youth. Woodcuts. Post 8vo. 7s. 6d.

PARKYNS' (MANSFIELD) Three Years' Residence in Abyssinia; with Travels in that Country. With Illustrations. Post 8vo. 7s. 6d.

PEEL'S (SIR ROBERT) Memoirs. 2 Vols. Post 8vo. 15s.

PENN (RICHARD). Maxims and Hints for an Angler and Chess-player. Woodcuts. Fcap. 8vo. 1s.

PERCY (JOHN, M.D.). METALLURGY. Fuel, Wood, Peat, Coal, Charcoal, Coke, Fire-Clays. Illustrations. 8vo. 30s.

——— Lead, including part of Silver. Illustrations. 8vo. 30s.

——— Silver and Gold. Part I. Illustrations. 8vo. 30s.

PERRY (REV. CANON). Life of St. Hugh of Avalon, Bishop of Lincoln. Post 8vo. 10s. 6d.

——— History of the English Church. See STUDENTS' Manuals.

PERSIA. [See BENJAMIN.]

PHILLIPS (SAMUEL). Literary Essays from "The Times." With Portrait. 2 Vols. Fcap. 8vo. 7s.

POLLOCK (C. E.). A book of Family Prayers. Selected from the Liturgy of the Church of England. 16mo. 3s. 6d.

POPE'S (ALEXANDER) Works. With Introductions and Notes by REV. W. ELWIN, and W. J. COURTHOPE. Vols. I.—IV., VI.—X. With Portraits. 8vo. 10s. 6d. each. (Vol. V., containing the Life and a General Index, is in preparation.)

PORTER (REV. J. L.). Damascus, Palmyra, and Lebanon. Map and Woodcuts. Post 8vo. 7s. 6d.

PRAYER-BOOK (BEAUTIFULLY ILLUSTRATED). With Notes, by REV. THOS. JAMES. Medium 8vo. 18s. *cloth.*

PRINCESS CHARLOTTE OF WALES. Memoir and Correspondence. By LADY ROSE WEIGALL. With Portrait. 8vo. 8s. 6d.

PRIVY COUNCIL JUDGMENTS in Ecclesiastical Cases relating to Doctrine and Discipline. 8vo. 10s. 6d.

PSALMS OF DAVID. With Notes Explanatory and Critical by Dean Johnson, Canon Elliott, and Canon Cook. Medium 8vo. 10s. 6d.

PUSS IN BOOTS. With 12 Illustrations. By OTTO SPECKTER. 16mo. 1s. 6d. Or coloured, 2s. 6d.

QUARTERLY REVIEW (THE). 8vo. 6s.

RAE (EDWARD). Country of the Moors. A Journey from Tripoli to the Holy City of Kairwan. Map and Etchings. Crown 8vo. 12s.

——— The White Sea Peninsula. Journey to the White Sea, and the Kola Peninsula. Map and Illustrations. Crown 8vo. 15s.

——— (GEORGE). The Country Banker; His Clients, Cares, and Work, from the Experience of Forty Years. Crown 8vo. 7s. 6d.

RAMBLES in the Syrian Deserts. Post 8vo. 10s. 6d.

RASSAM (HORMUZD). British Mission to Abyssinia. Illustrations. 2 Vols. 8vo. 28s.

RAWLINSON'S (CANON) Five Great Monarchies of Chaldæa, Assyria, Media, Babylonia, and Persia. With Maps and Illustrations 3 Vols. 8vo. 42*s.*

——— (SIR HENRY) England and Russia in the East; a Series of Papers on the Condition of Central Asia. Map. 8vo. 12*s.*

——— [See HERODOTUS.]

REED (Sir E. J.) Iron-Clad Ships; their Qualities, Performances, and Cost. With Illustrations. 8vo. 12*s.*

——— Letters from Russia in 1875. 8vo. 5*s.*

——— Japan: Its History, Traditions, and Religions. With Narrative of a Visit in 1879. Illustrations. 2 Vols. 8vo. 28*s.*

——— A Practical Treatise on Shipbuilding in Iron and Steel. Second and revised edition with Plans and Woodcuts. 8vo.

REJECTED ADDRESSES (THE). By JAMES AND HORACE SMITH. Woodcuts. Post 8vo. 3*s.* 6*d.*; or *Popular Edition*, Fcap. 8vo. 1*s.*

REMBRANDT. [See MIDDLETON.]

REVISED VERSION OF N.T. [See BECKETT—BURGON—COOK.]

RICARDO'S (DAVID) Works. With a Notice of his Life and Writings. By J. R. M'CULLOCH. 8vo. 16*s.*

RIPA (FATHER). Residence at the Court of Peking. Post 8vo. 2*s.*

ROBERTSON (CANON). History of the Christian Church, from the Apostolic Age to the Reformation, 1517. 8 Vols. Post 8vo. 6*s.* each.

ROBINSON (REV. DR.). Biblical Researches in Palestine and the Adjacent Regions, 1838—52. Maps. 3 Vols. 8vo. 42*s.*

——— (WM.) Alpine Flowers for English Gardens. With 70 Illustrations. Crown 8vo. 7*s.* 6*d.*

——— English Flower Garden. With an Illustrated Dictionary of all the Plants used, and Directions for their Culture and Arrangement. With numerous Illustrations. Medium 8vo. 15*s.*

——— The Vegetable Garden; or, the Edible Vegetables, Salads, and Herbs cultivated in Europe and America. By MM. VILMORIN-ANDRIEUX. With 750 Illustrations. 8vo. 15*s.*

——— Sub-Tropical Garden. Illustrations. Small 8vo. 5*s.*

——— Parks and Gardens of Paris, considered in Relation to the Wants of other Cities and of Public and Private Gardens. With 350 Illustrations. 8vo. 18*s.*

——— Wild Garden; or, Our Groves and Gardens made Beautiful by the Naturalization of Hardy Exotic Plants. With 90 Illustrations. 8vo. 10*s.* 6*d.*

——— God's Acre Beautiful; or, the Cemeteries of the Future. With 8 Illustrations. 8vo. 7*s.* 6*d.*

ROMANS, St. Paul's Epistle to the. With Notes and Commentary by E. H. GIFFORD, D.D., Archdeacon of London. Medium 8vo. 7*s.* 6*d.*

ROME (HISTORY OF). [See GIBBON—INGE—LIDDELL—SMITH—STUDENTS'.

ROMILLY (HUGH H.). The Western Pacific and New Guinea. 2nd Edition. With an additional Chapter on the Ghost in Rotumah. With a Map. Crown 8vo. 7*s.* 6*d.*

———(HENRY). The Punishment of Death. To which is added a Treatise on Public Responsibility and Vote by Ballot. Crown 8vo. 9*s.*

RUMBOLD (SIR HORACE). The Great Silver River: Notes of a Residence in the Argentine Republic. With Illustrations. 8vo. 12*s.*

RUXTON (GEO. F.). Travels in Mexico; with Adventures among Wild Tribes and Animals of the Prairies and Rocky Mountains. Post 8vo. 3*s.* 6*d.*

ST. HUGH OF AVALON. [See PERRY.]

ST. JOHN (CHARLES). Wild Sports and Natural History of the Highlands of Scotland. Illustrated Edition. Crown 8vo. 15s. *Cheap Edition*, Post 8vo. 3s. 6d.

——— (BAYLE) Adventures in the Libyan Desert. Post 8vo. 2s.

SALDANHA (DUKE OF). [See CARNOTA.]

SALE'S (SIR ROBERT) Brigade in Affghanistan. With an Account of the Defence of Jellalabad. By REV. G. R. GLEIG. Post 8vo. 2s.

SALMON (PROF. GEORGE, D.D.). An Introduction to the Study of the New Testament, and an Investigation into Modern Biblical Criticism, based on the most recent Sources of Information. 8vo. 16s.

——— Lectures on the Infallibility of the Church. 8vo.

SCEPTICISM IN GEOLOGY; and the Reasons for It. An assemblage of facts from Nature combining to refute the theory of "Causes now in Action." By VERIFIER. Woodcuts. Crown 8vo. 6s.

SCHLIEMANN (DR. HENRY). Ancient Mycenæ. With 500 Illustrations. Medium 8vo. 50s.

——— Ilios; the City and Country of the Trojans, With an Autobiography. With 2000 Illustrations. Imperial 8vo. 50s.

——— Troja: Results of the Latest Researches and Discoveries on the site of Homer's Troy, and other sites made in 1882. With Maps, Plans, and Illustrations. Medium 8vo. 42s.

——— Tiryns: A Prehistoric Palace of the Kings of Tiryns, discovered by excavations in 1884-5. with Preface and Notes by Professor Adler and Dörpfeld. With Coloured Lithographs, Woodcuts, Plans, &c., from Drawings taken on the spot. Medium 8vo. 42s.

SCHOMBERG (GENERAL). The Odyssey of Homer, rendered into English verse. 2 vols. 8vo. 24s.

SCOTT (SIR GILBERT). The Rise and Development of Mediæval Architecture. With 400 Illustrations. 2 Vols. Medium 8vo. 42s.

SCRUTTON (T. E.). The Laws of Copyright. An Examination of the Principles which should Regulate Literary and Artistic Property in England and other Countries. 8vo. 10s. 6d.

SEEBOHM (HENRY). Siberia in Asia. With Descriptions of the Natural History, Migrations of Birds, &c. Illustrations. Crown 8vo. 14s.

SELBORNE (LORD). Notes on some Passages in the Liturgical History of the Reformed English Church. 8vo. 6s.

SHADOWS OF A SICK ROOM. Preface by Canon LIDDON. 16mo. 2s. 6d.

SHAH OF PERSIA'S Diary during his Tour through Europe in 1873. With Portrait. Crown 8vo. 12s.

SHAW (T. B.). Manual of English Literature. Post 8vo. 7s. 6d.

——— Specimens of English Literature. Selected from the Chief Writers. Post 8vo. 7s. 6d.

——— (ROBERT). Visit to High Tartary, Yarkand, and Kashgar, and Return Journey over the Karakorum Pass. With Map and Illustrations. 8vo. 16s.

SIEMENS (SIR WM.), C.E. Life of. By WM. POLE, C.E. 8vo.

——— Selection from the Papers of. 2 vols. 8vo.

SIERRA LEONE; Described in Letters to Friends at Home. By MRS. MELVILLE. Post 8vo. 3s. 6d.

SIMMONS (CAPT.). Constitution and Practice of Courts-Martial. 8vo. 15s.

SMILES' (SAMUEL, LL.D.) WORKS:—

BRITISH ENGINEERS; from the Earliest Period to the death of the Stephensons. Illustrations. 5 Vols. Crown 8vo. 7s. 6d. each.

SMILES' (Samuel, LL.D.) WORKS—*continued.*

Life and Labour; or, Characteristics of Men of Industry, Culture, and Genius. Post 8vo. 6*s.*

George Stephenson. Post 8vo. 2*s.* 6*d.*

James Nasmyth. Portrait and Illustrations. Post 8vo. 6*s.*

Scotch Naturalist (Thos. Edward). Illustrations. Post 8vo. 6*s.*

Scotch Geologist (Robert Dick). Illustrations. Cr. 8vo. 12*s.*

Huguenots in England and Ireland. Crown 8vo. 7*s.* 6*d.*

Self-Help. With Illustrations of Conduct and Perseverance. Post 8vo. 6*s.*

Character. A Book of Noble Characteristics. Post 8vo. 6*s.*

Thrift. A Book of Domestic Counsel. Post 8vo. 6*s.*

Duty. With Illustrations of Courage, Patience, and Endurance. Post 8vo. 6*s.*

Industrial Biography; or, Iron-Workers and Tool-Makers. Post 8vo. 6*s.*

Men of Invention and Industry. Post 8vo. 6*s.*

Boy's Voyage Round the World. Illustrations. Post 8vo. 6*s.*

SMITH (Dr. George) Student's Manual of the Geography of British India, Physical and Political. With Maps. Post 8vo. 7*s.* 6*d.*

——— Life of John Wilson, D.D. (Bombay), Missionary and Philanthropist. Portrait. Post 8vo. 9*s.*

——— Life of Wm. Carey, D.D., 1761—1834. Shoemaker and Missionary. Professor of Sanscrit, Bengalee and Mara'hee at the College of Fort William, Calcutta. Portrait and Illustrations. 8vo. 16*s.*

——— (Philip). History of the Ancient World, from the Creation to the Fall of the Roman Empire, A.D. 476. 3 Vols. 8vo. 31*s.* 6*d.*

SMITH'S (Dr. Wm.) DICTIONARIES:—

Dictionary of the Bible; its Antiquities, Biography, Geography, and Natural History. Illustrations. 3 Vols. 8vo. 105*s.*

Concise Bible Dictionary. Illustrations. 8vo. 21*s.*

Smaller Bible Dictionary. Illustrations. Post 8vo. 7*s.* 6*d.*

Christian Antiquities. Comprising the History, Institutions, and Antiquities of the Christian Church. Illustrations. 2 Vols. Medium 8vo. 3*l.* 13*s.* 6*d.*

Christian Biography, Literature, Sects, and Doctrines; from the Times of the Apostles to the Age of Charlemagne. Medium 8vo. Now complete in 4 Vols. 6*l.* 16*s.* 6*d.*

Greek and Roman Antiquities. Illustrations. Med. 8vo. 28*s.*

Greek and Roman Biography and Mythology. Illustrations. 3 Vols. Medium 8vo. 4*l.* 4*s.*

Greek and Roman Geography. 2 Vols. Illustrations. Medium 8vo. 56*s.*

Atlas of Ancient Geography—Biblical and Classical. Folio. 6*l.* 6*s.*

Classical Dictionary of Mythology, Biography, and Geography. 1 Vol. With 750 Woodcuts. 8vo. 18*s.*

Smaller Classical Dict. Woodcuts. Crown 8vo. 7*s.* 6*d.*

Smaller Dictionary of Greek and Roman Antiquities. Woodcuts. Crown 8vo. 7*s.* 6*d.*

Complete Latin-English Dictionary. With Tables of the Roman Calendar, Measures, Weights, and Money. 8vo. 21*s.*

Smaller Latin-English Dictionary. New and thoroughly Revised Edition. 12mo. 7*s.* 6*d.*

SMITH'S (Dr. Wm.) ENGLISH COURSE:—

Copious and Critical English-Latin Dictionary. 8vo. 21*s.*

Smaller English-Latin Dictionary. 12mo. 7*s.* 6*d.*

School Manual of English Grammar, with Copious Exercises and Appendices. Post 8vo. 3*s.* 6*d.*

Primary English Grammar, for Elementary Schools, with carefully graduated Parsing Lessons. 16mo. 1*s.*

Manual of English Composition. With Copious Illustrations and Practical Exercises. 12mo. 3*s.* 6*d.*

Primary History of Britain. 12mo. 2*s.* 6*d.*

School Manual of Modern Geography, Physical and Political. Post 8vo. 5*s.*

A Smaller Manual of Modern Geography. 16mo. 2*s.* 6*d.*

SMITH'S (Dr. Wm.) FRENCH COURSE:—

French Principia. Part I. A First Course, containing a Grammar, Delectus, Exercises, and Vocabularies. 12mo. 3*s.* 6*d.*

Appendix to French Principia. Part I. Containing additional Exercises, with Examination Papers. 12mo. 2*s.* 6*d.*

French Principia. Part II. A Reading Book, containing Fables, Stories, and Anecdotes, Natural History, and Scenes from the History of France. With Grammatical Questions, Notes and copious Etymological Dictionary. 12mo. 4*s.* 6*d.*

French Principia. Part III. Prose Composition, containing Hints on Translation of English into French, the Principal Rules of the French Syntax compared with the English, and a Systematic Course of Exercises on the Syntax. 12mo. 4*s.* 6*d.*

Student's French Grammar. With Introduction by M. Littré. Post 8vo. 6*s.*

Smaller Grammar of the French Language. Abridged from the above. 12mo. 3*s.* 6*d.*

SMITH'S (Dr. Wm.) GERMAN COURSE:—

German Principia. Part I. A First German Course, containing a Grammar, Delectus, Exercise Book, and Vocabularies. 12mo. 3*s.* 6*d.*

German Principia. Part II. A Reading Book; containing Fables, Anecdotes, Natural History, and Scenes from the History of Germany. With Questions, Notes, and Dictionary. 12mo. 3*s.* 6*d.*

Practical German Grammar. Post 8vo. 3*s.* 6*d.*

SMITH'S (Dr. Wm.) ITALIAN COURSE:—

Italian Principia. Part I. An Italian Course, containing a Grammar, Delectus, Exercise Book, with Vocabularies, and Materials for Italian Conversation. 12mo. 3*s.* 6*d.*

Italian Principia. Part II. A First Italian Reading Book, containing Fables, Anecdotes, History, and Passages from the best Italian Authors, with Grammatical Questions, Notes, and a Copious Etymological Dictionary. 12mo. 3*s.* 6*d.*

SMITH'S (Dr. Wm.) LATIN COURSE:—

The Young Beginner's First Latin Book: Containing the Rudiments of Grammar, Easy Grammatical Questions and Exercises, with Vocabularies. Being a Stepping stone to Principia Latina, Part I. for Young Children. 12mo. 2*s.*

The Young Beginner's Second Latin Book: Containing an easy Latin Reading Book, with an Analysis of the Sentences, Notes, and a Dictionary. Being a Stepping-stone to Principia Latina, Part II. for Young Children. 12mo. 2*s.*

SMITH'S (Dr. Wm.) Latin Course—*continued.*

Principia Latina. Part I. First Latin Course, containing a Grammar, Delectus, and Exercise Book, with Vocabularies. 12mo. 3*s*. 6*d*.

*** In this Edition the Cases of the Nouns, Adjectives, and Pronouns are arranged both as in the Ordinary Grammars and as in the Public School Primer, together with the corresponding Exercises.

Appendix to Principia Latina. Part I.; being Additional Exercises, with Examination Papers. 12mo. 2*s*. 6*d*.

Principia Latina. Part II. A Reading-book of Mythology, Geography, Roman Antiquities, and History. With Notes and Dictionary. 12mo. 3*s*. 6*d*.

Principia Latina. Part III. A Poetry Book. Hexameters and Pentameters; Eclog. Ovidianæ; Latin Prosody. 12mo. 3*s*. 6*d*.

Principia Latina. Part IV. Prose Composition. Rules of Syntax, with Examples, Explanations of Synonyms, and Exercises on the Syntax. 12mo. 3*s*. 6*d*.

Principia Latina. Part V. Short Tales and Anecdotes for Translation into Latin. 12mo. 3*s*.

Latin-English Vocabulary and First Latin-English Dictionary for Phædrus, Cornelius Nepos, and Cæsar. 12mo. 3*s*. 6*d*.

Student's Latin Grammar. For the Higher Forms. A new and thoroughly revised Edition. Post 8vo. 6*s*.

Smaller Latin Grammar. New Edition. 12mo. 3*s*. 6*d*.

Tacitus, Germania, Agricola, and First Book of the Annals. 12mo. 3*s*. 6*d*.

SMITH'S (Dr. Wm.) GREEK COURSE:—

Initia Græca. Part I. A First Greek Course, containing a Grammar, Delectus, and Exercise-book. With Vocabularies. 12mo. 3*s*. 6*d*.

Appendix to Initia Græca. Part I. Containing additional Exercises. With Examination Papers. Post 8vo. 2*s*. 6*d*.

Initia Græca. Part II. A Reading Book. Containing Short Tales, Anecdotes, Fables, Mythology, and Grecian History. 12mo. 3*s*. 6*d*.

Initia Græca. Part III. Prose Composition. Containing the Rules of Syntax, with copious Examples and Exercises. 12mo. 3*s*. 6*d*.

Student's Greek Grammar. For the Higher Forms. Post 8vo. 6*s*.

Smaller Greek Grammar. 12mo. 3*s*. 6*d*.

Greek Accidence. 12mo. 2*s*. 6*d*.

Plato, Apology of Socrates, &c. With Notes. 12mo. 3*s*. 6*d*.

SMITH'S (Dr. Wm.) SMALLER HISTORIES:—

Scripture History. With Maps and Woodcuts. 16mo. 3*s*. 6*d*.

Ancient History. Woodcuts. 16mo. 3*s*. 6*d*.

Ancient Geography. Woodcuts. 16mo. 3*s*. 6*d*.

Modern Geography. 16mo. 2*s*. 6*d*.

Greece. With Coloured Map and Woodcuts. 16mo. 3*s*. 6*d*.

Rome. With Coloured Maps and Woodcuts. 16mo. 3*s*. 6*d*.

Classical Mythology. Woodcuts. 16mo. 3*s*. 6*d*.

England. With Coloured Maps and Woodcuts. 16mo. 3*s*. 6*d*.

English Literature. 16mo. 3*s*. 6*d*.

Specimens of English Literature. 16mo. 3*s*. 6*d*.

SOMERVILLE (Mary). Physical Geography. Portrait. Post 8vo. 9*s*.

———— Connexion of the Physical Sciences. Post 8vo. 9*s*.

SOMERVILLE (Mary). Molecular and Microscopic Science. Illustrations. 2 Vols. Post 8vo. 21*s*.

SOUTH (John F.). Household Surgery; or, Hints for Emergencies. With Woodcuts. Fcap. 8vo. 3*s*. 6*d*.

——— Memoirs of. [See Feltoe.]

SOUTHEY (Robt.). Lives of Bunyan and Cromwell. Post 8vo. 2*s*.

STANHOPE'S (Earl) WORKS:—

History of England from the Reign of Queen Anne to the Peace of Versailles, 1701-83. 9 vols. Post 8vo. 5*s*. each.

Life of William Pitt. Portraits. 3 Vols. 8vo. 36*s*.

Miscellanies. 2 Vols. Post 8vo. 13*s*.

British India, from its Origin to 1783. Post 8vo. 3*s*. 6*d*.

History of "Forty-Five." Post 8vo. 3*s*.

Historical and Critical Essays. Post 8vo. 3*s*. 6*d*.

The Retreat from Moscow, and other Essays. Post 8vo. 7*s*. 6*d*.

Life of Belisarius. Post 8vo. 10*s*. 6*d*.

Life of Condé. Post 8vo. 3*s*. 6*d*.

Story of Joan of Arc. Fcap. 8vo. 1*s*.

Addresses on Various Occasions. 16mo. 1*s*.

STANLEY'S (Dean) WORKS:—

Sinai and Palestine. Coloured Maps. 8vo. 12*s*.

Bible in the Holy Land; Extracted from the above Work. Woodcuts. Fcap. 8vo. 2*s*. 6*d*.

Eastern Church. Plans. Crown 8vo. 6*s*.

Jewish Church. From the Earliest Times to the Christian Era. Portrait and Maps. 3 Vols. Crown 8vo. 18*s*.

Church of Scotland. 8vo. 7*s*. 6*d*.

Epistles of St. Paul to the Corinthians. 8vo. 18*s*.

Life of Dr. Arnold. Portrait. 2 Vols. Cr. 8vo. 12*s*.

Canterbury. Illustrations. Crown 8vo. 6*s*.

Westminster Abbey. Illustrations. 8vo. 15*s*.

Sermons Preached in Westminster Abbey. 8vo. 12*s*.

Memoir of Edward, Catherine, and Mary Stanley. Cr. 8vo. 9*s*.

Christian Institutions. Essays on Ecclesiastical Subjects. 8vo. 12*s*. Or Crown 8vo. 6*s*.

Essays. Chiefly on Questions of Church and State; from 1850 to 1870. Crown 8vo. 6*s*.

Sermons and Addresses to Children, including the Beatitudes, the Faithful Servant, &c. Crown 8vo. 3*s*. 6*d*.

[See also Bradley.]

STEBBING (Wm.). Some Verdicts of History Reviewed. 8vo. 12*s*.

STEPHENS (Rev. W. R. W.). Life and Times of St. John Chrysostom. A Sketch of the Church and the Empire in the Fourth Century. Portrait. 8vo. 7*s*. 6*d*.

STREET (G. E.). R.A. Gothic Architecture in Spain. Illustrations. Royal 8vo. 30*s*.

——— Gothic Architecture in Brick and Marble. With Notes on North of Italy. Illustrations. Royal 8vo. 26*s*.

——— A Memoir of, by his Son, Arthur Edmund Street, Portrait. 8vo.

STUART (Villiers). Egypt after the War. With Descriptions of the Homes and Habits of the Natives, &c. Coloured Illustrations and Woodcuts. Royal 8vo. 31*s*. 6*d*.

STUDENTS' MANUALS. Post 8vo. 7s. 6d. each Volume:—

Hume's History of England from the Invasion of Julius Cæsar to the Revolution in 1688. Revised, and continued to the Treaty of Berlin, 1878. By J. S. Brewer, M.A. Coloured Maps and Woodcuts. Or in 3 parts, price 2s. 6d. each.

*** Questions on the above Work, 12mo. 2s.

History of Modern Europe, from the fall of Constantinople to the Treaty of Berlin, 1878. By R. Lodge, M.A.

Old Testament History; from the Creation to the Return of the Jews from Captivity. Woodcuts.

New Testament History. With an Introduction connecting the History of the Old and New Testaments. Woodcuts.

Evidences of Christianity. By H. Wace, D.D. [*In the Press.*

Ecclesiastical History; a History of the Christian Church from its foundation till after the Reformation. By Philip Smith, B.A. With numerous Woodcuts. 2 Vols. Part I. A.D. 30—1003. Part II.—1003—1614.

English Church History; from the Planting of the Church in Great Britain to the Silencing of Convocation in the 18th Cent. By Canon Perry. 2 Vols. *First Period*, A.D. 596—1509. *Second Period*, 1509—1717.

Ancient History of the East; Egypt, Assyria, Babylonia, Media, Persia, Asia Minor, and Phœnicia. By Philip Smith, B.A. Woodcuts.

——— Geography. By Canon Bevan. Woodcuts.

History of Greece; from the Earliest Times to the Roman Conquest. By Wm. Smith, D.C.L. Woodcuts.

*** Questions on the above Work, 12mo. 2s.

History of Rome; from the Earliest Times to the Establishment of the Empire. By Dean Liddell. Woodcuts.

Gibbon's Decline and Fall of the Roman Empire. Woodcuts.

Hallam's History of Europe during the Middle Ages.

Hallam's History of England; from the Accession of Henry VII. to the Death of George II.

History of France; from the Earliest Times to the Fall of the Second Empire. By H. W. Jervis. With Coloured Maps and Woodcuts.

English Language. By Geo. P. Marsh.

English Literature. By T. B. Shaw, M.A.

Specimens of English Literature. By T. B. Shaw.

Modern Geography; Mathematical, Physical and Descriptive. By Canon Bevan, M.A. Woodcuts.

Geography of British India. Political and Physical. By George Smith, LL.D. Maps.

Moral Philosophy. By Wm. Fleming.

SUMNER'S (Bishop) Life and Episcopate during 40 Years. By Rev. G. H. Sumner. Portrait. 8vo. 14s.

SWAINSON (Canon). Nicene and Apostles' Creeds; Their Literary History; together with some Account of "The Creed of St. Athanasius." 8vo. 16s.

SWIFT (Jonathan). [See Craik.]

SYBEL (Von). History of Europe during the French Revolution, 1789—1795. 4 Vols. 8vo. 48s.

SYMONDS' (Rev. W.) Records of the Rocks; or Notes on the Geology of Wales, Devon, and Cornwall. Crown 8vo. 12s.

TEMPLE (SIR RICHARD). India in 1880. With Maps. 8vo. 16s.

——— Men and Events of My Time in India. 8vo. 16s.

——— Oriental Experience. Essays and Addresses delivered on Various Occasions. With Maps and Woodcuts. 8vo. 16s.

THIBAUT'S (ANTOINE). Purity in Musical Art. With Prefatory Memoir by W. H. Gladstone, M.P. Post 8vo. 7s. 6d.

THIELMANN (BARON). Journey through the Caucasus to Tabreez, Kurdistan, down the Tigris and Euphrates to Nineveh and Palmyra. Illustrations. 2 Vols. Post 8vo. 18s.

THOMSON (ARCHBISHOP). Lincoln's Inn Sermons. 8vo. 10s. 6d.

——— Life in the Light of God's Word. Post 8vo. 5s.

———Word, Work, & Will: Collected Essays. Crown 8vo. 9s.

THORNHILL (MARK). The Personal Adventures and Experiences of a Magistrate during the Rise, Progress, and Suppression of the Indian Mutiny. With Frontispiece and Plan. Crown 8vo. 12s.

TITIAN'S LIFE AND TIMES. With some account of his Family, from unpublished Records. By CROWE and CAVALCASELLE. Illustrations. 2 Vols. 8vo. 21s.

TOCQUEVILLE'S State of Society in France before the Revolution, 1789, and on the Causes which led to that Event. 8vo. 14s.

TOMLINSON (CHAS.). The Sonnet: Its Origin, Structure, and Place in Poetry. Post 8vo. 9s.

TOZER (REV. H. F.). Highlands of Turkey, with Visits to Mounts Ida, Athos, Olympus, and Pelion. 2 Vols. Crown 8vo. 24s.

——— Lectures on the Geography of Greece. Post 8vo. 9s.

TRISTRAM (CANON). Great Sahara. Illustrations. Crown 8vo. 15s.

——— Land of Moab: Travels and Discoveries on the East Side of the Dead Sea and the Jordan. Illustrations. Crown 8vo. 15s.

TWINING (REV. THOS.). Recreations and Studies of a Country Clergyman of the Last Century. Crown 8vo. 9s.

——— PAPERS (Selections from the). Being a Sequel to the "Recreations of a Country Clergyman of the 18th Century." Edited by RICHARD TWINING. Crown 8vo. 9s.

——— (LOUISA). Symbols and Emblems of Early and Mediæval Christian Art. With 500 Illustrations from Paintings, Miniatures, Sculptures, &c. Crown 8vo. 14s.

TWISS' (HORACE) Life of Lord Eldon. 2 Vols. Post 8vo. 21s.

TYLOR (E. B.). Researches into the Early History of Mankind, and Development of Civilization. 3rd Edition. 8vo. 12s.

——— Primitive Culture: the Development of Mythology, Philosophy, Religion, Art, and Custom. 2 Vols. 8vo. 24s.

VATICAN COUNCIL. [See LETO.]

VIRCHOW (PROFESSOR). The Freedom of Science in the Modern State. Fcap. 8vo. 2s.

WACE (REV. HENRY), D.D. The Principal Facts in the Life of our Lord, and the Authority of the Evangelical Narratives. Post 8vo.

——— The Foundations of Faith. Bampton Lectures for 1879. Second Edition. 8vo. 7s. 6d.

——— Christianity and Morality. Boyle Lectures for 1874 and 1875. Seventh Edition. Crown 8vo. 6s.

WELLINGTON'S Despatches in India, Denmark, Portugal, Spain, the Low Countries, and France. 8 Vols. 8vo. £8 8s.

——— Supplementary Despatches, relating to India, Ireland, Denmark, Spanish America, Spain, Portugal, France, Congress of Vienna, Waterloo, and Paris. 15 Vols. 8vo. 20s. each.

WELLINGTON'S Civil and Political Correspondence. Vols. I. to VIII. 8vo. 20s. each.

—————— Speeches in Parliament. 2 Vols. 8vo. 42s.

WESTCOTT (CANON B. F.) The Gospel according to St. John, with Notes and Dissertations (Reprinted from the Speaker's Commentary). 8vo. 10s. 6d.

WHARTON (CAPT. W. J. L.), R.N. Hydrographical Surveying: being a description of the means and methods employed in constructing Marine Charts. With Illustrations. 8vo. 15s.

WHEELER (G.). Choice of a Dwelling. Post 8vo. 7s. 6d.

WHITE (W. H.). Manual of Naval Architecture, for the use of Naval Officers, Shipbuilders, and Yachtsmen, &c. Illustrations. 8vo. 24s.

WHYMPER (EDWARD). The Ascent of the Matterhorn. With 100 Illustrations. Medium 8vo. 10s. 6d.

WILBERFORCE'S (BISHOP) Life of William Wilberforce. Portrait. Crown 8vo. 6s.

—————— (SAMUEL, LL.D.), Lord Bishop of Oxford and Winchester; his Life. By CANON ASHWELL, D.D., and R. G. WILBERFORCE. With Portraits and Woodcuts. 3 Vols. 8vo. 15s. each.

WILKINSON (SIR J. G.). Manners and Customs of the Ancient Egyptians, their Private Life, Laws, Arts, Religion, &c. A new edition. Edited by SAMUEL BIRCH, LL.D. Illustrations. 3 Vols. 8vo. 84s.

—————— Popular Account of the Ancient Egyptians. With 500 Woodcuts. 2 Vols. Post 8vo. 12s.

WILLIAMS (SIR MONIER). Brahmanism and Hinduism, Religious Thought and Life in India as based on the Veda. 8vo. 10s. 6d.

—————— Buddhism. With a Chapter on Jainism. 8vo. [*In the Press.*

—————— Sakoontala; or, The Lost Ring. An Indian Drama Translated into English Prose and Verse. 8vo. 7s. 6d.

WILSON (JOHN, D.D.). [See SMITH, GEO.]

WINTLE (H. G.). Ovid Lessons. 12mo, 2s. 6d. [See ETON.]

WOOD'S (CAPTAIN) Source of the Oxus. With the Geography of the Valley of the Oxus. By COL. YULE. Map. 8vo. 12s.

WORDS OF HUMAN WISDOM. Collected and Arranged by E. S. With a Preface by CANON LIDDON. Fcap. 8vo. 3s. 6d.

WORDSWORTH'S (BISHOP) Greece; Pictorial, Descriptive, and Historical. With an Introduction on the Characteristics of Greek Art, by GEO. SCHARF. New Edition revised by the Rev. H. F. TOZER, M.A. With 400 Illustrations. Royal 8vo. 31s. 6d.

YORK (ARCHBISHOP OF). Collected Essays. Contents.—Synoptic Gospels. Death of Christ. God Exists. Worth of Life. Design in Nature. Sports and Pastimes. Emotions in Preaching. Defects in Missionary Work. Limits of Philosophical Enquiry. Crown 8vo. 9s.

YORK-GATE LIBRARY (Catalogue of). Formed by Mr. SILVER. An Index to the Literature of Geography, Maritime and Inland Discovery, Commerce and Colonisation. Compiled by E. A. PETHERICK, F.R.G.S. Second Edition, greatly enlarged, and Illustrated. 468 pp. Super-royal 8vo. Price 42s.

YULE (COLONEL). The Book of Ser Marco Polo, the Venetian, concerning the Kingdoms and Marvels of the East. Illustrated by the Light of Oriental Writers and Modern Travels. With Maps and 80 Plates. 2 Vols. Medium 8vo. 63s.

—————— and A. C. BURNELL. A Glossary of Anglo-Indian Colloquial Words and Phrases, and of Kindred Terms: Etymological, Historical, Geographical, and Discursive. Medium 8vo. 36s

—————— (A. F.) The Cretan Insurrection. Post 8vo. 2s. 6d.

BRADBURY, AGNEW, & CO., PRINTERS, WHITEFRIARS.